STATE OF OTHERS

NEW JEWISH PHILOSOPHY AND THOUGHT

Zachary J. Braiterman

STATE OF OTHERS

Levinas and Decolonial Israel

Elad Lapidot

INDIANA UNIVERSITY PRESS

This book is a publication of

Indiana University Press
Herman B Wells Library 350
1320 East 10th Street
Bloomington, Indiana 47405 USA

iupress.org

© 2025 by Elad Lapidot

First printing 2025

Cataloging information is available from the Library of Congress.

ISBN 978-0-253-07326-6 (hdbk.)
ISBN 978-0-253-07327-3 (pbk.)
ISBN 978-0-253-07329-7 (ebook)
ISBN 978-0-253-07328-0 (web PDF)

CONTENTS

PREFACE

THIS BOOK RECOGNIZES, AMONG OTHER THINGS, THE STATE of Israel and its war against the Palestinians as the defining challenge of contemporary Jewish thought. It was written before October 7, 2023. The long chain of events that have taken place in the months following has by now crystallized into a distinctive moment in time that feels increasingly like a turning point in Jewish history.

Contrary to what many claim, the center of the unfolding catastrophe is not anti-Semitism, if that term means, as it should, anti-Jewish racism, the attribution of imaginary vices to individuals because of their Jewish descent. Today's growing anti-Jewish sentiment would be better described as anti-Judaism or anti-Jewishness, which is hostility to what Jewish people as such actually do. But the deep crisis of the hour does not arise primarily from sentiments toward Jews. Rather, it arises from what is currently being done in the name of Judaism.

Following the atrocities of the Hamas attacks, the State of Israel, in the name of defending Jews and Jewish self-determination, has unleashed genocidal violence against millions of Gazans, killing tens of thousands, destroying neighborhoods, displacing masses of people, and condemning them to starvation. This extreme destruction casts an apocalyptic light that reveals—to those who have not experienced it firsthand—the history of the Jewish state as a decade-long history of repressive violence perpetrated against Palestinians.

All those who remember Jewish existence in the diaspora as a history of resistance to state violence; all those who perceive a call to moral responsibility, a prophetic vision of justice, and a messianic promise of peace as standing at the heart of Jewish tradition; all those who, like the French Jewish philosopher Emmanuel Levinas, care about the value of Judaism—the atrocities being committed by the Jewish state in Gaza must shake their moral constitution and unsettle their fundamental perceptions.

Does Jewish thought possess in its archives the conceptual, intellectual, and moral resources to counter, resist, or even simply critically reflect on its current appropriation for the purpose of justifying murderous state violence? The endeavors underlying this book were undertaken with the deep conviction that such resources do exist and that Levinas was one of the most prominent thinkers of our time to seek them.

The concerns that the following chapters raise about Levinas's metaphysical justification of Israeli politics, especially in light of the messianic celebration of the current war by circles within religious Zionism, suggest that our access to critical Jewish sources and our ability to draw a response from them to the troubles of the present hour are anything but certain.

Elad Lapidot
Berlin, June 2024

ACKNOWLEDGMENTS

T HIS BOOK IS THE RESULT OF MORE THAN twenty-five years of reflection. Somewhere in the late 1990s, when we were studying at the Hebrew University in Jerusalem, Michael Sfard gave me a book, *Postmodern Ethics*, by his grandfather, Zygmunt Bauman, and this is how I discovered Levinas and Bauman. Bauman's title fascinated me; it sounded timely. Shortly after, I took a seminar on Levinas with Shalom Rosenberg, and every Friday afternoon, while he was washing dishes, we would talk on the phone, and I would struggle to tell him what I understood from reading *Autrement qu'être*. Once we had a guest lecture by Daniel Epstein, who translated the *Talmudic Readings* into Hebrew. I gave him a ride back from Mount Scopus to the city. In the car, he spoke about Levinas in a soft voice with a French accent, and I decided to do a PhD on Levinas's philosophy in Paris.

I did go to Paris, a week after 9/11. My—vague—idea was to write about Levinas's logic. If, as Levinas argued, ethics should be considered first philosophy, what does the logic of this philosophy look like? What is the logic of ethics, in particular of "postmodern" ethics? Today I think this—the logics of ethics—is a good question, central to this book. But back then, I did not really understand its meaning. Since it was my guiding question, I was unable to understand Levinas, and so my adviser at Paris 1, Renaud Barbaras, was unable to understand me. On the brink of despair, I turned to Heidegger. My hope was to see what Levinas criticized in his master to better grasp his response to it. I ended up writing a PhD on Heidegger, the logic of *Sein und Zeit*, under the supervision of Jocelyn Benoist.

I did not completely abandon Levinas. A few years later, I translated *Le temps et l'autre* into Hebrew. But I never got back to my question, my project, my desire to write on Levinas. I turned to other things, started learning Talmud. At a certain point, Christina von Braun allowed me to lead a Talmud seminar at the Jewish Studies Center she founded in Berlin. The seminar went on for eight years. We were a lively group, with each semester a few students, a handful of scholars of all disciplines visiting Berlin, occasional interested visitors, and a small circle of regular participants, some expats, some locals. My focus was neither philological nor historical. I treated the text as a poetic medium for thinking. "Like Levinas did," one participant once told me. I had not even thought of that. It suddenly occurred to me that I had followed Levinas's footsteps, from Heidegger to Talmud. It was then that I felt ready to read him again. This book and the forthcoming one are what came out of this rereading.

I am grateful to all the people I encountered on this journey, those I mentioned and others. Over the years, I benefited immensely from conversations on Levinas with friends, colleagues, and teachers like Amir Engel, Eli Schonfeld, Dror Pimentel, Christoph Schmidt, Oded Schechter, Dror Yinon, Roi Bar, Itzhak Benyamini, Michal Ben Naftali, Leora Batnitzky, Daniel Boyarin, Jonathan Boyarin, Luca Di Blasi, Hans Ruin, Ulrika Björk, Sarah Hammerschlag, Gil Anidjar, Amnon Raz-Krakotzkin, Menachem Lorberbaum, Ivan Segré, Agata Bielik-Robson, Annabel Herzog, Cedric Cohen-Skalli, Willem Styfhals, Daniel Herskowitz, and Anoush Ganjipour. A special debt of gratitude I owe to colleagues who read parts or versions of this book and helped improve it, such as Adi Ophir, Itamar Ben Ami, Karma Ben Yohanan, Jayne Svenungsson, Michael Fagenblat, Vivian Liska, Elliot Wolfson, and Jan Eike Dunkhase.

Ideas and texts from this book were presented and discussed in lectures and talks organized by Manuela Consonni at the Hebrew University in Jerusalem, Cedric Cohen-Skalli at the University of Haifa, Jayne Svenungsson at the University of Lund, Vivian Liska at the University of Antwerp, Willem Styfhals at KU Leuven, Re'ee Hagay and Itamar Haritan at Cornell University, Adam Ferziger and Miri Freud-Kandel at the University of Oxford, and Agata Bielik-Robson at the Polish Academy of Sciences. I am grateful for these invitations and for the participants in the discussions.

Many thanks go to Steve Corcoran, who copyedited the entire manuscript with sensitivity and attention to details; Zak Braiterman, who kindly accepted this study into his series; Anna Francis and Dan Crissman from Indiana University Press for making the publication possible; and my academic homes, the University of Lille and the research center Cecille (Centre d'Études en Civilisations, Langues et Lettres Étrangères), for their generous support of the publication.

Beyond thanking, I am grateful to Eva and Alma for years of companionship, patience, and love.

STATE OF OTHERS

INTRODUCTION

WESTERN THOUGHT IS UNDER CRITIQUE. IT IS CRITICIZED for not living up to its claim of being universal and instead being precisely— Western. This critique is often mistaken as anti-Western or antiuniversal. But it has arisen within the Western academy and draws on modern European epistemology, which founds its universality through self-critique. The contemporary self-critique of Western knowledge concerns the historical performance of asserting the Western claim to universality by way of colonialism. Contemporary epistemology is a critique of colonialism, articulated through the difference, or break, between two epistemes, the colonial and the colonized. This horizon forms the epistemo-political space for various contemporary "Studies"—African, Black, Islamic, Women's, Gender.

Within this framework, Jewish Studies have an ambivalent status. *Jewish* may be described both as Other to Europe *and* as a foundational element of Europe. Does the Jewish episteme contest or constitute the West? The collective Jewish agency in history, traditionally known as Israel, is the proper name of what epistemo-political performance? How does Israel lay claim to universality? Was it, and is it still, a colonial or anticolonial figure? The ambivalence of Israel, the inner split of its political epistemology, opens a conceptual terrain on which fundamental questions of contemporary critical epistemology can unfold. This is the terrain on which this book situates the work of Emmanuel Levinas.

The Debate: Levinas versus the Others

In recent years, Levinas's work has become a site for debates on alterity and Jewish alterity, as well as on the relation between the Jewish Other and other Others, such as the non-European and the feminine.[1]

Levinas is not only a philosopher of the Other but also a thinker of Jewish epistemic otherness. The term *epistemic* or *episteme* is used here in a Foucauldian sense to refer to knowledge understood as a system of socially authorized truths and truth procedures, which determine not only theoretical but also practical, institutional, existential, and moral positions. The term *episteme* itself arises from the Greek culture of knowledge, and therefore, if we should acknowledge epistemic difference, the term ultimately may not be universally applicable to all cultures of knowledge, such as the Jewish. It is used here heuristically.

As one of Levinas's first readers, Jacques Derrida, noted in 1964, Levinas's thought stages a fundamental confrontation between "the Jewish" and "the Greek."[2] This epistemic distinction is embodied in the two major corpora of the Levinasian oeuvre, which is to say, in the split between his philosophical, or "Greek," writings and his Jewish ones.

Early on, however, the inter-epistemic constellation around which Levinas's oeuvre is structured was criticized for not fostering epistemic difference, instead suppressing it. The argument was put forward that in Levinas's work, Jewish otherness actually operates as the agent of a powerful, imperial sameness.

Derrida expressed his skepticism about the possible epistemic difference between the Greek and the Jewish. He suggested that Levinas ought to be seen as a "Jewgreek" or a "Greekjew." Indeed, there is much in Levinas that manifests not a clash but a harmony between what he calls "the Bible and the Greeks."[3] In his understanding, the Jewish episteme has at its core an ethics of the other person, which he presents as "first philosophy" rather than as antiphilosophy. The relationship to the Other does not break with universal rationality but instead constitutes it. As many have noted, Levinas found in the Jewish episteme the otherness of transcendence, which, like the monotheistic God, transcends all worldly sociocultural differences and grounds monouniversalism. The eyes of the Other have no color.[4] Levinas's Judaism is thus easily read as grounding European humanism.

The critique leveled against the notion that Jewish epistemic difference grounds the transcendence of difference points to the ambivalence of the Jewish figure. If Judaism means universalism beyond difference, then the Jewish—as episteme, tradition, culture, politics—emerges as the identity beyond all identities, namely as a second-order identity, a meta-identity not just superior to all others but in which all others are dissolved. In this way, a Jewish political epistemology of otherness would constitute the Jewish collective, Israel—so the critique goes—as the paradigmatic agent of imperialism.

I identify three main variants of this critique.

First is a universalist variant. Authors such as Judith Butler, Sarah Hammerschlag, and Ethan Kleinberg point out the dispersion or deracination of identities that Levinas finds in Jewish otherness but criticize Levinas's valorization of this ethics as specifically Jewish. They argue that the ensuing notion of exceptional Jewish morality, of a supermoral Israel, proves problematic precisely when it leads Levinas to justify the Jewish state's suppression of non-Jews. They suggest that true fidelity to Levinas's Jewish ethics requires de-Judaizing it, whether through translation, allegorization, or metaphor.[5] The idea of universalizing the Jewish episteme by detaching it from Jewish existence harks back to the Greek Jew Saul-Paul, "apostle to the nations," to whom Michael Fagenblat has indeed compared Levinas.[6]

The *second* variant of this critique is a postcolonial one. It reminds us that Paulinian universalization, namely the de-Judaizing of the Jewish episteme, did not historically solve the problem of a Jewish meta-identity. On the contrary, de-Judaized Judaism produced its ultimate imperial performance in the form of European Christianity. Authors such as Andrew McGettigan and Fred Moten criticize Levinas's Greco-Jewish Israel not for supporting the particularity of Jewish nationalism but for consolidating Judeo-Christian imperialism, for collaborating with Europe's humanist colonialism. "The Bible and the Greeks are the world the slaveholders made," Moten states.[7] Similarly to the universalist Levinasians, postcolonial Levinasians like John Drabinski also suggest that Levinas's ethics be decolonized through a process of de-Judaizing, which would mean not transcending difference but acknowledging it precisely by recognizing other Others.[8]

Finally, the *third* variant of this critique comes from authors such as Samuel Moyn, Leora Batnitzky, and Benny Lévy, all of whom subscribe to the postcolonial problematization of Levinas's Greco-Jewish Israel as the agent of a Paulinian suppression of difference. However, they point out that this, and indeed all, Paulinism effaces not only different Others but also, and primarily, the Jewish Other, which is precisely *not* Judeo-Christian.[9] As Robert Bernasconi suggests, to decolonize Levinas, to open his ethics of otherness to epistemic and cultural difference, does not require effacing the Jewish episteme from Levinasian thought; on the contrary, it requires turning intellectual attention more closely to the Jewish in Levinas's work[10]—and, I add, guarding it from Levinas's own Paulinian fusion of "the Bible and the Greeks."

The Argument of This Book: Levinas's Decolonial Turn

I agree with the basic observation underlying all three critiques. Levinas indeed asserts that the Jewish episteme is the foundation of Western universalism, such that in his thought, the historical, collective Jewish Other—Israel—emerges as the messianic agent, as a meta-identity able to transcend all cultural difference. I agree with the postcolonial critique that Levinas's Israel presents not the problem of Jewish particularism but instead the colonial problem of European universalism. Last, I agree with the Jewish critique that decolonizing Levinas's thought requires not de-Judaizing it but rather de-Judeo-Christianizing, or de-Europeanizing, it. I contend that what needs rethinking is the specificity of the Jewish episteme.

My central argument is that Levinas anticipated the postcolonial critique of his thinking and incorporated it through a process of self-critique. He responded by developing a decolonized conception of Jewish epistemic difference, which might be called decolonial Jewish thought. The following chapters are dedicated to showing, analyzing, and critiquing Levinas's decolonial turn.

The key to my reading of Levinas—and to the structure of this book—lies in paying close attention to two inner tensions or conversations around which Levinas's work is articulated. The first inner conversation is a synchronic, inter-epistemic one between his philosophical writings and his Jewish writings, what I call a conversation between philosophy and prophecy, between phenomenology and eschatology. The second is a diachronic one between the early and the later Levinas that takes place in both the philosophical and the Jewish writings.

Contemplating these tensions together reveals a shift in Levinas's work between two conceptions of Jewish epistemic difference vis-à-vis Western philosophy. This shift, I suggest, articulates a basic development of post-Holocaust Jewish thought, arising from a polemics between Jewish otherness and other Others. The turn in Levinas's oeuvre from the earlier to the later conceptual constellation can be very roughly dated to the years 1967 and 1968, or more precisely '67 seen in the wake of '68—what I call '67 after '68.

The next sections of this introduction are dedicated to clarifying the two hermeneutic keys to this book: the tension between Levinas's philosophical and Jewish writings and the tension between early and late Levinas. These hermeneutic perspectives are not obvious and constitute interventions in ongoing scholarly debates.

Between Philosophical and Jewish Epistemes

This book examines Levinas's work as fundamentally articulated through its staging of an inter-epistemic tension that is both a difference and an encounter. It is a tension between different worlds of knowledge, different epistemes: on the one hand is a Western or European episteme, paradigmatically represented by the tradition of Philosophy, and on the other, a Jewish episteme, epitomized by the tradition of Talmud. Accordingly, in contrast to readings that recognize in Levinas's work only a purely transcendental, nonworldly, and ahistorical figure of alterity (such as those of McGettigan, Moten, and Drabinski), one that stands for no knowledge, no episteme, but instead the ethical rupture of all knowledge, my reading identifies a foundational inter-epistemic difference at the basis of Levinas's entire project, which is firmly situated historically and culturally.

The obvious support for this reading comes from the most apparent architectural feature of Levinas's oeuvre, which is its division into two distinct corpora: the philosophical writings and the Jewish and talmudic writings. Levinas's work is not just about inter-epistemic tension; it is also a literary performance of this tension in the form of textual *separation*, which, as we will see, appears in Levinas's thought as the structure of the relation between the same and the other—that is, as the structure of relationality per se. It should be noted that the separation between Levinas's philosophical and Jewish writings, which I analyze as performing an epistemic difference, is not only textual but also sociopolitical, implying distinctions between publishers, institutions, communities, readerships, and scholarships.

Nonetheless, Levinas scholars have most often refrained from interpreting the division of his work between philosophy and Jewish writings as expressing an inter-epistemic difference, as being different worlds of knowledge. The reason for this refrainment lies in how readers understand the meaning of *the Jewish* in Levinas's work and its separation from philosophy. I indicate two main positions. *Either* the Jewish is understood as constituting no episteme at all, no specific system of knowledge and thought comparable or even relatable to philosophy, whereby the separation of the philosophical from the Jewish writings is understood as expressing no relation, a sort of irrelevance, *or* the Jewish is understood epistemically as Jewish thought but not as exhibiting any significant difference from philosophy, whereby the separation is understood as an expression of segregation and discrimination—merely artificial, not real.

The *first*, most common position, which dismisses the epistemic value of Levinas's Jewish writings and notions, considering them irrelevant to philosophy, is based on a secularist view of the Jewish intellectual tradition as a "religion" and of religion as belonging to the realm of particularism, of specific traditions, beliefs, and rituals, a realm categorically transcended by the universal reason of secular knowledge, which is to say, science and philosophy.[11] Levinas himself suggests this orientation when he describes the inner division of his writings in the following terms: "I always make a clear distinction, in what I write, between philosophical and confessional texts."[12] The designation of Levinas's Jewish texts as "confessional" has become commonplace, usually seen to imply that they pertain to religion and so are a matter of indifference to philosophy.[13]

The *second* position, as noted, does acknowledge the epistemic value of the Jewish intellectual tradition and its relevance to philosophy and refrains from dismissing Judaism as philosophically irrelevant religion. However, in order to recognize the philosophical relevance of the Jewish episteme, this second position dismisses any fundamental, epistemological specificity distinguishing Jewish thought from philosophy, thus focusing on elements within the Jewish intellectual tradition that display, or may be said to constitute, Jewish philosophy. Accordingly, any radical differentiation between philosophy and Jewish thought, such as Levinas's separation between his philosophical and Jewish writings, is understood as epistemically groundless, arising only due to some kind of prejudice or discrimination.[14]

The position I develop in this book differs. It consists in recognizing in Levinas's work a foundational differentiation between the basic epistemologies of the philosophical tradition on the one hand and the Jewish tradition on the other. Jewish thought or the Jewish episteme—and more specifically, the talmudic episteme—is philosophically relevant insofar as it is *different* from philosophy. It is no coincidence that this position recently emerged in two scholarly books, by Annabel Herzog and Ethan Kleinberg, respectively—the first works to focus on Levinas's talmudic readings.[15]

Before elaborating on my own perspective, I shall briefly respond to the aforementioned common positions by referring to the passage in Levinas's text in which he explains the separation between his philosophical and his Jewish writings. Notwithstanding his rather infelicitous characterization of the latter as "confessional," Levinas emphasizes that with respect to his Jewish thought, "I do not wish to talk in terms of belief or nonbelief." "I always make a clear distinction, in what I write, between philosophical and confessional texts. I do not deny that they may ultimately have a common source of inspiration. I simply state that it is necessary to draw a line of demarcation between them as distinct methods of exegesis, as separate languages." The demarcation between philosophical and Jewish thought is epistemic—that is, the Jewish episteme offers philosophy "an alternative approach to meaning and truth," a different form of universality. This is the sense in which this book speaks of inter-epistemic difference and encounter in Levinas's work.[16]

A structural insight of the present book is that the inter-epistemic drama in Levinas's work manifests performatively in the division of his work into philosophical and Jewish writings, into two separate corpora or conversations. Each corpus in fact operates in a different discourse. The two corpora do not just comprise different terms and themes, do not just refer to divergent authors, texts, and traditions; they actually unfold distinct kinds of logic, are woven by different textualities, as "separate languages." The basis for my comparing and contrasting these two epistemic corpora of Levinas is the different ways in which they address the question of inter-epistemic difference. My claim is that the inter-epistemic encounter takes place in Levinas's work not just *between* its two corpora, the philosophical and the Jewish writings, but as a formative event within each corpus. The inter-epistemic difference is, however, differently staged in each corpus. The difference between the two epistemes—the philosophical and the Jewish—manifests paradigmatically in the way in which the two Levinasian corpora, the two bodies of his kingdom, constitute distinct regimes of epistemic difference that differently stage the inter-epistemic encounter. In other words, in Levinas's writings there are two different encounters between philosophy and Jewish thought, one philosophical and one Jewish, and the difference between these encounters is a structural concern of this book. It belongs perhaps to the essence of encounters that they always take place more than once, or take more than one place, always simultaneously from different perspectives, ultimately never really taking place at all.

The first structural feature of the following chapters is therefore the division between—and comparison of—the discussion of the inter-epistemic difference in Levinas's philosophical writings and in his Jewish writings. I now introduce the general features and methodologies of these two discussions.

Philosophy versus Jewish Thought in Levinas's Philosophy

That the encounter between philosophy and Jewish thought is at the heart of Levinas's philosophical writings is far from self-evident. That these writings, which rarely make reference to Jewish texts, give any place at all to such an encounter is also far from obvious. As noted, readings of Levinas tend more commonly to interpret the division between philosophical and Jewish texts as categorically divesting the latter, "confessional" writings of all philosophical significance and, *vice versa*, as liberating the former, "rational" writings from any dependence on religious faith. I explained above why I think this position misunderstands the separation between Levinas's two corpora, which do not manifest epistemic indifference but instead inter-epistemic difference. However, *within* Levinas's philosophical writings, no distinction between philosophical and Jewish thought or epistemology seems to play any role whatsoever. On the contrary, philosophy appears to stand for the universal unity of thinking. Levinas's philosophical writings feature phenomenological analyses that focus on individual human subjectivity and interpersonal encounters to the seeming exclusion of all collective dimensions of history, culture, and politics, as Levinas's postcolonial critics have indeed argued. In his philosophy, there seems to be no visible sign of historical and political epistemology, no sign of inter-epistemic difference.

Nevertheless, this book demonstrates that Levinas's philosophical and phenomenological texts are deeply concerned with inter-epistemic difference. The following chapters show how the inter-epistemic encounter between philosophy and Jewish thought is a fundamental event staged in Levinas's philosophical writings, an event that articulates their narrative, structures their drama, and may therefore serve as a hermeneutic key for reading this corpus. Levinas is a philosopher of inter-epistemic difference.

Before I demonstrate this claim, it may be helpful to briefly situate Levinas in twentieth-century philosophy. I began this introduction by pointing out that the contemporary radical critique of Western philosophy has developed from within Western philosophy, that European philosophers were the ones who identified the limits of European philosophy and pointed toward possibilities of thinking beyond it, toward postphilosophical thinking. Within the contemporary Western episteme, critical thinking has to some extent spread or migrated beyond the disciplinary bounds of philosophy itself, becoming theory grounded in a multiverse of studies— literary, cultural, gender, religious, postcolonial.[17] Indeed, the impetus for this migration of Western thought beyond philosophy came from key figures of European philosophy, such as Martin Heidegger, one of Levinas's most influential teachers.

Jacques Derrida already outlined the ambiguous relations of Levinas's critique of Western philosophy and Heidegger's.[18] On the one hand, Levinas portrays Heidegger as epitomizing philosophy's fixation on being—Western philosophy as ontology. On the other, he reiterates central aspects of Heidegger's critique of philosophy as overly theoretical. Heidegger's existential turn in the 1920s made him attractive to young students such as Levinas and Hannah Arendt, as well as to Hans Jonas, who, like Levinas, was drawn away from Husserl's scientism and toward Heidegger's existentialism. Levinas shows his awareness of this debt to Heidegger insofar as he acknowledges that the philosophy of being does not necessarily have to conservatively reaffirm the being of philosophy, to preserve the tradition of Western philosophy; rather, it is "in its comprehension of being . . . concerned with critique."[19] Indeed, Heidegger deploys the notion of being not to consolidate the universal order of beings the philosophical tradition established but instead to question it.

Levinas goes a step further and qualifies this acknowledgment of the critical potential of ontology by indicating that "its critical intention then leads it beyond theory and ontology."[20] This is to say that philosophy has the potential to engage in a self-critique that would take it beyond itself—toward its epistemic Other. However, this trans-epistemic intention is also central to Heidegger's project insofar as his calling of our understanding of being into question is about arguing that *different* understandings—and thus different ontologies, epistemologies, and epistemes—are possible. In this schema, Heidegger problematizes Western philosophy and seeks to show that it only represents a specific episteme. Heidegger's basic effort is to go beyond—to "destruct"—the tradition of Western philosophy toward a radically different way of thinking and knowing, toward a radically different epistemology that is no longer either epistemology (focused on scientific knowledge) or ontology (focused on beings). For later Heidegger, thinking would no longer even belong to philosophy but to alternative historical sites, such as the pre-Socratic Greeks or Hölderlin's postmodern Germans.

Heidegger's late inter-epistemic thought looks for nonphilosophy not only before or after the West but also parallel with it, for instance, in East Asia, Japan, or China.[21] But his early lectures, given many years prior to the publication of *Being and Time*, already develop his critique of Western philosophy and lay the foundation for his alternative epistemology from a site of nonphilosophy situated within the West, one that speaks Greek but with an accent, a Judean one, namely in the epistles of the Greek Jew Saint Paul, also known, for Christians, as the Bible. Heidegger's doctoral student Hans Jonas proceeds in this same West-to-East direction in his trans-epistemic quest insofar as he recognizes a different, foreign, existential knowledge beyond Platonic ontology that in Greek is called not *episteme* but *gnosis*, a category in which Jonas also includes Christian and Jewish epistemes.[22] The exact same movement and vector are at work in Levinas's philosophical project, which confronts philosophy as a Western epistemic tradition with an alternative, which he often refers to as "the prophets."

However, though I argue that this inter- or trans-epistemic concern is constitutive for Levinas's philosophy, it is not evident in his philosophical writings. This is an important point that concerns the epistemic nature of philosophy. From the perspective of contemporary critical epistemology, the attitude toward epistemic difference is itself a defining feature of any given culture of knowledge. The type and degree of visibility that epistemic difference has within a specific epistemic discourse, the kind of knowledge or—to use Levinas's term—"optics" this discourse provides with respect to epistemic difference, belong to the fundamental epistemic settings of that discourse. Any such optics is at the heart of epistemic difference itself; the optics is the very matter of the dispute.

The specificity of Levinas's philosophical writings with respect to epistemic difference is that the inter-epistemic encounter they stage is for the most part presented as *intra*-epistemic tension within philosophy itself, between mainstream and subversive traditions. In such texts, epistemic difference is articulated as a distinction between different philosophical paradigms, namely paradigms of nondifference versus paradigms of difference: totality versus infinity, unity versus plurality, the true versus the good, ontology versus ethics. That these inner philosophical oppositions correspond to tensions between philosophy and Jewish thought is indicated in Levinas's philosophical work mostly through hints or code that my analysis claims to decipher.[23]

The coding of inter- as intra- here translates the rupture *of* thought *into* thought. From the perspective of the rupture between worlds of thought, these different worlds are by definition unable to be integrated into one coherent discourse, one purely conceptual *logos*, but may be indicated not by concepts but through proper names: Western philosophy, Jewish thought. But Levinas's philosophical works constantly work to convert names into concepts. This conversion arises from the essence of the philosophical episteme, which—as Levinas recognizes—always knows how to retrieve "the interrupted discourses of every civilization and of the prehistory of civilizations that were set up as separated" and so to "affirm itself to be coherent and one."[24] This coherent and unified discourse or reason, which is the epistemic principle of philosophy, is designated in this book as "logos," and the philosophical episteme is characterized accordingly as "logical." I show how a unified logos is generated in Levinas's philosophy through the phenomenology of the subject. Logos and subject, episteme and epistemic agency, are akin. The critical intervention of this book consists in showing how philosophy's power to dissolve epistemic difference into a single logos is operative in Levinas's own philosophical texts to such an extent that common readings fail, understandably, to locate any epistemic difference at all.

Nonetheless, my hermeneutic intervention consists in deciphering allusions and highlighting the significance of the underlying inter-epistemic drama that traverses Levinas's philosophical texts. The encounter between philosophy and Jewish thought, it turns out, lies at the heart of the phenomenological narratives Levinas develops. Accordingly, in examining Levinas's phenomenology, which appears to be centered on the individual subject and individual ethics, my readings underline the crucial role of the often neglected collective, political, and historical stakes in Levinas's argumentation. Inter-epistemology is, we shall see, political epistemology.[25]

Levinas's philosophical corpus is shaped by two kinds of difference, by difference at two different levels, each with distinct temporalities. The first difference is between philosophy and Jewish thought, which I claim structures the inner logic of his major works and constitutes the synchrony of their respective narratives. Next to this synchronic difference, Levinas's philosophical writings also feature an epistemic difference, a diachronic one, which does not synchronize but instead divides the time of his work into separate periods. Within the discourse of philosophy, this feature is so obvious that it is hardly visible as such. Philosophy is written by authors, philosophers, who produce multiple works, which are separate and independent and can be divided into early and late. This division is conditioned by the discursive paradigm of the work, taken as a complete and total unit, a perfected event or act of speech that has a beginning and an end and constitutes a systematic logos fully present to itself—in a word, a book. Philosophy is divided into books. Levinas's philosophy can be and is often perceived to be divided into two major books, the earlier *Totality and Infinity* from 1961 and the later *Otherwise Than Being* from 1974.[26]

My analysis of Levinas's philosophy in this book focuses on systematic readings of these two major works, which comprise the most coherent and comprehensive articulations of his phenomenology. The goal is to present the similarities and fundamental differences between these two interventions in order to trace a movement, an inner development in Levinas's philosophy, from the earlier to the later work, which I characterize as self-critique. Within philosophical discourse, this self-critical development is analyzed in purely conceptual terms, purely "philosophically." We will see how this philosophical self-critique corresponds to a similar development in Levinas's historical-political interventions in the context of his Jewish writings, which I trace in politico-historical terms as a shift from before to after 1967–1968. Needless to say, the development of Levinas's philosophy is far more complex than can be seen through a comparison of the two books, as I indicate in passing from time to time. This book, however, is less interested in tracing some genealogical nuance than in revealing a sharp conceptual turn.

The diachronic turn from Levinas's earlier to his later philosophy is related to the synchronic difference between philosophy and Jewish thought in these works. I claim that Levinas's two major books of philosophy can be read as different performances of a philosophical encounter between the philosophical and the Jewish episteme. They will be read as providing two constellations for the inter-epistemic encounter between philosophy and Jewish thought within the discourse of philosophy. The constellations are interrelated such that the later constellation, which Levinas stages in his second book, *Otherwise Than Being*, constitutes a critical reflection on the first constellation, seen in *Totality and Infinity*. In examining central motifs of the conceptual trajectory leading from Levinas's first book to his second, I present his basic conception of the inter-epistemic difference and the inter-epistemic encounter both in general terms and more specifically between philosophy and Jewish thought; I go on to present Levinas's own critical reflection on this initial conception and the fundamental revisions he undertook subsequently. This book therefore provides a theoretical framework not only for conceiving the inter-epistemic difference in question but also for critiquing it.

In a nutshell, I claim that Levinas's early philosophy asserts the inter-epistemic difference between philosophy and Jewish thought and—contra the philosophical episteme, which tends to totality—asserts the Jewish episteme as the episteme of difference. Nevertheless, these two assertions are countered by Levinas's own phenomenological narrative, which, in the logos of the subject, uses difference to ground unity. In his later philosophy, I argue, Levinas criticizes his use as an abuse that he ascribes to the fundamental operation of logos. Accordingly, Levinas's later philosophy develops a stronger epistemology of difference based on a fundamental epistemic shift from logics to hermeneutics. My critical observation is that, notwithstanding this powerful shift, Levinas's later phenomenological narrative reiterates the transformation of difference into unity—and to a significant extent, even enhances it—by means of a more "rigorous logic."

Philosophy versus Jewish Thought in Levinas's Jewish Writings

There is a basic methodological challenge in making any systematic or general statement concerning Levinas's Jewish writings, especially in attempting to have them emerge from, or relate to, a supposedly underlying Jewish episteme (or any episteme at all). These writings consist of dozens of relatively short texts about Talmud, Jewish thought, or Judaism, spanning over six decades, that Levinas never systematized into a book, as he did with his philosophy.[27] On the contrary, the mature form he gave his Jewish texts is explicitly fragmentary, dispersed, and multiple—in short, talmudic. Beyond the difficulty of searching within this rich textual multiplicity for common themes and epistemic features, and even more so for a fundamental narrative or message, the structure and history of this archive seem to explicitly speak against any search for a unified logos or epistemology.

The analyses herein nonetheless identify an inter-epistemic drama at the heart of Levinas's Jewish writings. In view of this drama, Levinas's Jewish writings can be examined through comparison with his philosophical texts. At first glance, the two corpora stage rather different inter-epistemic events. Levinas's philosophical writings, as noted, stage the inter-epistemic encounter between philosophy and Jewish thought as an intra-epistemic tension within philosophy, which "affirms itself to be coherent and one." By contrast, Levinas's Jewish texts explicitly seek to mark the distance between different worlds and cultures of knowledge, between epistemes. These texts constantly contrast not just concepts or epistemic paradigms but concrete historical traditions of knowledge, cultures, and collectives, which are not just alluded to but overtly named—hence the explicit cultural locatedness of these texts. Whereas Levinas's philosophy is never qualified as French, his Jewish texts clearly identify themselves as a *Jewish* performance. If these writings are "Jewish," it is not only because they mainly address Jews. Rather, they invoke and constitute the Jewish as a real historical, political, and social site of difference between philosophy and nonphilosophy.

This is why, as scholars like Annabel Herzog and Oona Eisenstadt have noted, the characteristic question of Levinas's Jewish writing is a political one.[28] Politics features in the Jewish writings not primarily as a branch of theory but as one of the names for the dimension in which theory, thought, and knowledge become reality, existing beyond theory, as human existence, as society, culture, and history.[29] Levinas's Jewish writings display political thinking because they *are* political—that is, they stage and actually unfold the epistemic, inter-epistemic drama never as a purely conceptual tension between different ideas or epistemologies but always as historical conflicts between concrete collectives, cultures, nations, and regimes: Jews, Greeks, Rome, Persia, Hitlerism, Stalinism, France, the State of Israel, and Arabs. These conflicts are not mere arguments. They erupt in violent struggles, wars, not because they are not epistemic but because they arise from radical inter-epistemic difference: they are political because they are struggles over the meaning of politics, and even over the meaning of meaning itself.

It may be helpful to think here of Carl Schmitt's concept of "the political" as the extreme degree of a conflict's intensity at which discussion is no longer possible, the unity of reason breaks down, the opposition becomes ontic, and the potential of physical violence—of war—becomes structural and permanent.[30] Or we might think of Levinas's own notion of ethics, which, as we see in chapter 1, is not a relation of knowledge but of "attitude." In any case, he stages inter-epistemic difference in the Jewish writings as something like a "clash of civilizations," a real rupture not just in thought but of thought, which takes place in a nonepistemic space of no thought, an open space of pure dispersion, ununified by any logos. Once again, it would seem that Levinas's Jewish writings talmudically resist any attempt to sketch a coherent story or clear message and even constitute resistance to such attempts.

But we must ask whether the political, social, and cultural discourse in which Levinas's talmudic and Jewish texts deploy inter-epistemic difference—as a discourse about reality that concerns concrete historical factuality—*necessarily* lies beyond the concept as such, that is, whether it can *only* function as a means of resistance to, and rupture of, logos. The contrary is arguably the case, since there is an entire tradition of philosophy stretching from Plato to Heidegger (to use Levinas's coordinates) for which concrete reality is always an enactment of ideas, for which beings arise from Being. Within this tradition, someone like Hegel, for instance, sees the discourse of concrete collective entities as existing in real time, and history, far from resisting logos, constitutes its completion.

To be sure, the Hegelian philosophy of history is one of the central paradigms Levinas's work—his philosophy and Jewish thought taken together—explicitly seeks to counter. However, let us not forget those who, like Karl Löwith and Jacob Taubes, suggested that the eschatological philosophy of history originally arose from the combination of philosophy and Judaism.[31] In fact, without wedding Levinas specifically to Hegel, I will demonstrate how the historico-political discourse deployed in Levinas's Jewish writings does not open a space of epistemic difference beyond comprehension, in which logical coherence is interrupted or fragmented. On the contrary, underlying Levinas's discourse is a conceptual constellation that can be clearly identified and articulated and of which Levinas's historical narrative is an expression. More specifically, the reality in which this narrative takes place is an already organized, calibrated, and determined space where concrete historical entities, collectives, and cultures function as avatars of epistemic structures.

If we compare Levinas's philosophical writings to his Jewish texts, we can say that the latter configure a discourse in which conceptual, philosophical positions appear embodied in concrete entities, in realia. Concepts become proper names, and philosophy becomes Philosophy. This shift from concepts to names both disintegrates the coherence of logos and interrupts phenomenology—whereby Philosophy interrupts philosophy. Levinas's discourse does not merely interrupt the conceptual coherence of phenomenology; it also orients us around another form of coherence, a discursive genre that unifies names rather than concepts, a logos that is not a pure logic and that coordinates historical entities by placing them in the narrative coherence of a story or a history, which can be called a historiography.[32]

In other words, with respect to Levinas's inter-epistemic project, my critical claim is that Levinas's Jewish writings carry out a similar operation to his philosophy, an operation that consists in synthesizing inter-epistemic difference into one panoramic exposition, one logos. The philosophical writings generate *this* logos by way of a phenomenology of the individual subject, which itself arises from an inter-epistemic encounter—one between totality and infinity, between being and other-than-being—and constitutes the site of epistemic convergence. By comparison, the Jewish texts generate synthesis through the use of historiography, where collective agents—cultures, civilizations, nations, states—constitute the sites of inter-epistemic drama. This historiography (or historiosophy), which, varying over the years, is elaborated in dozens of texts and ways, is nonetheless built on a basic narrative. It is crucial to note how, similar to his phenomenology, Levinas's historiographic narrative features a site of epistemic convergence in the figure of subjectivity, of the subject, this time a collective, concrete, historical one. Collective subjectivity, as that which embodies historiographical logos, which is world history incarnate, has two main avatars, bodies, and names in Levinas's Jewish writings: Israel and the West.

To better grasp Levinas's epistemic performance in his Jewish writings, it is helpful to characterize more precisely the relation these texts configure between historiography and subjectivity. In contrast to the philosophical writings, one basic feature of all of Levinas's Jewish texts is their explicit performativity. Their basic speech act constitutes their unity as arising from the unity of one collective subject. We saw that Levinas described these texts as "confessional," and I showed why it is a mistake to interpret this term as signifying for Levinas something like faith in contradistinction to reason. What could it mean, then, that Levinas's Jewish writings are confessional?

As "confessional," these texts are "Jewish" not just because they speak of Jewish themes but also because they identify themselves as Jewish. Namely, they subscribe to a specific point of view, embodying and performing a specific discourse and intellectual tradition, a specific "confession," to which they confess, which they are. In a more fundamental way, the gesture of these texts is not simply to affiliate or ascribe a preexisting subject to a certain idea or tradition but to constitute this subject through the very act of a confession. To be sure, this can be also said of Levinas's philosophical writings, the confession of which is philosophy. As Foucault observes, all discourse also performs a function of constituting its subject.[33] We will see that Levinas understands language as the medium of subjective existence, where subjects exist simultaneously as separate and in relation, as "interlocutors." And Levinas's later phenomenology has at its center the primary speech act of subject constitution, "here I am," the seminal confession, which Levinas calls *testimony*.

And yet, Levinas's Jewish writings not only constitute their subject far more explicitly and purposefully; this constitution, this confession and testimony, also emerges from their primary function. These texts, published in both Jewish and non-Jewish journals and venues, typically present themselves as self-reflectively embodying, enacting, and articulating the voice of the Jewish subject within a broader historical situation. They never speak just about Jewish themes indicatively, in the mode of objective, scientific, or theoretical observations. Whether they speak to Jews or non-Jews, they assert and affirmatively enact the Jewish voice. As Levinas declares in the first sentence of his "Essays on Judaism," titled *Difficult Freedom*, these texts "testify" to Judaism.[34]

This generative performance is significantly amplified by the specific speech act of the talmudic readings. These texts are styled as what they really were, namely as scripts of Levinas's talks in front of a live audience. The texts directly address the public. They are what Althusser calls "interpellations" insofar as they invoke the subject and call on a certain subjectivity to appear, to come into being.[35] Levinas's talmudic readings invoke the subject, namely *their* subject, to emerge as the underlying unity of their fragmented narratives, the principle of their history, the unity of their message. The basic mode in which these readings carry out their interpellation is by presenting themselves as the speech act of a collective subject, a "we" that encompasses Levinas together with his listeners/readers, a collective that speaks to itself, that constitutes itself by speaking to itself of itself—"How are we to read it?"[36]

The logos of Levinas's talmudic readings is produced by a reading that is a self-interpellation, a way of telling the self, self-testimony: confession. In this sense, Levinas's historiographical act in his talmudic readings may be said to reenact a constitutive Jewish collective ritual, a reading ritual of communal constitution by the narrating of self—a telling of the self, such as the ceremony of public reading of the Torah or family reading of the Passover *haggadah*, a word that signifies both "the telling" and "the tale" and so turns each act of telling into part of the tale. It could arguably be said that all historiography is haggadah, that is, an act that tells the tale of its telling and so constitutes subjectivity as a tale of the self, a self-telling, as telling itself "we."

Levinas himself does not designate the specific Jewish mode of speaking or the specific Jewish mode of knowing, which in his own Jewish texts is characterized by interpellative historiography, by the rabbinic term *haggadah*. The term he most often uses to name the Jewish episteme in contrast to philosophy, which I therefore also use in this book, is *prophecy*. Within the literary archive of the Jewish intellectual tradition, the notion of prophecy refers most clearly to the prerabbinic Hebrew Bible. It may therefore seem puzzling that Levinas, in situating his intervention in the Jewish textual tradition, chooses to engage not with the prophetic corpus, the Bible, but with the rabbinic corpus. And in this corpus, he does not focus on the more visionary, speculative rabbinical episteme, the Kabbalah, but on the almost antiprophetic Talmud. Nevertheless, and this will be examined critically in a forthcoming study, Levinas reads the Talmud as the Jewish reading of the Bible—that is, as providing authentic Jewish access to prophecy. In the framework of the prophetic episteme, the basic operation of Levinas's Jewish texts, the transformation of inter-epistemic difference into a confessional historical-political narrative, into interpellative historiography, can be designated by Levinas's own characterization of prophetic discourse: eschatology.

Who is the subject of Levinas's eschatology? Who is its "we"? And what *eschaton*, what end vision, does it prophesize? This is the basic question of the Jewish texts, the answer their underlying historiographical narrative seeks to provide. This answer, which is to say, the eschatological drama as such, is built on a fundamental tension between two main figures, which are figures of one split historical subjectivity, torn into two bodies and epistemes. The tensions between these subject-figures generate the story, which simultaneously constitutes an inter-epistemic and an intra-epistemic plot.

The first collective subject seems to be obvious, titular, namely the Jewish, embodied in the figure of Israel. A common reading of Levinas has, however, denied that "the Jewish" and "Israel" designate for him a specific historical collective or people. This reading is often based on Levinas's assurance, in his talmudic reading from 1969 titled "Judaism and Revolution," that the rabbinic notion of "Israel" is not a "racist idea": "each time Israel is mentioned in the Talmud one is certainly free to understand by it a particular ethnic group which is probably fulfilling an incomparable destiny. But to interpret in this manner would be to reduce the general principle in the idea enunciated in the Talmudic passage, to forget that Israel means a people who has received the Law and, as a result, a human nature which has reached the fullness of its responsibilities and its self-consciousness."[37] Scholars have interpreted Levinas's rejection of racism and ethnic particularism to mean the rejection of any peoplehood, such that Israel would become a universal concept or a metaphor detached from specific Jewish history.[38]

I explain in chapter 4 why I think this reading overlooks the main political thrust of Levinas's assertion of the Jewish contra the philosophical, that is, the Greco-Roman episteme, which is the transformation of the essence of collective being, the revolutionizing of peoplehood. In any case, the specific Jewish collective is the historical agency and embodiment of the Jewish episteme in Levinas's inter-epistemic eschatology. It is this concrete collective that Levinas, speaking at the "Colloquium of Jewish Intellectuals," seeks to invoke and regenerate.

However, the Jewish intellectual comprising this contemporary epistemic community is, as Levinas invokes it, alienated from itself and hence from its collective Jewish episteme, the Talmud. By identifying Jewish knowledge with the Talmud, Levinas invokes Jewish subjects who are self-alienated, who are also someone else, others, and thus refers to a split collective subjectivity. In other words, Levinas's Jewish writings, especially his talmudic readings, structurally posit the Jewish in complex relations to another collective subjectivity, which is both foreign and intimate, non-Jewish and Jewish, embodying both difference and unity between Jewish and non-Jewish. This second figure of collective subjectivity goes by different names and is invoked in various ways in Levinas's prophetic eschatology. Most often it is called *l'Occident*, the Occident, the West, or Europe, "our old Europe."[39]

The basic plot of Levinas's prophecy is indeed the complex, inter-epistemo-political relationship between Israel and the West. The principal contemporary collective figure that stands at the center of Levinas's prophetic-eschatological narrative and orients the evolvement of the dramatic encounter between Jews and the West is the State of Israel. One of the key claims that is made in this book and underlies its entire structure is that Levinas's Jewish writings tell two eschatological stories of Israel, corresponding to the two phenomenological narratives of the subject in his early and late philosophical work, and that the turn between the two versions of this logos can be dated to 1967, or 1967 as viewed in light of 1968.

1967 after 1968

Whereas Levinas's philosophical work more readily presents itself as articulated by breaks of books, a shift from early to late as a movement from the first book to the second, the analogous shift, which is actually the same shift, lies hidden in Levinas's Jewish writings. Paradoxically, these foundational historical texts work, in their dispersion and fragmentation, to conceal their own history to the point of appearing timeless.[40] And yet, a careful analysis allows us to identify a turn from one distinct historiography narrative to another, each of which corresponds to one of Levinas's two phenomenological narratives, that of 1961 and that of 1974. This analysis enables us to ascribe the shift to a more precise date between 1961 and 1974—the years 1967 and 1968.[41]

Talk about two narratives before and after 1968 should be understood within the textual complexity of Levinas's writings. I do not wish to argue that his work can be simply divided into two corpora, before and after 1968, which tell two different stories. I do not speak about two different works but two different discourses, which develop, as thinking and writing do, and often coexist within the same texts. The later narrative is already present, in *statu nascendi*, in Levinas's earlier texts, and earlier narratives persist or even unfold in later texts. Readers should therefore not be surprised to see references to post-1968 texts in my discussion of pre-1968 Levinas. The two narratives are structurally interrelated; they are two different, or even, as already said, conflicting, articulations of the same basic inter-epistemic constellation. Nonetheless, a transformation of the articulation or emphasis of these narratives produces dramatic effects.

This complex discursive drama translates also into a complex epistemic event within Levinas's Jewish writings. As I have emphasized, Levinas's Jewish texts are not neatly divided into two books, before and after 1968. Rather, their foundational epistemic event is structured by the dynamic status of the talmudic readings in the Jewish writings. Levinas's first talmudic readings date from 1960. However, they were first published in 1963 as one section in *Difficult Liberty*, his "Essays on Judaism," which go back to the 1940s and were republished in a second edition in 1976. It is precisely in 1968, in a moment between these editions, the first from 1963 and the second from 1976, that Levinas's talmudic readings were first published as such, as *Talmudic Readings*, no longer only a section of his Jewish texts but the very *topos*, discourse, or mode of text and utterance of Levinas's narrative. This change of textuality, discursivity, and framing, like the shift in the historiographic accentuation, is subtle but dramatic.

In the following chapters, my demonstration therefore discerns a movement between Levinas's two philosophical endeavors, between *Totality and Infinity* and *Otherwise Than Being*, which corresponds to a movement between two historiographical narratives in Levinas's Jewish writings, before and after 1968, and is manifested in the emergence of the *Talmudic Readings*. The critical meaning of this pivotal year of 1968 for Levinas—and the entire discourse he represents—will become clearer through the demonstration itself. This demonstration does not assume the meaning of the events that took place in 1968. It presupposes no ready-made historiography that would be of use in understanding Levinas. On the contrary, my analysis traces within the Levinasian text the contours of a historiographical break, a narrative rupture, a discursive crisis that takes shape around 1968. This discursive shift in Levinas's writings, I propose, constitutes one of the foundational acts of discourse in the production of 1968 as an event for Levinas's contemporaries, especially Jews, and for the future, especially Jewish.[42]

At this preliminary stage, I point out that the inner relation between Levinas's two historiographical projects corresponds to the inner relation between his two phenomenological projects, wherein the late work features a self-critique of the early work. The plot is animated by the tension between the collective subjectivities of the West and of Israel, where the latter comes to find its ultimate embodiment in the State of Israel. It is with respect to tension between the West and the State of Israel that the pivotal year of 1968, and more precisely the years 1967–1968, obtain their dramatic signification. The emergence of Levinas's *Talmudic Readings* in 1968, so the following chapters claim, marks a shift from an early colonial to a late decolonial eschatology of the Jewish state and from a colonial to a decolonial justification of its war.

In a nutshell, the transformation I have in mind is between two philosophical-eschatological narratives, before and after 1968, and it concerns, phenomenologically, the nature of subjectivity and, politically, the nature of the collective Jewish subject, Israel. I argue that in his *pre-1968* work, Levinas develops in his phenomenology a subject that arises from the ethical encounter with the other, from "prophetic," namely Jewish ethics, but then gives effect to this ethics by developing an assertive, happy, erotic, and generous existence, an active Greek being in the service of Jewish morality.

This Judeo-Greek subject of Levinas's early phenomenology corresponds to the figure of the collective Jewish subject, "Israel," as developed in Levinas's pre-1968 Jewish writings. These writings feature Israel as the historical agent of prophetic justice in Western history, such that Israel appears as the messianic avant-garde of Western humanism. In the spirit of Jewish-Greek harmony, Israel offers the vision of a prophetic *polis*, the State of Israel, founded according to Levinas's narrative in modernity as the European nation-state, exemplified first by the French Republic and then by the Jewish State of Israel, acting as the spearhead of Judeo-Greek humanism in the Middle East.

It is this figure of Israel as the agent of expansive Western humanism—"the Bible and the Greeks"—that is targeted by contemporary postcolonial critique of Levinas. This critique indicates how the ethics of otherness generates an imperial subject. I claim that Levinas acknowledged this critique, internalized it, and reformulated his position—both phenomenologically and politically—in his post-1968 writings.

Levinas's second philosophy rethinks the nature of the ethical subject. His later philosophical intervention no longer consists in asserting prophetic ethics as grounding Greek ontology. On the contrary, ethics now disrupts the order of being. Levinas's later phenomenology conceptualizes the subject constituted by this disruption of Western being, namely the decolonial subject. In contrast to the joyful, triumphant ethical self of his pre-1968 philosophy, Levinas's later philosophy portrays a suffering self whose moral, responsible existence consists not in generosity but in self-sacrifice, not in active works of justice but in the radical passivity of persecution, in martyrdom and passion.

The translation of Levinas's post-1968 philosophy into concrete political history is done once again in his Jewish writings. The novelty of Levinas's post-1968 Jewish texts is the conceptualization of a decolonial Israel. In contrast to the Davidic Israel of the earlier narrative, an active agent of justice, Levinas's post-1968 Israel is modeled after the suffering subject. This subject is moral not by enforcing justice but by subjecting itself to injustice, to persecution. The historical Jewish collective, in this narrative, attests to morality not by agency but by weakness, by martyrdom, in submitting to "the Passion of Israel." Decolonial Israel is no king messiah but the messiah as the ultimate victim, namely of Western civilization. The portrait of the Jewish collective as persecuted does not lead Levinas to embrace statelessness. On the contrary, Levinas develops a vision of the Jewish state not as realizing prophetic justice but as the persecuted, victim state.

Structure of the Book

Part I of the book is dedicated to Levinas's work prior to 1967–1968. Chapter 1 shows how *Totality and Infinity* (1961) stages a confrontation between Western philosophy and "the Prophets." Philosophy is guided by ontology, which tends to a totality that violently excludes individual morality. By contrast, prophetic episteme is based on an ethics of nonviolent respect for alterity. But Levinas does not pit the prophets against the philosophers or promote ethics over ontology. Rather, he suggests that prophetic ethics is "first philosophy" and Jewish ethics grounds Greek being.

Chapter 2 argues that the main concern of Levinas's early phenomenology is not the Other but the ethical self that leads a happy, Greek existence in the service of Jewish morality. But Levinas's prophetic ethics seeks to counter totalitarianism not only at the level of individual morality but also at the collective form of justice. Against the Greek polis as a totalitarian state, *Totality and Infinity* posits "the Family." I argue that this figure, commonly understood as referring to the private sphere, deploys, against the state, the prophetic people, Israel.

This reading is confirmed by Levinas's Jewish writings. The historiographical narrative woven in these texts features Israel as the historical agent of prophetic justice. Chapters 3 and 4 show how in the early, pre-1968 version of Levinas's story, just as prophetic ethics grounds Western philosophy, so, too, does Israel act historically as the avant-garde of Western humanism. In the spirit of Jewish-Greek harmony, Israel offers a model for a prophetic polis, namely the Davidic Kingdom of Justice. Chapter 5 shows how in Levinas's early eschatology, Jewish prophetic politics—"the State of Israel"—was first founded in modernity as the French Republic. Its further, more accomplished realization is the Jewish State of Israel, depicted as the avant-garde of the Western *mission civilisatrice* in the Middle East.

Part II of the book is dedicated to Levinas's post-1968 work. Chapter 6 discusses Levinas's second philosophy, formulated in *Otherwise Than Being* (1974), and demonstrates how late Levinas rethinks the nature of the ethical subject. The driving problem of Levinas's later thought is no longer the disappearance of moral individuality in the totality of being. On the contrary, the fundamental problem is now that the individual, once arisen from an ethical break with being, seeks to preserve itself in being. Ethics empowers higher-order ontology and generates higher-order violence in the form of just war. The primary epistemo-political problem that troubles the post-1968 Levinas, I show, is no longer totalitarianism but imperialism.

Accordingly, Levinas's later philosophical intervention no longer consists in asserting the prophetic ethics of the Jewish episteme as grounding Western ontology. On the contrary, prophetic discourse here works to *disrupt* the Western order of being by "unsaying" ontology. Chapter 7 shows how Levinas's late philosophy seeks to conceptualize the subject constituted by an anarchic prophetic ethics, namely the decolonial subject. In contrast to the joyful ethical self of *Totality and Infinity*, Levinas's later phenomenology portrays a suffering self whose morality consists not in active works of justice but in the radical passivity of persecution.

Similarly to the period before 1968, Levinas's translation of his post-1968 phenomenology into concrete political history occurs in his Jewish writings. Chapter 8 argues that the novelty of Levinas's post-1968 Jewish texts lies in his conceptualization of a decolonial Israel. In contrast to the Davidic Israel of the earlier narrative, as an active agent of Justice, Levinas's post-1968 Israel is modeled on the suffering subject. Decolonial Israel is a messiah not as king but as a victim.

Chapter 9 demonstrates how in his post-1968 Jewish texts, Levinas develops something like a decolonial Zionism, which advocates a Jewish state that does not realize prophetic justice but provides self-defense from persecution. Self-defense, I argue, does not end but perpetuates persecution: in Levinas's narrative, the decolonial State of Israel, attacked, terrorized, and criticized, emerges as the model of the persecuted, martyred, victim state.

PART I. STATE OF JUSTICE: LEVINAS BEFORE 1968

T HIS PART IS DEDICATED TO THE ENCOUNTER BETWEEN philosophy and Jewish thought in Levinas's work before 1968. The first two chapters read this encounter, which Levinas describes as a confrontation between philosophy and prophecy, as standing at the heart of Levinas's early philosophy as formulated in his first major book, *Totality and Infinity* of 1961. We will see how Levinas's philosophical work stages the encounter between philosophy and prophecy in terms of a phenomenology of subjectivity. In the following three chapters, the discussion turns to Levinas's pre-1968 Jewish writings, which are read as articulating the dynamics between philosophy and prophecy in historical and political terms, namely as eschatology. I show how Levinas's early phenomenology of the subject underlies his early eschatology of Israel.

A central motif that my analyses reveal in the inter-epistemic dynamics featured in Levinas's pre-1968 work is the assertion of Jewish thought—prophecy or Torah—as the foundation of Greek philosophy and Western civilization. Within the phenomenology of the subject, this constellation manifests itself in the way that the ethical encounter with the other constitutes the separate existence of the sovereign self. In Levinas's pre-1968 eschatology, the Jewish principle of the West translates into a messianic vision of the State of Israel as working for the realization of universal European justice. My critical reflection indicates how, in different moments and ways, the assertion of alterity transforms into the production of identity.

PHILOSOPHY

THE FOLLOWING TWO CHAPTERS EXAMINE LEVINAS'S EARLY PHILOSO-
PHY through his first major book from 1961, *Totality and Infinity*. This is
Levinas's most well-known and studied work, and it provides a systematic
formulation of the fundamental terms of his philosophical project. It has
already been the subject of many studies, to which I refer in my notes. My
analysis offers a view of the core intellectual endeavor undertaken by Levinas in this book. It presents its major concepts and operations as interrelated
elements within one structured intervention. It is in view of this overarching structure that my analysis also offers a critique of Levinas's book.

My reading emphasizes two basic albeit oft-neglected concerns of Levinas's project, which I claim shape its basic contours. In contrast to common
readings of the book as confronting knowledge with ethics, chapter 1 argues
that the book's foundational confrontation is inter-epistemic, in that it occurs between two different kinds of knowledge, one theory based, the other
ethics based: philosophy and Jewish thought, or "prophecy." In contrast to
the common understanding of Levinas's ethics as individual and nonpolitical, chapter 2 shows how the ultimate thrust of the book's argument concerns collective life and politics and so structurally points toward Levinas's
Jewish writings.

1

ETHICS AS OPTICS

THIS CHAPTER OUTLINES A READING OF LEVINAS'S *Totality and Infinity* as asserting an inter-epistemic difference between philosophy and Jewish thought, a difference that concerns the very question of difference. One basic observation of my analysis is that, in this book of philosophy, inter-epistemic difference features as intra-epistemic—that is, as an internal tension within the tradition of philosophy. Levinas codes references from extraphilosophical, Jewish, or prophetic traditions into philosophical concepts, which explains why they have often remained unseen by readers. The following pages are an attempt at decoding these references.

Between Philosophers and Prophets

The title *Totality and Infinity: An Essay on Exteriority* places two nouns side by side as names of two separate cultures, two different traditions—Totality and Infinity,[1] interrelated by a mere "and," a minimal relation of juxtaposition, a relation of exteriority, as the subtitle suggests. Yet these are not names. They are concepts; they are categories that belong to a single epistemic system, Philosophy, which is too present and obvious to be named. The juxtaposition of Totality and Infinity can be easily read not as disjunction or conflict but as pertaining to conjunction and systematicity, as bringing together that which belongs together, which is basically one and the same, like Being and Time. The "and" suggests not conflict, difference, or dissymmetry but rather the coherence and synthesis of a panoramic view.[2]

And yet, from the outset, Levinas describes the book as seeking to expose something often perceived as *intra*-epistemic, as an inner tension within one and the same knowledge system, within the essence of culture or nature of man. He refers to the tension between the true and the good, between knowledge and morality, theory and praxis, contemplation and action, between Kant's first and second critiques. He refers to this seemingly intra-epistemic tension as constituting a "split" between two traditions, as an *inter*-epistemic difference: "To tell the truth, ever since eschatology has opposed peace to war, the evidence of war has been maintained in an essentially hypocritical civilization, that is, attached both to the True and to the Good, henceforth antagonistic. It is perhaps time to see in hypocrisy not only a base contingent defect of man, but the profound split [*déchirement*] of a world attached at the same time to both the philosophers and the prophets."[3]

What appears to be one world—what *is* already one world, ours—would in fact be the indecision between two different, separate, and antagonistic poles. This bipolar tension is built not just on difference, which may also constitute the inner structure of a systematic whole, but on a split, disruption, disturbance of wholeness, a rupture of totality. Our world is torn between two incommensurable civilizations, which are not just two concepts or terms conjoined in one discourse, not just two philosophical, Latinate categories, *totalitas* and *infinitas*, and not even two modes of consciousness, but instead two separate figures of humanity marked by two antagonistic paradigms of epistemic agency: "the philosophers and the prophets."[4] These two paradigms are both designated by Greek categories. In this way, they trace an inner tension in a world, ours, that is built on Greek, the West. At the same time, however, they invoke one of the most common inter-epistemic distinctions both operative in and generative of Western discourse, which is to say the distinction between Greek and non-Greek cultures of knowledge—and, more specifically, the tension between Athens and Jerusalem, European and Oriental, Greek and Jewish, Plato and Moses, Philosophy and the Bible.

The tension between philosophers and prophets preserves the ambiguity of the epistemic difference around which the book's argument revolves: this difference operates both within one world and between two different ones. It is both a conceptual tension between totality and infinity, true and good, and a split between two civilizations, two historical, textual, and political projects, two separate traditions of knowledge and praxis—two epistemes.

The ambiguity between split and difference, between *intra*-epistemic and *inter*-epistemic, is foundational for Levinas's staging of the inter-epistemic encounter in his philosophical writings and commands the movement from his earlier to his later book, as I show later. Philosophical discourse is only able to refer to its epistemic other in code. It can acknowledge this other not with a proper name but only and always through the concept, thus rendering the other as always already meaningful, understood, domesticated, and de-othered. The reference is often made not by direct designation but by incidental association. In *Totality and Infinity*, the idea of the Infinite, which, given Levinas's explicit reference to Descartes, can be easily translated as "God," is occasionally associated, for instance, with the "monotheistic faith"[5] as well as with the ideas of "creation *ex nihilo*" and "sabbatical existence."[6] Philosophy's epistemic other is also associated with religion, but Levinas explicitly declines to identify it with theology.[7]

In contrast, Levinas unambiguously rejects the designation of nonphilosophical thought, which his book promotes, as "Oriental." He objects to this designation—"an alleged Oriental thought"—deeming it an accusation or insult.[8] This rejection is doubtless a reaction to an entire modern discourse of secularism, Orientalism, and Semitism that performs a mix of anti-Semitic slurs and philo-Semitic condescendence, fulfilling the role of devaluing or de-epistemizing the epistemic tradition to which Levinas lays claim.[9] But what Levinas seems to reject even more fundamentally in "Oriental" is not the adjective but the name. This is not because of what it means, for instance, non-Greek, but because it does not have any epistemic meaning; it is not a concept but a name. It does not mean but simply points—to the East. In contrast to its Western counterpart, which in Levinas's texts commonly serves to determine philosophy ("Western philosophy"), Oriental otherness is no longer epistemic. West would relate to East not as one world of knowledge to another but as knowledge to the lack of knowledge or as thought to thoughtlessness.[10]

Accordingly, on both occasions that Levinas rejects "Oriental" as an improper designation for the epistemic other of philosophers, he immediately assures us of the "dignity" of this alternative tradition of thought by associating it with a well-known motif in the constitutive text of the tradition of philosophy, namely Plato's Idea of the Good. Of this notion, which Levinas believes exceeds Philosophy, he writes, "That there could be a more than being or an above being is expressed in the idea of creation which, in God, exceeds a being eternally satisfied with itself. But this notion of being above being does not come from theology. If it has played no role in the Western philosophy issued from Aristotle, the Platonic idea of the Good ensures it the dignity of a philosophical thought, and it therefore should not be traced back to any oriental wisdom."[11]

Along with Plato's Idea of the Good, Levinas defends the philosophical dignity of nonphilosophy by identifying it in a second figure central to
philosophy, a modern one: Descartes's Idea of the Infinite. This move gives
to nonphilosophy its undercover philosophical code, "Infinity."

In *Totality and Infinity*, Levinas's first philosophical magnum opus, the
inter-epistemic encounter between philosophy and nonphilosophy, between
philosophers and prophets, takes place for the most part in the form of a
drama internal to philosophy. "Totality and Infinity" reads initially as con-
veying the tension or struggle between two currents within philosophical
tradition: a mainstream strand running "from Parmenides to Spinoza and
Hegel," or "from Plato to Heidegger," and an undercurrent, a subversive tradition, which surfaces only at specific moments, for instance, in some Platonic or Cartesian ideas.[12] The translation of the split between two separate
traditions of knowledge, an inter-epistemic split, into an intra-epistemic
tension between different conceptions in philosophy has the effect of turning philosophical concepts into code names for the divide between philosophy and nonphilosophy, between the Greek and the Jewish: ontology and
metaphysics, totality and infinity.[13]

Light

Under the titular distinction between totality and infinity, Levinas provides
multiple characterizations of these paradigms of knowledge. Two central
features ought to be highlighted. First, all epistemic characterizations concern the question of difference, such that the two worlds of knowledge
represent traditions of dealing with difference—they differ on difference
and are "others" to each other because each has another approach to otherness. Second, the epistemic difference between these two conceptions and
performances of difference is articulated by the internal relation between
knowledge and practice within each episteme. In other words, even though
the above-quoted passage presents the split between the two epistemes as a
tension between the true and the good, this tension is also *internal* to these
epistemes and constitutive of their epistemologies. The question concerning ethical aspects of knowledge is central to the entire Levinasian project.
Totality and Infinity is motivated by a tension between wisdom and morality from its very first line. As Levinas writes, "Everyone will readily agree
that it is of the highest importance to know whether we are not duped by
morality."[14]

In this constellation, the tradition of wisdom is *philosophy*. Levinas's basic characterization of the philosophical episteme is "totality." Totality here means a certain constellation of difference, one with interrelated epistemic and ethico-political aspects. As a constellation of difference, totality signifies a multiplicity of different elements that nonetheless constitute a whole. Totality is difference as unity of the different. Philosophy, as the tradition of totality, is "philosophy of unity" in that it promotes "the ancient privilege of unity that is affirmed from Parmenides to Spinoza and Hegel."[15] Accordingly, the basic act of philosophy—the fundamental operation of its knowledge, that which it knows how to do—is to generate totality by overcoming difference in unity.

Levinas indicates the two main epistemological paradigms that have served philosophy in generating totality: theory and ontology, which is to say theory as ontology.

Theory, which comes from the Greek θεωρεῖν, *theorein*, meaning "to look, to view, to observe," refers to a form of knowledge based on seeing, on vision. Both theory and vision, as well as light, have an ambivalent epistemic role in *Totality and Infinity*.[16] The split between the philosophers and the prophets, which translates into a tension within philosophy, appears in a condensed form as the ambivalence of theory.

On the one hand, theory is knowledge from a distance, which not only respects otherness and difference but also constitutes the very essence of the epistemology of difference as the opposite of totality—and thus of philosophy. On the other hand, however, theory has a second meaning that is the exact opposite of the first. Theory is "a way of approaching the known being such that its alterity with regard to the knowing being vanishes."[17] The ambivalence of theory here is the ambivalence of vision, or light. Light is a medium of nothingness that enables knowledge from a distance. Thanks to the same quality, however, light is also an absolute medium that overcomes all distance, connecting all different things into one total visibility, one see-all, which Levinas calls "the panoramic." It is this totalizing effect of light, vision, and theory that Levinas identifies as the epistemic core of philosophy, which, "from Plato to Heidegger," has thought and performed knowledge as an operation of "bringing to light (*mettre en lumière*)."[18] Using a Platonic metaphor, Levinas argues that the epistemically strongest light is not sunlight, sensual light, but the light of the mind, intelligence, reason, or logos. The logos that philosophy has deployed to generate total visibility is the "logos of being," or ontology.[19]

Note that Levinas's basic attitude toward this philosophical epistemology is from the outset *critical*. In other words, Levinas does not just describe philosophy as a specific world of knowledge, with its own principles and elements that may be and are in fact different from other worlds of knowledge. Levinas's own thoughts on philosophy are not simply *theoretical*, contemplative, phenomenological, but rather consist essentially in judgment, in evaluation not from a neutral but from an already specific point of view. Furthermore, Levinas's fundamental judgment of philosophy is itself not purely theoretical but moral, ethical. This moral critique, this lack of neutrality from Levinas's contemplation, does not necessarily undermine his presentation of epistemic *difference*, plurality, and diversity; on the contrary, as we shall see, for Levinas it is not objective observation that constitutes our basic knowledge of difference but ethical engagement.

Levinas's central critique of philosophy's epistemology is that by abolishing all difference, it leaves no epistemic room for individual beings. Totality renders the individual insignificant. This abdication of individuality concerns not only the object of knowledge, the known being, the Other. Rather, the main thrust of Levinas's critique of epistemic totality is that it fundamentally abolishes the individuality of the knower, indeed of the self. Western philosophy's paradigm of totality, Levinas writes, reduces every relation "to an impersonal relation within a universal order. Philosophy itself is identified with the substitution of ideas for persons, of the theme for the interlocutor, of the interiority of the logical relation for the exteriority of interpellation. Beings are reduced to the Neuter of the idea, Being, the concept."[20] The ultimate epistemic consequence of totality as overcoming difference is not the subjugation of all otherness, things, and persons to selfish and solipsistic knowledge but the absorption of both others and self, of all selves, into impersonal knowledge: it is the disappearance of all individuality in Being, which "destroys the identity of the Same."[21]

Levinas's project is animated by the *ethical* implications of this epistemic destruction of identity in totality. Similar to Hannah Arendt, Levinas describes the basic practical implication of totalizing thought as generating "movement," namely as bringing individual identities into sync with a total vision, which Arendt calls "ideology": "a casting into movement of beings hitherto anchored in their identity, a mobilization of absolutes, by an objective order from which there is no escape."[22] This loss of identity is the defining character for Levinas of violence—that is, of evil.

For Levinas, as for Arendt, the evil of total knowledge lies in abolishing individuality and thereby destroying the basic condition for human action as the realm of ethics, namely destroying "every possibility for action" as arising from individual moral agents who are responsible for their actions.[23] Totality negates morality by abolishing individual responsibility. *Totality and Infinity* begins by describing how "lucidity" (knowledge guided by light) knows a reality that is without morality, a world that is ontologically violent and in a "state of war": "The state of war suspends morality; it divests the eternal institutions and obligations of their eternity and rescinds ad interim the unconditional imperatives."[24] For totalitarianism, Arendt argues, "everything is possible."[25] Eternal obligations are based on unconditional imperatives, which, as Levinas understands it, require absolute individual responsibilities—eternity, or infinity, which is correlative to individuality. For total knowledge, in contrast, there is no meaning in individual decisions and actions. The only judgment philosophy can therefore know is not that of morality but that of history.

The paradigmatic form of praxis that arises from philosophy's epistemology of totality, the praxis that constitutes the impossibility of action, a praxis of nonmorality, of war, is for Levinas in *Totality and Infinity* what constitutes "politics." Politics then amounts to the performance of totality to the exclusion of individuality. Whereas for Arendt, twentieth-century total politics is epitomized in the image of the movement, Levinas's first book imagines totality as a total state, as "the tyranny of the State."[26] As state, the human world of action is without individuals; it is anonymous, impersonal. When Levinas therefore describes ontology as a "philosophy of power" or a "philosophy of injustice," when he speaks about "ontological imperialism,"[27] the basic immorality of these constellations lies most fundamentally not in the selfish disrespect of others but in the loss of individual self, of responsible moral agent. Even though the term is not mentioned in *Totality and Infinity*, the most adequate designation for politics as Levinas imagines it in this book—politics as the practical correlate of philosophy's epistemological totality—is indeed Arendt's concept of "totalitarianism."[28]

Optics of Ethics

In contrast to philosophy, *prophetic epistemology* stands for the *rupture of totality*. If totality—as the epistemological principle of philosophy—is the constellation of difference as overcome by unity, prophetic knowledge maintains difference in nonunity. It pertains to the essential paradox of Levinas's project that he presents this constellation of difference, which marks a rupture with the epistemic totality of ontology, in ontological terms, as the "ultimate structure of being." Nontotalized difference means a being "produced as multiple and as split in Same and Other."[29]

Formally, Levinas characterizes the fundamental difference he has in mind as a relation that "does not have the structure formal logic finds in all relations," wherein "the distinction of terms also reflects their union," but rather as a relation where "the terms remain absolute despite the relation in which they find themselves." Levinas designates this relation of absolute difference with the category of *separation*. He identifies the idea of separation in one of the basic categories that has been attributed to the prophetic tradition and has functioned as a central topos for the translation of prophecy to ontology, namely *creation*. Creation here is understood as that "in which the kinship of beings among themselves is affirmed, but at the same time their radical heterogeneity also, their reciprocal exteriority coming from nothingness."[30]

Based on the paradigm of separation, prophetic epistemology cannot be ontology. It cannot be guided by any uniting logos, any light, because it cannot be based on knowledge as theory, as vision. As Levinas writes, "otherwise the Same and the Other would be reunited under one gaze, and the absolute distance that separates them filled in." Accordingly, a knowledge of difference cannot lie outside of difference but must pertain to the very relation of difference: a knowledge of separation must also *perform* separation. Knowledge does not consist in positioning entities relative to one another in indifferent space; it is not a conjunction of one "and" another. Rather, the relation of separation constitutes a movement, or a vector, that goes from one separated being toward another, as the "orientation of being 'from oneself' towards 'the Other,'" as "being for the other."[31] Subsequently, the relation of difference is not experienced and enacted, not "known" at all, strictly speaking, as "difference," which assumes an external, objective, and comparative point of view. Difference is only experienced from within, from the perspective of sameness that encounters difference as *otherness*, as the Other.[32]

Accordingly, *prophecy*, the epistemology of real difference, is focused on the separated entity that, by virtue of its separateness from others, constitutes the nonother, namely that which always remains "the Same," the entity whose being consists in remaining identical to itself: the self.

Conceptually—and this is a fundamental paradox of any philosophy of difference—a rigorous commitment to difference requires an equally rigorous commitment to identity. For Levinas, being identical to itself, being self, is what constitutes subjectivity, such that his antitotalitarian project, which consists in affirming separation, is also described as "defense of subjectivity."[33] According to Levinas, the concrete existence of the subjective self is the individual self, which therefore constitutes the absolute point of view, the absolute individual perspective of knowledge, and is designated as the individual knowledge subject, the singular first person "me": "Alterity is possible only starting from *me*."[34]

Levinas describes the "me" as "interiority." The relation of separation signifies interiority open to the outside. For this reason, *Totality and Infinity* is, as a defense of subjectivity, "An Essay on Exteriority." Exteriority is difference, otherness as known from the self's inner point of view. In prophetic epistemology, knowledge constitutes the relation of an inner self "with a surplus always exterior to totality." The exterior, the other, is that toward which the self's knowledge is oriented. Levinas calls it "radical" or "metaphysical" exteriority, which means that it can never be interior, since it constitutes the absolute exteriority in relation to which—and in separation from which—interiority may exist as such. He designates this exteriority using the preposition "beyond," *au-delà*, or "transcendence," meta-. Most prominently, however, in his first book, Levinas designates the otherness of knowledge, which essentially remains beyond knowledge, never to be contained or totalized, using the Cartesian term "infinity," the philosophical code name for prophecy.[35]

For the sake of decoding, note that infinity, or the infinite, is the epistemo-ontological concept for what is often known as God in the prophetic archive, sometimes designated as *En Sof*, "the Infinite," in the kabbalist tradition.[36] Accordingly, Levinas often describes knowledge of the infinite by the category of knowledge received from God, properly prophetic knowledge, *revelation*. Since the infinite is the other of "me," another subjectivity or another person—in French, *autrui*—Levinas also describes knowledge of the infinite through the category of knowledge received from another person, namely *teaching*.[37] "Teaching" is a designation of knowledge in the more specifically *rabbinic* tradition, a tradition that approaches prophecy not primarily as revelation but as *torah*, literally "instruction." And the source of this knowledge, the Other, the epistemic giver, is neither a god nor a prophet but, as Levinas writes, a teacher, literally a *rav*, rabbi.

Levinas's main point is that prophetic knowledge, which constitutes a subjective interiority's relation to infinite exteriority, from me to the Other, is in essence not a relation of vision and thus not one of theory. Separation is rather generated by knowledge that constitutes an actual "being for the other," which does not *see* the other but is seized by the other and *goes* toward the other, outside of itself. A knowledge of otherness, or relation to infinity, is accordingly characterized by Levinas as "desire" or "attitude": "In order that a pluralism in itself (which cannot be reflected in formal logic) be realized there must be produced in depth the movement from me to the other, an attitude of an I with regard to the Other (an attitude already specified as love or hatred, obedience or command, learning or teaching, etc.)." The epistemology of difference is therefore not ontology but axiology—or, rather, ethics. In this epistemology, the medium of knowledge, the optics of vision, is not distant indifference or neutral observation. In it, knowledge is already behavior, engagement, *conduct*. As Levinas famously formulates it, "ethics is an optics."[38]

Levinas's central contribution to the epistemology of difference is indeed to have indicated that difference-based knowledge cannot exist in the indifferent space of theory, of the true and the false, but that it resides in ethics, namely in the dimension of *good and bad*. Not only does this kind of knowledge, as the basis of epistemic diversity, not exclude morality, in contradistinction to the totalizing paradigm of philosophy, nontotalizing knowledge *is* in essence moral, and so the very nature of this episteme transcends the "opposition between theory and practice."[39]

Beyond ethics, Levinas identifies *language* as another essential feature of any epistemology of difference. "Absolute difference," he writes in *Totality and Infinity*, "inconceivable in terms of formal logic, is established only by language. Language accomplishes a relation between terms that breaks up the unity of a genus. The terms, the interlocutors, absolve themselves from the relation, or remain absolute within relationship. Language is perhaps to be defined as the very power to break the continuity of being or of history."[40]

Levinas's work points to a deep affinity between ethics and language as central features of difference-based knowledge. We may say that such knowledge, which would be the constitutive episteme of the prophetic tradition, is in its primordial essence not pure theory but ethics, and its element is not pure logic but language. This insight into the significance of language becomes even more explicit and central in Levinas's later work, as we see in chapter 6.

At this early point in our discussion, we can start by raising the question of the exact nature and historical location of the prophetic episteme that consists in ethical language. What exactly is this language? How does it stand in relation to philosophical language, in relation to the discourse of theory and light, to *logos*? Would prophetic, ethical language break with all logos or simply feature a radically different kind of speech or a different mode of language? Would ethical language, for instance, consist not of logos but of nomos, the language of law or of commandment?

This question bears on the very essence of the prophetic episteme, namely of Jewish thought. It will remain central and challenging, as we will see, for Levinas's entire trajectory, not least for his understanding and reading of the Talmud. *Totality and Infinity* offers, as we already read, an answer, which features the ethical language of prophecy neither as legal nor as breaking with logos but rather as consisting in a specific kind of logos, which is not theo-logy, the logos of god, but *eschatology*, the logos of the end, or messianic speech. I already noted in the introduction that I think this category describes well the kind of historiographic narrative in which Levinas stages the inter-epistemic difference in his Jewish writings. In coming to this narrative, we will ask whether Levinas's eschatology in fact does what *Totality and Infinity* says is the doing of prophecy, namely "oppose peace to war." In the meantime, the next chapter examines Levinas's prophetic eschatology as translated in his early philosophy into the language of phenomenology.

2

THE PHILONIC ENCOUNTER

CHAPTER 1 PRESENTED THE INTER-EPISTEMIC DIFFERENCE THAT UN-DERLIES *Totality and Infinity*, which translates conceptually, in the language of philosophy, the split between philosophers and prophets, philosophy and nonphilosophy, philosophical or theoretical speech and prophetic, ethical language. But Levinas's book is not a mere presentation of this difference; it is an intervention in it. *Totality and Infinity* features Levinas's early attempt to perform, from within philosophy, an encounter with nonphilosophy, with Jewish thought. This chapter is devoted to examining how Levinas performs this inter-epistemic event.

My analysis shows how the encounter between philosophy and prophecy in Levinas's narrative transpires not as confrontation but as synthesis, whereby prophecy emerges as that which founds philosophy, a Greco-Jewish vision similar to the one suggested by Philo. In elucidating the epistemic meaning of this narrative as Levinas develops it, I emphasize the structural—even if not textual—centrality of its political significance.

Phenomenology as Eschatology

The event begins by the act of staging difference *within* philosophy. We now understand that approaching the difference between philosophy and nonphilosophy from the point of view of philosophy is no contradiction and is actually required by the above-outlined epistemology of difference: the other must be approached from the perspective of the same, not observed next to it from a presumed neutral point of view.

How does this approach work? The epistemology of difference requires not a theoretical but an ethical approach, an attitude, a desire. Yet the designation Levinas gives for his move from philosophical to prophetic episteme, from totality to infinity, is part of a highly theoretical discourse: "deduction."

Levinas says it pertains to "the phenomenological method," in line with the "essential teaching of Husserl."[1]

This method, Levinas explains, departs from vision-based, theoretical, objectifying thought to "reveal" it as "implanted in horizons unsuspected by this thought" in "a forgotten experience from which it lives": "The break-up of the formal structure of thought . . . into events which this structure dissimulates, but which sustain it and restore its concrete significance, constitutes a *deduction*—necessary and yet non-analytical." Deduction leads from theoretical knowledge *back* to something else—a horizon, experience, event, situation—from which theory "lives." Just as Husserl shows that our perception of objects arises from experiences of our conscience, Levinas wants to show how objectifying, that is, *totalizing*, knowledge lives from nontotality: "We can trace back [*remonter*] the experience of totality to a situation where totality breaks up, a situation that conditions totality itself."[2]

From the outset, I would like to mark the ambivalence of this exercise: by tracing back totality to nontotality, by deducing nontotality from totality, Levinas appears to establish a necessary or logical connection between the two and thus overcomes their difference, reuniting them in a new, even more comprehensive totality. More specifically, the deduction structurally presents nontotality not as the opposite of totality but as its very basis. What Levinas undertakes as resistance to epistemic and political totalitarianism, namely the demonstration that totality is conditioned by difference, at the same time leads to featuring difference as the basis *of* totality.[3]

The formal structure of Levinas's intervention entails the very nature of its concrete operation. Showing totality to be based on nontotality means integrating the two into a comprehensive total discourse, something like a total narrative or vision. Levinas identifies the paradigm of such a total logos as "the logos of being," and his demonstration—his deduction—in *Totality and Infinity*, inasmuch as it mounts an opposition to ontology, is itself deeply ontological. It speaks the language of beings and of Being and undertakes to look for the "ultimate structure of being."[4] Prophecy is revealed as the condition of philosophy, but this revelation itself is made in and on philosophy's terms. Levinas's first book may therefore be described as Jewish Greek, as Jewgreek, in the sense that it speaks the language of a Jewish philosopher. It constitutes a Philonic intervention.[5]

Levinas's explicit reference and model is not Philo, however, but Husserl. His total logos is not only a logos of being, or ontology, but also a logos of appearances, of phenomena, a phenomenology, which is to say an observation, description, and depiction of reality. This reality, which serves as the concrete incarnation of the ontological plot, where it can be observed and analyzed, is paradigmatically the singular individual subject, an "I," a self, a soul, a conscience. The subject defines a primary domain of the real—as Levinas says, "interiority" or "experience." The conceptual movement (the deduction of nontotality from totality) is accordingly described as a process that takes place in the subject, as some development or modification in its condition. The phenomenological demonstration proceeds as a *narrative*, a story of this event within the inner experience of the self, which emerges as the overarching totality of nontotality with totality.

This model is prominent in the classics of modern philosophy directly referenced by Levinas's *Totality and Infinity*, from Heidegger's *Being and Time* to Husserl's *Ideen II* and including, of course, Hegel's *Phenomenology* and Descartes's *Meditations*. Levinas's text more or less explicitly renders tangible the affinity of these modern philosophical narratives to prophetic narratives such as biblical myth. In the narratives of modern philosophy, the individual subject incarnates the totalizing form of the narrative, which integrates the other in the same, God in the world, Being in beings. Accordingly, and this is visible also in Levinas's narrative, the individual drama represents a broader, collective, political event; that is, it functions as a parable for history. Phenomenology epitomizes eschatology.[6]

My claim is that, more so than similar phenomenological narratives, Levinas's story is built on its own struggle to be a story. It is not only an illustration of logical relations, one that arises from formal necessity, but an *occurrence* of otherness. It seeks to produce within totality a breakup of totality, a real encounter, a revelation. Levinas often uses the term "event" or "situation" to designate this happening, suggesting a lack of necessity, a contingency incommensurable with any theory or objective calculation. In this, however, there is a fundamental difficulty: his description of the nonnecessary event is supposed to perform a *necessary* deduction from totality to nontotality.[7] If we take this difficulty as a hermeneutic key for reading Levinas's narrative, then, notwithstanding the structure of Levinas's book, his narrative can be shown to fall into two parts that, taken together, articulate a structural, inexplicit *reflection* of Levinas's inter-epistemic project on itself.

The *first part* comprises the main part of the book, where we are given a phenomenology of subjectivity that traces back "the experience of totality to a situation where totality breaks up." Since the experience of totality is narrated as what constitutes subjectivity, the key moment of this narrative is the subject's encounter with the other as the event par excellence. However, since this event is *deduced* from totality, rather than disrupting totality, it arises as the basis of a subjective totality. The main part of the book in fact demonstrates the unity of totality and infinity. It shows how Greek philosophy is based on prophetic ethics, how our world is not split between these but arises from their unity.

The *second part* of Levinas's narrative takes place in the last sections of the book and is consequently dedicated to showing how the problem of totality arises from the Greek-Jewish *unity* of ontology and ethics. It is here that the real and often overlooked story of *Totality and Infinity* transpires: this story is not about the individual, ethical encounter with otherness but about the history of this encounter's epistemo-political abuse.

"You Shall Not Commit Murder"

The first part of Levinas's narrative begins with the "experience of totality." This notion and the description to which it gives rise are built on an equivocation. On the one hand, it is an experience of totality; on the other hand, it is *an experience* of totality, namely a totality that is already predicated on experiencing, on individual subjectivity, and therefore, on difference. Accordingly, Levinas's portrayal of totality is a phenomenological description of the singular individual self, the "me," whose basic principle is to exist as an individual, separate being. *Totality lives from separation.* The main thrust of Levinas's narrative is to insist—against any narrative that has the individual self depend on a higher order—on the independent being of the individual subject, whose existence is defined through contentment, enjoyment, and happiness: "Life is *love of life*." Against both Heidegger and the theology of original sin, Levinas insists that human being is not "fallen" in worldly life. Levinas's self is, as it were, Greek, basically "at home" in itself and in the world, existing, as the title of this section puts it, as "Interiority and Economy."[8]

And yet, inasmuch as the self is independent of unworldliness, it also depends on the world. To exist in the world as an individual means to subsist as an individual in and *by means of* relation to worldly otherness. This is the essence of enjoyment: breathing, eating, reproduction. The self maintains itself through its relation to worldly others, which are accordingly *relative* others and thus only exist as a moment in the self-generation of the individual subject. Separate individual existence, subjective being, consists in a dialectical relation between self and world, which is by definition a relation of nonseparation. Inasmuch as Levinas describes a separate being, this description is at the same time designed to portray the "experience of totality," the effacement of the individual self—or rather self-effacement by the very force of self-generation through the world.

This phenomenology concretely illustrates Levinas's more formal, ontological argument: by the very power of being, the individual being, inasmuch as it *is*, as it participates and invests itself in being, loses its individuality to the general, total, anonymous principle of Being, or as Levinas famously calls it, the *il y a*, the "there is," which stands for anonymous, neutral, impersonal, "chaotic being."[9] Such is the ultimate experience of totality that effaces all individual existence, all subjectivity.

This dialectical logic—separation as totalization—underlies Levinas's rich narrative, in which subjective experience is portrayed as an evolution between two fundamental conditions. In the first, primal stage, the individual has more immediate, sensual relations to the world, a world experienced in the form not of objects or things but of "elements." The individual "bathes in" these elements: through them he enjoys himself (the male gender is explicit, as we shall immediately see). He lives on them but at the same time displays a constant insecurity and fear of losing himself in them, of becoming them, not by dying but by being absorbed into the anonymous "there is."

In the second, higher evolutionary stage of the individual's self-identification through the world, the subject establishes relations, beyond the elements, with another subject. This other person is, however, encountered not as an absolute Other but as a part or dimension of the subject's own world. Levinas's identifies this inner-worldly otherness as "the feminine" or the Woman, the familiar other, whom one addresses with the informal second person pronoun in French, *tu*, a familiar "you."[10] The relation to the feminine opens within the elemental world a dimension of tenderness and hospitality, of familiarity, where the individual finds his interior space out in the world, which Levinas calls "home." The home is no longer the immediate, semichaotic world of elements but a regulated existence, economy, the first form of "civilization."[11] Economic civilization "adjourns" elemental immediacy so that the individual no longer just "bathes in elements" but acquires possessions, comes to have things. Through the same basic dialectics of enjoyment, things are only relative others. They exist for my consumption, "for me" and not "in themselves"—that is, they exist as mere phenomena and not as actual beings. The economic world is still a form of interiority, one in which the self generates itself through identification with relative others and so at the same time dialectically generates an "experience of totality," signifying the effacement of the self in its own world.[12]

The main point of Levinas's demonstration is that totality, or fusion of the self and other, is always an "experience of totality." It is an entirely subjective experience, a state of separated self. Totality is thus a performance of difference. It follows—this is the *deduction*—that totality requires, as a precondition, difference, separation, "a situation where totality breaks up, a situation that conditions totality itself." This situation is the self's encounter with the absolute Other.

Levinas describes the passage from the "experience of totality" to non-totality, to relation with the absolute Other, as a "situation," "a new event," a "new energy," or even a moment of "grace."[13] This event transcends all necessity and logic. It is a contingency that enables the narrative, descriptive, phenomenological quality of Levinas's demonstration. My claim is that this contingency nonetheless follows a conceptual argument, a deduction that operates with the force of structural necessity. There is a correlation between the experience of totality, or interiority, and the relation to the infinite, or exteriority. Totality and the breakup of totality articulate one and the same constellation. This is the hermeneutic key I propose for reading the centerpiece of *Totality and Infinity*, the "situation where totality breaks up," the encounter with the other: I suggest reading it not as a new development beyond the "experience of totality" but as a complementary component that completes the first, static part of Levinas's narrative and accordingly features no story, only the *basis* for a story.

The encounter with the other is portrayed by Levinas as an epistemic event, a redeeming event of knowledge. This encounter shows parallels to other mythical revelations of redeeming knowledge, such as the "call" in Gnostic myths or in Heidegger's *Being and Time* that wakes the self from worldly self-oblivion. From within the philosophical archive, *Totality and Infinity* explicitly invokes as a reference the Cartesian ego's overcoming of doubt through the idea of the infinite. And another explicit acknowledgment in the text recalls the second stage in Rosenzweig's narrative from *The Star of Redemption*, concerning the specifically biblical revelation, which is indeed Levinas's primary reference, namely the prophetic myth.[14]

The appearance of biblical prophecy indeed forms the core of Levinas's demonstration. It appears as an explicit quote that, in the world of totality, in Greek immanence, produces the emergence (or reemergence) of Jewish transcendence—"another text, the text of the other," as Derrida notes.[15] What Levinas describes as the "situation where totality breaks up" features prophecy as an episteme of difference and is characterized by the epistemic elements I indicated above: an *ethical* relation of the self to the other, which takes place in *language*. It is revealing how Levinas's phenomenology modulates these basic elements such that prophecy appears as enabling the totalizing epistemology of Western philosophy. A central motif in this constellation is how the relation to the other, ethics, operates as the constitutive event in the existence of the separated, independent self.

The encounter with the other is an event of language. For Levinas—and this remains unchanged in his later work—the paradigmatic phenomenon of language, language par excellence, which is the element of prophecy, is the act of *spoken* language, the speech act, the living word, or *parole*. Language, as the original relation to the other, the breakup of totality, is a relation between speakers, interlocutors. Voice is the fundamental phenomenon of language for Levinas. The other appears as a "voice coming from another shore."[16] Voice constitutes the other's presence for me. For Levinas, this vocal presence of otherness is the original experience of presence, of being, namely of something that exists not for me but for itself, *an sich*, objectively: the vocal is the unequivocal. As speaking voice, language is the experience of presence, where the speaking other is encountered as the paradigm of objective being. In *Totality and Infinity*, otherness paradoxically means presence, or being. Accordingly, the relation to the other is the relation to something present. In Levinas's phenomenological depiction of this relation, the auditory experience of voice is famously translated into the encounter with a paradigmatically visual object—namely, the *face*. Phenomenologically speaking, language is a relation of vision.

Here lies the significance of Levinas's notion that, in the epistemology of difference, "optics is ethics." The encounter with the other is the original event of objective knowledge. The other is the primal object and thus the primal source of knowledge—as Levinas puts it, *le Maître*, "the Master" or "the Teacher," addressed not by the familiar pronoun *tu*, the informal "you," but by the formal *vous*. Knowledge is essentially teaching. Even as Levinas invokes Descartes (God teaches me the idea of infinity) against Plato (the teacher only helps me to recall what I already know) in this context, his analysis of teaching and teacher clearly echoes the notions of "torah" and "rabbi" as two basic Jewish epistemological categories.[17]

Yet the basic teaching of the other, the basic knowledge they dispense, lies not in what they say but in the very speech act itself, in the voice that means nothing but itself, namely being as absolute presence. The revelation of absolute being in the interior experience of the self, which is an experience of totality, of permanent effacement of the difference between the self and—relative, worldly—others, means an encounter with *resistance* to this logic. The encounter with the absolute being of the other means an encounter with something that may not be dialectically made part of the self. As Levinas puts it, it is an encounter with the possibility of "total negation of a being," with something that is not only relatively but absolutely different from me, which has an absolutely independent existence and is therefore the first thing I—through my constant appropriation of the world—may completely negate, annihilate. The concrete phenomenon of absolute negation of being is killing. When Levinas therefore writes that "the Other is the sole being that I can wish to kill," this arises *analytically* from the notion that the other is the only absolute being. Being is being exposed to killing, which means that the other, as absolute being, is encountered as absolute vulnerability.[18] Levinas expresses this idea by invoking a biblical trope, describing the other not only as teacher but also as "the foreigner, the widow and the orphan."[19]

Consequently, the self's experience of the other, as absolute being, is an experience of resistance to the self's own being, to totalizing self-identification in all others. The absolute Other, as an absolute object, is encountered as objection, as opposition, as a "no." "No" is the original word spoken by the face, the original prophecy or first torah. In *Totality and Infinity*, the original speech act that constitutes the encounter with the other appears as a biblical quote from the torah of Moses, that Jewish arch-prophet and teacher. The original words are presented in the Torah itself already as an explicit quote not from Moses but from God, a quote of His—only—occasion of direct speech to the entire community without the intermediary of "professional" prophets, Moses included, namely the Ten Commandments. The Ten Commandments would be the core of the Torah, and the core of the Ten Commandments, God's primal word—this is the "no" Levinas quotes—is, to follow *Totality and Infinity*, the sixth commandment: לא תרצח, *lo tirtzach* (Exodus 20, 12), "You shall not commit murder."[20]

Positing commandment six as first prophecy is in itself far from obvious but has grounding in rabbinic exegesis.[21] In terms of Levinas's narrative, "killing" arises as the possibility of absolute negation, namely of the only being that absolutely *is*, the other. This possibility, the essence of my encounter with the other, is experienced as a resistance to my own being, a "no" that marks an end to my power, my possibilities. The experience of the other is one of impossibility. As Levinas makes clear, this limitation of my power is imposed not by a stronger power against whom I am too weak but, in contrast, by absolute weakness. The other, as absolute being, is experienced as something essentially beyond my power, that I cannot access *with* power and may therefore only access through a self-limitation of my power.

Self-limitation generates an experience Levinas calls "ethical impossibility."[22] This experience constitutes the moral conscience, a knowledge of good and bad, which Levinas refers back to Plato's idea of the good. In this ethical optics, certain entities, or speaking others, may only be encountered—that is, known—*as* a self-limitation of my power, as objects with respect to whom I can act but *should* not. The very being of these others, their objectivity and presence, their resistance to me, their "no," constitutes a commandment: "You shall not." This limitation of my action arises not because this act is not in my power to perform but because it is bad; it constitutes violence. Only in the optics of ethics do we *see* certain acts as violent, as crime: killing is murder. This is why the basic experience of the other as absolute being is the encounter with my possibility of killing the other, experienced as a negative commandment—"You shall not commit murder."[23]

The phenomenological analysis of the sixth commandment as articulating our fundamental experience of being, as fundamental ontology, is one of Levinas's most powerful and famous interventions. In the narrative of *Totality and Infinity*, this analysis marks the moment in which, within the subject's interior "experience of totality," totality breaks up through the presence of the absolute Other. Since the experience of totality is nothing but the existence of the self as self-identifying in (relative, worldly) others, the breakup of totality marks the limitation of the self. This self experiences power as violence, which essentially implies self-negation, a restrained, moral attitude of "nonviolence"—in other words, ethics.

It should be noted, however, that the very logic of Levinas's deduction indicates that this moment of rupture of totality is also the *condition* of totality. It is crucial to grasp the necessary function of ethical self-restraint in the structure of separation, the separate being of the self. Nietzsche famously points out the self-empowering force of ascetic morality. In Levinas's plot, too, the encounter with the other, as an event of ethical impossibility, of self-limitation, precisely marks the emergence of self-consciousness, of the explicit experience of being an individual, the experience of a "me." One fundamental insight of Levinas's work is that the encounter with the infinite other is the encounter with an infinite invocation—assignation, summoning, accusation, or "election"—of the self as infinite correlation to the other, as infinite responsibility.[24]

This is how the situation where totality breaks down—that is, the ethical encounter with the other—generates the individual self, whose immanent experience is the condition of totality. However, as revelation stories go, the emergence of the separate self as the condition of totality leads not to a mere repetition of the "experience of totality" but to a higher level of experience found in self-consciousness.

The first part of Levinas's story concludes with the developed form of his epistemology of difference. Jewish in origin, this epistemology is nonetheless visibly Greek. It is founded on the constitutive relation to the absolute Other, which, as we saw, is built on the paradigm of objective knowledge and has the structure of vision. The episteme of difference exists in the medium of language. However, just like original language—living speech—means the presence of the face, an encounter with objective being, so does developed language constitute the medium of generality, of objectivity, language as logos. Prophetic revelation would be the foundation of theory, a "divine veracity that sustains Cartesian rationalism." Rationalism figures in *Totality and Infinity* as the very performance of ethics because, as Levinas explains, generalization means generosity, "the offering of the world to the Other."[25]

Thus, Levinas's epistemology of difference, which seems to present a subversive, prophetic, Jewish alternative to the Greek epistemology of totality, rather reveals itself as a fusion of Moses and Plato, a Philonic vision whose modern embodiment, in *Totality and Infinity*, is the Judeo-Greco-French Descartes. "What is Europe?" Levinas writes a quarter of a century later, "It is the Bible and the Greeks."[26]

The State against God's People

This vision features in Levinas's narrative as the conclusion of a drama, the completion of the psychological development of the individual subject or of the historical formation of Western civilization. Yet as already noted and demonstrated, notwithstanding its situational, evental, dramatic language, Levinas's phenomenological portrait, due to its deductive methodology, outlines a static constellation of necessary conceptual correlations, a constellation of separation. Within the structure of separation, the emergent relation to absolute otherness, in the face of the other person, generates the absolute point of departure for this relation, namely the separate, individual self, who exists as interiority. In other words, Levinas's narrative, even up to this advanced point of *Totality and Infinity*, does not really feature any story. We get instead a point of departure for a story that must tell us about the birth of totality. Totality is not born in the "experience" of a singular subject but comes about as a historical episteme, a tradition of knowledge, Western Philosophy, that stands not only on Prophecy but *in opposition* to it. The last part of Levinas's account in *Totality and Infinity* must tell the story of how the episteme of totality arises *from* the episteme of difference.

My claim is therefore that the actual drama of *Totality and Infinity* takes place in its last sections. This drama extends "Beyond the Face," as per the title of the final section, beyond the momentary situation of the individual encounter between self and other. Its concern is designated in the title of the subsection that immediately precedes it: "The Ethical Relation and Time." It may be read as a direct conversation with Heidegger's *Being and Time*. Levinas here acknowledges that the phenomenological constellation described in the first part of his narrative, which culminates in the Other's revelation in inner experience as the ethical event that generates the separated self, Levinas acknowledges that this constellation, the ethical relation, in order to exist, must persist, namely in time. The second part of Levinas's narrative thus deals with the episteme of difference not only as a structure of individual conscience but as a tradition, culture, or world of knowledge. This is what I call a *historical episteme*, a form of civilization.

Concerning the inter-epistemic happening, one point should be carefully noted. My initial reading of *Totality and Infinity* suggests that this book stages a confrontation between two distinct traditions of knowledge, two conflicting epistemes—Totality and Infinity, Philosophers versus Prophets, Greek versus Jewish. My analysis of Levinas's narrative, however, produces a more complex picture. The point of departure for history—for *time*—in Levinas's narrative is not a conflict between two competing epistemes, Greek and Jewish; it comprises a Jewish Greek (French) episteme. It is a fusion of Moses and Plato whereby philosophy is founded on prophecy, resulting in moral rationalism. The actual inter-epistemic drama in *Totality and Infinity* does not play out between the Greek and the Jewish but between two different performances of their composition, or, to put it differently, between two different configurations of *the West*.

The possibility of different or multiple performances of the same constellation—the Self in relation to the Other—indicates a certain contingency, a moment of nonnecessity within the conceptual structure. The possibility of multiplicity, where something like an event or history, something like time, takes place, as the possibility par excellence, marks the real location of otherness in the narrative. The emergence of otherness is a constitutive moment in all narratives, as it establishes the very possibility of a story, furnishing the mythical foundation of myth. As the emergence of contingency, of freedom, this event is marked by a moment when things do not work as they should, when something happens that should not, when things go wrong. History begins with evil. Biblical mythology is based on a story of sin and fall. Fall, *Verfall*, is also a foundational moment in Heidegger's narrative, set in motion by Dasein's fall into improper existence. *Totality and Infinity* uses a different Heideggerian category, a more epistemic one: "forgetfulness."

The possibility of *forgetting* the other arises from the nature of otherness. The separate, individual self, constituted in correlation to the other, *can* indeed forget the other. Accordingly, Levinas identifies this oblivion as the possibility of forgetting God, or "atheism,"[27] which attests to the very power of creation to create a creature so independent it is capable of forgetting its creator.

In Levinas's analysis, by forgetting the other, the self closes on itself and becomes oblivious to ethics, generating "the possibility of injustice and radical egoism."[28] Herein lies the origin of evil and also of history. However, the historical evil *Totality and Infinity* is concerned with is the rise of totality, which is to say the *disappearance* of individual ego and with it the condition for individual responsibility and morality. This epistemo-political pathology is the one Levinas diagnoses in Western philosophy "from Plato to Heidegger"—it produces a total logos and a total state. One of the important insights *Totality and Infinity* unfolds at every level is that totality, or the forgetting of individuality, arises from self-identification. *Totality arises from radical individualism.* We saw this in the "experience of totality" generated by self-identification through others. The same dynamic now repeats in the new dimension opened by the relation to otherness, in the realm of reason. By forgetting the ethical foundation of reason, the uninhibited self perverts reason, making it an instrument of self-identification, a totalizing ontology. This perversion constitutes the being of the separate self in time, "beyond the face," as history.[29] Philosophy, as episteme of totality, would be the historical episteme of a Jewish Greek knowledge that has forgotten its Jewish origins, its foundation on ethical transcendence, and restored immanence. We may think here of a re-Hellenized Judeo-Greece, a Christianized Roman Empire, something we also come across as a central figure in Levinas's Jewish writings.

This episteme of totality, Levinas suggests, is the first problematic historical configuration of difference epistemology, problematic because it is perverted. The pathology appears in both constitutive dimensions of difference epistemology—in language and in ethics.

We saw that "language" is Levinas's most fundamental characterization of the medium in which the episteme of difference exists. Separation is a relation pertaining to language. Accordingly, the perversion of this relation is a perversion of language. Language enables evil, forgetfulness, history, ontology, and totality. In the context of the inter-epistemic tension between philosophers and prophets, *Totality and Infinity* repeatedly identifies the perversion of language in *writing*.

I recall that the paradigmatic phenomenon of language for Levinas is the living, spoken word—*parole*. It is in speech, through voice, that the other becomes present and is encountered as *is*, in coming to stand as the paradigmatic being, as face. Levinas refers to Plato's notion that in oral speech, the speaker is present, such that speech, *logos*, is "true discourse" because it "comes to its own assistance" and "supports itself," as the speaker explains himself. Oral speech presents the other *an sich* and therefore is rid of ambiguity: "as though by speech alone the multiple concurrent possibilities of the symbol, which symbolizes in silence and in twilight, could be sorted out and give birth to the truth." The "return to univocal being from the world of signs and symbols of phenomenal existence" in the situation of speech, in "the straightforwardness [*droiture*] of the face to face," is the advent of ethics, of "being good."[30]

It is easy, in these arguments, to see how the excellence of oral speech casts a shadow of negativity on writing. Written language is cast as language in a diminished form, as speech fallen from grace. The fall of spoken language, its perversion and thus the origin of evil and history, is marked by *the sign*. In the sign, language loses its quality of encountered presence, or voice, which for Levinas is its glory. The presence of the interlocutor in voice, Levinas writes, "measures the surplus of spoken language over written language, which has again become a sign. The sign is a mute language, an impeded language." It is noteworthy that Levinas portrays the lack of immediate presence, the distance between sign and object, as an impediment of language. It can just as well be claimed that this distance, this absence constituting the sign, is the very *essence* of language. But we already saw how language functions in *Totality and Infinity* as a paradigm of the relation to immediate presence, as the paradigmatic vision. Thus, the absence that constitutes the sign, which "only reveals by concealing" and so needs to be made sense of, understood, interpreted, or—as Levinas often writes—"deciphered," is the very site of negativity.[31]

That writing, hermeneutics, is the realm of negativity is a significant notion in the inter-epistemic tension between philosophy and Jewish thought as Talmud. Yet, as aforementioned, *Totality and Infinity* identifies the perversion of language in writing, where the relation to the other shifts from presence to absence. The spoken word that was his face, his living immediacy, becomes a worldly thing produced by the other, that traces back to him, a phenomenon Levinas calls "work," but that for this very reason attests to his disappearance, like his remains. In work, in writing, Levinas writes, "the Other signals himself, but does not present himself." And further, "the works symbolize him," such that the author is no longer to be found in the work as a living personal presence, as a "who," only as content, as a "what." Since the other encountered in speech is original presence, writing, as work and the absence of the other, arises as the original absence, as death. "The surplus that language involves with respect to all the works and labors that manifest a man," Levinas writes, "measures the distance between the living man and the dead."[32]

The perversion of language in writing is simultaneously for Levinas a perversion of ethics. *Totality and Infinity* identifies the fallen form of justice in *politics*. Language as writing, as "work," Levinas notes, constitutes "the tyranny of the State."[33] In the context of the encounter between philosophers and prophets, more specifically in view of the history of the prophetic tradition, it is remarkable how Levinas's discourse problematizes the notion of work through the double figure of writing and state, letter and law. These constitutive human creations, veritable paradigms of civilization, have famously played a central role in the Christian theological critique of the Jewish reception of prophecy, Paul and Luther being two canonic instances.

Levinas acknowledges the need to set boundaries to the tyranny of individual will, where freedom functions as arbitrariness. We have already seen how, in the encounter with the "no" spoken by the absolute Other, rationality limits and thereby defines the individual self. On the level of being in time, Levinas therefore sees good reason in what he attributes to Hegel's notion of mediated freedom, which is precisely inscribed in institutions and laws, in works. It is noteworthy how, in subscribing to Hegel, Levinas at this point writes, "Freedom is engraved on the stone of the tables on which the laws are inscribed. . . . Freedom depends on a written text."[34] This is an obvious, albeit silent, reference to a famous rabbinic exegesis of the biblical verse according to which the tablets of the law "were the work of God, and the writing was the writing of God, engraved upon the tablets" (Exodus 32, 16). The rabbis read the Hebrew word *charut*, "engraved," as the word *cherut*, "freedom." Freedom requires justice, which requires that the commandments, such as "You shall not commit murder," be written in stone and thus become letter and law.

However, in this overcoming of individual tyranny through the works of law, Levinas discerns another tyranny, one that arises from a perversion of these works when they become "alienated." The dynamic of idolatry is clearly at play here. Idolatry effects a fundamental perversion of human action, in which human creation—often depicted as paradigmatic of human work, the artifact, namely the human-made human form or statute (*eidolon*), but basically meaning culture, civilization—overpowers its human creator to be worshipped as divine. As aforementioned, Levinas portrays this perversion in two central paradigms. The first is language, which, in the fall from live speech to dead letter, degenerates into "impersonal reason" and constitutes "rational institutions," thus producing the second figure of degeneration in *Totality and Infinity*, namely the state: "In becoming a discourse universally coherent, language would at the same time realize the universal State, in which multiplicity is reabsorbed and discourse comes to an end, for lack of interlocutors."[35]

The state, the *polis*, what Levinas refers to as "politics," is understood as a perverted form of justice. The explicit problem here is totality. For Levinas, the state is the materialized manifestation of impersonal logic, which suppresses difference through a total system and thus "reduces all ethics to politics," generating "a tyranny of the universal and of the impersonal."[36] Once again, the historical figure that comes to mind here is Rome, the Judeo-Greek Empire, and, closer to Levinas, all the phenomena analyzed by Hannah Arendt as pertaining to twentieth-century totalitarianism.

It is important to insist that totalitarianism, or evil, in Levinas's analysis is indeed a perverted good, law turned into stone. The state pursues the

commandment "You shall not kill" through a legitimization of violence—
police—for whom killing is no longer murder, no longer a crime but the pre-
vention of crime. The state thus observes the commandment "You shall not
kill" by enforcing the commandment "You shall kill." Like writing, state law
for Levinas is a manifestation of death, of lost presence, of disappearance
and absence. State justice is a judgment made by a total reason, the "judgment of history," which "is always pronounced *in absentia*."[37] The state is
the perverted relation to the other in time and therefore the disfiguration
of the Jewish Greek or prophetic-philosophical episteme. It seeks to fulfill
ethics through historical reason, abolishing all individuality in the process.

Against this pathology, Levinas proposes an alternative, more authentic West, one committed to difference. This figure functions as the telos, or
destination, of Levinas's demonstration. It emerges as the dramatic denoue-
ment, the rectification of evil, the return of the fallen. It is the—happy—end
of history. In Heidegger's narrative, this kind of eschaton appears as proper
existence, as *Eigentlichkeit*; in Rosenzweig's drama, it appears as redemption. In the plot that Levinas charts, this ultimate figure embodies a nonperverted, authentic *historical* performance of the Jewish Greek episteme of
difference. In opposition to Christian Rome, the enactment of otherness in
Hellenic means, we must envisage here an enactment that is more Jewish,
that indicates a dissenting tradition of prophetic agency within the ontolo-
gized West. In contrast to the temporal performance of the ethical relation
to infinity in the improper form of the state, as politics, *Totality and Infinity*
identifies authentic ethical existence in time as *religion*.[38]

Against the impersonal tyranny of politics, "the religious order" is
"where the recognition of the individual concerns him in his singularity."
The essence of "religious conscience" is the acknowledgment of a moral
judgment beyond or outside of history, a "judgment of God." Against time
as totality, against history, against the time of states, religion requires a configuration of time as nontotal, a temporality predicated on infinity, which
Levinas refers to as an "infinite and discontinuous time."[39] Infinite time
means "infinite being," which is the temporal being of the infinite. The infinite being of the infinite can only be the infinite existence of the individual
self's *relation* to infinity, the relation that constitutes individuality. Infinite
time signifies the infinite being of the separate self, in other words, the infinite individual.

The infinite individual is the individual beyond finitude, beyond the
mortal, singular self, beyond the "I." The self beyond the singular is the

plural self. Religion is accordingly the dimension in which the relation to the other, that Levinas calls ethics, is enacted in time, in infinity, beyond the finite singular individual, not as a state but as a plural subject, a plural self: as a "we." *The authentic performance of the prophetic episteme of difference for Levinas is that of a "we," a people.* Against the common reading of Levinas's religion in *Totality and Infinity* as based on individual ethics, I suggest that religion is the authentic dimension of collective existence, of society, and also of politics.[40]

It is instructive to note how Levinas's epistemic configuration of this prophetic collective performance, to which the last section of *Totality and Infinity* is dedicated, challenges the structure of separation this configuration is nonetheless called to perform. This episode of redemption takes the narrative back to its first stage, before the situation where totality was ruptured, before the encounter with the voice, the face, the absolute Other, before revelation. It takes us back to interiority. More precisely, it takes us back to the encounter with the *relative* other, the feminine, the other that remains interior to the self's experience of totality, the other who is no master, no *vous*, but a familiar *tu*. It is in the familiar relation of the (essentially masculine) subject to the woman, prior to absolute separation, where infinite being is generated, where infinity comes into being.

Let us look at how this realm of being is configured with respect to the two basic features of Levinas's epistemology of difference—language and ethics. The feminine face does not speak. It signifies through its "feminine beauty," which signifies the lack of signifying and therewith the "disfigurement" of the face. The feminine face expresses "its renunciation of expression and speech," an expression that "sinks into the equivocation of silence."[41] The feminine other is encountered in silence. Since otherness exists in the voice, the silent relation to the feminine does not bring the subject into contact with any presence or absolute being, which means that it is no longer—or not yet—a relation of separation.

The ethical essence of this relation, as an attitude of the self toward the other, is not performed in moral self-restraint, through a "no," but through voluptuosity, sexuality, eros.[42] In Levinas's analysis, eros supersedes separation and thus unites the self and the other, man and woman, to generate the child, who is "at the same time other and myself." In fecundity, relating to the other, transcendence, means becoming the other through "transubstantiation." This is how the singular individual becomes a plural individual, which is to say, family. Family is the existence of individuality beyond the finite individual; it is the infinite individual being, the "ultimate structure" of being, "produced as multiple and as split into same and other."[43] Against the temporal performance of ethics as politics, as state, which is a universal totality devoid of individuality, Levinas thus posits the "we" of the family, a performance of ethics in *religion* as plural individual subject.[44] "The family does not only result from a rational arrangement of animality; it does not simply mark a step toward the anonymous universality of the State. It identifies itself outside of the State, even if the State reserves a framework for it."[45]

The ultimate figure of *Totality and Infinity* is indeed the family, as the paradigm of authentic ethical existence in time. The family is not a total state but a plural, individual, self-identifying subject, a "we." I therefore contest readings of Levinas's "family" as asserting the "private" sphere against the public sphere of politics.[46] As I read it, the family is the paradigm of collective, social ethical existence based not on the category of the *polis*, not "political," but instead on subjectivity, which is to say not on state institution but on a collective person. Levinas's family therefore provides the conceptual basis for the notion of the people as a collective individual subject, what in modern categories is often called the *nation*. The latter category is not one that Levinas uses here, and, as I have noted, common reading situates Levinas's family in the sphere of individual or private ethics, whose political corollary, "fraternity," is simply the universal bond of all humankind.[47] Nevertheless, it is my contention that the family functions in *Totality and Infinity* as the very epitome of people as the infinite collective individual being of the infinite, of God's people. God's people here is the multitude that becomes individualized, unified in a specific collective identity by being collectively subjected to commandments through the election for an infinite responsibility for the infinite, chosen for the good, for God. Levinas does not state this explicitly. But his text can, once again, be easily decoded to indicate that there is, against a Greek state-based social thought, a Jewish people-based social thought, and against a Greek performance of the Jewish Greek episteme of difference in the historical-political figure of Rome, a Jewish performance in the figure of Israel, whose historicity is not properly historical and whose politics is not properly political. This reading has the advantage of connecting *Totality and Infinity* to the contemporaneous discourse of "Israel" in Levinas's Jewish writings, as I show in the next chapters.[48]

At this point, which is to say, in the realm of metapolitics, we find a surprising affinity between Levinas and Heidegger.[49] Levinas's positing of the family as a counterfigure to the state, a collective subject against a total object, indeed calls to mind the famous §74 of *Being and Time*, in which Heidegger portrays Dasein's authentic existence as "destiny," one that comes to contrast inauthentic, objectified, and deindividualized "they" (man) with "the event of the community, of the people."[50] Critics of Heidegger have often pointed to this passage as proof of his early attachment to nationalism.[51] Heidegger, like Levinas in our passage, does not use the term *nation* in this context, and §74 offers different, more nuanced readings of the nature of the community Heidegger is speaking of, which do not necessarily lead to *völkisch* ideology.

Nonetheless, let us think with Levinas, whose project explicitly seeks to turn away from Heidegger as an alleged representative of the entire Western philosophy, as based on the paradigm of unity. In so doing, we ask whether positing the family as a corrective to the state does not raise any fundamental difficulties. Hannah Arendt, whom I have already paralleled to Levinas as a contemporary antitotalitarian thinker, certainly did not consider the genealogical conception of the collective subject, the nation-family, as a figure of resistance to totalitarianism but, on the contrary, through the category of "race," as the main ideological vehicle of modern totalitarian movements. She shows how it was precisely the combination of divine election ("God's people") with statelessness that made the Jewish people into a source of inspiration for race-based colonial imperialism.[52] Arendt identifies this inspiration as a perversion, but her answer to imperial perversion is not a better politics of the chosen people. On the contrary, her response to Western totalitarian imperialism is to return to the Greek politics of the *polis*, which is no infinite being but a territorially—and metaphysically—limited state.[53]

It is worth noting that *Totality and Infinity* provides a last, very brief indication, that there may be a horizon in which the notion of the plural subject as infinite being regains the structure of totality. The collective self remains—this is the whole point—an individual self, which, by the very logic of separation, exists in self-identification, namely in generating a collective "experience of totality." "Truth," Levinas writes in the last lines of his narrative, "demands both an infinite time and a time that it may seal—a completed time. The completion of time is not death, but messianic time where the perpetual is converted into eternal. Messianic triumph is pure triumph. It is secured against the revenge of evil whose return the infinite time does not prohibit. Is this eternity a new structure of time, or an extreme vigilance of the messianic consciousness?"[54]

"Truth" here represents the epistemic core of religion as the people's collective self-conscience. It demands more than the sense of surpassing finite individual destinies, more than infinite time. It demands "a completed time," namely a notion of ultimate purpose, a destination, an *eschaton*, an end of time. In this vision, infinity becomes eternity. Redemption is complete and final—total. "Pure triumph" leaves no place for "evil," which is, as I indicated in Levinas's own narrative, precisely the other in logos. Levinas leaves open—"the problem exceeds the bounds of this book"—the question of whether this total vision of eternity is "a new structure of time, or an extreme vigilance of the messianic consciousness": to read these words with Rosenzweig in mind,[55] a new Christian Israel or an eternal Jewish people.

* * *

In Levinas's phenomenological narrative, totality and individuality do not contradict each other. Instead, totality consists in the experience and very being of the individual, of a separate self-identity. This is why separation can be deduced from the experience of totality. According to the same logic, the totality of the state, too, inasmuch as it erases singular individuality, must at the same time imply a radical performance of individual identity, an amplified form of subjectivity. For this reason, I suggest that the subjective figure of the people (family) that Levinas presents in the concluding movement of his narrative as opposite and corrective to the state, as redemption from politics, in fact functions as corresponding to the state. The state is the state *of* the plural individuality of a "we."

As Hannah Arendt argues, the notion of God's peoples, of the religious, eschatological, messianic collective, did not contradict state totalitarianism but provided the foundation and paradigm for a totalitarian, imperialist subjectivity. In the history of the West, the Judeo-Christian people of Israel were for the most part not the enemies of Rome but its citizens. Seen from this perspective, *Totality and Infinity*, by tracing back totality to the prophetic episteme of difference, to the chosen people, does not so much overcome the problem of Western politics as articulate its origins. I now show how the political implications of Levinas's early phenomenology, only implied in his philosophy book, explicitly unfold in his early Jewish, "prophetic" writings, prior to 1968.

PROPHECY

THE PRECEDING TWO CHAPTERS OFFERED A READING OF Levinas's early philosophy as staging an inter-epistemic difference and encounter between philosophy and Jewish—"prophetic"—thought. My analysis problematized, in Levinas's discourse, the paradoxical dynamic by which difference generates a higher form of identity: the difference between Greek philosophy and Jewish prophecy generates a higher Greco-Jewish episteme of prophecy-based philosophy, and the ethical encounter with the other grounds a higher separate identity of the self as a self-conscious individual and a religious collective. In Levinas's philosophical discourse, in his phenomenology of the subject, political corollaries, albeit central, remain mostly tacit—and historical references remain coded in abstract categories.

The next three chapters demonstrate how the historical-political meanings of Levinas's early philosophy are formulated explicitly and in detail in his early, pre-1968 Jewish writings. In these texts, the ideas underlying Levinas's phenomenology take historical shape and are expressed in the language of prophecy, that is, to follow *Totality and Infinity*, in eschatology. We will see how the basic eschatologos of Levinas's discourse features prophetic ethics, the Jewish ethics of the other, as grounding the messianic mission of the State of Israel in the service of Western humanism.

3

OUR OLD EUROPE

T HE NEXT TWO CHAPTERS BEGIN THE JOURNEY INTO the eschatological narrative of Levinas's early Jewish writings by presenting the central protagonists of its inter-epistemic plot. The presentation of the actors already portrays the eschatological act as a movement from non-Jewish to Jewish. This chapter focuses on the non-Jewish epistemes featured in Levinas's narrative, which are, alongside and before Greek philosophy, Christian theology and Hitlerian racism. The chronicle of their emergence in Levinas's texts corresponds to their role in his developing historiographical as well as historical drama.

1934: The End of the West—Hitlerism

The story—both the telling and the tale—here begins at the end. It is perhaps the apocalyptic law of all historiography that it emerges with the perceived demise of its object, which reveals itself for what it is only at the sight of what it is not, its termination, the end that defines it and gives it a principle and beginning, gives it history. Historiography is apocalypse. Both Levinas's historiographical writing and the narrative it develops, that of the history of the West, begin with Levinas's sight of the non-West that rises within the West to end it—and so to show it for what it is. His later Jewish writings feature multiple non-Western figures, figures of the non-West, bearing a variety of apocalyptic ends and definitions. But before that, in 1934, Levinas identified the end of the West in what he called and would continue to call "Hitlerism."[1]

As the term suggests, Levinas perceives the rise of Hitler as epitomizing the rise of a certain constellation of thought, which he does not simply dismiss as "ideology" but provocatively calls "philosophy." Indeed, in offering "Some Reflections on the Philosophy of Hitlerism,"[2] Levinas claims to see in Hitler not just the leader of National Socialism, not only a certain politics, but a figure of philosophy. This figure is indeed an extreme one, a liminal phenomenon that is "primal," "elementary," but also terminal. It is a figure of philosophy's end, at least to the extent that philosophy is Western, European. It is worth noting that Levinas describes Hitlerism not primarily as anti-Semitic, not as specifically anti-Jewish, but as anti-European. To be sure, the establishment of an anti-Semitic Nazi regime is clearly the historical event to which Levinas's essay responds. However, his response consists in arguing that anti-Semitism—and thus anti-Judaism—is not just about politics but also has philosophical meaning; philosophically, anti-Semitism is anti-Europeanism.

"European civilization," a twenty-eight-year-old Levinas argued in his 1934 essay on Hitlerism, is based on the "European concept of man," which the essay identifies also in Socrates but mainly describes as Judeo-Christian. The Greco-Jewish-Christian—prophetic-philosophical—anthropological principle of Europe is the "absolute liberty of man vis-à-vis the world."[3] Humans are not entirely determined by their circumstances, by politics, culture, and nature, but have the absolute freedom to choose—there is no determinism. To use Levinas's later philosophical language, the human is not all being; it is fundamentally also different, separated from the world. The human arises from (some relation to) absolute otherness. As commentators have noted, the essay's strongly dualistic description of—supposedly European—human unworldliness is evocative of Gnostic acosmism.[4] The main two attachments to being, from whose tyranny Levinas claims Europe liberated man, are history and the body. Fostering an "ascetic ideal" of retreat from carnal existence, Judaism and Christianity broke nature's iron law and introduced the possibility of pardon and renewal. The short essay posits this "Judeo-Christian *leitmotif* of liberty" as underlying modern Europe's liberalism of autonomous reason. If, Levinas underscores, Marxism challenges liberalism by claiming that being determines consciousness, it nonetheless remains committed to liberating man from social fatalism through revolutionary consciousness. Marxism remains committed to the ideal of European politics, namely, the community of free agents united by a common idea, a polity of truth that is universal and egalitarian, and whose Judeo-Christian politics it is to "create its peers," to propagate truth.[5]

In contrast, Levinas argues that the "philosophy of Hitlerism" promotes a radically "new conception of man," a non-European one. The newness of Hitlerism, which Levinas philosophically traces back to Nietzsche, is not a

Judeo-Christian renewal. It is not a revolutionary break with the past but, on the contrary, a reactionary return to the principle of past determination, a principle Levinas's essay identifies in two pre-Judeo-Christian historical cultures that are non-European for being pre-European: "the tragedy of Greek *Moira*" (ancient mythological figure of destiny) and "the Germanic ideal of man." As opposed to the European anthropology of human freedom from the world, based on human absolute otherness vis-à-vis being, non-European man, who is both pre-European and the end of Europe, is entirely immersed in being, all being with no other. As opposed to the Greco-Judeo-Christian spirit of liberty, Germanic man is "chained" to the world. Not only do these worldly chains limit freedom, but Hitlerism turns these chains into the very principle of human being by turning man's physical, bodily, organic predisposition, his "biological" being, into "the essence of spirit."[6]

This anthropology of immanence, diametrically opposed to Jewish-Christian transcendence, has clear political consequences for Levinas. Biologism does not dissolve society. Rather, it biologizes society, conceiving of it "on the basis of consanguinity," not as community of consciousness, of idea, but as "community of blood." Hitlerism marks the end of Judeo-Christian Europe with its racial politics, the alleged opposite of modern liberalism. Remarkably, however, if liberal, Jewish-Christian politics is universal, if it aspires to "create its peers" and spread truth, then Hitlerian race politics, Levinas notes, is not simply particularistic in the sense of concerning itself only with itself while forgetting all others. Hitlerism is a figure of philosophy, a constellation of knowledge, an episteme, so its particularistic race politics preserves in it the formal structure of universal truth. Racism does not think only of itself but aims at the "creation of a new world." In contrast to universalistic Greco-Judeo-Christian politics, which spreads by gaining new Judeo-Christians, by persuading and converting to truth, Germanic race spreads by "expansion," namely by physically overpowering all others, by the subjugating and enslaving through war and conquest. Like Hannah Arendt after World War II, in 1934 Levinas identifies racism as the basis of imperialism. It is as racist imperialism that Hitlerism embodies the non-European that brings Judeo-Christian Europe to its end.[7]

It should be recalled that Arendt's *Origin of Totalitarianism* explicitly points to the ambivalence of imperialist racism insofar as it entails a form of universalism, suggesting that racism and imperialism do not simply stand in opposition to Judeo-Christian Europe but also have something in common with it. Both in relation to the Boers, in the "African experience" of imperialism, and in relation to later "continental imperialism"—the great "pan-movements," Pan-Germanism and Pan-Slavism—Arendt shows how racist imperialism's explicit historical paradigm related to Judeo-Christian messianism, and, more specifically, to the Jewish notion of the "chosen people." She does not see racist imperialism as simply an instance of Judaism but rather "a complete reversion and perversion . . . so that chosenness was no longer the myth for an ultimate realization of the ideal of a common humanity—but for its final destruction."[8] In Levinas's analysis, the same perversion links Hitlerian racial expansionism to the Judeo-Christian mission of universal truth, complicating the antinomy between European civilization and its Germanic end.

These complications resurface and shape Levinas's later historiographical endeavors, starting with his critique of Christianity, as we shall immediately see. And yet, even though, in Levinas's 1934 account, Hitlerism emerges from within Europe as a self-perversion of, or at least a Nietzschean reaction to, its Jewish-Christian heritage, it nevertheless emerges as an extreme, liminal figure, which Levinas marks as the limit of the West. It can thus serve conceptually—and bibliographically—as the negative point of departure for his Western eschatology. Hitlerism, the philosophy and politics of man's total immersion in being, of being without otherness, is the non-Western in opposition to which the West as such makes sense. Indeed, Hitlerism, for Levinas, embodies the fundamental *evil* to which Western civilization is the resistance, and where it accordingly stops. In the talmudic reading of 1966, he writes in a passage that evokes his ethics of infinite responsibility for others that man is a "hostage of all the others." Yet Levinas adds one condition: this responsibility is for those "others who are not Hitlerians." Infinite responsibility is not unlimited. It applies only to "all those who are not Hitler."[9]

That Hitler signifies evil is obvious. But what is less evident is the philosophical, ethical, political significance of the exclusion from responsibility, which suggests that conceptually, there are two kinds of others: others for whom we are responsible and other others, the Hitlerians. The problem becomes more palpable and acute if we understand "Hitlerians" not only—as the English translation reads—as "followers of Hitler," or Nazis, but also, as Levinas suggested in 1934, as adherents of anything similar to "the Philosophy of Hitlerism," that is, of the non-West.[10] We will see that non-Western Hitlerism emerges as a decisive figure in Levinas's narrative concerning the State of Israel and the Arab-Israeli conflict. But first, let us turn west.

If the non-West—that is, the epistemo-political principle in opposition to which Levinas defines Western civilization—arises from the evil of pure immanence with no transcendence or distance, of being with no otherness, then the West, "our old Europe," is the *civilization of the other*. This notion expresses in historical-political terms the seminal tension in Levinas's discourse of difference as analyzed in the context of his philosophy, namely of identity based on otherness. Just as Levinas's phenomenology consists in describing subjectivity as constituted by the relation to otherness, his historiography, too, is centered around the historical performance of a collective subjectivity, around a "humanity," as Levinas sometimes says, which is to say a culture, a world, a civilization, a sociopolitical order built on alterity. Europe is the civilization *of* the other, with all the ambivalence this genitive contains. Europe is at once devoted to the other and—precisely by virtue of this distinguished devotion, by virtue of this outstanding ethics—the very embodiment of the other, which commands eminent devotion.

1947: The Love of Evil—Christianity

For Levinas, Hitler's rise in the mid-1930s reveals the end of Europe and marks the negative point of departure for his inter-epistemic historiography, the "no" to which Europe must be the "yes," the evil it is called to cure—by historiographical means, in retrospect. However, the affirmative tale of Europe itself, its self-constituting Haggadah, is a narrative that Levinas mostly relates after World War II, after the *Libération* and the defeat of Hitlerism. If opposition to Hitlerism revealed a united West, an epistemo-political alliance, then the disappearance of Hitlerism raised the question of how to secure this victory, how to prevent Hitler from returning and Europe from ending—how best to be the West. In other words, after the war, Levinas is confronted with internal differences within the opposition and resistance to Hitler, different and conflicting figures of the Occident.

Levinas's phenomenological response to the question of the West elaborates an ethics of the other, which is what Europe should be; his historiographical response says what Europe, as the civilization of the other, already embodies. More precisely, Levinas's postwar historiography consists in showing how internal differences within the West feature different constellations of otherness-based humanity. His narrations translate what he considers to be the major forces in the Occident into such constellations, enabling him to express their respective positions and conceptual interrelations as well as determine their point of convergence, the West's innermost self, the West within the West. By identifying and interrelating the different Western epistemic actors conceptually, Levinas is also able to relate them to each other narratively, thus generating a story, a Western history, which tells how the West comes to be. Levinas's historiography of the West is therefore not told as a history of the West but as the history of the West's innermost self: a specific—particular—position within the West that nonetheless holds its essence and carries the West as vocation and promise, the point where all Western forces ideally converge and from where the unity of the West will arise. Levinas's logos is an eschatology that constitutes the essence of prophecy in *Totality and Infinity*.

The point of convergence in this postwar eschatology, that which marks its innermost self, is the specific Western constellation that Levinas's texts explicitly designate as their subject—the specific collective they speak about and the collective that speaks in them, their "we," namely the "Jews" or "Israel." If the 1934 reflections on Hitlerism identify the anti-Hitlerian West as Greco-Judeo-Christian, then post-Hitlerian reflections on the West begin by tracing, within Western civilization, within the civilization of the other, its primary inner difference as one between two cultures of the other, Judaism and Christianity, two traditions of Israel. Conceptually, narratively, and textually, the identification of that which is specifically *Jewish* does not begin in the opposition to Hitlerism but in the opposition to Christian anti-Hitlerism. As Levinas writes in the foreword to *Difficult Freedom*, his "Essays on Judaism" from 1963, "In the aftermath of Hitler's exterminations, which were able to take place in a Europe that had been evangelized for fifteen centuries, Judaism turned inward towards its origins. Up to that point, Christianity had accustomed Western Judaism to thinking of these origins as having dried up or as having been submerged under more lively tides. To find oneself a Jew in the wake of the Nazi massacres therefore meant once more taking up a position with regard to Christianity."[11]

The defeat of Hitlerism provoked the Western subject to reflect on its inner split between Jewish and Christian, two fundamentally different responses to Hitlerism understood as being without otherness. The Jewish and the Christian thus feature as the two modes of relating to the other and of enacting this relation as ethics, society, politics, culture, history—the two Western religions. Islam remains almost entirely absent from Levinas's narrative. From the Jewish perspective, which Levinas's texts voice and generate, Christianity emerges as the primary inner-Western counterfigure. And if Judaism is affirmed, if it affirms itself as the better West—which, I argue, is the basic operation of Levinas's historiography—then Christianity comes to be positioned as the lesser West, something like the non-Western element inside the West, the inner-European figure of Europe's end.

To be sure, after the war Levinas never ceased to pay tribute to Christian acts of charity toward Jews during the dark years of persecution. In "Judaism 'and' Christianity," a disputation-like exchange between Levinas and Bishop Klaus Hemmerle of 1987, Levinas speaks of two facts he realized with respect to Christianity after the Holocaust. The second, he emphasizes, is "very, very important: during that period, what you call charity or mercy appeared to me directly. Wherever the black robe was to be seen, there was refuge."[12] Levinas's acknowledgment of Christian charity was not least a matter of personal obligation: "I have a debt toward that charity. I owe the life of my little family to a monastery in which my wife and daughter were saved. Her mother had been deported, but my wife and little girl found refuge and protection among the nuns of St Vincent de Paul."[13]

This personal debt to personal charity, however, is interlinked in Levinas's texts with a fundamental conceptual critique of Christianity. In his polemics with Hemmerle, prior to acknowledging the refuge offered by the monastery, Levinas points to "the fact that all who participated in the Shoah had, in their childhood, received a Catholic or Protestant baptism; and they found no interdiction in that!"[14] The above-quoted foreword from 1963 speaks of "Hitler's exterminations, which were able to take place in a Europe that had been evangelized for fifteen centuries." Indeed, Levinas's conception of Christianity positions it as the *inner* limit of the West, the shadow cast by the non-Western within the Western, which accordingly features a structural complementarity, a historical complicity with the non-West, with Hitlerism. To be sure, Christianity is not Hitlerism but anti-Hitlerism. Yet it is a kind of anti-Hitlerism that can coexist with Hitlerism, at least without disturbing it, can give it a place, live with it, always at the risk of loving it. In Levinas's narrative, Christian anti-Hitlerism indeed presents the danger of responding to evil with love, which risks the monstrosity of loving evil.

In ontological terms, or in terms of Levinas's antiontology, if Hitlerism, the non-West, is a philosophy and civilization based on the principle of pure immanence, of pure being without otherness, then Christianity, as the first, liminal Western figure, stands for otherness without being. This symmetry between being without other and other without being provides structural complementarity between Christianity and Hitlerism.

Levinas articulates this conceptual complicity soon after the war in his essay "Being Jewish" from 1947.[15] As the essay's title suggests, Levinas performs in it the exact operation described above of self-asserting the Jewish perspective not directly against Nazism but in opposition to Christian resistance to Nazism. In other words, and this applies more broadly to Levinas's later historiography, he does not assert Judaism primarily against the threat of anti-Semitism but instead against the threat of Jewish assimilation to the non-Jewish, Christian West. What Levinas in 1947 understands as "Christian" is very similar to the position that in 1934 he described as the "Judeo-Christian *leitfmotif* of liberty," namely a notion of strong, dualistic, Gnostic-like separation between the human and the world, a principle of "absolute liberty," of "interior life that can be infinitely renewed."[16]

Similar to his essay of 1934, in 1947 Levinas identifies his Christian principle of liberty not only in nominally "Christian" theologies, traditions, and cultures but also as foundational for the modern world, for (a now non-Jewish) Europe. "Being Jewish" argues that the Christian idea of man's absolute otherness vis-à-vis worldly immanence, radical otherness without being, extreme detachment from the world, underlies a modern temporality based on the abstract "present," which is absolutely detached from all history and origin.

It is noteworthy that within the modern episteme, Levinas more specifically identifies the Christian principle of absolute liberty at work in existentialism—not only Sartre's but also Heidegger's, wherein human existence is conceived as "contingent," subject to choice or decision.[17] To some extent, we may say that for Levinas, Christianity stands more generally for the foundation of liberalism.[18] Interestingly, the second Christian figure of modern knowledge Levinas points to in his 1947 essay is the active, *technological* essence of modern science, which, by virtue of human unworldliness, grants to human power all liberty with regard to nature. Levinas here unites existentialism and technology insofar as they both arise from the same Christianity, with the exact same argument—radical unworldliness—that, a few years later, Hans Jonas would use to identify them both as arising from Gnosticism.[19]

The main point is that, whereas Levinas's 1934 "Reflections on the Philosophy of Hitlerism" posits a fundamental opposition between the absolute worldly immanence of Hitlerism on the one hand and the Judeo-Christian principle of absolute human liberty from the world on the other, in 1947, in contradistinction to "Being Jewish," Levinas identifies the dualistic separation between man and world as specifically *Christian* and indicates its structural complicity with the philosophy of immanence: "There is something of a kinship between two forms of existence that at first glance are contradictory. One of these is absolutely free, liberated from all constraints, having at its disposal all the resources of an interior life that can be infinitely renewed, countlessly re-initiated. The other unfolds like something eternal: a human nature defined forever, classed into stable kinds amid a world of regular rhythms, of pre-existing forms, of implacable laws."[20]

Indicated here is a conceptual kinship between absolute freedom and absolute necessity, between extreme transcendence and extreme immanence, pure otherness and pure being—between Christianity and Hitlerism.[21] Levinas already identified this complicity between radical transcendence and radical immanence in his early essay on Hitlerism from 1934. This text shows how excessive emphasis on human liberty from worldly necessity led European civilization to undermine any existential or bodily engagement in the world, thus abandoning the world and the body to biologist racism—to Hitler.[22]

In a series of texts from the 1950s that were published in his "Essays on Judaism," Levinas diagnoses the specific element in European thought that enabled complicity with Hitlerism as Christian and develops the ethical, political, and historical implications of this complicity. In the essay "Place and Utopia" from 1950, he argues that by radically separating human freedom from worldly existence, Christianity perceives the world as "total resistance to human action," meaning that worldly action—ethics and politics—is pointless and the only hope and commandment of morality lies in passively awaiting the "total transfiguration" of reality, the emergence of a world of an entirely different nature: utopia.[23] Christian dualism, pure other versus pure being, accordingly "separates the reign of God from the reign of Cesar, reassures Cesar. Utopia does not only seem to us as vain in itself, dangerous in its consequences. Utopian man wills unjustly. To the hard task of just life, he prefers the lightness of solitary salvation." By placing justice in unworldly otherness, Christianity cooperates with—"reassures"—the world of injustice. Absolute transcendence signifies absolute immanence. In his talmudic reading from 1964, "The Temptation of Temptation," Levinas restates the complicity between pure *Realpolitik*, which is perfectly amoral, "beyond good and evil," and the Christian conception of morality as "naïve spontaneity," as resisting injustice with childlike faith, countering politics by avoiding it and, by this avoidance, letting evil be.[24]

Christianity's structural complicity with evil is denounced by Levinas most radically in his essay "Simone Weil against the Bible" from 1952. Levinas identifies in Weil's biblical readings a radical version of Christian ontological dualism between man and world, metaphysical and physical, that translates into an ethics of nonpolitics and more radically of inaction, namely a "metaphysics of passion." In this radical metaphysics, the good—God's—is "an absolutely pure idea, excluding all contamination or violence," utterly unworldly. Once again, Levinas indicates how this utopianism surrenders reality to evil by pointing to Christian Europe's failure to uproot pagan—which is to say, racial—Hitlerian nationalism. But Levinas takes a further step. Metaphysical passion not only tolerates, or facilitates, worldly evil but also feeds from it, thrives on suffering. And an ethics that consists in suffering evil is never far from loving it. "God's supernatural love, in Simone Weil's Christianity," he writes, "if it's anything beyond compassion for creation's misery, can signify only love of evil itself. God loved evil; this is perhaps—we say it with infinite respect—the most fearful vision of this Christianity and the entire metaphysics of passion."[25]

Not only does Christianity, pure otherness, coexist with pure ontic immanence, the very principle of Hitlerism, but this latter evil ends up being the ultimate object of Christian love: passion loves suffering. The distance and distinction between Christianity, the non-Western within the West, and Hitlerism, the non-West, narrows further. "The exaltation of sacrifice for the sake of sacrifice, faith for the sake of faith," Levinas writes two years later, "the call to a gratuitous—that is to say, heroic—act: this is the permanent origin of Hitlerism."[26] The absolute passivity of good veers toward the absolute activity of evil.

In his polemics against Simone Weil, Levinas has her Christianity not only complement but actually *merge* with Hitlerism in anti-Judaism. The metaphysics of passion, he notes, generates "anti-Semitism of the Gnostic type."[27] From the perspective of Gnostic dualism—which Levinas understands as the specific principle of the Christian episteme, separating man, God, and the good from worldly being—real evil consists not so much in the evil of worldliness but rather in the impudence of trying to make it good, in mixing together God and world, in confusing other and being, that is, from the Christian perspective, in being Jewish: "evil is specifically Judaic."[28] Real evil is evil made good. It is the perverse worldly assertion of a transcendent good that compromises this good and risks turning the good itself into an accomplice, or ultimate agent, of evil. Note that this logic applies equally to Christian anti-Judaism and to Levinas's own Jewish anti-Christianism. History, however, from a European post-1945 perspective, makes anti-Jewish evil more evident and the condemnation of Christian anti-Hitlerism for conceptual collaboration with Hitlerism easier to sustain.

Christianity is the historical episteme that arises from the principle of otherness, the principle of the West. Yet it consists in asserting otherness by negating the world, by negating being, and more precisely by resisting all attempts to assert otherness, transcendental goodness, within being or in the world. Christianity figures as the inner anti- of the West, the inner-Western non-West, and is thus structurally akin to the non-West per se: to absolute immanence, racial imperialism, Hitlerism. The dualistic, Gnostic world negation that underlies the Christian episteme, as Levinas understands it, applies not only to the assertion of the good in being in the form of politics but also more fundamentally to the assertion of the good in being in the form of knowledge: reason, science, philosophy. Christian human action is passion; it is faith. This passion is antipolitical and antiepistemic. As founded on an anti-, Christianity becomes perceptible for Levinas very often as the principle at work in historical instances of self-negation, self-destruction, perhaps even self-hate, within the opposite, *positive* constellation of the Judeo-Christian West—that is, Judaism. Simone Weil is a case in point, but a similar operation takes place in Levinas's texts on the subject of the Gospels ("the figures of the gospels leave us cold and stupid. . . . we no longer recognize our own verses"), in Spinoza ("subjugated the truth of Judaism to the revelation of the New Testament"), and in Mendelssohn (emancipation as "dejudaization"). Christianity consequently appears as a perversion of Judaism, the radical exclusion of metaphysical ethics and of religion from being, knowledge, and politics.[29]

In contrast, Judaism emerges in Levinas's work as the authentic principle of the West. It is the better Israel, real anti-Hitlerism, that does not merely oppose the other to being, good to reality, and God to the world but overcomes all dualisms insofar as it accepts the complexity and challenge of asserting otherness within being. In contradistinction to Christianity, Judaism proves to be, as the title of one of Levinas's famous essays on Judaism from 1957 would have it, a "Religion of Adults"—not the passion, "the Pathetic" of pure, absolute, innocent liberty, but a *Difficult Freedom*.[30] Judaism counters pure immanence, Hitlerism, within immanence, in the world. The inner drama of Judaism, the drama of the West, revolves not around antagonism between pure metaphysics (Christianity) and pure physics (Hitlerism) but around the complex relations of affinity and tension between efforts to give being to the good and efforts to generate goodness in being. Levinas's haggadah of the West is accordingly the story of the relations between two major figures of otherness in being, namely the Jew and the Greek, or the Greco-Roman. Discursively, it is the story of the relations between two epistemes, an inter-epistemic drama, the one I indicated as subtending *Totality and Infinity*: a drama that plays out between prophecy, ethical knowledge, or the Bible, on the one hand, and properly epistemic, scientific philosophy, on the other. Yet the prophetic episteme, which is properly Jewish, is the Bible correctly understood, nonperverted, namely not Christian.

For Levinas, "it is the Talmud that allows the Jewish reading of the Bible to be distinguished from the Christian reading."[31] And so it is that the central plot in Levinas's narration of the West takes eminent place in his talmudic readings. This plot is based on Judaism's tension not vis-à-vis Hitlerism or Christianity but vis-à-vis Greco-Roman civilization. It is a conflict between different fundamental strategies of asserting the other in being, the good inside the world. It is a conflict about the state.[32]

1960: The State of Cesar—and Stalin

Levinas's talmudic readings, prior to becoming the *Talmudic Readings* of 1968, most centrally contemplate Judaism as a political question. The Jewish question is a question of politics. Oriented by the inner conversation of the talmudic text, Levinas understands the talmudic self, the Jewish episteme, far less in contradistinction to Christianity than vis-à-vis the figure of the Greco-Roman state. The defining epistemo-historical polemics in which Levinas situates the Talmud is a disputation less with the New Testament than with Philosophy. The polemics vis-à-vis Christianity only serve as a prequel to Levinas's main dilemma about the right response to Hitlerism, the right "Model for the West" (title of the talmudic reading from 1976), namely the tension between Jewish and Greek performances of the Greco-Jewish Occident. It is therefore here that Levinas's early Jewish writings most intimately correspond to his early philosophical work as presented in the two preceding chapters.

The Jewish-Greek tension arises from the great intimacy of the Jewish and the Greek with one another. Against the non-Western immanence of being without otherness and in contradistinction to the Christian radical transcendence of otherness without being, the Jewish and the Greek, in Levinas's narrative, share the basic performance of giving otherness an effect in being, of deploying metaphysics in the world.[33] Greece's metaphysical distinction is already noted in Levinas's 1934 "Reflections," which against Hitlerism's complete surrender to corporeality posits Socrates as the first reference in the long European tradition of absolute human liberty from the tyranny of *physis*. Levinas's later work consistently identifies as "Greek" all the great achievements of the West—projects of bettering being, civilization, reason, science, and good governance.

For instance, Levinas's talmudic reading from 1983, which deals with the Greek translation of the Hebrew Bible, the Septuagint, describes Greek as the language of "European civilization," "our academic language of the Western world," the "language of deciphering. It demystifies. It demythizes. It also depoetises" through the "prose of commentary, of exegesis, of hermeneutics."[34] An essay from 1980, "Assimilation and New Culture," indicates how the intelligible language of philosophy, "which has been able to sublimate metaphors into concepts and to express all lived experience," founded "the spiritual excellence of universality, the norm of feeling and thinking, and the source of science, art and modern technology, but also the thought of democracy and the foundation of the institutions linked to the ideal of freedom and the rights of man." Greek universality was developed in the West as "the common patrimony of humanity: every man and all peoples can enter it on the same level and occupy a place there."[35] Greece is the source of the West as the project of making the world a better place, of making being good.

This is why Levinas's Jewish writings basically relate to philosophy not as an enemy but as an ally. In chapter 1, we saw how Levinas identifies within the philosophical tradition, against its mainstream, a subversive undercurrent that bears Jewish ideas. His Jewish writings express a corresponding desire for Greekness. In his first talmudic reading from 1960, he assures us that rabbinic thought is radical enough "to satisfy the demands of philosophy"; in the introduction to the Talmudic readings from 1968, he calls for the renewal of early rabbis' contact with "Greek thought," which has been "forgotten by contemporary Talmudists." The above-mentioned reading from 1983 finds in the Talmud's great appreciation of the Greek translation of the Torah evidence that "rabbinic Judaism wishes to be a part of Europe," a desire Levinas prophesizes to be fulfilled in the "translation 'in Greek' of the wisdom of Talmud," which—we will get to that—"is the essential task of the University of the Jewish State."[36]

From the great Jewish-Greek intimacy, however, a profound difference arises, which is the topic of the current book. In the first two chapters, I analyzed Levinas's early critique of the philosophical tradition as expressed in philosophical discourse itself. His early Jewish writings express the same critique in epistemic terms, paying greater attention to its political ramifications and its concrete historical and contemporary manifestations. Within the narrative underlying Levinas's Jewish writings, as analyzed here, the problem can once again be formulated in terms of a resistance to Hitlerism—and *the perversion of this resistance.* For Levinas, as we saw, against Hitlerian being without otherness, Christianity asserts otherness without being, a vision of radical transcendence that nevertheless leaves the evil of immanence intact. Greco-Roman civilization, on the other hand, asserts otherness *within* being, transcendence *within* immanence, and seeks to counter worldly evil with worldly goodness. The perversion it consequently risks—and, according to Levinas, has historically fallen prey to—is not, like Christianity, resignation, but *corruption*: namely, that otherness, once brought into being, would join immanence instead of countering and disturbing it, becoming entity, essence, a superior force of being—superior because exercised in the name of transcendence, in the name of the good. Greco-Roman civilization presents the fundamental problem of otherness turned into being—the problem of *totality.*

The initial and basic discourse of the Jewish writings articulates the epistemological and political aspects of this problem more or less along the lines of Levinas's earlier philosophical work, *Totality and Infinity.* An especially precise analysis of the *epistemological* problem of Greek knowledge, of philosophy, is offered in the talmudic reading from 1964, titled "The Temptation of Temptation." The reading examines a famous rabbinic exegesis of the biblical scene of the Torah's giving at Mount Sinai, an *ur*-scene of rabbinic knowledge. Levinas reads the exegetic passage as a reflection of talmudic knowledge on itself, a piece of talmudic epistemology. He characterizes talmudic epistemology in a way that contrasts it with "a certain conception of knowledge, occupying a privileged position in Western civilization," namely philosophical, Greek epistemology, the critique of which frames his entire discussion.[37]

In this talmudic reading, Levinas characterizes Greek knowledge as based on "total lucidity." This characterization employs the same basic categories used in *Totality and Infinity* for describing the epistemology of Western philosophy—light, totality—and evokes the same dialectics that

Levinas deploys in order to criticize this conception of knowledge. On the one hand, light—as the element of knowledge as seeing, as theory—is a relation of distance, a relation to otherness, enabling Western philosophy to transcend Germanic immanence. On the other hand, light is a universal medium, which connects all particulars in a panoramic vision, absorbing all alterity in totality and thus regenerating immanence at a higher level. Accordingly, philosophy, as Levinas writes in the first talmudic reading from 1960, generates "one coherent discourse that embraces all," which a year later *Totality and Infinity* calls the "logos of being," ontology.[38]

It is interesting to see how the 1964 talmudic reading problematizes this Greek epistemology of lucidity, which stems back, as Levinas suggests, to "Luciferian origins," namely to a fall from an original glory in a perversion of virtue, an abuse of knowledge. This perversion is the same one that, a few years later, the 1971 reading describes as an "excess of knowledge": "a Jewish perversion, that is to say, the perversion of all those able to rise to the true, of all those who assemble at the foot of Mount Sinai." The Greek episteme, he thus suggests, arises from an original sin of Jewish knowledge, a seminal idolatry. To explain this epistemic pathology, the 1964 reading, similarly to *Totality and Infinity*, deploys an existential phenomenology of the individual subject to provide a brief description of the "the condition of Western man."[39]

The Western existential condition is, as the reading's title states, a "temptation of temptation." This temptation, Levinas emphasizes, is an epistemic condition, and indeed the very condition of Europe's Greek knowledge: "the temptation of temptation is the temptation of knowledge," and "the temptation of temptation is philosophy." Temptation here is the existential expression of *knowledge as a relation to otherness*, as that which attracts, draws, or tempts the subjective self to venture out, to experience. The "temptation of temptation" expresses the dialectic perversion of the Greek episteme, wherein the other is approached through light, theory, and reason, all of which abolish the other's otherness, "including it in the whole." The argument Levinas employs is familiar from *Totality and Infinity*. Indeed, the effacement of the other in this talmudic reading poses not only an ethical problem ("the inability to recognize the other person as other person, as outside all calculation, as neighbor") but an existential one; it is a threat to the very existence of the self. The abolishment of otherness abolishes the essence of experience. European consciousness, which Levinas sees epitomized in Ulysses, "can listen to the song of the sirens without compromising the return to its island. It can brush past evil, know it without succumbing to it, experience it without experiencing it, try it without living it, take risks in security." "To know," in Greek epistemology, "is to experience without experiencing, before living." The temptation of temptation is thus indeed *only* the temptation of temptation, merely an inner reflection, an illusion, devoid of actual temptation, of real experience, of real life, of any actual self.[40]

Levinas underlines how the perversion of excessive knowledge precludes all *action* through "the subordination of any act to the knowledge that one may have of that act." In contrast to the Israelites at Mount Sinai, who declared "we will do and hear" (Exodus 24, 7)—meaning, as the Talmud notes, that they will do *before* they hear—in Greco-European humanity, "we," says Levinas, "want to know before we do." The epistemic suppression of individual action suppresses individual responsibility, which is precisely the suppression of morality by philosophy, of the good by the true, described in the first pages of *Totality and Infinity*: "Does not lucidity—spirit's openness upon the true—consist in catching sight of the permanent possibility of war?" In "The Temptation of Temptation," Levinas concludes by saying that Greco-European knowledge is "beyond good and evil." This Nietzschean formulation seems to connect the Greek with the Germanic. However, against Nietzsche and against Hitlerism, Levinas analyzes the Hellenic effacement of moral responsibility *not* as empowering the subject by unchaining the egoistic power to will, the power to live, but, on the contrary, as the *disappearance* of subjectivity, the *effacement* not only of the other but of the individual, particular self. In other words, the perversion of the Greek response to Hitlerism, philosophy's perverted response to racism, does not consist in reproducing racism, particularism, and egoism but, on the contrary, in effacing all ego, wiping out all subjectivity through a totalizing universalism.[41]

Indeed, the problem of totality and totalitarianism characterizes the basic *political* corollary of Greek epistemology in Levinas's talmudic readings, just as in *Totality and Infinity*. Nevertheless, whereas in Levinas's philosophy book, the political question of totality, of the state, even as it frames the entire discussion (politics vs. morality), receives a rather marginal and rudimentary articulation within his phenomenological analysis (as shown in chap. 2), it becomes central in the epistemic historiography developed by Levinas through his readings in the Talmud.

His very first reading from 1960, titled "Messianic Texts," is built on a fundamental distinction between two projects of universalism: the messianic, namely Jewish, and the "universality that might be called catholic, which is sought by political life and formulated by Aristotle."[42] Aristotle here epitomizes the link between Western philosophy's universal logos ("one coherent discourse that embraces them all") and its universal polis, "the universal State." Accordingly, it is crucial to note how, in Levinas's analysis, the West, in its Greco-Roman performance, deploys radical universalism against racist expansionism, against the non-Western principle. This universalism primarily poses the danger not of imperialism but rather of totalitarianism, which Levinas views less as the empire and more as the state: the "Greco-Roman State," "the State of Cesar."

In Levinas's talmudic readings, the state is indeed the epitome of politics. Politics, as already noted, is the paradigmatic form in which the Greco-Roman heritage of the West, in contrast to Christianity, does not assert otherness in radical opposition to being—morality as absolutely separate from worldliness—but endeavors to assert otherness and morality *within* being. In one of his later readings, Levinas writes about the "ancient Western confidence in rational practice ensuing from political and religious institutions and that need to allow man to be the fellow of the other, the faith in human institutions through which the *good* would come to *be*."[43] Greek rationality is the epistemic basis for the Western *institution* of morality in the world, and the paradigmatic Western institution is the state, which accordingly constitutes the ontic hypostasis of morality, of good made entity.

Several texts from the 1970s articulate this idea through rabbinic passages. In "The State of Caesar and the State of David" from 1971, a seminal essay on Western—that is, Greco-Roman and Jewish—politics, Levinas quotes a rabbinic exegesis of Genesis 1, 31, "And God saw everything that he had made, and behold, it was very good": "R. Simeon b. Lakish said: 'It was very good' alludes to the kingdom [*malkhut*] of heaven. But the 'behold' which precedes 'it was very good' signifies the Roman kingdom [*malkhut*]. Is then the Roman kingdom very good? How strange! Rome earns that title because it exacts Law and justice [*dikayon*] for men."[44]

In this passage, the Creator himself is portrayed as pleased by his own creation of two reigns, two *malkhuyot*, one on heaven and one on earth, the latter being the Roman reign, which stands for worldly justice, *dikayon* (the original, Hebrew rabbinic midrash uses the Greek word for justice). The Greco-Roman state is basically a manifestation of the good. The rabbis, Levinas notes, pay "homage to the State represented by Rome."[45]

The specificity—and moral complexity—of the Roman model of state is indicated in the talmudic reading from 1978, "Who Plays Last?," concerning a talmudic passage (Yoma 10a) Levinas describes as "a reflection on the outcome of the political history of the world."[46] Commenting on Rome's high standing in rabbis' political eschatology—"Persia will fall into the hands of Rome"—Levinas quotes a statement from the Mishnah's collection of rabbinic maxims, *Pirkei Avot* (Chapters of the Fathers): "Pray for the State [*malkhut*]; for were it not for the fear it inspires, men would swallow each other alive."[47]

Levinas's analysis situates the Roman state explicitly vis-à-vis what I characterize in this historiographical narrative as the non-Western principle of pure immanence, of corporeality and racial particularity, which he early on identifies with Hitlerism and represents in this text with Persia. We will return to the orientalist significance of opposing Western, Roman civilization to Persian "animality." At this point, it is crucial to see that, for Levinas, Rome's victory over Persia, as predicated by the Talmud, does not simply mean that Rome is the stronger race. Rather, against Persian particularistic politics, Rome stands for a *different* political order altogether, one that is "more and better than the unfurling of warrior forces and the opening out of being in its wild vitality."[48] Against animalistic, ontic particularism, Rome stands for universal justice, law.

However, and this is the crucial point, the Roman performance of universalism—of metaphysics and otherness—is essentially *negative*: it consists in *breaking* with the ontic reign of warring particularities. This negativity has two important consequences. *First*, the paradox of Rome is that, in order to end war, it has to win war. In order to end violence, it must become the greatest violence. Rome is the state that institutes justice on "fear." Rome's universal reign, inasmuch as it transcends animality, nonetheless develops "through animality," "out of a condition in which 'man is a wolf for other men.'" In order to "keep in check the animality of human hordes," it must become the most violent animal, the monster, the Leviathan. Talmudic Rome thus presents itself as the model of the modern state, "as Hobbes would have it."[49]

The *second* consequence of Roman negative universalism is its formalism. Roman law is a "legalism." The Roman state is "a State which would not have reached the ethical law that ensues from the life of a man for the other man: but a law which will have gone through animality to end up dialectically in the formal universality of the law itself."[50] Roman universalism established the negation of all particularity, generating only the *form* of generality, of universal law. In response to particularism, both individual and collective, the Greco-Roman state categorically effaces all individual subjectivity. It does not *change* humanity but *suppresses* it. Rome's response to egoism is totalitarianism, which stands for Levinas as the politics of philosophy, political philosophy's very paradigm.

The Greco-Roman inscription of the good in being suffers from a lethal pathology. Before we turn to Levinas's talmudic explication of this pathology and the remedy it requires, it is worth noting that the 1978 reading discusses a third rabbinic source, one actually placed at its center, which underlines the rabbinic embrace of Rome *notwithstanding* its deficiency. We already saw that the passage from *Pirkei Avot*, the acknowledgment that Rome's justice is instituted on fear, nonetheless puts forth this acknowledgment as the reason why one should "pray for the State." The third, central passage in Levinas's talmudic reading states that "R. Judah said in the name of Rab: The son of David will not come until the wicked kingdom of Rome will have spread (its sway) over the whole world" (Yoma 10a).

"The son of David" is the rabbinic Messiah, which means that the ultimate victory of Rome "over the whole world" is, notwithstanding its "wickedness," a necessary condition for the completion of talmudic eschatology. Rome's negative, formal universalism "begins the order of the West," says Levinas commenting on this passage, indicating the necessity, for talmudic eschatology, "of a planetary West for the coming of the Messiah."[51] Note that Rome's crucial importance for the Talmud, in Levinas's reading, exceeds the role of a *katechon*, a "restrainer" of the anti-Christ in the absence of Christ, which is Rome's role in Christian political theology, as explained, for instance, by Carl Schmitt.[52] Talmudic Rome is not just the anti-anti-Christ. It does not represent politics in a world absolutely devoid of goodness. Rather, it constitutes the *commencement* of salvation, the initial rise of ethics, albeit as formal, earthly, Greek justice, *dikayon*, which heralds "a world pregnant with a new future! Politics, such as Rome represents it, is a preliminary gestation for Messianic generosity itself."[53]

This form of justice is, however, only preliminary. The Greco-Roman institution of goodness as a universal state—the "politicization of truth and morality"[54]—suffers from a fundamental pathology, which Levinas diagnoses in his 1978 reading as formalistic legalism and which easily falls into inhuman totalitarianism. In his 1971 essay, Levinas describes this pathology of Roman politics, of "the State of Cesar," of the "pagan State," as *idolatry* of the state: "jealous of its sovereignty, the State in search of hegemony, the conquering, imperialist, totalitarian, oppressive State, attached to realist egoism. Incapable of existing without self-adoration, it is idolatry itself."[55] In the Roman state, the—metaphysical, moral—otherness of being is perverted into the most brutal, total form of immanence, where Leviathan is God.

The talmudic reading from 1977 offers a vivid illustration of this perversion through the figure of the "Cities of Refuge." This rabbinic notion stems from a provision of God's instructions to the Israelites while in the desert as reported in Deuteronomy. According to this provision, on settling the Promised Land, the Israelites are called to designate as part of their political organization a number of cities that function as safe havens for people who have accidentally or "unwittingly" occasioned the death of others (Deut. 19, 2–10). The Bible illustrates this eventuality with the example of "a man goes with his neighbor into a grove to cut wood; as his hand swings the ax to cut down a tree, the ax-head flies off the handle and strikes the other so that he dies" (Deut. 19, 5). Levinas's reading presents the "city of refuge" as a trope for the Greco-Roman state, which provides a safe haven to the West as a civilization of unwitting murderers, of "semi-innocents." The Western, Roman state, he explains, wards off "barbarity"—that is, counters animality—by instituting justice. However, this justice is only formal, a mere enforcement of order: it represses desire without creating a just society. But state repression does not solve injustice; it also *generates* it. State repression itself becomes the cause of "wars and killings" and in its turn generates a "popular rage, spirit of revolt or even delinquency in our suburbs," which ramps up repression and so forth. The ingenuity of Levinas's interpretation is that it portrays the city of refuge itself as the device of unwitting murder, or even as a form of murder with good intentions.[56]

Where does Levinas see Rome, "a wicked State, but perfectly a State,"[57] existing in the years after 1945? What concrete Western politics represents the Greco-Roman response to Hitlerism? This universalist albeit formalistic politics, a philosophical politics and political philosophy, constitutes the main challenge and rival for Levinas's Jewish-Talmudic response. It is the main rival because it is the closest to his own response not only theoretically but also politically, a rival in the attempt to win over the hearts and minds of Levinas's immediate public, his immediate "we," the French Jews. Throughout Levinas's Jewish and talmudic writings from the 1930s to the 1980s, the one figure that stands out clearly time and again as this intimate adversary is Marxism, especially in its Soviet, Stalinist manifestations, which, during the Cold War era, arise as Western civilization turned against itself, as West turned East—as perversion or revolution.[58]

As early as in his 1934 "Reflections on Hitlerism," Levinas identifies Marxism as the first Western movement to break with Judeo-Christian liberalism, a break that nonetheless rejected Hitlerian racism and remained committed to Western universalism. In the postwar period, especially in the 1960s, several of Levinas's essays portray Western Jews as facing a fundamental choice between Judaism and Marxism. In his "Jewish Thought Today," published in 1961, he writes of the new rise of the non-West in "the arrival on the historical scene of those underdeveloped Afro-Asiatic masses who are strangers to the Sacred History that forms the heart of the Judaic-Christian world." He nonetheless goes on to state that "in this enormous world now rising up before us, Marxism still unites us in an immediate and unique way, as a doctrine in which we can glimpse its Judeo-Christian legacy."[59]

In other texts of his, this vision of solidarity transforms into an existential dilemma. For example, in "Judaism and the Present," an essay from 1960, Levinas argues that Western Jews "displayed their essence" after 1945 in that they "carried on the Resistance, in the absolute sense of the term"—against not just Nazi occupation but injustice. The essay portrays Jewish political resistance as facing the choice between two basic visions of social justice: on the one hand, Judaism, which Levinas advocates, and on the other, the philosophical vision of history's rational end in a "universal and homogenous society" of global industrialism, an unmistakable reference to historical materialism, which Levinas criticizes as "inhuman dogmatism." The totalitarian tendency of socialism is also clearly targeted in "Education and Prayer" from 1963. This essay specifically condemns the suppression of Jewish difference through dreams of uniform social equality, which Levinas allegorically portrays as the enslavement of the Israelites by a materialistic, rational Pharaoh: "the builders of a better world—who, in the name of Reason, ignore the Judgment—are enclosing and walling up our sons like the living bricks of biblical Egypt spoken of by the Talmud."[60]

Some of Levinas's texts direct their criticism more explicitly at concrete manifestations of Marxist politics. "Freedom of Speech" (1957), a short comment on the debates around Khrushchev's anti-Stalinist "Secret Speech," denounces Soviet propaganda as the "absolute discredit of language," linking it to the totalizing ideal of the Western logos "from Socrates to Hegel": "political totalitarianism rests on ontological totalitarianism."[61] In a short text from 1960, Levinas analyzes the Sino-Soviet split as a conflict between, on the one hand, a de-Stalinized Russia that reasserts its commitment to a European, Greco-Judeo-Christian civilization of cultural particularities and, on the other, the uncompromising and totalitarian universalism of Chinese—"Asian"—Communism: "a gospel without Old Testament."[62] In the Talmudic reading from 1985, which discusses Western politics as the institution of goodness in being, Levinas pays tribute to Vasily Grossman's critical portrayal of Stalin's regime in his novel *Life and Fate* and describes Stalinism as a perversion that turns "revolutionary generosity" into "dehumanization."[63]

The key text for Levinas's Jewish disputation with the Marxist Left, composed in a key moment for the development of his historiography, as we shall later discuss, is the talmudic reading from 1969, "Judaism and Revolution." This reading can be seen as a deep—and, as we will see, painful—confrontation with the discourse of '68. This confrontation is what Levinas means when he suggests to his French Jewish "we" that "the entire acuity of our current dilemma" is whether to "serve the ideal," to seek justice, through Judaism or "common politics." A central gesture of this reading is to raise the question whether politics, "as it emerged from the Greco-Roman State," can be the means or even the end of the revolutionary struggle "against Evil" without state violence itself becoming the greatest evil. This dilemma can be translated into the question, Is Stalinism better than Hitlerism? "I do not think that revolutionary action is to be recognized by the massiveness of victorious street demonstrations," Levinas critically commented on Greco-Roman motifs in the student movement of May '68: "The fascists knew more successful ones."[64]

If Christianity accommodates Hitlerian racism, Greco-Roman philosophy, through Marxism, converges with Hitlerism in Fascism. Both Christian and philosophical performances of the Western episteme accordingly lead to the collapse of Western humanity, to the apocalypse. However, one collective figure, one epistemo-political performance within the West, carries the power of salvation. It is to this messianic, prophetic figure that we now turn.

4

THE STATE OF DAVID

THE CENTRAL CONCERN OF LEVINAS'S JEWISH ESSAYS IS the exposition of the Jewish episteme. Prior to 1968, Levinas's basic politico-historiographical gesture involved presenting this episteme as the optimal—albeit hitherto unacknowledged—constellation of Western, European civilization. Accordingly, in Levinas's intellectual historiography, the Jewish episteme is delineated in contradistinction from the non-Western (Germanic Persian), Christian, and Greco-Roman epistemes. In a nutshell, in contrast with the non-Western episteme of pure immanence, or being, the Jewish episteme asserts transcendence, metaphysics—the other. In contrast to Christianity, Judaism asserts the other not in absolute opposition to being but within being, in the world; in contrast to Rome, Judaism asserts the other in being not *as* a worldly being, even the supreme one (the state), but as another *sense* of being altogether, as another mode to be, namely as being for the other, which configures another kind of world, a radically other civilization, a civilization of others. This chapter presents the major elements of this conception in early Levinas.

What and where is the Jewish episteme?

The first thing to note is that within the archive of Jewish textual and intellectual history, it is specifically rabbinic tradition, and more specifically, the Talmud, that Levinas takes to embody the Jewish episteme vis-à-vis philosophy. This is not an obvious choice for a European philosopher. A more obvious choice would have been to turn to medieval Jewish philosophy (as Hermann Cohen did), to Kabbalah (as Gershom Scholem did), to Hassidism (as Martin Buber did), or to the Bible (as Franz Rosenzweig and André Neher did). Levinas's polemics against Christianity are key to understanding his turn specifically to the Talmud. For Levinas, the Talmud expresses the *Jewish* reading of the Bible, namely in contrast to the Christian.

We should reflect critically on Levinas's biblical reading of the Talmud. At this point, suffice it to say that, in opting for the talmudic paradigm, Levinas explicitly posits a model of Jewish episteme, of torah, oriented by halacha, namely, as Levinas calls it, law or ethics.

Torah

Levinas's analyses identify the concept of torah as a fundamental category of Jewish-talmudic knowledge. This is the central category used in talmudic discourse to designate its own specific episteme—not just the Pentateuch, the torah scroll, but also, even mainly, the Talmud itself and the entire universe of rabbinic knowledge and praxis. Torah is the episteme of Judaism, like philosophy or science—or the very category *episteme*—is the episteme of Greek civilization.

What is the torah's epistemic specificity? I have shown how Levinas, in his first philosophical book, *Totality and Infinity*, posits a prophetic episteme of difference wherein knowledge, aimed at infinity, is not contemplative but ethical—hence his formula "ethics is optics," which runs counter to the totalizing episteme of Western philosophy based on objectifying vision. The formulation "ethics is optics" is one Levinas uses already in his early essays on Judaism prior to *Totality and Infinity* to characterize the specificity of the Jewish episteme, the torah, whose knowledge and "vision" are directed toward divine infinity.[1]

The talmudic reading of 1964, "Temptation of Temptation," which we have seen provides an epistemic articulation of Greco-Roman knowledge, also offers two different accentuations of the Jewish principle of "ethics is optics," accentuations that define torah respectively vis-à-vis Christianity and philosophy. Against the Christian assertion of divine otherness as absolutely opposed to worldly immanence, morality as opposed to politics, faith as opposed to reason—a position Levinas describes as naive or childlike—Judaism, as a "religion of adults," posits ethics *as optics*, namely as the foundation of worldly knowledge. Conversely, against philosophy's lucid knowledge "beyond good and evil," the Torah provides optics *as ethics*, namely knowledge that is inherently axiological.

In multiple places throughout his Jewish texts, Levinas points to a fundamental phenomenological observation through which he justifies his categorical characterization of torah as axiological knowledge. This body of knowledge, most conspicuously in its rabbinic manifestations, subsists in a discursive universe that can be described as normative, juridical, or legal, as *law*. Torah is law or, as translated in the Septuagint, *nomos*. This translation is not literal, as "torah" literally means "guidance" or "instruction." I leave open here the critical question as to the epistemic accuracy of translating the word *torah* by "nomos" and *nomos* by "law." Levinas often mentions the rabbinic category used for the specific kind of norm that characterizes torah knowledge: *mitzvah*, "commandment." The main point here is the fundamental normative or practical modality of rabbinic discourse, which is to say its *ethical* essence—as Levinas uses the word, that which contrasts to pure theory. The basic text of the rabbinic torah, the Talmud, is in fact built on a juridical corpus, the Mishnah.

Levinas asserts torah as law in a critical operation that defines his polemics against the Gnostic tendency of Christian faith. However, insisting on torah as law is not enough to distinguish torah from philosophy, since the political manifestation of the Greek episteme, the Greco-Roman state, is founded on countering "barbarian," Persian Germanic racial particularism with the universal law. For Levinas, law, or justice, is the form in which divine otherness takes effect in worldly immanence, in being, which is the basic operation that *unites* Judaism and philosophy in contrast to Christianity. To distinguish torah from philosophy, then, it is necessary to make a distinction *within* the notion of law itself. In the framework of Levinas's analysis, the epistemic distinction of torah thus requires a concept of law that is not totalizing, one that does not counter particularism by means of the total state, whereby Greek ethics does not simply lead onto Roman politics and imperialism is not simply restrained by the Leviathan. Law, the Jewish, the mitzvah, must not prolong the *logos* in the *polis* but challenge both.

In the first post-1968 talmudic reading, "Judaism and Revolution," Levinas stages a crucial contrast. He sets the formalistic universalism of the Greco-Roman state, which asserts the general idea of "man" as that which overcomes particularistic egoism, against "Jewish humanism," that which counters egoism not through generality but through the particularity of the other. Torah is thus defined as a law based not on formal justice but on justice for the other person, a "Humanism of the Other."[2] This conceptualization, it should be noted, corresponds to a phenomenological contemplation of the normative essence of the rabbinic halacha, which consists less in "law" in the sense of a formal distribution of rights and obligations and more in a mitzvah, a "commandment" or "imperative," an absolute obligation that calls for an unconditioned response, which Levinas calls

"infinite responsibility." It is this responsiveness to mitzvoth that constitutes the Jewish person, such that the greater one's responsiveness, the more
one takes on themselves, the more one exists. The collective subjectivity
constituted by Jewish law is the center of Levinas's interest.

My analysis of *Totality and Infinity* has articulated the broader epistemic
implications of his ethics of the other. One central implication is ontological: the infinite responsibility for the other requires—and constitutes—the
existence of the individual self as separate. The law, the commandment "You
shall not commit murder," gets translated in Levinas's philosophy into *ethics* as the epistemo-ontological foundation of subjectivity. My analysis has
demonstrated how, against the total being of the state, *Totality and Infinity*
posits the infinite being of the subject as the collective subject, or family,
which I suggest we read against more common non- or even antipolitical
readings as the epitome of the people.

My claim now is that the talmudic readings explicitly articulate the affinity between law and people as the epistemo-political essence of Judaism.
The point I wish to indicate here is the dynamic at work in Levinas's texts,
which generates a shift or transformation from the law to the (collective)
subject—to put it in theological terms, from law to spirit.[3]

Let us return to the "Temptation of Temptation" of 1964, which critically describes the Greco-Roman episteme of philosophy, of theory and
light, of Luciferian knowledge "beyond good and evil."[4] This talmudic
reading contrasts the antiethical Greco-Roman episteme with the Jewish
episteme, with torah. To do so, Levinas reads a talmudic passage that contains a series of rabbinic exegeses, called midrashim, on the biblical text
that narrates the giving of the Torah at Mount Sinai, the mythical *urscene*
of the rabbinic episteme. The midrashim on the torah event at Sinai can be
read as featuring a rabbinic epistemology. Levinas's reading of the talmudic
midrashim in 1964 describes the epistemic encounter between the people
of Israel and God at Mount Sinai in terms of the self's encounter with the
other as portrayed phenomenologically in 1961, a portrait that, as I have
shown, quotes Sinai.

Totality and Infinity describes the self's encounter with the other, with
the face of the other, not as an encounter with an object, as doxical, theoretical perception of some existing thing, but as an axiological encounter with
a limitation on one's own will. The face voices a commanding "no": "You
shall not commit murder." This "no," which founds ethics by exposing my
action as violence, is posited in the 1964 talmudic reading as the essence of

the torah: "nothing can be more exposed to violence than the torah, which says *no* to it."[5] This "no," as the inaugural limitation of will, as the first commandment, is by definition *not* voluntarily chosen but *imposed* from the outside. The midrash Levinas reads interprets the *giving* of the torah at Mount Sinai as an *imposition*.

Commenting on Exodus 19:17, which begins the Sinai event by situating the people of Israel "at the foot of the mountain," the Talmud states that "Rav Abdimi bar Hama bar Hasa has said: This teaches us that the Holy One, Blessed be He, inclined the mountain over them like a tilted tub and that He said: If you accept the torah, all is well, if not here will be your grave" (BT Shabbat 88a). That torah is law means that it is knowledge not acquired through the free consent of a willing subject, that it does not arise from autonomy or self-legislation, which Levinas instead considers to be the epistemic principle of philosophy. Rather, "the torah is an order to which the I adheres without having entered it, an order beyond being and choice."[6]

Yet in *Totality and Infinity* Levinas also argues that the encountered "no," which limits the self's powers, primordially *constitutes* the self as such, as a separate individual. Similarly, in "Temptation of Temptation," the imposition of the torah at Sinai is at the same time the constitution of a self-conscious subject, of a collective subjectivity. Levinas's demonstration follows the talmudic midrash on Sinai, which, immediately after interpreting the expression "at the foot of the mountain" (Ex 19:17) to mean that the torah was forced on Israel, interprets Israel's response to this imposition as "we shall do and hear" (*na'ase ve-nishma*, Exodus 24:7). These words can be read as expressing absolute commitment—absolute in the sense of blind, of committing to something before it is known to what one commits: "we shall do" before "we shall hear." However, the midrash describes the notion of "we shall do and hear" as having arisen from an angelic "secret" revealed to the Israelites at Sinai. "We shall do and hear" expresses not blindness but, on the contrary, supreme knowledge, or, as Levinas says, a "knowledge of angels, of which all later knowledge would only be commentary." "For such knowledge," he continues, "its messenger is simultaneously the very message." The message is the messenger. In other words, "we shall do and hear" expresses a form of agency, a mode of subjectivity—more precisely, the principle of subjectivity. The divine "no" of the law generates an "unconditional yes," namely the very position of a self, the constitution of an individual subject.[7] In Levinas's later phenomenology, this self-positioning of the subject is performed through the words "here I am."

In contrast to the universal law of the Greco-Roman state, which, to counter the egoistic particularism of self-interest, *suppresses* individuality and instates formal universality, torah law *positively* intervenes into the existence of the individual. Torah law institutes an individual subjectivity of another kind, a human existence endowed with another mode of being. The subjective existence founded by torah is ethical: it is a self that exists not only for the sake of itself but also for the sake of others, a being-for-the-other—*responsibility*. Beyond philosophy as ontology, the revolutionary operation of the Jewish torah consists in the "inversion of the essence of being."[8]

Levinas is here in agreement with Nietzsche that Judaism produces the *Umwertung aller Werte*, the transvaluation of all values. For Levinas, however, the Jewish transformation is not just of values, namely of the attitude toward being, toward life, but, more radically, a transformation of life itself, of being. This is perhaps *the* paradigmatic answer of Judaism to Nietzsche. The "man of Torah transforms Being into human history."[9] Torah law humanizes being, transforming subsistence into history. It does so not by oppressing subjectivity but rather by grounding subjectivity—that is, by laying the ground for the position of an individual self, in perfect accordance with the phenomenology of *Totality and Infinity*.

Israel

The transformation of being, inasmuch as it operates on the individual level, is not only an individual event. Torah law generates a new *kind* of individual, a new *form* of human existence. The subjectivity instituted by the giving of the torah at Sinai is not singular but plural. It was received by a collective subject, a "we": "We will do and hear."

My analysis of *Totality and Infinity* has shown how Levinas's phenomenology of the ethics-based subject does not conclude with the constitution of the individual self through the encounter with the face of the other. It proceeds "beyond the face" to the plural subject of "infinite being," described by Levinas in terms of family, paternity, filiality, fraternity. This plural subject, I suggest, points toward the collective constellations of people or nation. The talmudic readings offer a historiography of the West where torah, just like philosophy, is indeed a collective epistemo-political project. More precisely, the proper social deployment of torah is strictly speaking not "political." Unlike philosophy, it does not institute a polis, a state. Rather, torah law constitutes a form of collective human being, a plural ethical subjectivity, which has historically manifested itself in the "difficult liberty of being Jewish."[10]

For Levinas, being Jewish or Jewish being is the otherness in being as an other—inverted—mode of being.[11] In contrast to the universalist Greco-Roman state, the episteme of torah counters self-centered particularism by *inverting* it into other-centered particularism. Other-centric particularism, the claim goes, has been the founding principle for the concrete, historical form of the collective Jewish subject. Consequently, torah in its essence exists in the collective body of the historical subjective agent of Jewish law, namely Israel.

The figure of Israel stands at the center of Levinas's epistemo-political historiography, both early and late. Israel is a particular, individual collective, a people, but it is also the Jewish paradigm, which, for Levinas, means it is the *better* paradigm of the West, in the same way that the West is the better paradigm for humanity. This tension between particularity and universality, the tension of *exemplarity*, commands Levinas's entire discussion.[12]

We have seen that, according to Levinas, the project of the West seeks to counter the egoistic particularism of racism, which is riveted to immanent being and takes on the universal form of imperialist expansion rather than remaining discrete. Against non-Western egoistic being, Christianity asserts an otherness beyond being, and the Greco-Roman episteme asserts otherness in being as universality beyond particularity. Through its assertion of Israel, of a particular people, does Judaism not, rather than offer a better Western paradigm, undermine the entire Western project and return to particularistic egoism?

Indeed, since the basic thrust of the Jewish project, as Levinas understands it, is to counter egoistic particularism *not* with total universalism but with the transformation of the mode of being of particular subjectivity, and thus with *another* kind of particular collective existence, one central vector of his intervention involves a departure from formal universalism back toward particularity. This movement initially leads his Jewish episteme closer to the problematic site that Christianity and Greco-Roman Philosophy attempted to ward off, namely Germanic or Persian racism. This ensuing proximity is a delicate and challenging motif in Levinas's thought, especially to Greco-Roman ears. As explained in the introduction, my reading diverges from common interpretations in contemporary scholarship.

We encounter this motif in various texts and contexts, as we shall see, most provocatively in the above-mentioned essay "Being Jewish" from 1947. I have already indicated how in this text Levinas departs from his prewar embrace of a Judeo-Christian alliance and criticizes Christianity (and modernity, portrayed as Christian-like) for espousing an unworldly otherness that does not counter but, on the contrary, dualistically separates itself from worldly racism and thus accommodates it. Judaism, by contrast, directly counters racism on its own ground, asserting otherness not beyond but within the realm of worldly immanence, in materiality, corporeality, and history. Judaism is marked, according to Levinas, by "facticity" beyond any idea or belief. Being Jewish is a *fact*, not a matter of individual choice, constituting an "irremissible" belonging. For this reason, Levinas argues, even after complete assimilation, the Jew retains a sense of "mystery," which attracts racial hatred. Anti-Semitism does not arise from a mere anti-Semitic fantasy, as Sartre had thought, but from a reaction to the ineluctable Jewish fact, this unchosen chosenness. "The recourse of Hitlerian anti-Semitism to the racial myth," Levinas writes in 1947, "reminded the Jew of the irremissibility of his being."[13] Racism echoes Jewish corporeality.

However, Levinas also insists that the particular Jewish facticity is *not* racial and that anti-Semitic hate "is different than the one provoked by a persecuted race or some minority."[14] The nature of Jewish particularity, the essence of Israel's existence, is a central theme of the first talmudic reading of 1960, "Messianic Texts." In it, Levinas emphasizes, as he continues to do in future texts, that the particularity of Israel is not "ethnic" or "national" in the sense that it does not arise from mere ontic identity, from the self-sameness of substantive being, such as race.[15] Rather, Israel arises from the Western project of otherness, which transcends ontic egoism and is universalist. Yet Jewish universalism, in contrast to Aristotelian (that is, Greco-Roman) or Catholic (that is, Christian) versions, does not simply transcend or abolish all particular collective subjectivity. Rather, Judaism features a complex composition of universality and particularity, which Levinas calls "universalist particularism."[16]

The collective Jewish subject, "Israel," features a universal vision in a particular embodiment. Its particularity therefore does not consist in being an individual case, a specific instance of the general model of collective particularism—ethnic, national, racial. Rather, the particularity of Israel consists in featuring a different model of collective existence altogether, a different kind of peoplehood. Israel is not a people among peoples but "a people outside peoples."[17] We may say that Israel—like Heidegger's Dasein—is distinct from other historical collectives not just ontically but ontologically: it is not only different; it *is*, as a collective, differently.

Israel's ontological difference consists precisely in its existing *not* for itself (as Levinas understands Heidegger's Dasein to be) but in the mode of being for the other, all others, namely in infinite and universal responsibility, in "serving the universe."[18] Paradoxically, the particularity of Israel is the particularity of the nonparticular among the particulars; it is the collective that, unlike common collectives (like Germanic or Persian groupings), is *exceptionally* founded not on self-care or the nonself (like the Greco-Roman state) but on the selfhood of caring for others. This is the specificity of torah law as Levinas understands it, namely that it is built not on the person's "rights" toward others but on mitzvoth, on "commandments" each person assumes individually toward the King of the World, toward God. This law, albeit an obligation toward "the universe," is nonetheless not universal in the sense that it obligates no one else but Israel. Torah is not formal justice but a law that only obligates Jews.[19] Israel consists of those who assume exceptional, asymmetrical, and nonreciprocal obligations.

The particularity of Israel arises from its exceptionality, and the Jewish exception features difference and *excellence*. That Israel is based on responsibility for the world rather than on collective self-preservation means that Jews are posited not only as a "people outside of peoples" but also as an "elite," a people *above* peoples, elevated—as Levinas writes in the talmudic reading of 1966—by the "superhuman demand of morality."[20] Here we touch on the paradox of ethical excellence, whereby zealous subservience, as humble as it may be, is simultaneously self-affirming. This insight reinvokes the dialectics of otherness and self, what in chapter 2 of this book I identified as a fundamental difficulty that arises from *Totality and Infinity*, namely the entity that is ontologically founded on the ethical interruption of being. Israel's self-subjection to the mitzvoth, namely its subjugation of being to responsibility, of ontology to ethics, is structurally retranslated into ontology, that is, into the ethical existence of the Jewish collective, whose moral excellence also implies ontic, existential excellence. The "superhumanity" of Israel is, according to Levinas in 1969, an "accomplished humanity": a "people who has received the Law and, as a result, a humanity which has reached the fullness of its responsibilities and its self-conscience . . . a self-conscious humanity, no longer in need of being educated."[21]

Israel's exceptional excellence is, however, not absolutely exclusive. Its particularity is "universalist" not only in the sense that Jews "serve the universe" but also insofar as this moral and existential excellence is *exemplary*, which is to say, a model offered and available to everyone. Israel is an open elite.[22] This is a crucial point for Levinas, as it marks the critical difference between a racist particularism and an exemplary one. Already his "Reflections on Hitlerism" from 1934 distinguishes between the perverse universal drive of racist "expansion," the individual will to power of which seeks to universally subjugate all others by force, war, and conquest, and the universality of the humanist idea, which seeks not to subjugate but to *convert*, not to enslave but to create equals, "peers." As I have noted, decolonial insights cast doubt on the political implications of this Greco-Judeo-Christian distinction.[23] Yet this idea of Israel as a model for humanity underlies Levinas's notion of "universalist particularism" as something eschatological or *messianic*. The exceptional excellence of Jewish subjectivity as based not on self-preservation but on responsibility features a new type of existence, a new kind of world, a new humanity: "man of a new type."[24] Israel prefigures the West that prefigures a humanity to come.

Levinas's Israel is comparable to other eschatological figures, to other "universalist particulars"—that is, to other collectives with universal missions, other Israels, such as the Church. We saw, however, that Levinas understands Christianity as embracing the other beyond the world. He therefore prefers to compare the Jewish Israel to the worldly, materialist messianic figure of the Marxist proletariat, albeit emphasizing, in "Judaism and Revolution" from 1969, that the accomplished self-consciousness of Israel exceeds any proletarian "revolutionary consciousness" and bears a "superior universality to that of the exploited class."[25] What Levinas means, I suggest, is that the exploited class presents the *negative* embodiment of the eschaton: it incarnates the victim of the class system. It is the identity of those whom the system oppresses and exploits. Accordingly, through its very collective *being*, the proletariat embodies the *end* of the class system— including the end of the proletariat itself. Israel, by contrast, embodies the "new man," namely the positive "end," the ultimate destination, *telos*, or "accomplishment" of humanity. The Jewish project of Israel is that of a collective, a people who "has no longer any need of being educated" and thus already stands at the end of history, negating historical injustice not only by victimhood but also through the affirmative episteme of torah law, which Levinas refers to as a "science of justice."[26] Rather than the proletariat,

Levinas's Israel is epistemo-politically closer to the universalist particularism of Marx's own communist party as a collective agent of a world to come.[27]

The State of Israel

Where Levinas breaks with Marxism, as he understands it, is on the question of the state, which is deeply connected to the question of history. Torah, as a Jewish "science of justice" based on ethics and subjectivity, counters the Marxist science of historical materialism, itself based on Greco-Roman formal ontology. Similarly, the collective subjectivity of Israel counters the formal universalism of the polis, epitomized for Levinas in the totalitarianism of the Stalinist state. We see this double rejection of history and the state in *Totality and Infinity*, in which Levinas's fundamental critique of politics leads him to postulate a religious-moral social bond founded on the collective subject of the family as that which, I suggest, epitomizes the people, in the sense of the people of the infinite, or God's people—Israel. The Jewish texts make this inference and historiographical identification explicit.

The Jewish project of a just society prototypically embodied in the particular collective of Israel aims "beyond the State."[28] "The man who is entirely human," Levinas writes in "Judaism and Revolution" from 1969, asserting the Jewish ideal against the '68 movement, "should not concern himself with politics, he should concern himself with morals."[29] Against politics, which fights immanence with immanence, violence with greater violence, racial imperialism with a Leviathan, Jewish otherness inverts the essence of being. It introduces a new mode of existence, a new kind of human being, or as Levinas writes in the talmudic reading of 1978, "another order"—that is, an order of religion that marks the "end of the political history of the great empires."[30] This end of political history, which is not only negative but also a positive, messianic end, exemplarily embodied by Israel, "still belongs to History," as Levinas emphasizes in that reading, echoing a Maimonidian, sober vision of the messianic times.[31]

A more radical vision is offered in Levinas's earlier "State of Cesar and State of David" from 1971. Noting that Maimonides's messiah is a king and thus still a "political form," Levinas invokes the talmudic idea, voiced by Rabbi Hillel, that "Israel has no Messiah, since it already ate him during the days of Hezekiah" (Sanhedrin 99a).[32] Levinas follows Rashi's commentary here ("the Holy blessed be he will govern and redeem them by himself") in claiming that Israel has no king but "God himself."[33] This means, Levinas continues, that "salvation by the Messiah is salvation by another, as if, arrived at my complete maturity, I could be saved by another, as if, in contrast, the salvation of all others would not be incumbent upon me, according to the most exact signification of my personal existence! As if the completion of the person would not be the possibility of only listening to my own conscience, and to refuse the reasons of State!"[34]

Israel is not a project of state, that is, of a universal institution of justice beyond subjectivity, but one of "new possibilities of the human Spirit," of "new relations with the other person," of a new kind of—accomplished—human being.[35] This radical otherness, one not beyond being (Christianity) or in being (Greco-Roman philosophy and state) but *of* being, is the Jewish project *beyond* messianism, beyond politics and history—namely, Levinas suggests, the talmudic project of *ha-olam ha-ba*, "the world to come." The world to come is completely new, beyond any existing form, and thus even beyond any possible projection, a project beyond all project, beyond all prophecy, which "no eye has ever seen" (Sanhedrin 99a). This radical otherness of the world to come is—paradoxically—embodied, carried, and to some extent rendered present in *this* world through the collective Jewish subjectivity of Israel. As stated in the Talmud, "All Israel has a share in the world to come" (Sanhedrin 90b).

Israel is the connection between the new being, the new world, the world to come, and the current state of being, the present world, this world (*ha-olam ha-ze*). Israel is the new man in the old world. The crucial, urgent question concerns the mode of existence of the Jewish collective subject in this *transitional* situation. How does an ethical superhumanity, otherwise put, a responsibility-based collective subjectivity, exist vis-à-vis and *within* given humanity, which still functions on the basis of self-interest? What is the nature of the relation between the postpolitical—moral, ethical, or religious—and the political? Is it a political or postpolitical relation? Can *any* relation with the political be nonpolitical? Would this relation not require some disposition, some faculty or accommodation to allow effective communication or at least interface with politics, such that the nonpolitical or postpolitical must take some political form?

Concerning the postpolitical—which is not simply apolitical and indifferent to politics but *alternative* to politics, to the new world that will follow this one—it seems that the nonpolitical, inasmuch as it represents the accomplished positivity to come, would have to take a negative political form to communicate or coexist within the world of politics. This dialectics is akin to the deficient functioning of the enlightened person in the world of darkness in Plato's allegory of the cave. Similarly, Israel, as the people of humanity beyond the state, insofar as it exists, subsists within the history of states and thus must appear as a negative form of statist existence. In his seminal "Religion of Adults" from 1957, Levinas accordingly contrasts Judaism to peoples and cultures attached to immanence, to land, to "houses, temples and bridges"—in this context, he invokes Heidegger's view of ancient Greece, but the Talmud's view of Rome is equally discernible.[36] Israel, by contrast, he characterizes in terms of its *detachment* from any land, from any self-assertion such as that of the Greek polis, as "exiled on this earth." A few years later, Levinas will write in the "Messianic Texts," the first talmudic reading from 1960, that Israel, this eschatological elite of "a people outside of the peoples," is "capable of diaspora."[37] He would thus appear to suggest that, within the world of states, Israel, as humanity beyond the state, exists as the negative of the state, in exile, in diaspora—*stateless*.

However, such is *not* Levinas's position on Jewish politics. Here we arrive at a central element of Levinas's political thought, one that is crucial for his entire intellectual project. This element concerns the political implications of his ethics of the other. In my analysis of *Totality and Infinity*, I traced the ethico-political question of Levinas's project back to its ethico-ontological paradox, which is that the being of the self, as the ethical being whose essence is infinite responsibility, is conditioned by the relation to the other. Ethics, then, at once restricts the self ("You shall not commit murder") and grounds and empowers it. In *Totality and Infinity*, this syndrome is described on the individual level in the process whereby infinite responsibility constitutes rationality (generosity as generality), which moves from the face to the third person, from the other to the others, and so transforms responsibility into justice, which is also "justice for me."[38] As Levinas reiterates in the talmudic reading of 1964, "the me may be called in the name of unlimited responsibility to take care also of himself."[39] And on the level of collective or plural individuality, we have seen how infinite responsibility requires infinite being in the subjective form of the family or—in accordance with my reading—the *people.*

The question we might now ask is about the *political* form of the people. How does the people exist vis-à-vis the state, for which the people, according to *Totality and Infinity*, is the alternative? Is the people, insofar as it is based on infinite responsibility—that is, insofar as it is God's people—necessarily antithetical to the state and so necessarily stateless? It is a question *Totality and Infinity* leaves open, or rather does not raise. By contrast, in Levinas's Jewish and talmudic texts, which transpose the conceptual-phenomenological question onto the concrete political historiography of Jewish Israel, this question becomes pivotal. Must Israel, as the eschatological figure of the project that is the West—must the Jewish people, in order to be Jewish, which is to say, to embody the epistemo-political project of Judaism—exist essentially without a state, as diasporic, exilic? A major plank of Levinas's post-1948 project is to *reject* this proposition.

The *first* moment of Levinas's rejection of diaspora is negative, precisely the negation of (exilic) negation. This moment consists of the insistence that, even though the ethical subject exists not as self-preservation but as responsibility for the other, in self-offering—which in Levinas's later work is called self-sacrifice—the *collective* ethical subject, the ethical people called *Israel*, which is founded on the "superhuman demand of morals" and "serves the universe," is nonetheless *not* based on self-denial, is not "a people of martyrs."[40] To be sure, Israel is an "accomplished humanity," "a humanity which has reached the fullness of its responsibilities and its self-consciousness," "a consciousness more conscious than consciousness."[41] However, as we see, for instance, in "Promised Land or Permitted Land," Levinas's talmudic reading from 1965, which discusses Israel's (or *Israeli*) politics and to which we return below, Levinas vehemently rejects any "conscience that is too pure," any "moral delicacy" of "beautiful souls," something he attributes to the position of "leftist intellectuals."[42]

Levinas's categorical rejection of the notion that Israel must be stateless is clearly linked to the destruction of the Jewish diaspora in Europe by Hitlerism. I claim that he considers, after the Shoah and even as a *response* to it, the idea that Jews must refuse the affirmative political form of the state as too Christian. We have already seen how Levinas criticizes what he understands to be the Christian response to the world of Hitlerian racism by affirming unworldly otherness. Levinas insists on worldly confrontation, on confrontation with the being of the world. Israel, the Jewish one, he argues, must affirm itself not only beyond but also against Hitlerism and do so from within being. In the talmudic reading of 1963, "Towards the Other," which deals with the question of *forgiveness*—a notion that, in the 1934 essay on Hitlerism, signified the Judeo-Christian spirit of absolute liberty from history—Jewish worldly self-affirmation manifests itself in the *rejection* of unlimited forgiveness to Germans: "One can forgive many Germans, but there are Germans whom it is difficult to forgive. It is difficult to forgive Heidegger." To reject forgiveness means to insist on justice, to hold persecutors accountable for their deeds. Three years later, in the reading of 1966, Levinas emphasizes that, notwithstanding Israel's "superhuman demand of morals," infinite responsibility, and charity, "for all eternity a place [in hell] must be reserved and kept hot for Hitler and the Hitlerians." If *Otherwise Than Being* suggests a radically self-sacrificing subject, one who "bears even responsibility for the persecuting by the persecutor," in the Talmud Levinas reads that Israel's responsibility is "for all those who are not Hitler."[43]

The theological underpinnings of Levinas's position are explicitly articulated in a couple of texts from the 1980s. In "Judaism and Kenosis" from 1985, a reading in Chayim Volozhyn's *Nefesh Chayim*, Levinas reflects on the notion that Jewish prayer consists in self-abnegation, or "offering oneself." Levinas suggests that this notion of prayer goes back to the sacrificial ritual at the Jerusalem Temple, to the offerings of *olah* sacrifice, which is "burned completely away, leaving nothing behind for the giver of the sacrifice," and which Levinas calls "daily holocausts." Does this mean that the Jewish collective lives from self-sacrifice? Does it imply that, by destroying Jews, the Holocaust nonetheless corresponds to an inner-Jewish principle of ethical self-affirmation through persecution, for which Israel's infinite responsibility must ultimately answer? Levinas categorically rejects this conclusion. First, in a footnote, he doubts whether any such proposition "can still be said since the passion of Auschwitz."[44] Second, he suggests more generally that, since the people of Israel are the worldly manifestation of divine glory, the persecution of Israel is "the profanation" of God and for this reason must be prevented.[45] In a 1987 polemic with Bishop Klaus Hemmerle in "Judaism 'and' Christianity," Levinas strongly criticizes, in view of crimes like Auschwitz, the latter's notion of a "defenseless" Christ, protesting that the "kenosis of powerlessness costs man too much! Christ without defense on the cross eventually found himself leading the armies of the Crusades!"[46] This last remark recalls Levinas's observation, for instance, in his polemics against Simone Weil (1952), of the ultimate complicity between worldly racial evil and unworldly Christian morality.

This brings us to the *second* moment in Levinas's rejection of statelessness as the political form of Israel. The second moment is a positive, affirmative moment. A key text here is the essay "State of Cesar and State of David" from 1971. Levinas's argument sets out precisely from the critique of Christian dualistic separation between being and otherness, world and God, religion and politics. If, as we have seen, Judaism seeks to go beyond politics, "beyond the state," then, in contrast to Christianity, it does not seek to disengage itself from politics and invest itself in some nonpolitical religion, in an otherness beyond being. Rather, Judaism seeks to *confront* the Greco-Roman state. It seeks to challenge statist, formal law (that which effaces egoistic subjectivity) with torah law (that which constitutes ethical subjectivity). Judaism therefore cannot say, like Christianity, "render unto God that which is God's, and unto Caesar that which is Caesar's," for torah law applies to the same reality as the state, which is therefore not extraterritorial to the jurisdiction of torah. No state is "removed from the Law."[47] The project of Israel is not apolitical but postpolitical—it takes place within politics, within the state.

Judaism's intervention in politics, however, is not merely negative: it does not simply work *against* the state. Rather, in order to go beyond the state, the Jewish project of Israel, as a project for a new humanity, neither ignores nor negates but instead *requires* a state. This is the heart of Levinas's political epistemology: *the state of beyond the state, the poststatist state.*[48]

Once again, in accordance with the notion of "universalist particularism," Levinas explains the paradox in terms of temporality, of eschatology. As he writes, the "penetration of the Law into the world requires education, protection and thus history and the State," describing politics as "the road of this long patience and great precautions."[49] What "protection" does torah law require? Basically, in contrast to Christianity, which abnegates being, and Greco-Roman universalism, which oppresses being, torah law seeks to change or "inverse" being, to reconfigure the essence of human existence away from self-interest toward a responsibility for others. As such, Israel stands in conflict with the world.

The first level of conflict between Israel and all other peoples is structural: it is not about the common war between competing particularities but about the principle of particularity itself, a conflict between self-interest and responsibility, ontology and ethics. In order to change the world, to end racial warfare, Israel must first situate and assert itself in the world, *within a state of war*. Israel must therefore seek to ally itself with an element of the world it endeavors to change. In order for responsibility for others to come about, this responsibility must first preserve itself. Paradoxically, in order to exert its action, which will *eventually* abolish all violence, Israel must *in the meantime* defend itself against all violence by embracing the greatest violence, the state. This logic reinvokes the figure of the Leviathan, now in its precise theo-political, eschatological function, according to which the empire is not absolute justice but instead the relative evil that the church must embrace *prior to* a final redemption through Christ in order to prevent or restrain (*kathechon*) absolute evil, the anti-Christ.[50]

However, as we saw, in contrast to a Christian Israel, Levinas's Jewish Israel cannot ally itself with the Greco-Roman state. It is precisely the law of this state, universalist totalitarianism, that torah law seeks to counter. Accordingly, in view of its postpolitical vision of humanity, of the world to come, Judaism develops for *this* world a *different* kind of politics, a different model of polis. In contrast to the "State of Cesar," Levinas argues in his 1971 essay that the properly political project of Judaism is the "State of David." The State of David is the proper State of Israel, the polis of postpolitical humanity, a state outside states for a people outside peoples. Levinas understands this Jewish *kalopolis*, this State of David, as constituting the messianic state, Israel's project in this world.

What distinguishes the messianic State of Israel from the Greco-Roman state is that its law is torah law. We already saw that by "torah," Levinas understands not so much rabbinic law, halacha, but rather ethical conscience, a superior, accomplished mode of subjectivity, of human being. Accordingly, he describes David's torah-cratic state in Platonic terms, evoking Maimonides's description of the Messiah as a king who is "educated in this knowledge," a rabbi-king. A few years later, in the talmudic reading from 1977, he posits, in contrast to the Western Greco-Roman "cities of refuge," the idea that Jerusalem is a city of torah governed by the "science of justice," which implies "a consciousness more conscious than consciousness," a superhuman people. The Jewish project of the State of David, otherwise known as Jerusalem, a project that holds "the aspiration to Zion, to Zionism," Levinas writes, "is not another nationalism or particularism; nor is it a simple search for refuge. The State of Israel is the hope of a science of society and of a society that are entirely humane."[51] Judaism for Levinas is the political project of postpolitical humanity, of the Messiah king who prepares the world to come, of a state for the people beyond the state.

This is the State of Israel that Levinas, in his pre-1968 narrative (which he continues to develop in post-1968 texts, as we have seen), reads in the Jewish project of the West, which should be acknowledged by the West as its response to the crisis of Hitlerism, as the reemergence of the non-West within the West, and as a result of the failure of Greco-Roman Christianity. The messianic State of David can thus be made manifest as the epistemo-political project of Levinas's Jewish texts. What are the concrete implications of this project for post-1945 politics? How do they concern the actual State of Israel founded in Palestine in 1948? What do they mean for Jews in France?

5

STATES OF ISRAEL

WHAT IS THE MEANING OF READING THE STATE of David as the epistemo-political project of the Jewish episteme, of rabbinic torah? The Davidic state is doubtless a central political figure of the Bible, a focal point of its theo-historical narrative. As the theo-polis, the city of God, Zion, it is arguably *the* epistemo-political project of the prophets. The Bible, the Hebrew one, is not merely the theory or constitution of the Davidic state; it is its myth.[1] To posit the image or vision of the State of David as key to a political reading of the Jewish episteme articulated in the Talmud requires seeing the Talmud as a reading of the Bible, which is indeed the basic operation of Levinas's talmudic hermeneutics. In this chapter, I show how Levinas's early Jewish and talmudic writings transform rabbinic torah law into the life of the collective subjectivity of Israel as the citizenry of the Davidic state.

The Negation of Galut

One of the major challenges facing this operation is that the Talmud, like the entire rabbinic tradition, is a postbiblical discourse that emerged and developed in the absence of a Jewish state—that is, in diaspora or exile, in *galut*. The Talmud is historically and existentially a project of statelessness. To be sure, talmudic discourse refers in a variety of ways to aspects of biblical narrative, including its political, statist elements. All these references, however, are arguably diasporic acts and perform *galut* as such. This condition is reflected in the hermeneutic quality of the references, which work to deconstruct the Bible. The same deconstructive operation of the biblical state through talmudic *galut* is also evident thematically.[2] Questions as to what this deconstruction means precisely, what diaspora or *galut* signify politically, and how to understand their negative and positive performances vis-à-vis the state are all difficult to answer. Levinas does deal with the talmudic critique of the state when it comes to Rome, as I have shown. However, my own critical analysis shows that he does not extend the same critique to Jerusalem, rather posits that the pre-talmudic State of David is the Talmud's response to the State of Cesar. This operation excludes, as a possible response to the state, the Talmud's own political work of diaspora. Stated differently, within this perspective, the historical talmudic Israel, in *galut*, is posited as a purely *negative* political project, as an apolitical absence of state.[3]

The negation of talmudic *galut* through a portrayal of Jewish diasporic history as politically negative is a central operation of Levinas's historiography, in both his talmudic readings and his Jewish writings more broadly. Franz Rosenzweig and Hermann Cohen interpret historical statelessness as the uniquely positive social condition of the Jewish people. In contrast, for Levinas, diaspora means the condition of impossibility, or suspension, of torah.[4] This basic position manifests in his understanding of both the *genealogy* of Jewish diaspora—how it came to be, its sources and causes— and the *nature* of Jewish diaspora, namely of the quality of diaspora as the epistemo-political condition of historical Jewish culture.

Concerning genealogy, Levinas does not describe Jewish diaspora as having arisen from inner development of the Jewish episteme beyond the biblical project of the state. He therefore implicitly rejects a common feature of rabbinic narrative, namely that which ascribes the destruction of Jerusalem to internal failures of Jewish politics, such that statelessness, *galut*, is referred to as Jewish agency and diaspora is thought of as a positive, self-critical project of Jewish politics. This approach is legible first and foremost in the prophets themselves. The prophetic books of the Bible are based on a Deuteronomistic logic that repeatedly holds the kingdoms of Israel and Judea responsible through their sins for their own demise and consequent exile. This basic idea recurs frequently in the Talmud as well, for instance, in the "stories of destruction" in the Gittin tractate, which provide a narrative account of the destruction of Jerusalem as resulting from corruption. And it persists in modern accounts, such as that of Moses Mendelssohn, which Levinas discusses.[5] By contrast, Levinas narrates the destruction as having arisen not from any inner deficiency of the Jewish state but as the work of outside forces.

The historiographical argument is first formulated in an essay from 1961: "Not imposing its thought through war, but also not seeking, in its contact with different civilizations, the shocks from which clarity leaps—this earns prophetic Judaism a solid reputation as a particularism that cannot be shaken."[6] Israel, an accomplished and ethical humanity that requires no further education, neither forces itself on other nations nor seeks to learn from them. Israel chooses isolation, such that its universalist particularism is perceived by others as radical particularism and leads to universal anti-Jewish persecution—both by other particularist nations and by the universalist empire. In the 1980s, Levinas described this process as a historical "misunderstanding" whereby Israel's exemplary moral superuniversalism became perceived as nationalistic and racist superparticularism—the "paradox of Israel."[7] According to this narrative, the biblical Jewish state had nothing wrong with it; it was just too good for this world. Jerusalem's demise followed from no inner deficiency and signifies no fault. On the contrary, it manifests its absolute excellence.

From this genealogy of diaspora results its political meaning. If the biblical Jewish state was an instance of political perfection, its absence—which is to say, the postbiblical Jewish condition of statelessness, or diaspora—signifies an absolutely negative political condition. Diaspora has been the sheer absence of Jewish politics, a long period of Jewish existence outside of history.

The motif of diaspora as political negativity is recurrent in Levinas's work. In an important early essay of 1951, "The State of Israel and the Religion of Israel," to which we will return, he contrasts the social engagement of the young Israeli state with "the fervent mysticism that overexcites the orthodox or liberal tendencies of the diaspora living alongside Christianity."[8] The apolitical nature of the Jewish diaspora assimilates it, in Levinas's mind, to Christian Gnosticism, which abandons the world and simply lets it be. In a short text from 1961, Levinas interprets the image of the little bottle of oil the Talmud describes as the real miracle of Hanukkah in contrast with the celebration of the Maccabees' military triumph in nationalistic versions. This oil, Levinas writes, signifies a "nocturnal existence turned in on itself within the narrow confines of a forgotten phial," symbolizing the talumdic diaspora as "existence sheltered from all uncertain contact with the outside, a lethargic existence traversing duration, a liquid lying dormant on the edge of life like a doctrine preserved in some lost yeshiva, a clandestine existence, isolated, in its subterranean refuge, from time and events, an eternal existence, a coded message addressed by one scholar to another, a derisory purity in a world given over to mixing!"[9]

Ten years later, in 1971, Levinas published "State of Cesar and State of David," in which he clearly states the political nullity of the Jewish diaspora: "For two thousand years, Israel was uninvolved in History. Innocent of all political crime, as pure as the purity of the victim, a purity whose sole merit was perhaps its long patience, Israel had become incapable of thinking a politics which would bring to perfection its monotheistic message."[10] The postbiblical Jewish history of diaspora—the history of the Talmud—is for Levinas a history of no history, a collective existence of no politics, of no social investment in the world or in being, a time of Christianized Israel, "lying dormant on the edge of life," in the shadow of the empire.

France as a Modern State of Israel

Levinas's historiography marks a dramatic turn at the advent of European enlightenment. "Since the eighteenth century," he declares in his first talmudic reading from 1960, "reason has penetrated history."[11] "Reason" here cannot mean the formal ontology of Greco-Roman knowledge. Rather, the reason that first penetrates world history with enlightenment is that which does not oppress individual ethics but, on the contrary, is grounded on the ethical individual. Remember how in *Totality and Infinity*, the constitution of the self through relation to the Other was epitomized in Descartes's idea of the infinite. What enlightens Europe is the Jewish episteme—torah. In other words, the first *positive* political figure of Israel after the destruction of biblical Jerusalem is modern, enlightened Europe. This Europe, "ours," is where the West recreates itself on the model of Jewish Israel.

Levinas formulated this idea early after World War II, for instance, in his 1947 essay "Being Jewish," where he describes how Jews rediscovered "the mission of Israel" in the "Christian and liberal world."[12] In a text from 1952, he suggests how, before the advent of Hitler, Jewish morality had become "European moral consciousness" in the nineteenth century: "Never has prophetic morality seemed more in consensus and the famous mission of Israel closer to its destination."[13] In his seminal "A Religion of Adults" from 1957, Levinas identifies the revolutionary principle of Jewish collectivity, founded not on self-preservation in being (like Heidegger's Germanic ethos of land, "houses, temples and bridges") but instead on exiled existence in responsibility for others, as the very principle of "modern nations, defined by the decision to work together much more than by the obscure ways of legacy."[14]

Here Levinas echoes Ernst Renan's famous definition of the modern nation not as an "ethnographic" entity based on objective reality of ethnicity, language, religion, soil, or culture but as a "spiritual family" based on subjective will, on "a daily plebiscite." Whereas, however, Renan narrates the birth of the modern nation as arising *against* Semitic racial particularism from the marriage of Christianity with the Germanic national principle, Levinas inverts the story by identifying race as German and "spiritual family" as Jewish. It was Judaism's "concrete universalism," he writes elsewhere, that attenuated "the alternative national-universal" and inspired nationality as the political principle of an enlightened Europe.[15]

If the modern European nation embodies the people of Israel, then the modern European nation-state, which emerged from the demise of Rome, the State of Cesar, is the postbiblical avatar of the Davidic State of Israel. Diaspora, as the negative political life of Israel, ends with the rise of the European nation-state. In "The State of Israel and the Religion of Israel" from 1951, Levinas describes the modern nation-state as possessing the same features as his ethically "superhuman" Israel, as an "accomplished humanity": "the state is not an idol because it enables full self-consciousness. . . . In the sovereign state, the citizen may finally exercise will. He acts absolutely. Leisure, security, democracy: these mark the inversion of a condition, the beginning of a free being. This is why modern man recognizes his spiritual nature in his civic dignity or, even more so, when acting in the service of the state. In the destiny of the Western peoples, the state represents their human accomplishment. . . . Modern man, man of humanism, is a man in a state."[16]

Although Levinas disagrees with Renan on the historical inspiration for the European nation-state, he nevertheless agrees regarding which is the *paradigmatic* nation-state in Europe, the first among firsts, the European State of David. "It is France's glory," Renan declares, "to have proclaimed, through the French Revolution, that a nation exists by itself. . . . The principle of the nations is ours." For his part, Levinas concurs that, prior to the Dreyfus affair, for "Jewish people of Eastern Europe France was the country in which prophecies came to pass." The French Republic was the first modern State of Israel, the emergent kingdom of the Messiah.[17]

Nevertheless, this emergence of the messianic age was only in its beginnings and as such was germinal, rudimentary, incomplete. The budding, fragile European State of David was exposed to the fundamental evil that threatens any attempt to introduce otherness into being, namely the evil of ontic abuse. The messianic coming risks the perversion of messianism. In an essay on Rosenzweig from 1959 titled "Between Two Worlds," Levinas describes the age of enlightenment as "the end of philosophy," not because philosophy disappeared but, on the contrary, because "everything is philosophy" in the sense that reason became the very foundation of individuality. We already saw how this messianic subject, with its full self-consciousness, is the emancipated modern subject, "man in a state." Levinas indicates, however, that this accomplished individuality risks losing itself in reason, in ontology, and thus risks abandoning all individual responsibility in favor of a total understanding of the "march of history." According to the logic articulated in *Totality and Infinity*, then, this accomplished individuality risks perverting the modern republic by turning it into "totalitarian tyranny."[18] We already saw how Levinas identifies modern totalitarianism, the perversion of the good, in Stalinism and Fascism, two tendencies he also recognized in the movement of May 1968.

Nonetheless, some of his texts from the 1960s evoke another figure of perverted messianism, one that does not arise from totality's suppression of individuality, from Greco-Roman totalitarianism, but, on the contrary, from the overempowerment of individual collective subjectivity, namely from a perversion of the modern, enlightened, Israel-like nation: the nationalistic perversion of Israel. Just like Israel, Levinas states in the talmudic reading from 1966, "every nation believes it is at the center of the world! The very idea of nation emerges whenever a human group believes that it sits in the center of the world." Accordingly, as we find in a text from 1960, "every nationalism carries a messianic message and every nation is chosen," the upshot of which is that the nation-state system of European modernity has produced "premature messianic claims." Another text from 1963 bemoans "the tragic error of [Judaism's] interrupted lesson" to "the political peoples" who, in their haste to redeem history, became "violent with messianism." Here Levinas comes close to Arendt's analysis of imperialist racism, which she deems a perverted Judeo-Christian messianism.[19]

Levinas concludes in these early Jewish essays that European nation-states, as budding modern States of David, need the older, original, Jewish Israel to resume the "interrupted lesson." European Israel needs to learn Judaism's "special patience," which dismisses "all premature messianic claims." Europe needs to learn a kind of messianism that knows how to avoid submitting justice to history. In the enlightened age of "everything is philosophy," this means learning a form of thought, of reason, of Jewish *episteme* that "becomes life instead of becoming politics."[20] In the contemporaneous terminology of *Totality and Infinity*, to counter the threat of Stalinism and racism, the Western nation-state needs an ethical rationality that does not dissolve in the state or turn into nationalism. Instead, this ethical knowledge, or law, materializes in an individual collective subjectivity based on responsibility. Ethics should become embodied in an ethical nation, a moral superhumanity set on rebuilding the city of justice, Jerusalem, on forging a torah-based Israel that will serve as a state for cultivating a poststatist humanity.[21]

Who Is *Not* Modern Jewish Israel

We thus come to the most burning and central question of Levinas's historiography: what and where is modern Jewish Israel? And how can it resume humanity's "interrupted lesson" and intervene in the European nation-state to remedy its totalitarian and nationalistic deficiencies, thus helping the State of David attain modern perfection?

Levinas begins his reply by stating who is *not* modern Jewish Israel, what modern Jewish project does *not* invest the superhumanity of Israel in the messianic age of the European nation-state. His negative answer negates the existing Jewish diaspora in its two basic forms of assimilation and isolation. It is worth noting that Levinas's negative indication of which Jews participate in what he considers to be the modern fulfillment of the messianic mission of Israel entails a political and ontic negation. Not only does the modern diaspora mark a negative, Gnostic-Christian form of political existence—leading an apolitical existence like some premodern, "mystic" diaspora living "in a lost yeshiva"—but it can also be characterized as ontically negative, namely as doomed to inexistence. For the assimilated diaspora, this negation occurs through disappearance, and for the isolated diaspora, through extermination. We can say that the messianic age of modern Europe, inasmuch as it is redemptive for Jews, is also eliminatory—it terminates their unredeemed form of existence. Israel's redemption from diasporic nonpolitics, its ascent to the polis, signifies the termination of *galut*.

This crisis stands at the center of Levinas's first talmudic reading, "Messianic Texts," from 1960. The messianic event of modernity, insofar as it reunited reason and history, subjectivity and polis, the fall of Rome and rise of the European nation-state, opened stateless Jewish Israel "to the political forms of this humanity." Emancipation abolished the distance between the state and the Jew, with the latter becoming a Jewish citizen, a man in a state. Emancipation marked the first end of the nonbelonging or statelessness of the Jewish diaspora. European nation-state messianism absorbed Jewish messianism. In this absorption, Levinas notes, "messianism in the strong sense of the term," the specific Jewish messianic project, became "compromised."[22]

The first form of dissolution of Jewish Israel within the European nation-state is *assimilation*. Assimilation means that Jews, in becoming citizens, leave behind their Judaism, their "universalist particularism"—their specific Jewish episteme, the torah, and their specific Jewish political project, the State of David. Assimilation means that Jews abandon the "mission of Israel" and in this sense become non-Jewish. In his 1982 essay on Mendelssohn, Levinas analyzes assimilation as "dejudaization" or "conversion." In essays dated 1955 and 1966, Levinas fleshes out the epistemo-political meaning of modern dejudaization in the figure of Baruch Spinoza. Criticizing the secular Jewish—and also Zionist—trend of reconciliation with the excommunicated seventeenth-century philosopher, Levinas accuses Spinoza (and Mendelssohn) of having separated Judaism from philosophy, reason from political history, and thereby "subjugated the truth of Judaism to the revelation of the New Testament." On several occasions, Levinas more specifically points to the abandonment by Jews of torah law, or the mitzvoth, an abandonment that can "compromise the mysterious Jewish sense of Justice in us." The assimilated Jew becomes a citizen with no Jewish practice but only Jewish faith, which is a private matter that has nothing to do with society, politics, the world, otherness without being, or—in Levinas's terms—Christianity.[23]

Next to dejudaization by assimilation, Levinas identifies, especially in the talmudic readings, another form of how redemptive emancipation eliminates the Jewish diaspora. This time, elimination arises not through an abandonment of torah but, on the contrary, through an exclusive fidelity to it. Too zealous an attachment to torah amounts to a refusal to acknowledge the modern opening of Jews to politics and embrace emancipation, which means the end of diasporic existence. Instead, this attachment leads one to remain outside of the state, to persist in the traditional, premodern, and orthodox "ghetto." This traditional diaspora is none other than the historic talmudic civilization, which, as I have shown, Levinas considers to be apolitical, alienated from the world in "mysticism." In his Mendelssohn essay, Levinas describes this nonassimilated diaspora as a "minority of strict observance": "Throughout all the adventures of dejudaization, it was in these groups, which were indifferent to the changing times and as if devoid of any relationship with history, that the energy of the tradition and its invisible irradiation has been preserved."[24] Nonetheless, asserting the demise of talmudic diaspora in enlightened modernity is critical for Levinas's talmudic readings, which seek to read in the Talmud not statelessness but the constitution for the Davidic nation-state. In Levinas's narrative, the destruction that enlightenment inflicted on the traditional talmudic diaspora as a matter of necessity was not just conversion, or dejudaization, but extermination.

In the introduction to the first volume of talmudic readings published in 1968, Levinas presents the double destruction of the Jewish diaspora as a "contradiction that tears" asunder modern Judaism. Next to the problem of assimilated Jews, doomed to disappearance (dejudaization), Levinas raises the opposite problem of how "loyalty to a Jewish culture closed to dialogue and polemic with the West condemns the Jews to the ghetto and to physical extermination."[25]

A further articulation of this thought is unfolded in the talmudic reading from 1975, "Damages due to Fire," with Levinas's comment on the following: "As soon as freedom is given to the angel of extermination, he no longer distinguishes between the just and the unjust; moreover, he even begins with the just" (BT Baba Kama 60a). For Levinas, the word *extermination* refers, beyond all war insofar as it is still governed by reason, to an abyss of nonsensical violence that indistinguishably devours both the just and the unjust. However, the fact that extermination "begins with the just," Levinas continues, may suggest otherwise: "Does the madness of extermination retain a grain of reason? That is the great ambiguity of Auschwitz."[26] His commentary offers a possible grain of reason for the extermination of the just—that is, of talmudic Judaism—in Auschwitz: "Saints, monks, and intellectuals in their ivory tower are the righteous subject to punishment. They are the Pharisees, in the non-noble meaning of the term which the Jewish tradition is the first to denounce. The righteous subject to punishment may also be the Jewish people when it closes itself off in its community life and contents itself with its synagogue like the Church satisfied with the order and harmony which reign within its precincts."[27]

Once again, diaspora is understood as depolitization, which amounts, for Levinas, to the Christianization of Judaism. Depolitization after emancipation in the form of assimilation leads to dejudaization; in the form of self-isolation, it leads to extermination. As already noted, for Levinas, state-lessness refers to a negation of politics, such that throughout the centuries of its diasporic existence, "Israel became incapable of thinking a politics that would perfect its monotheist message." As Levinas concludes in his 1968 introduction to his talmudic readings, "Diaspora, injured in its living forces by Hitlerism, no longer has the knowledge or courage necessary for the realization of such a project," namely the project of the messianic State of Israel, the Davidic Jerusalem of Torah.[28]

The Greek-Jewish State of Israel

Who, then, constitutes modern Jewish Israel, if not diaspora Jews? Levinas's answer is that modern Jewish Israel emerges with dediasporized Jews or, more specifically, with *disassimilated* Jews—Jews who were assimilated to modern Europe, left the ghetto of tradition to become citizens of the modern nation-state, and then disassimilated from it. Citizens already, they became estranged from their states and disassimilated.

The initial production of disassimilated Jewish subjectivity, the creation of modern citizens without a state, is presented in several of Levinas's texts as the work of modern anti-Semitism. We noted above how anti-Semitic racial persecution "reminded the Jew of the irremissibility of his being." For Levinas, the anti-Semitic contestation of emancipation manifests the failure of assimilating the Jews, who remain "Marrano." State persecution of Jews paradoxically redeems Israel, rescuing it from oblivion: "once again, Israel found itself at the heart of religious history." Unlike Sartre, Levinas does not interpret this revival through persecution as the rise of the Jewish subject *qua* pure victim and mere opponent of anti-Semitism, the anti-Semitic subject whose essence is to fight anti-Semitism in the name of assimilation. On the contrary, what Levinas highlights in the Jewish reaction to anti-Semitism is the disillusionment of the promise of assimilation, a self-disassimilation that consists in a retreat from total identification with the modern European episteme and a return to the specific Jewish episteme, manifest for Levinas in the generalized return to talmudic sources—"the authentic access to the Bible."[29] Anti-Semitism thus generates modern Jewish citizens who discard their states and rediscover the Jewish Bible.

For Levinas, these disassimilated Jews constitute the modern Jewish Israel. They are called not to abolish but to perfect the project of the modern European nation-state, which features the preliminary realization of the State of David in modern times. The concrete project that fulfills this call is the state of disassimilated Jews, a nation-state for a stateless nation of European citizens, the State of Israel. In Levinas's historiography, the State of Israel is accordingly the messianic site for the completion of the Jewish project—a Western project for a new, responsible humanity in a novel ethical world.

The first basic feature of the State of Israel as the state of disassimilated Jews is that it perfects disassimilation, namely the break of Jewish citizens, as *citizens*, with the European nation-state. As citizens, Jews break with non-Jewish states by becoming citizens of a different state, a Jewish one. In the first talmudic reading from 1960, Levinas describes this operation as the "Israeli solution" to the challenge of modern Jewish messianism, that is, as performing a "collaboration with history" (becoming modern citizens) through "a movement of withdrawal, by exiting this history, in which, since emancipation, we exist as assimilated Jews."[30] As Israelis, Jews enter modern political history by withdrawing from non-Jewish states and setting themselves apart.

It is worth noting that Levinas recognizes the disassimilating isolation the State of Israel operates for modern Jews not only in the general territorial, cultural, and political separateness of a sovereign nation-state. More specifically, on different occasions, Levinas points to the "danger" Jews expose themselves to by living in Israel, a clear reference to the violence of the Israeli-Arab conflict, which he compares to "the danger of persecutions." We will see how Levinas's portrayal of the geopolitical conflict facing the Jewish state as a reenactment of historical persecutions inflicted on diaspora Jews comes to play a more significant role in Levinas's post-1968 historiography. At this point, however, the important motif is how, for Levinas, the revival of Jewish politics requires or implies not only separation but also, in a Schmittian vein, engagement in actual hostility against a mortal *enemy*. "Building a just state on an arid and dangerous land," he writes in 1959, "brings back to Israel the Jews who left the synagogues." Israeli disassimilation in the wild Middle East generates Jews as modern citizens who are liberated "from an obsession with the Western, Christian world" and can accordingly return not to apolitical diaspora but to "autonomous political and cultural existence."[31]

At the same time, we see the second basic feature of the State of Israel as the state of a disassimilated Judaism, according to Levinas's early historiography, alongside the perfection of disassimilation from the European nation-states: to present the contemporary site for the Jewish perfection of the European nation-state as the modern State of David. *In the State of Israel, Jews withdraw from Western history in order to complete Western history.*

This eschatological, messianic vocation, which Levinas ascribes to the independent Jewish nation-state, is articulated in its main aspects in a key text from 1951, "The State of Israel and the Religion of Israel." In this essay, Levinas describes the young Israeli state as the "resurrection" of the collective project of Israel from its political death in diasporic statelessness, wherein the Torah and Talmud languished for two millennia in mystical paralysis. It is only in the form of the modern nation-state, as a Jewish nation-state, that the Jewish episteme is reactivated; Jews can "finally begin the work of their lives" and, namely, are given "finally the opportunity to carry out the social law of Judaism." "The masterpiece has now finally come," that masterpiece being the messianic project of the Davidic State of Torah, the incarnation of "God in social enterprises." The State of Israel, Levinas writes ten years later, gives "body once more to the spirit that animated the prophets and the Talmud," presenting Judaism with its "first opportunity to move into history by bringing about a just world."[32] The State of Israel is where the people of Israel, as a moral superhumanity performing in and through its own collective flesh the inversion of the essence of being from selfness to ethics, will proceed to the ethical recreation of the entire world.

Levinas's texts offer two central images of projects designed to realize this messianic vision of the Israeli state. Notably, some early texts evoke the Israeli project of the *kibbutz*, that is, agricultural community settlements established in Palestine from the early twentieth century by groups of young European Jews who saw in Zionist colonization the opportunity to realize a socialist utopia. For Levinas, the small kibbutz settlements epitomize *first* the danger to which Jews expose themselves in the State of Israel, which disassimilates them from Europe. As he puts it in the first talmudic reading, the "Messianic Texts" of 1960, "Israeli Judaism has accepted danger through its life in the State of Israel and what the State of Israel is to the whole of Jewry, its vanguard groupings are to the State itself." He further writes, "Within the State, in its small grains scattered in the desert, in the remote frontier kibbutzim, men established themselves, who are indifferent to the seething world whose human values they nonetheless serve. They display their indifference in their daily lives of work and risks." *Second,* the strictly regulated social life in kibbutz communities appears to Levinas precisely as a political return to the uncompromising ethical demands of Jewish law. As he argues in the essay from 1951, "it is in the justice of the kibbutz that the nostalgia for ritual is once again to be felt." *Third*, by realizing the Jewish ideal of social justice, of responsible humanity, the kibbutz supposedly provides Europe, and the West, with the ultimate model for a socialist nation-state: "Socialism in one country?" Levinas writes in 1961, "The collectivist society of the kibbutz attempts socialism in one village!"[33]

As the fundamental condition for kibbutz humanity as Levinas envisions it, his texts indicate the necessity of another messianic enterprise, beyond the kibbutz, for realizing the eschatological vocation of the State of Israel. This other, more fundamental project is properly epistemic; it constitutes a direct intervention of knowledge in knowledge, an epistemological intervention. The epistemic project takes place not in the fields, carried out not in "remote frontier kibbutzim" but instead in collectives such as the Colloquium of Jewish Intellectuals in Paris. It is in the epistemic project of the State of Israel that the essence of Levinas's own messianic intervention lies, an intervention that may be considered as animating not only his talmudic readings but also the entire inter-epistemic event of his oeuvre.

The nature of this epistemic enterprise is discussed in his 1951 essay. The Davidic State of Israel, the city of justice, whether in the form of the kibbutz or something else, arises not from mere faith (like the Christian project) but (like the Greco-Roman project) from positive knowledge of the world, from torah as a proper episteme, as "science." "Between the Jewish state and the doctrine which should inspire it," Levinas declares in the first-person plural, "we must establish a science, a formidable one." This "high science of justice," he explains, is a scholastic science of study that elaborates contemporary sociopolitical knowledge out of ancient Jewish sources: "the social and political situation described by the Bible and the Talmud is the example of a given situation that is rendered human by the law. From it we can deduce the justice required for any and every situation."[34] The messianic State of Israel is thus deemed to arise from the development of the Talmud, which Levinas understands as the ethical and legal constitution of the biblical State of David, and its adaptation to the needs of the modern nation-state. The creation of this modern Talmud, which constitutes the dediasporization and repolitization of the Jewish episteme through transformation of torah law into state law, is the messianic project of knowledge in which Levinas's talmudic readings seek to partake.

Levinas's contribution to this project is focused not on the scholarly aspect but rather on the conceptual constitution. He seeks to lay down its theoretical foundations, to think it through. Formative thought is necessary, since the epistemic renewal of the Talmud Levinas envisions does not consist in mere repetition or reactivation, in the reinstitution of old traditions. Instead, it consists in creating something new: a new form of Jewish knowledge to serve a new form of Jewish existence. In an essay from 1959, "How Is Judaism Possible?" Levinas correlates the repolitization of Jewish thought in the State of Israel with the "renewal of Jewish studies" not in the university but among Jewish youth movements in France. This return to Jewish texts, of which Levinas's own talmudic readings constitute a central manifestation, is not merely academic but communal, producing "a Jewish school of a new type."[35] The novelty of this Jewish school nonetheless consists in the basic direction of its epistemo-political vector: beyond the Talmud in France and toward the biblical land. The high science of justice that comes from the new Torah for the modern Jewish State of David, as Levinas writes in "The State of Caesar and the State of David" from 1971, signifies "the formulation of political monotheism that no one has yet formulated. Not even the Talmudic scholars. Only the responsibility of a modern State, exercised on the land promised to Abraham's descendants, should allow his heirs to elaborate patiently, by comparing formulas to facts, a political doctrine suitable for monotheists."[36] The new Jewish episteme is not a prerequisite for the Jewish state but rather the state's *telos*, its finality, its basic vocation. The new Torah is to come from Zion.

The messianic vocation of the State of Israel for Levinas is thus an explicitly epistemic one: to produce the science of justice, ethical knowledge, law not only for Israelis or Jews but for the world. "The Judaism of Diaspora and an entire humanity astonished by the political renaissance of Israel await the Torah of Jerusalem," he declares in the introduction to his first collection of talmudic readings. This same introduction also expresses the trans-epistemic nature of the event of messianic knowledge the State of Israel represents: "The translation 'in Greek' of the wisdom of Talmud is the essential task of the University of the Jewish State."[37] As we saw, in Levinas's historiography, the project of the West, which consists in affirming otherness in being, has been split between the tendency to separate the Other from being (Christianity) and the tendency to submerge the Other in being (Greco-Roman civilization). Judaism seeks to transcend this split, to unite otherness and being, transcendence and polis, by recreating being on the basis of otherness, by creating a moral world. The statelessness of the diaspora, however, kept Judaism in check, out of being, in a condition of apolitical mysticism—which is to say, Christianized and de-Hellenized. In this vision, by producing the "Torah of Jerusalem," the new State of Israel, in which we see the long-awaited activation of the Jewish project, finally mends the break between Christian *pistis* and the Greco-Roman *polis*, between otherness and being, by dediasporizing the Jewish episteme and reconfiguring the Talmud as a nation-state project.

Such is the trans-epistemic event that Levinas's messianic project envisions. His own work in France sought to prepare the stage for an encounter between Talmud and Philosophy, "to give to such a study all the breadth it requires, to translate into a modern idiom the wisdom of the Talmud, to confront it with the problems of our time devolves, as one of its highest tasks, upon the Hebrew University of Jerusalem."[38] Levinas's vision reads as an epistemic eschatology, one that features the Hebrew University as a temple of wisdom and justice for all nations and thus harks back to Isaiah's prophecy of Jerusalem in the end of days: "For out of Zion shall go forth the law. And the word of the Lord from Jerusalem" (Isa 2, 3).[39] Levinas's version has the word of the Lord, namely the talmudic reading of the Bible, spread from Zion through its translation into Greek in the worldly form of science and philosophy; torah law spreads in the form of the polis, as a modern state. Levinas later calls this messianic union of Talmud and philosophy the "end of misunderstanding," the reconciliation of Israel with Greco-Roman civilization. Such an epistemo-political union in modern Zion would engender a new, integrated, and complete human subject. The "most noble essence of Zionism," the 1968 introduction to the talmudic readings concludes, "in the form of an autonomous, political and cultural existence, makes possible a Western Jew, Jewish and Greek, *everywhere*."[40] The State of Israel stands here as the womb of a new, ethical humanity, a Western-Jewish humanity—that is, a humanity that is fully Western because fully Jewish, everywhere.

Just State

The State of Israel is to become the State of David, the messianic state for preparing a world-to-come beyond all states, a state for poststatist humanity. Levinas draws from this conception of the modern Jewish state the basic principle that should guide its existence as a polis. The politics of the State of Israel, according to its noblest essence, should be based on the principle whereby its existence as a state, its being, is not absolute, not a purpose in itself, but rather conditioned by a higher purpose of justice and responsibility, of being for others. In the Israeli polis, as Levinas writes in 1979, "self-assertion is responsibility for everyone. It is both politics and already non-politics."[41]

This principle, which conditions the state through morality, is inherently ambivalent. It posits morality as both grounding and justifying the state. It is the same ambivalence indicated in Levinas's earlier philosophical work, in *Totality and Infinity*'s demonstration of how the experience of totality (the self) is conditioned by the rupture of totality (the encounter with the other) while ontology is conditioned by ethics, which means that ethics grounds ontology and the relation to transcendence grounds totalitarianism.

In relation to the State of Israel, Levinas's messianic vision of this state as fulfilling the eschatology of justice allows him to develop a critical position against certain forms of statist, chauvinist, or nationalistic ideologies concerning the young Jewish state. I have already noted his rejection of nationalistic or racial understandings of the nature of the collective "Israel." The articulation of this position with respect to the Israeli state is the heart of the 1951 essay "The State of Israel and the Religion of Israel." Since, as we saw above, Israel's religion, Judaism, means "justice as the raison d'être of the state," then the State of Israel, Levinas argues, "will be religious or it will not be at all": "The subordination of the State to its social promises articulates the religious significance of the resurrection of Israel as, in ancient times, the practice of justice justified one's presence on the land. It is in this way that the political event is already surpassed. And ultimately, it is in this way that we can distinguish those Jews who are religious from those who are not. The contrast is between those who seek to have a State in order to have justice and those who seek justice in order to ensure the subsistence of the State."[42]

Levinas's critique condemns all conceptions of the State of Israel, all Israeli politics, that consider the state's existence, its territorial sovereignty, an end in itself rather than an instrument for realizing the Jewish science of justice. Some passages are more specific. The talmudic reading from 1963, for instance, warns against contemporary ideological idolatry that forgets God, the ultimate ideal of justice, and instead worships human agency called to realize justice, such as the working class or the Jewish people, "as some young people in Israel do."[43]

Levinas elaborates this critique two years later in the talmudic reading of 1965, "Promised Land or Permitted Land," first delivered at a meeting of the Colloquium of Jewish Intellectuals dedicated to the State of Israel. The reading refers to the talmudic midrah about the biblical story of the twelve spies Moses sent to explore the land of Canaan (Numbers 13, 1–33). Levinas comments on the spies' "evil report" according to which the dwellers of the land "are very powerful, and the cities are fortified and very large": "They are stronger than we . . . are men of a great stature . . . giants, the sons giants: and we were in our own sight as grasshoppers" (Numbers 13, 27–33). Canaan stands here for "building, dwelling, being—a Heideggerian order," Levinas comments, going on to imagine the Canaanites as "magnificent beings, very tall, blond, I suppose." It was the image of these Germanic pagans that terrified the biblical Children of Israel, "who had just come out of the Egyptian ghettos."[44]

But Levinas also suggests a second contemporary interpretation of the stately dwellers of Canaan: "Perhaps the spies caught a glimpse of *sabras*. Fear seized them; they said to themselves: this is what awaits us there; these are the future children of Israel, those people who make holes wherever they set foot, who dig furrows, build cities, and wear the sun around their necks. But that is the end of the Jewish people!"[45]

Levinas's reading is playful, but the rhetorical approximation of the Germanic and the Sabra marks a concrete target for his critique of Jews who put state above justice. Levinas's remark may have been specifically directed at the subculture known as *ha-knaanim*, "The Canaanites," which emerged in Mandatory Palestine out of intellectuals, such as Yonatan Ratosh and Adya Gour Horon, who had renounced their affiliation to the Jewish people, whom they criticized as inherently exilic. These intellectuals cultivated an autochthonous identity of "Hebrews" harking back to the supposedly ancient, pre-Judaic Semitic peoples of the land.[46] The explicitly anti-Jewish position of the Canaanites for Levinas clearly arises from the analogy he draws between the Sabra and the Germanic peoples, both of whom spell "the end of the Jewish people." In contrast to the Canaanite Ratosh, the end of Judaism for Levinas does not mean the happy end of diaspora; on the contrary, it means the catastrophic demise of the messianic project of the just state, the State of David. Like the new Hebrews, Levinas rejects diasporic Judaism and projects his vision back to biblical Israel, where "the practice of justice justified one's presence on the land."[47] The relation to the land, as we saw, is central to Levinas's conception of the State of Israel.

We may even wonder where one could go in the 1950s to see an authentic Sabra if not to a kibbutz. Would Levinas's talmudic readings prevent the kibbutznik from turning into Canaanites? Or would the translation of the Talmud into Greek return the Sabras to Judaism?

The proximity of Canaan and the kibbutz renders visible the aforementioned ambivalence inherent to Levinas's messianic vision of the State of Israel as conditioned by the quest for justice. As noted, the very positing of justice or morality as a condition for the state, inasmuch as it deabsolutizes the state's existence and subjugates it to the ethical demand of responsibility, simultaneously provides the grounds on which to justify the state and render it, as a *just* state, absolute. Furthermore, if the state's being is conditioned by the principle of justice, would the state's existence not *prove* its morality, serving as evidence that it is just? Would justice not be ultimately translatable into existence and otherness into being? If, for the State of Israel, "self-affirmation is immediately responsibility for all," would not the primary form of this state to exercise universal responsibility be to affirm itself, to ensure its own presence on the land?[48]

Just Conquest

Here we encounter the paradox of ethical egoism which, as I have shown, arises from *Totality in Infinity*, namely from the claim of being, of a justified self-preservation based on ethical superiority. We will see that Levinas's late book epitomizes this paradox in the political figure of violence exercised in the name of nonviolence, of war fought in the name of peace, of war against war, *just war*. This is the paradox that I claim underlies Levinas's early historiography in his Jewish writings, with respect to its central epistemopolitical figure, the messianic Judeo-Greek project that is the State of Israel.

Just like in Levinas's phenomenology, in his historiographical narrative the political drama of this collective ethical subject, of the Jewish state, emerges most clearly in his account of this state's *war*. The war that has been interlinked with the historical existence of the Jewish State of Israel since its foundation on the territory of Mandatory Palestine and even before—which is to say that the violent conflict with non-Jewish Palestinians may be considered, hermeneutically speaking, as a moment of truth for twentieth-century Jewish thought. My claim is that in Levinas's earlier, pre-1968 Jewish texts, the Israeli war is conceived of and portrayed as a just war. Israel's is a moral, ethical, good war waged against an immoral, illegitimate war, namely against a violence that is, properly speaking, not part of war but a crime against the fundamental ethical commandment "You shall not commit murder," a fundamental crime against ethics itself. The war waged by the State of Israel, as a project for a good state, is portrayed by Levinas as a war against *evil*.

My analysis here diverges from the standard debate concerning Levinas's position on the Israeli-Palestinian situation, which highlights and problematizes Levinas's distinction between politics and ethics. The locus classicus for this debate has been Levinas's 1982 interview with Shlomo Malka, conducted in the aftermath of the Sabra and Shatila massacre. In view of the mass murder, Malka suggested that the Palestinians are Israel's Other. Levinas dismissed this proposition, noting, somewhat obscurely, that "in alterity we can find an enemy, or at least we are faced with the problem of knowing who is right and who is wrong, who is just and who is unjust. There are people who are wrong."[49]

Why did Levinas deny the Palestinians otherness? Judith Butler interprets Levinas as saying that "the Palestinian had no face."[50] Her remarks have been criticized as misquotes showing that she misunderstood the categorical distinction Levinas made between ethics and politics, with respect to which the relation between Israel and the Palestinians is not ethical but political. Butler's rejoinder to the criticism is that the distinction between political and ethical is precisely the problem that led Levinas to deny ethical responsibility toward the massacred Palestinians. Howard Caygill has offered a more precise analysis according to which Levinas's ethical commitment to the State of Israel, his "responsibility for the other," takes precedence over his political responsibility to the Palestinians, which is a "responsibility for the third."[51]

Caygill's analysis reveals how the State of Israel actually features in Levinas's work as a collective, or political, figure of otherness, as a State of Others. Accordingly, as I will now demonstrate in the broader scheme of Levinas's Jewish writings, his position concerning the Israeli-Arab conflict is not predicated on a separation between politics and ethics but, on the contrary, on the politics of ethics. The State of Israel is understood to be the other because it stands for the ethics of responsibility to the other. In contrast, the Arabs, as enemies of Israel, paradoxically play the role of the egoistic, pagan "I," who is deaf to the commandment "You shall not commit murder" and blind to the face, which is to say, "has no face"—has no ethics of otherness and therefore is not worthy to be considered other in terms of such ethics.

In his 1981 introduction to the collected talmudic readings *Beyond the Verse*, Levinas warns against analyzing the Israeli-Palestinian or Israeli-Arab conflict in purely political terms, that is, using categories of democracy or human rights detached from "their prophetic and ethical depths." The Zionist project of the Israeli state, he claims, is not just political; its purpose is not the state itself. Rather, it serves the biblical "eschatology of Israel," seeking to create a new humanity founded not on self-interest but on responsibility for others. And this, he continues, "cannot be the cause of wars."[52] In other words, the eschatological quality of the Jewish state, its commitment to the messianic vision of the State of David, of Jerusalem as the city of justice, situates it beyond politics and thus precludes any justification of violent resistance to it.

Recall the 1959 description of the Jewish state as disassimilating, as reisolating Jews from Europe by situating them "on an arid and dangerous land." In Levinas's discourse, the Arab and Palestinian armed struggle against the State of Israel is often portrayed not so much as a political conflict with an enemy, a rival, but rather as an objective "danger" arising from the natural, climatic, geographical properties of the land. Arab violence is the inherent violence of the land, of land in general; it is the brute force of being. A text of 1969 referring to the war speaks of Palestinian refugees as representing the "call of the land," in contrast to the "call of consciousness" represented by Jews, and invokes "the vast spaces inhabited by the Arabs" or "the Arab Fatherland." Another text from 1979 makes a contrast between the State of Israel as "one of the most fragile things in the world" and Arab countries as "uncontested nations, rich in natural allies, surrounded by their lands."[53]

The Arab collective subjects, including Palestinians, are presented as natural peoples, based not on ethics but on ontics, on subsistence and expansion. In other words, the Arabs—whom Levinas never conceives of as Muslims, as a configuration of God's people, of Israel, just like Christians, an Islamic configuration that is absent from Levinas's work—constitute no modern European nations ("defined by the decision to work together much more than by the obscure ways of legacy") but rather particular peoples that arise from the Germanic (and Persian) principle, the principle of race. And considering that the Western project, as understood by Levinas from 1934 on, consists in opposing racial politics, the Arabs and Palestinians become embodiments of the non-West, which for the Western project, spearheaded by the State of Israel, stand for evil. The Palestinian cause is accordingly conceptually affiliated to Hitlerism, such that the struggling Palestinians are placed beyond the scope not only of politics but of ethics, beyond the limits of Israel's superhuman infinite responsibility for others—which, as aforementioned, is limited to "others who are not Hitlerians."[54]

The above elements of Levinas's conceptualization of the Israeli-Palestinian conflict come together most coherently and render clearly visible the ambivalence of his early eschatological understanding of the State of Israel in the aforementioned talmudic reading from 1965, "Promised Land or Permitted Land." In this text, Levinas chooses to contribute to that year's colloquium discussion on the State of Israel a reading that relates to the biblical episode of the conquest of the Holy Land, the seminal instance of a holy war—"a remarkably contemporary passage."[55]

As we saw earlier, the text studied by Levinas approaches this episode through the story of the twelve spies who were sent by Moses before the conquest of Canaan to explore the land and brought back discouraging reports about the Canaanites, who were "stronger than we." Levinas offers two interpretations for the Canaanites' power over Israel. The *first* interpretation concerns *physical* power, such that the Canaanites are portrayed as a material people of the land, an ontic, self-interested people opposed to and constituting the enemy of ethical Israel. I have already shown how Levinas portrays these Canaanites in the contemporary political situation as a figure for the Germans and the Sabra, both of whom spell, in different ways, the end of the Jewish people.

Levinas's *second* interpretation reads the Canaanite power over Israel not as physical but as *moral*, arising from the same "ethical impossibility" that in Levinas's phenomenology in *Totality and Infinity* the face of the Other posits against my own violence. On this reading, the fear reflected in the spies' description of the dwellers of Canaan concerns "moral qualms": "they may have asked themselves whether they had the right to conquer what had been so magnificently built by others."[56] Translated into contemporary terms, "into Greek," the spies' apprehension pertains not to the Jewish people's fear of being subjected to violence of the Germans or the Sabra but, on the contrary, the Jewish fear of Jewish violence against existing non-Jewish dwellers of the Holy Land—Palestinians. Are not the Jewish people, the people of infinite responsibility for others, the people of the superhuman demands of morality, *constituted* by the "ethical impossibility" of exercising violence against others? Would not the armed occupation of Palestine from Palestinians contradict the moral essence of Judaism? Would not military conquest turn Jews into Sabras, into Germans, such that the State of Israel itself would constitute "the end of the Jewish people"?

The main thrust of Levinas's Talmud reading is to answer these questions in the *negative*. Quoting Rabbi Johanan's phrase about the spies' "bad intentions," Levinas comments, "bad intentions which were good intentions: those of an overly pure conscience." Moral qualms in view of the conquest of the land, in the face of the Canaanite dwellers of Palestine, arise from a good conscience that has turned bad, from a perverse sense of morality, from "moral delicacy that is rather condemnable and morally twisted." Levinas's text harshly condemns the moral perversity of "beautiful incorruptible consciences." It castigates "the tears of beautiful souls" and the more sinister "plot of the righteous." Morality becomes twisted for Levinas when fear of immorality leads to resignation, namely to refrainment from taking any action, to the pursuit of *purity*. In contemporary terms, Levinas scolds the "purity of egalitarian consciousness," which seeks to be "pure like leftist intellectuals." He also speaks of the "purity of atheism" and describes the spies' ethical misgivings as "a crisis of atheism, a crisis much more serious than the crisis of the Golden Calf."[57] If worshipping a false god leads to a false politics (state idolatry), then a godless morality, Levinas appears to be saying, *cannot justify any politics at all*. Atheist goodness precludes political action and consists in rejecting politics, in rejecting worldly justice. The apolitical atheism of "leftist intellectuals" is tantamount for Levinas to worshipping an a-worldly god, which is how Levinas understands Christianity.

In contrast to the leftist, Christian spies, Judaism—represented in the story by the two dissenting spies, Joshua and Caleb, who favored the conquest of Canaan—understands that God commands "what is above our strength or what is beneath our conscience." In view of the ontic immanence of the Canaanites, Judaism asserts otherness not through apolitical morality but through a moral politics, through the people of Israel acting within the State of Israel on the land of Israel: "We will not possess the land as it is usually possessed; we will found a just city in this land," which will thus be "sacralized," become holy.[58] In other words, Levinas considers violent conquest of the land, violence against its dwellers, as justified by the cause, by the inversion of being, the conversion of reality from self-interest to responsibility, from violence to justice.

It is easy to observe here the violence done in the name of nonviolence that goes by the name of just war. In his 1965 reading, Levinas recognizes this concern, which he sees as an abuse of justice whereby a claim to moral

superiority is turned into a justification of colonialism. Nonetheless, he insists that such abuse is not a necessary but only a possible outcome, one
that arises from false messianism and does not concern the real, Jewish
messianism.

> You will say that everyone can imagine that he is founding a just society and
> that he is sacralizing the earth, and will that encourage conquerors and colo-
> nialists? But here one must answer: to accept the Torah is to accept the norms
> of a universal justice. The first teaching of Judaism is the following: a moral
> teaching exists and certain things are more just than others. A society in
> which man is not exploited, a society in which men are equal, a society such as
> the first founders of kibbutzim wanted it . . . is the very contestation of moral
> relativism. What we call the Torah provides norms for human justice. And it
> is in the name of this universal justice and not in the name of some national
> justice or other that the Israelites lay claim to the land of Israel.[59]

Invoking the inner-Jewish term for designating Jewish immigration to
the Holy Land, also used for Jewish immigration to the State of Israel, not
"conquest" but "ascension," *aliyah*, Levinas concludes that "those who are
about to conquer a country the way heaven is conquered, those who ascend,
are already beyond delicate tears."[60] The message is clear: just as the messianic vocation of the Israelites justified the dispossession of the Canaanites, the messianic vocation of the Israelis justifies the dispossession of the
Palestinians.

Levinas underscores the idea that the mission to create a just society
not only justifies Israel's political existence but also *conditions* it. The justice
of the Jewish states is a condition of its legitimacy. The State of Israel "will
be religious or it will not be at all," he declared in 1951. In his 1965 reading,
he notes with respect to the biblical conquest of Canaan that the Israelites'
"right to that country" arises from their willingness "to accept the consequences of their actions and to accept exile when they are no longer worthy
of a homeland": the land of Israel "is a country which vomits up its inhabitants when they are not just," and the people of Israel "assume a responsibility without indulgence and are summoned to pay for their own injustice
with their exile."[61] Here we see the *critical* potential of Levinas's ethical
messianism vis-à-vis the concrete politics of the State of Israel.

Yet the position of moral superiority is, as we saw, ambivalent. To subject Israel's existence to the condition of justice quickly shifts toward a
perception of the sole fact of Israel's existence as justice, meaning that its
enemies are by definition enemies of justice—not opponents but evildoers,

not fighters but murderers. Do the conquering and violent taking possession of the land not *already* constitute acts of injustice toward its Canaanite or Palestinian dwellers? Is not their violent struggle against this occupation at least as justified? According to the logic of just war, the enemy is precisely precluded from having any justification to fight: a just war is fought by definition against unjustified violence, good against evil. Israel's moral superhumanity *categorically* casts subhuman shadows on those who stand in its way. When Levinas chastises the biblical spies, who, "in the purity of their egalitarian consciousness, denounced as antidemocratic the wisdom which excluded from freedom the murderers of freedom," he immediately qualifies this remark by saying "that in all this we are not dealing with a problem of history": "Were the Canaanites actually so mean? This is the hypothesis or the initial given within which we must place ourselves. Without it, everything we have just said is perfectly meaningless!"[62] The Canaanites are by definition "murderers of freedom."

This criminalization of Canaan's dwellers does not remain a mere literary observation about the biblical narrative but extends into Levinas's own contemporary geopolitical analysis. I have already indicated how his texts characterize the Arabs as peoples of the land, of immanent being, akin to Germanic race-based peoplehood, which in Levinas's intellectual historiography stands for the non-Western evil against which the ethical quest of the West is defined. In the 1965 reading, Levinas finds the literary trope of the murderous Canaanites to be "remarkably contemporary."[63] Commenting on the biblical spies' report according to which the Israelites looked to the Canaanites "like grasshoppers" (Numbers 13, 33), Levinas notes, "Didn't someone say recently: 'We are one hundred million strong to crush you.' When Israel arms itself against its neighbors, pacifists ask: How do you know that your neighbors do not want to make peace with you? Did they say so? Yes, they did say so; they told us we were like grasshoppers. It is a remarkably contemporary passage. That way of taking human faces for grasshoppers! Or that way of taking the historical act of Return for a movement of grasshoppers."[64]

It is unclear who Levinas is quoting here, and it is also unimportant. The alleged quote is a rhetorical device that puts words in the mouth of Israel's neighbors. It reproduces the language of bellicose speeches a Jewish audience would expect to hear from Arab leaders.[65] The important point is that, within the context of the geopolitical conflict in the Middle East, Levinas sees Arab hostility toward the State of Israel as arising from a profound moral and civilizational attitude that consists in "taking human faces for grasshoppers." The Arabs are portrayed as rejecting, according to Levinas's philosophy, the constitutive experience of human consciousness, namely the ethical encounter with the face of the other as speaking the moral commandment "You shall not commit murder." This violence done to the human face marks out Israel's neighbors, including the Palestinians who struggle against Israel, as enemies of humanity, as evil.

Levinas's 1965 talmudic reading thus deploys the biblical story of the Holy Land's conquest by the Israelites from the Canaanites as a parable for the contemporary Israeli-Palestinian and Israeli-Arab conflicts. The messianic-ethical vocation that Levinas's narrative transposes from biblical Israel to the State of Israel, as a state of justice, is not used to ground a prophetic, inner-Jewish moral critique against Israeli politics. On the contrary, Israel's mission of justice projects a mission of injustice on its foes, such that Israeli violence against them takes the form of holy war. Levinas's early eschatology corresponds to his early phenomenology by featuring the Jewish people as the redeeming epistemo-political figure of the West, and the State of Israel as the spearhead of the Western *mission civilisatrice*. The prophetic ethics of the Other thus works here to ground the messianic justification of Zionism as a form of colonialism.

PART II. STATE OF PERSECUTION: LEVINAS AFTER 1968

THUS FAR, I HAVE PRESENTED THE INTER-EPISTEMIC PLOT in Levinas's early work, the unfolding tension between philosophy and Jewish thought staged in his phenomenology and eschatology, including the epistemic and political consequences of the ethics of the other to the State of Israel. Major elements of this drama continue to feature in later texts. Yet Levinas's narrative has its own essential history insofar as his narration responds to its time and shapes the latter in turn. The drama told corresponds to the drama of the telling, which is articulated through its own events. If the story of Levinas's telling begins with the pivotal moment of 1934, the center around which its meaning takes shape—retroactively—is 1968. My claim is that this year marks a watershed in Levinas's work that constitutes not just a shift but a trauma akin to the wound of 1934.

The year 1968 refers here to a series of events that took place in that year, such as the student demonstrations in Paris and elsewhere in May '68, that are commonly perceived as epitomizing a set of deep transformations in the intellectual, discursive, cultural, and political texture of Western societies after World War II. These transformations redefined the self-understanding of the West in many ways that are still foundational today.[1] Some of these central shifts relate directly to the basic concerns of Levinas's project. As we saw, Levinas's endeavor responds to the crisis in European civilization after World War II, seeking to revisit the disoriented project of Western humanism and reorient it using Jewish coordinates. Correspondingly, the moment of 1968 may be described—and is registered in Levinas's work—as a moment where Western self-critique, not unlike the self-critique developed by Levinas himself, attains a level of intensity at which it begins criticizing not only the distortions, shortcomings, or side effects of Western civilization but also its very foundations. As *self*-critique, 1968 marks the emergence of an anti-Western West.

The anti-Western West criticizes itself not for failing to realize its ideals but for holding them as ideals in the first place. In other words, this critique perceives the evil of the West as residing in its very perception of what is good. Accordingly, if the Western project had consisted, as Levinas himself occasionally indicates, in promoting *human* well-being, in developing and spreading "humanism," then the radical Western self-critique that came about with 1968 may be called, as Levinas occasionally does, "antihumanism." From a different perspective, that which is allegedly good—humanism—is perceived as a historical evil, its promotion through Western humanism as the expansion of Western man, and Western universal humanism (including its dissemination in the Judeo-Christian message) as *colonialism*, so that the radical self-critique of 1968 takes the guise of a discourse of anticolonialism, decolonialism, and, later, postcolonialism.

That the Western project of spreading humanism around the globe amounted to a violent project of colonization, that the *mission civilisatrice* was a project of violence—was it ever really in doubt?—became a central concern in France in view of the wars of decolonization that took place in the aftermath of World War II, especially in Vietnam (1946–1954) and Algeria (1954–1962).[2] Frantz Fanon, a prominent spokesperson of the non-Western world who was engaged in the Algerian National Liberation Front and gave voice to colonized peoples in the language of French colonizers, famously called the colonized, in his 1961 book of the same name, *Les damnés de la terre*, translated into English as *The Wretched of the Earth*.[3] More accurately, *les damnés* are not just wretched; they are damned, which is to say fated to demise by a higher power, here through a verdict of eschatological violence. "Pure violence" is how Fanon describes colonialism.[4] Colonialism's violence arises directly from its so-called humanist mission, which, by asserting the West as the human, eo ipso posits the non-West as less than human. Accordingly, Fanon wrote, "the colonized world is a world split in two,"[5] two species, two races: the human and the nonhuman. Humanism is racism.[6]

In his 1961 preface to Fanon's *Les damnés*, Jean-Paul Sartre converts the non-Western gaze on the West into a new Western self-conscience. Sartre transforms the non-Western critique of the West into an internal Western self-critique, generative of a new anti-Western Western collective conscience. "We too, people of Europe, are being decolonized," he translates Fanon's gospel: "A bloody operation removes the colonizer inside each one of us." In Sartre's sermon, Europe's redemption from its own colonialism requires a radical *metanoia*, a total conversion in which the Western sinner not only denounces evil and commits to good but also, more radically, confesses as evil what he has so far held for good. "Our beautiful souls are racist," Sartre repents, "We are the enemies of the human kind; the elite shows its true nature: it is a gang." This self-denunciation, or Western self-unmasking, this "striptease of our humanism," exposes it as "a deceptive ideology, the exquisite justification of pillage": "the European was only able to become human by producing slaves and monsters."[7]

It is easy to see how, conceptually, this call for self-decolonization directly concerns the "superhuman demands of morals" that stand at the center of Levinas's vision of the West as portrayed in his Jewish writings and early philosophy. As I showed in the introduction to this book, postcolonial critiques of Levinas's work have been increasing in number in anglophone scholarship over the last two decades.

However, already in the 1960s, the French critique of Western humanism was explicitly applied to Levinas's early work in Jacques Derrida's famous essay "Violence and Metaphysics" from 1964.[8] In contrast with the indication Levinas makes in *Totality and Infinity* of a difference within the West between philosophers and prophets, totality and infinity, theory and ethics, Greek ontology and Jewish metaphysics—a difference that, it is argued, stands for a conflict between war and peace, violence and non-violence—Derrida's "Violence and Metaphysics" points to the violence *of* metaphysics.

If, as Levinas argues in *Totality and Infinity*, Western philosophy, as logos and light, as ontology, as phenomenology, has been producing violence, Derrida reminds us that the philosophical logos itself emerged as a form of resistance to a more fundamental violence—namely "the worst violence,

the violence of the night which precedes or represses discourse," "the violence of primitive and prelogical silence," "when one silently delivers oneself into the hands of the other in the night." Derrida's notion of prelogical
violence, which the Greek logos resists, brings to mind Levinas's notion of
animalistic violence, which his historiography attributes to non-Western
epistemes such as the Germanic or Persian ones. But Derrida does not refer
to this narrative. His point is that if discourse and light resist prelogical
violence, "the worst violence," then any attempt to resist light as violence,
such as Levinas's critique of Western philosophy, must reproduce light, discourse, reason: "If light is the element of violence, one must combat light
with a certain other light, in order to avoid the worst violence, the violence
of the night which precedes or represses discourse." Accordingly, any attempt, such as Levinas's, to assert a discourse of infinity, transcendence,
and metaphysics—be it innerphilosophical or prophetic—against the discourse of totality, immanence, and ontology, according to Derrida, must
remain light and violence. This violence is necessary to avoid the worst
violence, such that metaphysics must always be "violence against violence.
Economy of violence."[9]

Discourse, Derrida argues, cannot seek to abolish violence but only to
minimize it. Indeed, "the least possible violence, [which is] the only way
to repress the worst violence," requires acknowledging this situation; it
requires the "avowal of violence" in discourse. All discourse, as nonviolent as it may seek to be, must acknowledge its own necessary violence. To
overlook this irreducible violence, Derrida admonishes, means to overlook
"the responsibility for [one's] own finite philosophical discourse." Derrida's
critique addresses the *disavowal* of discursive violence by a discourse such
as Levinas's, which, against the violence of philosophical logos, seeks to
assert a prophetic language of nonviolence (as in *Totality and Infinity*)—or
which, I add, seeks to assert the superhuman morality of Israel, as paragon
of Western humanism (as in the early Jewish essays) against the violence
of the Greco-Roman state. "The very elocution of nonviolent metaphysics
is its first disavowal," Derrida observes, since elocution is discourse and
therefore a violent break with nondiscursive violence.[10]

But Derrida says more. He indicates that the disavowal of violence, the
"elocution of nonviolent metaphysics"—which may serve as a title for Levinas's early philosophy—is not just self-refuting: worse still, it *increases* violence. How so? Clearly the avowal of discursive violence "is not yet peace"
or the end of violence but rather the avoidance of the worst violence, of

perpetual war. The avowal of violence, Derrida writes, is "the opposite of bellicosity"—"the bellicosity," he continues, "whose best accomplice within history is irenics."[11] In other words, the worst violence, that which discursive violence seeks to avoid, not only arises from prelogical, prehistorical primitivism but is also generated *within* history, within discourse, by "irenics," that is, by the pacifist discourse that disavows its own necessary violence. This disavowed violence of nonviolence, we may say, is precisely what constitutes the "bellicosity" of Western humanism. The worst war is the war against war, the just war, and with it just conquest, colonialism.[12]

This critique was not lost on Levinas—far from it.[13] It is one of my central claims in this book that, though Levinas was initially a *target* of radical Western self-critique, of the Western anti-Occidentalism of the French 1960s, he was quick to absorb and assimilate this attack and transform it into a productive *self-critical* development of his early, pre-1968 work into his later, post-1968 work, especially in view of the Six-Day War of 1967. In what follows, I demonstrate this claim in both main corpora of Levinas's writings, first in his philosophy, in the language of phenomenology, and then in his Jewish texts, in the discourse of eschatology. The following chapters show how, in his later work, Levinas manages to formulate the basic elements of a decolonial Jewish thought—and a decolonial Zionism.

PHILOSOPHY

THE DECOLONIAL TURN IN LEVINAS'S POST-1968 PHILOSOPHY IS articulated here through a reading of his second major philosophical book from 1974, *Otherwise Than Being*, whose core chapter on "substitution" was first published in 1968. This book is less studied and understood than the earlier *Totality and Infinity*—no doubt due to the more demanding linguistic style of *Otherwise Than Being*, which, as we shall see, constitutes a central part of its conceptual performance.

Otherwise Than Being is often understood as a reformulation of the same basic ideas as in Levinas's earlier book.[1] And to some extent, this is true. In general, anticolonialism's radical critique of Western civilization is intellectually akin to Levinas's original project of fundamentally calling into question Western philosophy "from Plato to Heidegger." Nonetheless, the next two chapters show how *Totality and Infinity*'s critical gesture against Western philosophy was radicalized after 1968 by a gesture of self-critique in *Otherwise Than Being*. Whereas Levinas's early book asserts ethics of nonviolence as breaking with the violence of ontology, his later book (self-)critically reflects on how this break with being reinscribes itself in being, such that nonviolence asserts itself as war on violence, as just war.

Chapter 6 analyzes the fundamental, self-critical turn in Levinas's project that takes place in *Otherwise Than Being*. My analysis locates the deepest point of this turn in the question of language and in a shift from logics to hermeneutics, which leads to an important revision in Levinas's conception of the inter-epistemic tension between philosophy and prophecy. Chapter 7 examines—and problematizes—Levinas's decolonial turn in terms of his later phenomenology of subjectivity.

6

UNSAYING

THIS CHAPTER TRACES AND ANALYZES LEVINAS'S PHILOSOPHICAL TURN after 1968, the self-critique this turn generates vis-à-vis his earlier philosophy, and, most importantly, the new horizon it opens for the question of epistemic difference. This horizon is the realm of hermeneutics, or, to use Levinas's terms, the realm of difference between what is said and the event of saying. Levinas's most important idea in this context is expressed in his notion of "unsaying,"[1] which opens up in thought, in logos, a horizon of epistemic otherness. Within this horizon, the logos of philosophy enters into relation with the hermeneutics of talmudic thought. The idea of unsaying thus marks, in my view, Levinas's most penetrating insight into inter-epistemic thought.

Beyond

My claim is that Levinas's late work *Otherwise Than Being* involves a fundamental self-critical reflection on his early work *Totality and Infinity*, specifically concerning inter-epistemic difference and its political implications. This self-critical development is indicated in the titles of the works themselves. Both titles suggest a difference between one thing or concept and another. The first expresses this difference through a juxtaposing "and" that provides us with a synoptic, panoramic view. This integral vision, as per Levinas's own analysis in the book, reincorporates the differing components, totality *and* infinity, into one structure, which I have shown emerges in the figure of the Jewish Greek world, the West.

The title of the second book eschews the panorama and presents a different act of signifying—and knowing—difference, one closer to what Levinas suggests in *Totality and Infinity* as an alternative to vision, namely ethics, a desire that goes from the one toward the other, a movement of "otherwise than." This ethical movement of knowledge does not just go toward something else, toward some undetermined "otherwise"; it recognizes something as superior, higher, or commanding, having a dimension of *hauteur*, of height and transcendence—as the subtitle of the second book adds, a dimension of the "beyond." Beyond, *au-delà*, signifies a relation of transcendence and forms the fundamental preposition of Levinas's text.[2] It is the basic operator of what *Otherwise Than Being* calls the logic of "the superlative."[3] In contrast to the formal logic of vision, where difference is presented as difference, as a relation between a "one" and an "other," such that this very presentation abolishes difference, the superlative presents difference as otherness or alterity, as a condition of one entity whose other is not presented as another entity but as simply "beyond," such that the presentation of difference does not abolish but *performs* difference.

This logic guides the new constellation of inter-epistemic difference in philosophy that Levinas formulates in his second book as a critical reflection on his first book. *Totality and Infinity* stages—panoramically—a fundamental difference between two performances of difference, between totality and infinity, the philosophic and the prophetic, politics and morality, the Greek and the Jewish. This staging itself, as I have shown, generates a synoptic vision that conceptually links totality to infinity, synthesizing the Greek and the Jew, ethics and theory, and thus presenting a certain totalitarianism or suppression of difference as the very performance of the Jewish Greek episteme of the West. The total state is a performance of God's people. To be sure, totalitarianism is a perverse performance of metaphysics, an abuse of prophecy. But herein lies the problem. If the West has a problem with respecting difference, this problem arises not from a split between a Greek episteme centered on totality and a Jewish one centered on difference but from an inner tension within one and the same Jewish Greek episteme, something like a Jewish-Christian tension between different performances or interpretations of prophecy. The problem of Western civilization arises not from an absence of prophecy but from its presence in pathological form. If *Totality and Infinity* is dedicated to showing this presence, *Otherwise Than Being* focuses on the pathology.

My claim is that Levinas's motivation in his later book remains what he perceives as a Western problem of respecting difference. However, the problem is no longer diagnosed as the forgetting of prophetic wisdom, where the stress is on the importance of morality and unconditional individual responsibility over and against totalitarian universality, which suppresses individuality and difference. Rather, *Otherwise Than Being* diagnoses the problem of the West, of European civilization, as an abuse of the ethics of prophecy. This abuse arises from the very constellation *Totality and Infinity* presents as the core of prophetic epistemology and morality, namely the ethics-based self. My analysis has pointed out how the dialectic of self and totality is structurally embedded in the logic of *Totality and Infinity*, which posits the separated self as the precondition of totality. This structural dialectic becomes the explicit theme of *Otherwise Than Being*, in which the focus is shifted from totality to the self. The suppression of difference is no longer analyzed primarily as a tendency toward totality—that is, toward suppressing the individual by means of the universal, morality by politics—but, on the contrary, as the radical, *moral* assertion of individuality, an ethics-based *egoism* in the singular and plural senses.

Abuse

The dedication and epigraphs that open Levinas's second book already announce the self-critique it contains. Levinas dedicates the book to the memory of his family members who were murdered in the Holocaust, and to all the victims of the Nazis and "of the same hatred of the other man, the same anti-semitism."[4] The next page has five epigraphs. The second is a quote of a prophecy from Ezekiel (Ez. 9, 4–6). In it, God is said to have commanded a mass slaughter of all of sinful Jerusalem's inhabitants, bar the righteous ones who criticized sinful behavior. The quote depicts a prophetic self-critique in which God's people, Israel, is portrayed as responsible, thanks to its sins, for its own demise. The third quote expresses a rabbinic reflection on this prophetic passage in the form of a rabbinic exegesis, a midrash. According to this midrash, when the prophecy says that the slaughter of Israel should begin "at my sanctuary," *mi-mikdashi*, it should be read as *mi-mekadshai*, "with those who sanctify me," with the righteous. In this reading, not only are God's people punished for their sins, but the righteous among them are also executed first, since it is they who bear the greatest responsibility. The nature of the sin is expounded in the last two quotes, both of which are from Pascal. The first points to individual self-affirmation ("This is my place under the sun") as the beginning of the "usurpation of the whole earth," namely imperialism. The second identifies erotic love, "concupiscence"—which some, like Levinas in *Totality and Infinity*, present as the basis of a good society—as a "false image of charity," which is to say as a perversion of love that is in fact "hate," "the same hatred of the other man, the same anti-semitism."

This tragic perversion of the relation to the other, of prophecy, defines the European episteme and its sins. This is the underlying insight of *Otherwise Than Being*. In the book, Levinas articulates the pathology of this episteme using the same basic epistemological operators as in *Totality and Infinity*: ontology, ethics, and language.

I begin with ontology. Similar to *Totality and Infinity*, Levinas's later book also characterizes the episteme of the West as problematic due to its commitment to ontology, to the logos of being. "Being" here is similarly understood as a totalizing notion that abolishes all difference, integrating the diversity of disparate entities as beings into a total system that suppresses individuality. The totality of being suppresses all difference between beings and between being and nonbeing. It therefore liquefies every substantive, dissolving all solid being into the pure verb "Being," recreating the state of chaos prior to the distinction between being and nonbeing, which Levinas in his early philosophy designates as *il y a*, "there is"—in *Otherwise Than Being* using the more ontological term *essence*.[5]

However, in contrast to *Totality and Infinity*, the opposition to Being is no longer sought in individual being, in a separate entity. Levinas now takes a more radical distance from ontology. He notes that the constitutive conceptual difference that regulates ontological discourse, namely the difference between Being and being, between the total verb and the individual agent, which Heidegger calls "onto-ontological difference," is *no difference at all*. Rather, Being and being are two aspects of the same thing; their distinction constitutes an "amphibology." Levinas now shifts the focus of the problem from the total Being to the individual being. The problem with Being is no longer that it suppresses all individual being. On the contrary, Being is now understood precisely as the deed of the individual being, as the singular entity's existence as such, its remaining itself. Essence is "persistence in essence": "The essence is performed as an invincible persistence in essence, filling up every interval of nothingness which would interrupt its exercise. *Esse* is *interesse*; essence is interestedness."[6]

"*Esse* is *interesse*" means literally that the act of essence, *esse*, being, consists in surmounting the distance between beings, in "filling up the interval of nothingness" that separates them, *inter-esse*, fusing them together into one *interesse*. However, this fusion does not simply mean the disappearance of individualities or totality, like it did in *Totality and Infinity*. Rather, Levinas now recognizes that Being, *interesse*, is also interestedness; it is not the suppression of the individual self but, on the contrary, its very

performance. The self abolishes its separation from the other as an enactment of existence, self-identification, and self-preservation: interestedness
"is confirmed positively as the *conatus* of beings."[7]

In other words, the individual being, the separated, happy self that *Totality and Infinity* posits as the rupturing of totality, now emerges as the
agent of totality. I have shown how this constellation can already be traced
in the inner logic of *Totality and Infinity*, where totality is posited as the
"experience of totality" itself conditioned by individuality. *Otherwise Than
Being* explicitly features individual being as the main problem of Western
ontology, where the individual, the "disturbance of essence," becomes—this
is the key phrase of the book—the "essence of disturbance."[8] The essence of
disturbance is the ontological totalization generated by the performance of
individuality, Being as effected by being.

Accordingly, the constellation of difference as presented in *Totality and
Infinity*, namely the breakup of totality in individual self-consciousness and
rationality, comes, in *Otherwise Than Being*, to constitute the very performance of essence, or totality. Levinas speaks of the "unity of conscience and
essence."[9] Objective knowledge, the relation of conscience to being, which is
the heart of the relation to the other in *Totality and Infinity*, is now conceived
as the performance of the separate self in which the self, the subject, functions
as the inner difference *within* the totality of being. Knowledge, or conscience,
functions as a difference that being generates within itself in order to overcome this difference and become total. Totality is generated as the relation of
being to itself in self-manifestation, which takes place in the self as consciousness. Consciousness is what reunites being with itself.[10] The basic operation
of Western knowledge consists in re-presentation, in "collecting dispersion in
one presence."[11] Consciousness re-presents through reminiscence, through
recollection, through memory and history, through the force of time as always remaining the same time—time as synchronicity and simultaneity. It
is crucial to see the dialectics at work here: individual consciousness, which
ruptures totality, maintains itself by (re-)generating totality. Totality is generated for the sake of the individual rupturing of totality—it is not simply suppression but perversion of individuality.

War on War

This onto-epistemological observation has dramatic *ethical* implications.
First of all, it means that totality is not simply the absence of individuality

and therefore not simply the—political—absence of morality. Rather, totality is a form of morality, a perverse form. We have seen how my analysis of the narrative of *Totality and Infinity* clarifies this point, demonstrating how totalitarianism arises structurally from a perversion of justice. *Otherwise Than Being* makes this insight explicit.

One manifestation of this insight is seen in Levinas's use of Gnostic terminology. Throughout the book, the subject, the self, is understood most fundamentally not as consciousness, (objective) knowledge, or psyche—as in *Totality and Infinity*, which denotes an affinity and belonging of the subject to the world, to being—but as spirit, *pneuma*, unworldliness. We return to this issue below. The point now is that Levinas also uses a Gnostic term to describe the totality that suppresses the self: "eon."[12] Eon, the world into which spirit falls and becomes lost, is itself a spiritual creation, which is to say, a transformation, a materialization of spirit, a necessary hypostasis. Spirit, the individual self as an "interruption of essence," according to Levinas, "must spread out and assemble itself into *essence*, posit itself, be hypostasized, become an eon in consciousness and knowledge, let itself be seen, undergo the domination of being."[13] The totality of being, as eon, is not just a neutral, impersonal, anonymous universality, the utter nonexistence of moral agency, but a perverted form of good, an evil that, just like good, implies a specific agency.

In this way, the fundamental ethical deficiency Levinas identifies in the Western episteme is significantly redefined in *Otherwise Than Being*. Just like in *Totality and Infinity*, the problem arises from a perversion of ethics, of the moral relation to the other, in the temporal being of politics. However, just as the West's ontological pathology no longer lies in the suppression of individual being in Being ("there is") but, on the contrary, in Being as the persistence of individual being, in Levinas's post-1968 book the West's basic political pathology no longer lies in totalitarianism—the total state as absence of individuality—but, on the contrary, in a universalism deployed in the service of particularism, in *just war*.

In both of his books of philosophy, Levinas correlates ontology with war. However, whereas in *Totality and Infinity*, war signifies the suppression of individuality in totality,[14] in *Otherwise Than Being* war arises from individual existence as *interesse*, as self-interestedness, as the *conatus* of egoism, the struggle for existence: "War is the deed or the drama of the interestedness of essence."[15] Levinas problematizes his earlier defense of singular and collective individuality. I have shown how *Totality and Infinity* asserts the collective individual subject, the family, or—as I argue—the nation against the impersonal state. *Otherwise Than Being*, however, explicitly posits nationalism as the origin of political evil. Furthermore, as I also claim, national individuality cannot be simply opposed to the state, as the nation *is* the collective subject of the state. Just like the singular individual exists as the "experience of totality," so the collective asserts itself in total politics. In other words, totalitarianism, universalism, the seeming abolishment of individuality are powerful instruments of the collective individual. This is what Levinas acknowledges when he writes about the "violences of nationalism, even when it hypocritically pretends to be but *at the service of Essence* and not willing the will."[16]

The implicit critique of Heidegger here is clear. Heidegger is both a thinker of Being and *the* philosopher of National Socialism. Levinas dismisses the attempt made by Heidegger and Heideggerians to point at Heidegger's efforts—especially after 1934—to counter the Nazi and Nietzschean biologistic will to power by asserting, through Hölderlin, the notion of Germans as a people of poetic and philosophical devotion to the truth of Being.[17] This seeming sacrifice of all particularism does not lead to an impersonal universalism, Levinas argues, but in fact operates as an instrument of more powerful, higher nationalism, of a collective philosophical egoism, as it were. It is remarkable that when problematized not as totalitarianism but as nationalism, political ontology suddenly shows a troubling affinity to the tradition of prophetic ethics, as do the people of Being to the people of God.[18] Levinas warns not only of nationalism "in the service of Essence" but also of politics made "in reference to God—to a God who is always deniable and in permanent danger of turning into the protector of all egoisms."[19] It is not simply nationalism, by contrast to the state, that, in *Otherwise Than Being*, becomes the fundamental problem of Western politics; it is, more specifically, Judeo-Christian nationalism, the ethical-religious collective of Israel, *Totality and Infinity*'s unspoken messiah and the protagonist of Levinas's Jewish texts.

Consequently, Levinas's later work portrays the West's political pathology as correlative to the ontological pathology of persistence in essence, *conatus*—not merely as the natural struggle for existence between selfish individuals but as the confrontation of individual assertions of universality, namely war as a struggle between moral collectives or civilized nations, waged in the name of justice and ethics: not simple war but just war. The position Levinas adopts here is not the Hobbesian claim of war as a natural, prepolitical evil abolished by politics but one closer to Carl Schmitt's idea of politics as regulated, "hedged" war, where the real evil is antiwar politics, which, in the name of peace, morality, and humanity, wages war on war. Just war, Schmitt argues, is not merely violence but total war, a war of destruction, a *Vernichtungskrieg*.[20] Similarly, in *Otherwise Than Being*, Levinas articulates a clear critique of *Totality and Infinity*'s basic effort to found the individual through the ethical rupturing of totality—that is, in "You shall not commit murder"—when he problematizes the "disturbance of essence" through moral repulsion from violence: "This repulsion attests only to the stage of nascent or savage humanity, ready to forget its disgusts, to be inverted into 'essence of disturbance,' to surround itself like every essence, inevitably jealous for its perseverance, with military honors and virtues."[21]

If Levinas's early diagnosis of Western onto-political pathology is the totality of Being without beings, his subsequent diagnosis can be summed up as the "essence of disturbance," being as based on the interruption of being, politics as based on ethics, leading to "war in good conscience."[22] *Totality and Infinity* argues that "the state of war suspends morality; it divests the eternal institutions and obligations of their eternity and rescinds ad interim the unconditional imperatives."[23] It thus posits morality against political violence. *Otherwise Than Being*, however, engages in a critical reflection on Levinas's earlier analysis, identifying the political problem in "the institution of violence out of this very struggle" against violence: "Does not the war on war[24] perpetuate that which it is called to make disappear, and consecrate war and its virile virtues in good conscience?"[25]

Said and Saying

The most dramatic site of Levinas's self-critique in *Otherwise Than Being* is language. *Totality and Infinity* identifies language as constituting the relation to the other and, accordingly, as the primary realm of difference, prior to abstract thought. Yet the main point of *Totality and Infinity* is to show how the relation of language is the true basis for rationalism, logics, and objective perception. Thus, the very paradigm of language is live speech, which constitutes the encounter with the face, a relation structured as vision. I have pointed out how Levinas brings language into harmony with logos and logics, how he brings Moses into perfect understanding with Plato and Descartes. I have also problematized the way in which the motif of evil enters into (and so begins) the narrative of *Totality and Infinity* as a perversion of speech, a relation to presence, working its way into phenomena like writing, signs, and works, which admittedly relate only through absence but, for this very reason and in contrast to vision, also feature proper linguistic phenomena.

Otherwise Than Being places language at the very center of its analysis, casting it not simply as the distinctive feature of an epistemology of difference, in contrast to systems of totality, but as the primary site of perversion—as Levinas now calls it, of "abuse." The pathology of the Western episteme arises most fundamentally from an abuse of language. Accordingly, language becomes the explicit realm in which the epistemological drama of *Otherwise Than Being* takes place. On the conceptual level, the constitutive difference that underlies Levinas's discourse in the book no longer arises directly from ontology, from the discourse of being; it is no longer the difference between Being and being. Rather, it is the difference between two other concepts, Saying and Said, which arises from discourse on language itself, or self-reflective discourse, namely a self-referential performance of language. To the extent that this discourse calls into question the very act of making sense, including its own, we may say that in *Otherwise Than Being*, Levinas shifts not only the terminology of philosophical discourse but also its operation, including Levinas's own, *from the operation of logics to that of hermeneutics*. We will return to this point.

Levinas notes that his meditation on language in his later book "owes much to Heidegger."[26] Similar to Heidegger's later essays on language, Levinas also argues for the foundational role of language in constituting our most fundamental forms of experience. If *Totality and Infinity* acknowledges a domain of interiority, where the self bathes in sensations and ambiguous phenomena prior to the uprightness of the spoken word, *Otherwise Than Being* insists that even our sensations arise from language: "Experienced sensation—being and time—is already heard/understood [*s'entend*] in the verb."[27] What we feel, all the more what we see, is already discourse, already said, that is, logos: "The phenomenon itself is phenomenology."[28]

As constitutive of our experience, of our world, the form of language that Levinas, like Heidegger, considers paradigmatic is the perfected speech act, namely a speaking that has become articulated speech, *das Gesagte, le Dit*, "the Said," in the sense of that which has been said and has become "a saying." Language, so understood, manifests primarily not as an abstract set of grammatical rules and vocabulary but as a materialized operation of verbalizing and informing existence—not just as discourse but as tale, story, epos, what Heidegger calls *Sage*, which means both the saga and "the saying." Whereas Heidegger identifies this creative paradigm of language—in contrast to the theoretical logos—as *Dichtung, poiesis*, that is, as art and poetry, Levinas designates it with another Greek category, one arising from the Christian reception of the prophets, namely *kerygma*, proclamation or preaching. The difference between Heidegger and Levinas in identifying the historical-discursive location of nontheoretical, generative language—Classic Greek or Jewish-Christian Hellenism—also reflects their different choices of textual corpora for their interventions in nonphilosophy, with Heidegger turning to Hölderlin and Levinas to the Talmud.

The main thrust of Levinas's conception of language in *Otherwise Than Being*, however, consists in a fundamental critique of both Heidegger's philosophy of language and his own earlier analyses in *Totality and Infinity*. Inasmuch as language, in the figure of the Said, features the original epistemic realm, where sensation, experience, perception, and knowledge arise, language, as the Said, also generates *essence* in the problematic sense this term has for Levinas. It bears recalling that in Levinas's later book, essence is the basic category of a Western epistemology of nondifference and indifference against which he proposes the notion of nonindifference. *Totality and Infinity* attempts to counter—what it claims is Heidegger's notion of—Being by affirming individual being, rupturing all ontological totality in the situation of speech. In contrast, *Otherwise Than Being* takes a critical distance from ontological difference. It diagnoses the difference between being and Being not as an absolute distinction but rather as an "amphibology" or "ambiguity" constituting the generative dialectics of essence *within language as Said*.

This is how Levinas describes the amphibology of the Said. As a body of expressed meaning, as that which has been said, language is "a system of nouns identifying entities."[29] Language is about naming. However, language is not just a set of names; it also *says*. As speech, as *verb*, it sets nouns in motion and relates them to each other such that in the "predicative proposition," the *apophansis* or logos, "substances dissolve into modes of being."[30] In the verb, the underlying movement that fuses together distinct substantives into the elements of one coherent event, the noun no longer designates an independent, separate entity—to use Levinas's example, "red." Instead, the noun becomes the description of a certain condition, a certain "mode" of the underlying event, ultimately the event of existence: red means being redly. Every noun is simultaneously an adverb of being, and all being is a mode of Being.[31] In terms that resonate with Heidegger's philosophy of language ("language speaks as the peal of stillness"), Levinas thus describes the verb of language as "the silent resonance of essence": "There is neither *essence* nor any being behind the Said, behind Logos. The Said as a verb is the *essence* of *essence*."[32]

Accordingly, whatever individual, separate entities language names, the Said, by the power of verbal essence, generates a "gathering," a totality. The noun is already a theme interconnected with other themes into an integral whole, a system, a story, a history, a world, which is an "eon"—"the source of a tyranny exercised by totality."[33] Here, Levinas takes a self-critical distance from the confident rationalism of *Totality and Infinity*, where logos signifies a break with totality. Even as *Otherwise Than Being* continues, like the earlier book, to identify totalizing language in writing, the problem identified in written language is no longer absence—of object, of speaker—but, on the contrary, excess of presence, of essence: the "simultaneity of writing, eternal present of writing."[34] Accordingly, although speech, the act of speaking, preserves its superiority in the narrative of the later book, as we shall see, it is no longer because it constitutes "the presence of interlocutors to each other, in a dialogue, where they are in peace and agreement with each other."[35] Language, as the Said, is still the place and paradigm of presence, of being. However, presence and being no longer constitute a rupture in totality; they are no longer the elements of separation but instead stand as the *interesse* of essence.

Yet inasmuch as language generates essence, totality, nondifference, it is also, as in *Totality and Infinity*, the original (or "pre-original") realm of epistemic difference. As already noted, one of the most crucial interventions of *Otherwise Than Being* consists in shifting the foundational distinction of the epistemology of difference from the ontological difference between being and Being to a difference of language itself, more precisely between language as nondifference (essence, totality) and language as difference. We saw that Levinas identifies the essence of essence in language as the Said, the perfected act of saying, a systematic whole of meaning, or logos, maintained by the inner amphibology of noun and verb, of being and Being. By contrast, as the realm of nonessence, nonpresence, nonbeing, and difference, language is posited as the pure act, the infinitive underlying the perfect "Said," *Dit*—that is, *Dire*, "Saying." Language as Saying is the original realm of difference, a dimension that lies beyond (*au-delà*) or before (*en deçà*) all system or totality, before or beyond all order of consequences and origins, a "pre-original" domain regulated by no principle, united by no recollection, both "anarchic" and unmemorable. Saying is language before logos, or, as Levinas puts it, "anterior to all civilization and to all beginning of signification in spoken language."[36]

What the Saying *is* exactly—what paradigm or form of language it concretely signifies, in what real or historical phenomena of language it shows itself—emerges as the main question of Levinas's later project of an epistemology of difference and inter-epistemic encounter. Before we come to this, however, it is crucial to note how *Otherwise Than Being* posits language as the realm of both difference and the suppression of difference, as both Saying and Said. Language arises as the space where the transformation—more specifically, the *perversion*—of difference to essence takes place. Indeed, in Levinas's later book, language becomes the explicit and central stage of the phenomenological story, of all stories, of history, and of politics, the original scene of original sin, the site of the *abuse* that has been generating the West, which is essentially an "abuse of language." This generative abuse consists in a transformation of language as difference, as infinite action, as Saying, into language as perfected deed, as essence, as Said. This transformation of Saying to Said is the foundational manifestation of what I designate as the basic pathology addressed in *Otherwise Than Being* through its critical reflection on *Totality and Infinity*, namely the essence that arises from the disruption of essence, "the essence of disturbance."

Levinas describes the emergence of essence from difference, the transformation of Saying into Said, in terms of inscription, of the speech act become sign or writing.[37] This move, as already indicated, reiterates *Totality and Infinity*'s gesture of contrasting speech to writing, as life contrasted to death. In *Otherwise Than Being*, however, Levinas uses another, more explicitly hermeneutic trope, describing the abusive transformation of Saying into Said as an act of translation, which—as the classic saying goes, *traduttore, traditore*, "translator, traitor"—is at the same time an act of treason, of betrayal.[38] It should be noted, however, that the transformation or perversion in question here is located deeper than the passage from the original to the translation or even from spoken to written language. Rather, the passage from Saying to Said constitutes (or perhaps is one with) the very emergence of language as a world of meaning. The "abuse of language" is the abuse that generates language, the abuse language essentially *is*.

In my analysis of *Totality and Infinity*, I indicated how the pathology Levinas identifies in written language, the sign—that is, absence—concerns the very essence of language (in contrast to vision). *Otherwise Than Being* makes this connection between pathology and the essence of language explicit. Language (as Said) consists in the abuse of language (as Saying). This constitutive, inherent abuse recalls Heidegger's *Being and Time*, which analyzes spoken language (*Sprache*) as a compromised form of discourse (*Rede*).[39] To be sure, Levinas's "Saying" is more primordial, more "pre-original" than Heidegger's *Rede*, which is already the articulation of a coherent totality of meaning, of a world, and so already features the essence of what Levinas calls "the Said." Nevertheless, the analogy to Heidegger is instructive because it highlights the *necessary* character of the abuse. Both in *Being and Time* and in *Otherwise Than Being*, the existence of language, as a coherent realm of meanings, requires an act of betrayal, a translation or inscription of Saying into Said, a conversion-perversion of difference to essence.

The exact nature of this necessity is clarified by another analogy to Heidegger. A basic motif in Heidegger's later work is the ambivalence of the process or event by which Being reveals or unconceals itself—becoming truth by bringing forth beings that, even as they manifest Being, simultaneously conceal it, such that the very revelation of Being effects its concealment.[40] Similarly, "the subordination of saying to the said, to the linguistic system and to ontology," Levinas writes, "is the price that manifestation demands. In language qua said everything is summoned to appear [*se traduit*, also 'translated'] before us, be it at the price of a betrayal."[41] Like Being, Saying shows itself, or *is*, properly speaking, only in its abuse and betrayal: "the anarchical [i.e., Saying] is not possible but as contested by the discourse that betrays, but translates, without cancelling, its an-archy with an abuse of language."[42] Like Being, Saying exists and shows itself in its absence from its own manifestation, a form of appearance Levinas calls the "trace." The trace presents an absence, that which conceals itself, through "betrayal."

This figure epitomizes Levinas's self-critical gesture in *Otherwise Than Being*. *Totality and Infinity* confronts, as a defining split of the West, a Greek episteme of totality with a Jewish episteme of difference—totalitarianism versus individual morality. The later book, as a second thought, identifies the civilization of nondifference, of essence, of the system and the "eon," as the very performance, meaning both manifestation and existence, of the rupturing of essence, as the *necessary* abuse of difference. The Said betrays—simultaneously manifests and abuses—the Saying; essence betrays individuality; just war betrays morality. Accordingly, the evil in Western civilization, in the European eon, does not arise from total oblivion, from the complete forgetfulness of the episteme of difference, of the relation to the Other, to God. On the contrary, the Jewish Greek West is the eon that *betrays* prophecy.

Second-Degree Disturbance

What is the *alternative* epistemology *Otherwise Than Being* seeks to assert against the epistemo-political evil of the West? Unlike in *Totality and Infinity*, the conflict is not about totality versus difference, Greek versus Jewish, two renditions of difference. Rather, it is about the very performance of the Jewish Greek episteme of difference that underlies the West. Against this West, Levinas comes to posit an other that is not merely non-West, not completely unrelated to the West, but invoked from within the West itself as the voice of an inner question, an other inside the West: "The true problem for us Westerners,[43] is not so much to refuse violence as to question ourselves about a struggle against violence which, without blanching in non-resistance to Evil, could avoid the institution of violence out of this very struggle. Does not war on war perpetuate that which it is called to make disappear, and consecrate war and its virile virtues in good conscience?"[44]

The other West does not simply assert difference against totality; it does not posit ethics—"You shall not commit murder"—against ontological violence. Such was the doing of the West itself, the Greco-Jewish West, which instituted violence as a struggle against violence, war against war—just war. The evil of the West is already instituted in the form of the struggle against evil. European ontology is already the essence that arises from the disruption of essence, totality based on the breaking up of totality. To counter this ontology, it is not enough to assert otherness. The other West requires another otherness; it must be other *otherwise*. Levinas explains that this other otherness "needs a disturbance of essence, by which it will not only be repelled by violence. This repulsion attests only to the stage of nascent or savage humanity, ready to forget its disgusts, to be inverted into 'essence of disturbance,' to surround itself like every essence, inevitably jealous for its perseverance, with military honors and virtues. For the little humanity that adorns the earth, a relaxation of essence to the second degree is needed: in the just war waged against war to tremble or shudder at every instant because of this very justice."[45]

The other West stands for a second-degree disturbance of essence, a *second degree of difference*. What is this second-degree disturbance, which shudders before its own justice, self-criticizes its own self-criticism, deactivates its own nonviolent passivity, "more passive than any passivity"?[46] What is this ethics that undermines the very subject that arises from ethics? On what level and in what dimension does the disturbance of the essence of disturbance take place? Here lies Levinas's most profound insight.

This operation of double disturbance, which *Otherwise Than Being* identifies as foundational for the alternative episteme of difference, takes place in the same dimension Levinas indicates as the primary scene of both difference and the perversion of difference through transformation into the indifference of essence, namely the realm of *language*. Language is the realm in which Saying, *Dire*—the preoriginal condition of difference, of nonessence, of "otherwise than being"—is inscribed thanks to its own inner dynamics, the movement of its own self-fulfillment, its own self-perfection as Saying in the Said, *le Dit*, logos, that which constitutes essence. In the perfection of Saying in Said, of difference in essence, the "otherwise than being" translates into the inner amphibology of the Said, inscribed in the ambiguity of noun and verb, of being and Being. To *counter* this process, in which the disturbance of essence (Saying) is betrayed or abused by essence (Said)—that is, to generate a second-order disturbance, an abuse of abuse, a disabuse—Levinas points toward an operation of reversal, of de-essentializing difference by deinscribing the Saying in the Said, an operation of *dé-dire*, of *unsaying*.

As Levinas says, "The *otherwise than being* is stated in a saying that must also be unsaid [*se dédire*] in order to thus extract the *otherwise than being* from the said in which it already comes to signify but a *being otherwise*."[47] Unsaying de-essentializes otherness; it reconverts otherness as a mode of being, a "being otherwise," to an otherness before being, an "otherwise than being." Unsaying does not mean not saying, not speaking, suspending language altogether. Rather, it means defrosting the solidified system of meanings, the coherence of logos and narrative, the perfected worldview, in order to break with the Said and thus to revitalize, to put into motion, into action once again, to reactivate the preoriginal, anarchic happening of Saying.[48] Levinas describes this operation of unsaying as that which leads the Said back to "the Saying *before* [*en deçà*] the Said," an operation of *re-duction*.[49]

Unsaying means reducing Said back to Saying. This operation may be referred to as a second-order disturbance or difference because it does not generate difference on the first, common level of language—language as a realm of perfected meanings, concepts, logos, of what is said—by insisting on the plurality of different beings versus the total, neutral, anonymous Being, as Levinas does in *Totality and Infinity*. Rather, unsaying performs difference at the higher or deeper level of language, that is, at the level of language as a happening of saying, of making sense and signifying. Unsaying suspends language as logos, as a movement within meaning, as thinking, and reveals the more fundamental happening of language that takes place as a movement from no meaning to meaning, as an action not of thinking but of making sense, of identifying the very existence of meaning, an action of rendering intelligible, of acknowledging signs and deciphering them, of understanding or *reading*. In other words, unsaying shifts the performance of difference—and thereby the entire epistemic question—from the level of logics to the level of hermeneutics. The basic operation of unsaying consists in revealing this difference of epistemic levels between logics and hermeneutics, thinking (or speaking) and reading.

Unsaying Philosophy

Unsaying emerges as the key category of epistemic difference in Levinas's later philosophy. Unsaying designates not only the epistemic difference between betraying difference (Said) and the preoriginal performance of difference (Saying), between signifying as thinking and signifying as reading; it designates not only the passage—by reduction—from betrayed difference to performed difference, from Said to Saying, or even the performance of this preoriginal difference, unsaying as saying. More profoundly, unsaying marks the difference between two temporal, historical, cultural performances of epistemic difference, two difference-performances of the West. If the evil of the West, in its mainstream, hegemonic, dominant variant, consists in perverting the disturbance of essence into the essence of disturbance, in betraying the Saying in the Said, in a certain abuse of language, then unsaying is the performance that undoes the West, *the anti-Western operation*. If this performance is in fact hermeneutical or consists in enacting the difference between the logical and the hermeneutical, then the category of unsaying is especially suggestive for contemplating, with Levinas, the epistemic split between philosophical thought and talmudic readings.

Yet the epistemic discipline *Otherwise Than Being* identifies as the generic and historic site for the exercise of unsaying, this second-order disturbance of essence that constitutes the essential performance of the other West, is *philosophy*. Philosophy is, on this account, the discipline and tradition that has been generated, summoned, or, as Levinas says, "called" on within the West to counter the perverse rending of difference as essence, the abuse of language, the betrayal of Saying through the Said. This betrayal, Levinas repeatedly writes, is one "philosophy is called to reduce,"[50] namely through an exercise of unsaying. It is far from trivial that philosophy represents here the episteme of a dissident West, considering the sweeping condemnation made in *Totality and Infinity* of "Western philosophy" from Parmenides to Hegel, from Plato to Heidegger, as the historical agent of totality. Indeed, as I have shown, *Totality and Infinity* stages the confrontation between philosophers and prophets as an internal tension within the philosophical tradition, a tension between a mainstream and a subversive undercurrent. *Otherwise Than Being* reiterates this inner tension in the history of philosophy. However, instead of opposing philosophy, Levinas now *occupies* the position of philosophy, as it were, by reclaiming its inner essence in defiance of its hegemonic deployment throughout history, in defiance of what philosophy has mostly *said*.

This reconfiguring of philosophy's epistemic status from an agent of totality to an agent of disruption repositions philosophy on Levinas's interepistemic map. Philosophy is no longer held to be a Greek episteme opposed to Jewish prophecy. Rather, within the Judeo-Greek episteme of the West, which betrays prophecy in just wars, philosophy is a second-degree interruption, a second rupturing of totality. This second-order prophetic event of interruption counters the betrayal of the first, undoes abuse through disabuse, recovers the preoriginal Saying from the Said not through an operation of resaying but by the deconstructive, reductive operation of undoing the Said, Unsaying.

Understanding philosophy as that which is called to exercise something like a second-order prophecy, a second-order Judaism, requires Levinas to retell the history of philosophy as commonly told, including in *Totality and Infinity*. The historiography of *Otherwise Than Being* is, like that of *Totality and Infinity*, not presented linearly but fragmentarily, and often in code, through the different strategies of unsaying that Levinas articulates conceptually and indicates in concrete historical figures. All the strategies of unsaying Levinas identifies in and as philosophy have as a commonality the disturbance of the Said, the undermining of logos, a movement that runs counter to the Platonic-Cartesian rationalism put forward in *Totality and*

Infinity. In *Otherwise Than Being*, Descartes cedes his place as the French patron of philosophy to Pascal.

Levinas identifies a *first* type of strategy of unsaying in what he calls "some instants of clarity" in the history of philosophy.[51] All of these instances perform unsaying through an act of Saying that immediately regenerates logos; they all fight logos with logos, such that their act of unsaying is immediately reinscribed in the Said. One example Levinas names is Husserl's *epoché*. Inspired by the Stoic "suspension" of judgment, the *epoché* consists in a suspension of our perception of how things really *are*, of our set of rational beliefs about beings. Inasmuch as Husserl literally understands this suspension as a "reduction," his *epoché* does not just interrupt the order of beings or logos of being; by suspending the reality of things, it also converts them into elements of consciousness, into phenomena. Through what Husserl calls "bracketing," a judgment about the being or nonbeing of a thing is suspended such that this thing is now perceived, regardless of its external existence, as a content of my conscience, as (a thing). Levinas says bracketing remains a "way of writing," by which he means that it remains inscribed in the system, in the realm of essence.[52] Husserl's *epoché* unsays being in order to write the science of phenomena; it translates ontology into phenomenology and reinstates the Said.

Another example Levinas discusses, one more central to his own endeavor, is the Heideggerian reduction of beings to Being. That this should be a strategy of unsaying, of second-order disturbance, is remarkable, considering that in *Totality and Infinity*, the reduction of beings to Being is construed as the paradigmatic operation of totalization, whereby the aim is to seek the interruption of the total Being by individual beings. This reversal manifests the critical self-reflection that marks the passage from Levinas's first major work to *Otherwise Than Being*. Rather than an as affirmative totalitarian act, Levinas now understands Heidegger's destruction of Western ontology, of the established order of beings through a raising of the question of Being, as Heidegger himself does: as an act of critique, of iconoclasm, that liberates Being from its oblivion in ontotheology.

This (partial) rehabilitation of Heidegger extends to the second archvillain of modern philosophy in *Totality and Infinity*, namely Hegel. Hegelianism, Levinas notes at one point in his later book, shakes anthropocentric pride in "the exceptional form of the *cogito*" by exposing behind individual reason "the dialectical structures of being," that is, by reducing being to Being. Hegel thereby anticipates all "modern forms of distrust of the immediate data of consciousness," which "in our days," Levinas indicates, manifests in—here we are reminded of Foucault—the "effacing of the living man behind the mathematical structures that think themselves out in him, rather than he be thinking them."[53]

All these modern projects of reducing beings to Being, ranging from Hegel to Foucault and including Husserl and Heidegger, that *Totality and Infinity* features as the essence of Western episteme of totality, the basic problem of our civilization, now appear in another light—no doubt closer to their own self-perception—as carrying out philosophy's subversive, critical task of calling into question the established Western order. By exposing the inherent ambiguity of the Said, of logos, they counteract the eon, unearth the abuse, and, undoing it, disabuse us.

Nonetheless, just like Husserl's phenomenological reduction, Heidegger's ontological difference and—especially—Hegel's dialectics stay inside the Said despite exposing its ambiguity, remaining in the space between being and Being, noun and verb. In analogy to later Heidegger's distinction between the reduction of beings to beingness (*Seiendheit*), which is what Western metaphysics has been doing, and the reduction of beings to Being (*Sein*), which is how Heidegger understands his subversive project, we may say that, for Levinas, Heidegger only reduces the Said to Saidness. This reduction does not break open the Said but, in fact, reinforces it and so fails to go beyond essence or uncover Saying. Heidegger's and Hegel's resistance is accordingly failed or even fake, actually reproducing the Western "essence of disturbance" and ultimately reinforcing the powers to be—both epistemically and politically.

Skepticism

A *second* type of strategy of unsaying that Levinas identifies in the history of philosophy goes further than reducing Said to Saidness, noun to verb, beings to Being, remaining within the inner ambiguity of logos, of essence. The second type of unsaying reduces logos not just to ambiguity or double meaning but to *nonsense*. This kind of unsaying, therefore, does not simultaneously regenerate the Said; rather, it produces a more sustainable second-order disturbance. The modern protagonist of this strategy in *Otherwise Than Being* is Nietzsche. Beyond Husserl's (and Heidegger's) reduction, which stays a "way of writing," Levinas claims, "one should have to go all the way to the nihilism of Nietzsche's poetic writing, reversing irreversible time in vortices, to the laughter which refuses language."[54] Nietzsche's murder—or burial—of the ontotheological God, it is claimed, is more iconoclastic, more anarchical than Heidegger's. It does not recreate the logos but instead breaks with it and with philosophy, which becomes poetry. This poetry is not foundational, such as in the way that Heidegger understands Hölderlin's poetry, but rather nihilistic. It is not even *poiesis* but nonsensical laughter. This nonsense is not nothing, not just destruction; it reveals the very trace of Saying, of difference beyond or before essence.

For this second strategy of unsaying through the radical interruption of language's basic function of making sense, Levinas identifies, beyond Nietzsche (and Derrida), a more general figure in the history of philosophy, one that is both conceptual and historical, namely *skepticism*. Skepticism, as the episteme of doubt,[55] features in *Otherwise Than Being* as a central category of the epistemic operation of philosophy as a second-degree disturbance of essence. The positing of skepticism as the epistemic core of philosophy entails a revision of the standard historiography of philosophy, one that remains mostly implicit in Levinas's book. This revision consists in shifting the emergence of (that which goes as) *proper* philosophy—that is, philosophy as a consolidated historical episteme, a discipline, a school - from classical Greece to Greco-Roman Hellenism. Skepticism follows classicism; doubt reacts to dogma, revisiting, reducing, retracting, and unsaying logos. Philosophy is accordingly a post-Greek, even counter-Greek, Greece. At one point, reflecting on otherness as the foundation of philosophy, Levinas invokes "the Stoic nobility of resignation to the logos."[56]

Otherwise Than Being's main figure of unsaying through resignation to logos is, however, not Stoicism but skepticism. In contrast to the Heideggerian or Hegelian reduction of logos, a skeptic unsaying of the Said does not also regenerate the Said or re-create logos. Rather, skepticism consists in doubting, namely in calling into question the very possibility of making sense, of perfecting Saying to Said. Skepticism says the impossibility of logos, which makes skepticism itself an impossible logos, a logos of no logos, a contradiction. As such, the skeptic logos is untenable. However, Levinas observes, this does not mean that skepticism cannot exist. On the contrary, we know how frequent and insistent its historical incidence has been. Skepticism is not inexistent but untenable. Its existence consists in interruption, in a disturbance of essence, in disrupting the continuous existence of thought, the continuous time of consciousness. The self-contradictory nature of skepticism, which says the impossibility of saying, does not mean that it does not exist, but that its existence—and thereby, philosophy's own existence—is an inherently disrupted existence; it is discontinuous, nonsimultaneous, *diachronic*.

Skepticism is unsaying with no simultaneous resaying. It is doubting without the simultaneous reassuring, meaning that it exposes the preoriginal, presynchronic temporality of logos as anarchic happening of saying: "It is produced out of time or in two times without entering into either of them, as an endless critique, or skepticism, which in a spiraling movement makes possible the boldness of philosophy, destroying the conjunction into which its Saying and its Said continually enter."[57]

In other words, only as inherently skeptic can philosophy have an actual history, one that is made not of continuity but of discontinuities, of permanent doubts, of gestures of unsaying that consist in a split between saying and unsaying—or, as Levinas describes it, in an "alternating movement" of skepticism and reason, of doubt that stands as a refutation of logos as well as a refutation of doubt, a refutation of refutation.[58] Yet, and this is the main point, doubt and its refutation are *not simultaneous*. The act of skeptic discourse is pure unsaying; it dissolves the Said and undoes sense without restoration. It disabuses without reconstruction. As such, similar to Nietzsche's laughter and Heidegger's Being without beings, skepticism, as impossible methodical doubt or discipline of nonsense, exists as a second-order disturbance, a trace of difference in essence, a trace of Saying in the Said.

Once again, similar to those modern "instants of clarity" that occur with Hegel, Nietzsche, Husserl, and Heidegger, skepticism, too, Levinas observes, has never been able to fully awaken the philosophical tradition of the West to its true calling, namely the reduction of the Said to the Saying by unsaying. "The history of Western philosophy," he writes, "has been nothing but the refutation of skepticism as much as the refutation of transcendence."[59] This observation undermines the resolute Platonism of *Totality and Infinity*, in which Plato is presented as the marshal of philosophical truth in the battle against sophist skepticism.[60] It is further noteworthy how transcendence, that is, the (ethical) relation to the absolute Other, to what *Totality and Infinity* calls the infinite, is associated here with *skepsis*, with doubt, which is to say with the first movement of Descartes's *Meditations*. Criticizing Western philosophy for having been nothing but the refutation of doubt and thereby of the Other, Levinas directly criticizes Descartes, whose project consisted in overcoming doubt through the "idea of the Infinite."

Whereas *Totality and Infinity* features Descartes's idea of the infinite as a central moment in the *subversive,* so to speak "Jewish," undercurrent in the tradition of philosophy, *Otherwise Than Being*—in taking a critical position vis-à-vis both Descartes and early Levinas—identifies the moment of subversion in the gesture of doubt, such that the idea of the infinite becomes the suppression or refutation of skeptical disturbance by the force of logos and essence, the power of the Said.

Books

This brings me to the *third* strategy of unsaying that Levinas indicates. This strategy is literally the most dramatic of the three; it is also the most important for the drama of inter-epistemology, and even more so for the drama between Philosophy and Talmud. We saw that the first strategy of unsaying, which Levinas identifies in exceptional moments in the history of philosophy (Hegel, Husserl, Heidegger), consists in undoing logos by reducing it to the internal ambiguity of the Said, to the inherent double sense of being/Being, noun/verb, said/saidness. The second strategy, skepticism, consists in undoing logos by reducing it not to the internal double sense of the Said but more radically to the nonsense of anarchical Saying as preoriginal to any meaning, as pure disturbance of essence. The third strategy of unsaying also reduces the Said to Saying, however not only as the negative dimension of nonsense, of categorical and radical doubt, of nihilistic laughter, but also as a positive event, as drama, the drama of language as negotiation of meaning, as *conversation.* Unsaying is not carried out here as a specific position, conception, or theory, that is, as an act of logos. It does not operate on the level of the Said, of language as a set of meanings, but instead on the level of language as a practice, as ethics. Unsaying as practice does not articulate some position of skepticism, for, through it, "language is already skepticism."[61]

The concrete historical figure Levinas provides for this third strategy of unsaying within the history of philosophy is the very existence of philosophy as history, as tradition, as an ongoing conversation. Philosophy, he writes, is "a drama between philosophers and an intersubjective movement which does not resemble the dialogue of teamworkers in science, nor even the Platonic dialogue which is the reminiscence of a drama rather than the drama itself. It is sketched out in a different structure; empirically it is realized as the history of philosophy in which new interlocutors always enter who have to resay [*redire*], but in which the former ones take up the floor to answer in the interpretations they arouse."[62]

This portrayal of philosophy as a historical conversation is already a feature of Levinas's description of the "alternate movement" between skepticism and reason. The exchange between skepticism and reason, however, remains a relation between two positions, two correlated theories or formulations of logos. The exchange, that is, remains a dialogue that involves a dialectics—"the reminiscence of a drama rather than the drama itself." The crucial point here, the one that generates a new strategy of unsaying, is that the history of philosophy is not only the temporal enactment of a cyclical alternation between doubt and certainty, skepsis and ratio, saying and unsaying. It is an *open* conversation, discontinuous and diachronic, between new and old interlocutors who essentially coexist not in any simultaneous or nontemporal dimension of logos, of reason and concept, but in the irreducibly interrupted space of difference.

The nature of the drama, of the language event that forms the actual temporal existence of philosophy, is not, therefore, a dialogue or conversation in the sense of the articulated development of some reasoning; it is not the unfolding of a thought process through different but coordinated thinkers ("teamworkers"), a series of Q & As, or the phenomenology of spirit. The basic interaction in the conversation underlying philosophy as a tradition of thought does not consist in pure thinking, in a movement between concepts and meanings, but more fundamentally in saying—in producing, maintaining, and performing the very domain of meaning in the making, remaking, and unmaking of sense. Before being thinkers who think, philosophers are interlocutors who listen and speak: all logos, all logical positions, if they are to exist, must be said and resaid, each time newly restated, articulated, repeated, read, interpreted, and understood. In other words, the basic event of philosophy as a subversive tradition of unsaying is fundamentally not logical but hermeneutical.

Here we touch on yet another critical revision by Levinas of his earlier work. My analysis has shown how *Totality and Infinity* tends to portray the hermeneutic domain, the realm of the sign, of writing, work, interpretation, that is, of *absence*, as constituting the dissimulation, the perversion of living, fully present speech and thus as an instrument of totality. The motif of writing as totalization is preserved in *Otherwise Than Being*, in which the abuse of Saying arises from its "inscription" in the Said. Nonetheless, inasmuch as hermeneutics remains a site of abuse of language, it is now revealed also as the site of disabuse, of Unsaying. Both functions arise from the same defining feature of the hermeneutic space, of the preoriginal event of Saying, namely from its being a space of difference, of otherness, of absence. Absence enables totalization and simultaneously *disables* it.

A text, Levinas writes, always refers to a reader, who is an absent interlocutor.

> This reference to an interlocutor permanently breaks through the text that the discourse claims to weave in thematizing and enveloping all things. In totalizing being, discourse qua Discourse thus belies the very claim to totalize. This reversion is like that which the refutation of skepticism exposes. In writing saying does indeed become a pure said, a simultaneousness of the saying and of its conditions. Interrupted discourse catching up with its own breaks—this is the book. But books have their fate; they belong to a world they do not include, but recognize by being written and printed, and by being prefaced and getting themselves preceded with forewords. They are interrupted, and call for other books and in the end are interpreted in a saying distinct from the said.[63]

It is crucial to see how the hermeneutic space, the realm of text, writing, and interpretation, emerges in this description as the scene for the drama of saying and unsaying, of language, politics, and history—as the drama of Western civilization itself. The essential configurations of this drama are translated into hermeneutic figures.

The central figure here embodies the fundamental configuration of the mainstream West understood as the perversion of prophecy, as that which inverts the disturbance of essence by converting the relation to the Other, or ethics, and absolute individual moral responsibility into the essence of disturbance, or total just war. We have seen how, in the general terms of language, Levinas analyzes this perversion as arising from the "inscription" of preoriginal Saying within the system of the Said. This inscription now shows itself literally to signify inscription, writing, text. The text systemizes; it totalizes by "weaving" all the elements of discourse together. However, and more specifically, the hermeneutic figure of the essence of disturbance is the peculiar text, the perfected phenomenon of writing, "the Written," as it were. The Written explicitly presents itself as a total, complete, self-containing semantic universe, a "simultaneousness" of all dispersed elements of Saying, which is to say as a *book*: "interrupted discourse catching up with its own breaks." The Book is the basic epistemic figure of the West seen as a perversion of prophecy. Inversely, the agents of a second-order disturbance, as the people of unsaying, take the hermeneutic form of resistance to, or interruption of, the Book.

This hermeneutic, deconstructive image of the Other West begins to evoke motifs of talmudic epistemology or grammatology as a text-based culture of knowledge. Is the Talmud true philosophy? Does it rise to the call to reduce the Western betrayal of the prophetic disruption by capturing it in the Book of Books, the Bible? In a forthcoming study, I will follow Levinas in exploring this horizon, leading away from the traditional textual environment of philosophy and toward the talmudic text.

At this point, however, from within Levinas's properly philosophical discourse, we receive no more than an initial indication, a mere hint. The above quote continues to speak of a world of *books*. The book is interrupted by "other books" and by the intersubjective, social events that form the existence of books: writing, printing, prefacing, introduction, interpretation. In other words, the dominating episteme or hermeneutic paradigm here remains the Said, that is to say, logos. We remain in the landscape, in the "say-scape," of the Western philosophical tradition. Even in its "instants of clarity," even with its permanent skepticism, this tradition remains a tradition of logos, of refutation of skepticism, of books. Its ultimate, hermeneutic interruption operates structurally, that is, through the event of Saying that constitutes philosophy as a tradition and history. However, this structural interruption of philosophy as Saying operates against the philosophical mode of Saying itself, which constantly aspires to restore logos.

Saying Otherwise

In Western philosophy, Levinas writes,

> The logos said has the last word dominating all meaning, the word of the end, the very possibility of the ultimate and the result. Nothing can interrupt it. Every contestation and interruption of this power of discourse is at once related and invested by discourse. It thus recommences as soon as one interrupts it. In the logos said, and written, it survives the death of the interlocutors that state it, and assures the continuity of culture. But does it not die with the end of civilizations, which recognize themselves to be mortal? The question can be raised. But the philosophical discourse of the West knows how to find again, under the ruins or in the hieroglyphs, the interrupted discourses of every civilization and of the prehistory of civilizations that were set up as separated. This discourse will affirm itself to be coherent and one.[64]

Philosophy, called to reduce the betrayal of Saying in Said, to generate a second-order disturbance of essence, to unsay, has, in its actual deployment in and as Western history, betrayed its calling, generating a second-order betrayal and so becoming an even higher agent of perversion, of essence and logos. This second-order betrayal of difference not only consolidates and synchronizes the structurally dispersed and diachronic saying of philosophy into one ahistorical logos but also further *abolishes the difference between Western philosophy and other civilizations of knowledge*—it betrays inter-epistemic difference, converting it into second-order essence.

Is a third-order disturbance of essence thus required? Is there a need to disturb not only the inner essentialization of the intersubjective happening of language, the tradition of texts, the conversation, but also the outer essentialization of the conversation between conversations, namely inter-epistemic happening? In any case, it is conceptually possible to outline another strategy of Unsaying, understood as philosophy's call to reduce the Said to Saying, one that goes beyond the historical performance of the philosophical tradition itself. This tradition, as we have seen, inasmuch as it gives rise to various forms of unsaying—ontology, skepticism, and hermeneutics—nonetheless remains committed to logos, to the perfection of Saying in a total Said. Are there other kinds of commitment, other performances of Saying and Said, traditions built on different modes of Saying, on other forms of the Said? Is there a Said, a corpus of meanings, a text, perhaps based not on the paradigm of logos but on a paradigm of disturbance?

At one point in *Otherwise Than Being*, Levinas not only suggests this possibility but also specifically names two nonphilosophical traditions that would answer philosophy's calling beyond the tradition of philosophy. In the philosophical tradition, as we have seen, Saying, grasped as the irreducible event of difference, is necessarily betrayed by the Said, understood as logos of essence, and made to disappear. The structural equivocation of language, however, leaves behind traces of Saying beyond the Said, of otherness beyond essence. "And yet," Levinas asks,

> Cannot this very beyond become a notion, while undoing itself? Language would exceed the limits of what is thought, by suggesting, letting be understood without ever explicitly saying, an implication of a meaning distinct from that which comes to signs from the simultaneity of systems or the logical definition of concepts. This possibility is laid bare in the poetic said, and the interpretation it calls for ad infinitum. It is shown in the prophetic said, scorning its conditions in a sort of levitation. It is by the approach, the-one-for-the-other of saying, related by the said, that the said remains an insurmountable equivocation, where meaning refuses simultaneity, does not enter into being, does not compose a whole. . . . A subversion of essence, it overflows the theme

it states, the "all together," the "everything included" of the said. Language is already skepticism.[65]

There seems thus to be a mode of language that not only makes it possible to formulate a theory or argumentation of skepticism, a skeptical logos, but also already performs skepticism—or unsaying or hermeneutics—in and through the very *mode* of saying. At this point, a comparison with Heidegger's ontology might be helpful. By calling into question the Being of beings, Heidegger does not simply seek to conceptualize in general categories (and so to naturalize, to "essentialize," as Levinas says) the way things actually are (what Heidegger calls their "beingness"); rather, by calling Being into question, by showing how Being can and should be a *question*, Heidegger ultimately suggests that things can be or can be understood as being *otherwise*. "To be," for instance, could mean not primarily to be in my presence (as that which is physically close to me) but to be in my horizon, in my future (as that which is important for me, what I care for and aspire to). Similarly, by reducing Said to Saying, by unsaying, *Otherwise Than Being* does not merely offer to conceptualize the—ethical—conditions of logos, as in *Totality and Infinity*; it also suggests the possibility of saying *otherwise*, that is, of a different kind of Said, a different mode of speech. This other kind of Said does not just abuse Saying by reducing it to absence, to implicit ambiguity, but "lays it bare," generating a Said that is not *logos*, not a systematic simultaneity of meaning but "an insurmountable equivocation, where meaning refuses simultaneity, does not enter into being, does not compose a whole."

Levinas names two concrete kinds of nonphilosophical Said that manifest such a performance: the poetic Said and the prophetic Said. Both forms neither abolish Saying nor are abolished by unsaying. Rather, their performance consists in *enacting* the preoriginal difference of language. Does the reference to any of these forms of Said point, beyond philosophy, toward the Talmud? Interestingly, it is the *poetic* Said, which is at the center of Heidegger's readings of Hölderlin—also in a bid to answer philosophy's calling beyond itself—that Levinas identifies here as constitutively *hermeneutic*, as essentially self-unsaying through "the interpretation it calls for ad infinitum."

The other form and tradition of nonphilosophical Said, the prophetic, which *Totality and Infinity* posits as a countertradition to philosophy—the Jewish against the Greek—is described here, more enigmatically, as "scorning its conditions in a sort of levitation." It is this second mode of nonphilo-sophical, prophetic Said that Levinas seeks to deploy in the intervention that constitutes *Otherwise Than Being*; the prophetic becomes the language of his post-1968 phenomenology. This language thus functions as an inherently inter-epistemic kind of unsaying and seeks—we may conclude—to interrupt the philosophical logos with another mode of Saying, another kind of Said. The next chapter closely examines this intervention in order to understand the nature and operation of this prophetic kind of Said, which performs un-saying by way of "levitation," or, as Levinas also says, through the "superla-tive." The point will be to grasp more precisely the role that Levinas's second book plays in its staging of the encounter between philosophy and Jewish thought.

7

THE SELF AS OTHER

T HE PREVIOUS CHAPTER INDICATED THE SELF-CRITICAL TURN IN Levinas's post-1968 philosophy. This turn radicalized Levinas's critique of Western ontology through the insight that the main problem of this ontology consists not in being oblivious to otherness and to nonviolence but, on the contrary, in abusing them, in transforming the very disturbance of essence into a higher essence, into an "essence of disturbance." I have shown how this realization led Levinas to seek a disturbance of being at a higher level, a second-order disturbance, which he detects, beyond the disturbance of being by Being, in the disturbance of the Said by Saying—in unsaying. Unsaying calls into question not just specific categories or given meanings in light of others (being vs. Being) but the very mode of sense making, the mode of saying that generates what is said. Levinas's ultimate insight, as I have suggested, points to a mode of saying different from the philosophical, different from logos, namely the prophetic, which consists in an *inherent* element of unsaying. The fundamental project of *Otherwise Than Being* aims precisely at interrupting, or unsaying, the philosophical logos, phenomenology, by having the prophetic said resonate within it.

This chapter examines how Levinas carries out this project in the phenomenology developed in *Otherwise Than Being*. The main concern of this chapter is the exact nature of the mode of speech, the kind of saying, deployed by Levinas. I thus attempt to understand what kind of unsaying, what kind of interruption, Levinas's language sets out to generate. The following analysis sheds doubt on whether Levinas's exposition in fact produces this interruption—or any kind of interruption at all.

More Rigorous Logic

In a key part of his second book titled "The Exposition," Levinas "aims to disengage the subjectivity of the subject from reflections on truth, time and being in the amphibology of Being and being which is borne by the Said; it will then present the subject, in Saying" as something different, something other than being.[1] *Otherwise Than Being* moves from said to saying; the book is an act of unsaying. And yet, its unsaying is achieved precisely by means of "exposition," suggesting a discourse of vision, a logos, which for Levinas is paradigmatic of the said.

This difficulty reminds us of *Totality and Infinity*, which, as I have analyzed, unites totality and break of totality into one whole through an exercise of phenomenology. Exposing totality (the subject's immanence) as conditioned by difference (the encounter with otherness) at the same time reveals difference at the basis of totality. *Otherwise Than Being*, according to my critical observation, repeats the same operation. The reduction of said to saying, of essence to disturbance, does not undo the coherence of logos; on the contrary, it generates a more comprehensive narrative, uniting said and saying such that, as Levinas further describes in his exposition, "it will be necessary—based on this *Saying* . . . —to account for the order of *the Said*" or, as he puts it later, to observe within Saying "the latent birth of cognition and essence, of the Said."[2] Levinas's second book, I argue, notwithstanding its critical reflection on the first book, reiterates the operation of deductive phenomenology, asserting otherness only to generate a higher sameness. Levinas's second intervention in the philosophical discourse for the cause of difference, even as it differentiates between said and saying, remains on the level of said, of logos—of a book.

Nonetheless, *Otherwise Than Being* does perform unsaying. As noted with respect to *Totality and Infinity*, like all phenomenology, Levinas's "Exposition" may be read not only as a description of immediate experience but also as an act of reading, a hermeneutic intervention on a given logos, on a transmitted said. More specifically, Levinas's exposition may be read as a phenomenological unsaying of phenomenology itself, namely of the paradigmatic said, which combines logos and mythos, concept and narrative, in the body of the subject. This act of counterphenomenology is performed by *Otherwise Than Being* primarily on the body of *Totality and Infinity*.

Levinas does not explicitly describe his exposition as unsaying and only hints at the nature of his *inter-epistemic* strategy. As I have suggested, the inter-epistemic strategy of unsaying consists in undoing logos not by reducing it to ambiguity (ontology) or to nonsense (skepticism) but by confronting it with another kind of said. It confronts the philosophical logos with another voice, a voice of otherness: "A voice comes from the other shore. A voice interrupts the saying of the already said." Making this nonphilosophical voice heard in philosophical discourse entails a disturbance of language, which Levinas describes as "introducing some barbarisms in the language of philosophy." A hint as to the identity of the barbarians is provided when Levinas describes the exclusion of otherness by "dogmatism and the mathematical and dialectical relation (attenuated only by a strange sensibility for a certain apocalyptic poetry)." This "apocalyptic poetry," a designation that covers a broad archive from Genesis to Hölderlin, combines the two aforementioned kinds of nonphilosophical discourse mentioned by Levinas: the poetic and the prophetic.[3]

What is the nature of the confrontation between the philosophical *logos* and the poetic-prophetic said? What kind of unsaying takes place when the latter is introduced into the former? Within the language of philosophy, the barbarism of the resistance of the nonphilosophical to logos manifests in the type of discourse that *Totality and Infinity* already asserts as characterizing the relation to otherness, namely, *ethics*. It is "ethical language," Levinas writes, that "phenomenology resorts to in order to mark its own interruption." When phenomenology seeks to unsay itself, to undo its own logos, as *Otherwise Than Being* attempts to do, it resorts to "the tropes of ethical language."[4]

What is ethical language? What is its distinctive characteristic as a specific form of said, as that which may operate within and against logos? "The significations that go beyond formal logic" and thus "show themselves in formal logic" in order to "break with formal logic" do so, Levinas notes, by the power of "a more rigorous logic," one based on "the structures of *beyond being.*" Ethical language is based on the preposition "beyond," meta-, trans-, *au-delà.* The operation of the beyond, Levinas underlines, is not negation. This operation differs from the contrasting between being and nonbeing, that is from the dialectics of essence. Rather, "it is the superlative, more than the negation of the category, which interrupts the system."[5] Ethics unsays logos by speaking in superlatives. It is, as Levinas puts it, "in the hyperbole, the superlative, the *excellence* of signification from which they derive—the transcendence that passes in them or surpasses itself in them, and which is not a mode of being showing itself in a theme—that notions and the *essence* they articulate break up and get woven into a human plot. The emphasis of exteriority is excellence. Height, heaven. The kingdom of heaven is ethical."[6]

Otherwise Than Being does not say much more about its own mode of saying, which constitutes its fundamental intervention in philosophy. But let us reflect. What exactly is the logic or hermeneutic of the superlative? How does it undo formal logic and dialectics? How does the structure of the *super* relate to metaphysics and the hermeneutic constellation of *meta*phor, or *trans*lation? The notion of a logic of excess, which breaks with essence by indicating a beyond of essence, by surmounting, exceeding, transcending, or outdoing being, reminds of the linguistic strategy of apophasis, which consists in saying by way of negation, a common form of unsaying. Apophasis has been systematically used in negative theology to point toward God or the One not by affirming Him but by stating how He surpasses all supreme predicates, how He exists beyond being.[7] Levinas similarly deploys a discourse that disrupts its own coherence by dissolving the solid essence of its theme, such that it is no longer reducible to any unity of subject or presence: the "strange discourse entertained here does not pass from one term to the other only by searching the 'subjective' horizons of what shows itself, but embraces conjunctions of elements in which concepts overstretched as *presence* or *subject* break up."[8]

To better understand, let us look at the basic phenomenological operation performed in *Otherwise Than Being* on *Totality and Infinity*. Both interventions make the same kind of demonstration, showing nondifference to be based on difference, the experience of totality to be based on the break with totality (*Totality and Infinity*), and Said to be based on Saying (*Otherwise Than Being*). In both books, this demonstration is based on a phenomenology of the subject, described—through an invoking of prophecy—as "created." Both of Levinas's books feature a story of creation. In *Totality and Infinity*, the subject is posited as the paradigm of being, as the very principle of an immanent, worldly existence. The account portrays man as soul of the world, as the protagonist of what I have characterized as Greek phenomenology. The story of Levinas's first book is thus a story of revelation that leads from the Greek to the Jewish, from the Parthenon to Sinai, from worldliness to otherness, from essence to its disturbance by the ethical "no," "You shall not commit murder," that restrains the subject's power.

As I showed in the previous chapter, *Otherwise Than Being* acknowledges how ethics, as that which initially limits the subject's power, nonetheless becomes an even more powerful instrument of self-assertion in that it produces the idea of just war. The disturbance of essence then becomes the essence of disturbance. Levinas's response to this perversion is to argue for a second-order disturbance of essence, a higher disturbance, in and through the superlative. This superdisturbance of the subject's power is a superpassivity, a "passivity more passive than all passivity."[9] Superpassivity signifies superotherness and no longer affects the subject through mere limitation, by means of the ethics of "no." Rather, superpassivity *constitutes* subjective existence, forming the very principle of subjectivity. Accordingly, against his first book, Levinas's second book deploys what may be called a *counterphenomenology of the subject*. In this counterphenomenology, a being-based subject, an onto-ontological individual, that of Greek anthropology, is unsaid by Jewish anthropology, by a subject that is no longer soul of the world but now unworldly, spirit: *otherwise than being, beyond essence*. More precisely, and more provocatively, it is the Jewish Greek subject, Philo's Moses, that is unsaid by a Greek Jew, Paul's Abraham, who structurally prefigures Jesus.[10] The basic logos or message, the kerygma of *Otherwise Than Being*, is that ethics, as individual responsibility for others, does not negate but *generates* subjectivity.

We will examine this counterphenomenology more closely. But before doing so, we need to ask the following questions: How does counterphenomenology overcome logos, rupture the language of essence, of nondifference, and open up another mode of saying, a mode of difference? Does it do this at all? My critical claim is that it does not open another mode of saying but instead does precisely the opposite. "Otherwise than being" remains within the discourse of being, ontology. Inasmuch as Levinas's conceptual argument suggests a hyperbolic notion of subjectivity beyond being, his phenomenology presents a hyperbolic *exposition*, namely of the *being* of his paradoxical subject: a phenomenology of the other of being, or even, I dare-say, a phenomenology of spirit. This phenomenology is structurally negative, as it describes manifestations in being of what is otherwise than being. All the phenomena are generated by the logic of the essence of disturbance. *Otherwise Than Being* does not tell a story of revelation, moving from essence to disturbance, as we see in *Totality and Infinity*. Instead, it tells a story of fall that goes from disturbance to essence. It is a story of betrayal, the self-betrayal of the other than being through its own ontic incarnations or hypostases.

The radicalization of otherness as the principle of subjectivity in Levinas's narrative thus paradoxically entails an *interiorization of the other in the self*. Accordingly, Levinas's later phenomenology is no longer revelation, also in the sense that its exposition, the phenomena and concrete situations it displays, point to no encounter, articulate no dramatic event of facing the Other, as in *Totality and Infinity*. Rather, the exposition of *Otherwise Than*

Being features a phenomenology of what may be literally called ex-position or emanation, in which all phenomena, all concrete realities depicted in the narrative, are manifestations of the subject and exteriorizations of an interior otherness, generated not by an event but through a development, through not an encounter but a self-exposition, and thus as manifesting not duality but unity.[11]

The phenomenological effect of interiorizing otherness, the shift from revelation to emanation, from dualistic to monistic dynamics, is coupled with a logical effect, namely on the mode of speech, on the form of the Said that constitutes *Otherwise Than Being*. I already noted that Levinas's discourse remains logos, a book of philosophy. We saw that the book's intervention in the philosophical logos consists in the disruption of "formal logic" by ethical language, which nonetheless, according to Levinas, features "a more rigorous logic." Paradoxically, this rigorous logic is produced by the very structure of the "beyond" that, by radicalizing otherness and pushing transcendence (the Other) completely out of view, transforms transcendence through its exposition into the *interior* principle of the subject, such that otherness becomes integrated within immanence and reinforces essence—and logos. Emanation offers a much more coherent phenomenology than revelation. It generates, as it were, a superlogos in which all themes are one, where the thematic is essentially *systematic*. "The different concepts," Levinas notes, "echo one another."[12] Indeed, even as the book's discourse suggests, as I will show, a certain narrative of progression, it often unfolds less as a linear development than as a semantic space where conceptual constellations appear and disappear to reappear from various angles and articulations like "waves on a beach," as Derrida describes it.[13] The happening here consists so little in action and so much in echo that Levinas's text often advances not through verbs but through a long series of nominal phrases immediately related to one another, made to signify one another ontologically, without so much as an "is" between them, thus generating, as it were, essence beyond being.

An example is in store: "A disclosing of being—disengaged from its identity, from itself (what we are here calling a getting out of phase) and rediscoveries of truth; between what shows itself and the aim it fulfills—monstration. The Same as this aim and the Same as discovered, only discovered and *amounting to the same*—truth."[14]

Another example describes "absolution that reverses essence: not a negation of essence, but a *dis-interestedness*, an 'otherwise than being,' which turns into a 'for the other,' burning for the other, consuming the bases of any position for oneself and any substantialization which would take form in this consummation, consuming even the ashes of this consummation, in which there would be a risk that everything be born again. Identity in the total patience of the one assigned, who, patient, despite himself, dies continually, lasts in his instant, 'whitens under the harness.'"[15]

Otherwise Than Being displays an intense texture that is *dicht* (dense) like *Dichtung*, poetic and rigorous in its semantic coherence; it is, indeed, super-Said. Within this rigorous logos, "the Said" and "the Saying" themselves appear as themes that, far from disturbing the system or unsaying it, are perfectly embedded in it. As we will now see, even as these (and other) notions operate ("echo") throughout the book, the Saying and the Said emerge quite late in the process, as derivative figures of the basic plot. Ultimately, the Saying and the Said, and especially unsaying, which, according to my analysis, is the most powerful intervention in *Otherwise Than Being*, play a limited, even marginal role as themes in the exposition itself.

The Book of Books

Before looking at Levinas's exposition more closely, I wish to briefly reflect on the genre to which it belongs, namely on its affiliation with other discursive projects in the inter-epistemic history of the West. As noted above, Levinas's intervention operates beyond any reduction of logos to ambivalence or nonsense, deploying another voice, ethical, poetic, and prophetic, against formal logic. However, *Otherwise Than Being* does not just set prophets against philosophers, as *Totality and Infinity* did. Rather, Levinas's second book intervenes on a second level by disturbing the essence of disturbance, disabusing the Western abuse of prophecy. Levinas's second phenomenology does not deploy prophecy against logos but sets prophecy against prophecy, one Western, Greek Jewish voice against another. This operation of the superlative, of beyondness, generates, as I have indicated, the paradox of counterlogos as superlogos, counterprophecy as superprophecy, which in hermeneutic figures emerge as one book superseded by another, old superseded by new. *Otherwise Than Being* is in this sense a book of books.

Similarly to his first book, Levinas's second book also provides few, often coded historical references for its own speech act. At one point toward the end of the book, after having pointed out that Western philosophy, save for "exceptional hours," has mainly neglected its call, remained essence, stayed "at home," and that European history has remained "conquest and jealous defense," Levinas states that, nonetheless, "we would not here have ventured to recall the *beyond essence* if this history of the West did not bear, in its margins, the trace of events carrying another signification, and if the victims of the triumphs which entitle the eras of History could be separate from its meaning."[16]

This passage resonates strongly with Walter Benjamin's idea of a "history against the grain."[17] The Other of the West is not the non-Western but the Other West, the failed *inner resistance to the West*, the *victims* of its triumph, whose demise makes possible the West's culture. The voice of prophecy here is not harmonized with logos, as in Philo; it is the voice of the suppressed, the persecuted, the victims of Europe, like those to whom *Otherwise Than Being* is dedicated—victims "of all confessions and of all nations, victims of the same hatred of the other man, the same anti-semitism." We will see how this notional victim of counter-Western prophecy materializes in Levinas's later Jewish writings as the figure of persecuted Israel, functioning as the archetype that unifies diaspora Jews with the Jewish nation-state.

Another pointer of the specific, modern positionality of Levinas's post-1968 phenomenology in *Otherwise Than Being* is provided in the first pages, where Levinas states: "To hear a God not contaminated by Being is a human possibility no less important and no less precarious than to bring Being out of the oblivion in which it is said to have fallen in metaphysics and in ontotheology."[18]

I already noted the complex relation in late Levinas to the antimetaphysical projects of Nietzsche and Heidegger. His notion of philosophy as unsaying acknowledges the value of their disturbing of the established discourse of Western metaphysics, namely, Heidegger's reduction of beings to Being and Nietzsche's reduction of sense to "nihilistic laughter." However, as in the above quote, Levinas requires a further movement, a going beyond of antimetaphysics, in order to assert a superlative metaphysics, more metaphysical than metaphysics itself, more forgotten than Being in beings, a God before or beyond Being. For Levinas, this movement does not so much extend Nietzsche and Heidegger as turn against them. To hear the forgotten God beyond Being is not just the next act after recalling forgotten Being beyond beings; it is also an act that runs counter to the question of Being, demanding that Being be (re-)forgotten through a forgetting that is "noble," "a forgetting that would be an ignorance in the sense that nobility ignores what is not noble, and in the sense that certain monotheists do not recognize, while knowing, what is not the highest."[19] *Pace* Nietzsche, it is those monotheists, those supermetaphysicians or super-Jews who hear God not only out of the world but also beyond Being, who constitute the real aristocracy.

Levinas's exposition in *Otherwise Than Being* is accordingly related to postmodern endeavors that attempt, from within philosophical discourse, to open access to a non-ontotheological divinity, a God before or after the West, a God whose absence Western civilization embodies. Once again, this feature places Levinas's second book in noticeable proximity to Heidegger's reading in Hölderlin of the West (*das Abendland*) as the "desolate time" of godly absence, after the gods who have flown and before the gods to come.[20] If Heidegger's "gods" remain too attached to being and the world, as Levinas claims, then we might see greater kinship to his thinking in the twentieth century in the theology of the "other God," represented, for example, by Karl Barth's "crisis theology," notably in his hyper-Paulinian commentary on Paul's Epistle to the Romans.[21]

As an attempt to "hear a God not contaminated by Being," Levinas's exposition can be read as belonging more generally to the discourse of the Other God, to the logos of God as the Other, that is, as a theology of otherness, or even—to quote the subtitle of Hans Jonas's book on the Gnostic Religion—as "a message of the Alien God."[22] If we follow Levinas's explicit references to Greco-Roman Hellenism, his exposition in *Otherwise Than Being*, a counterphenomenology, harks back not only to stoic or skeptic critics of classic Greek reason but also to the Hellenistic *Gnostic* discourses. Gnosticism sought to counter Greek Jewish prophecy by offering a counterprophecy that disabused the Jewish essence of disturbance, the Jewish eon, by the power of superior otherness.

In Gnosticism, we discover the same paradox operative in Levinas's exposition, the paradox according to which the attempt to break with immanence and radically disturb essence and logos ends up generating a more rigorous logos, a supersystem. Hans Jonas has rendered this paradoxical dynamic visible by showing the relationship between the Gnostic myths of acosmic dualism—that is, of a supermetaphysical, Alien God—and neo-Platonic systems from Philo to Origen and Plotinus: the relation between extreme transcendence and extreme immanence, extreme otherness and extreme oneness. Situated in this discursive climate, Levinas's *Otherwise*

Than Being bears resemblance to different genres of Jewish mysticism, such as Kabbalah.[23] There is, however, a more powerful precursor to the attempt to disabuse Greek Jewish prophecy with some counter- or superprophecy, to unsay the Greco-Jewish book by generating a counterbook that is at once an antibook, a new book, and a superbook. I am referring to the Greco-Roman project of the New Testament, which is simultaneously the project of the Old Testament and the project of the Book of Books—the Bible.

I have already noted the Greek Jewish, Pauline anthropology of the self as other, which *Otherwise Than Being* contrasts to the Jewish Greek, Philonic phenomenology of *Totality and Infinity*. I now add the hermeneutic affinity between Levinas's second book and the operation of the New Testament. This affinity will become central in my forthcoming study of how Levinas hermeneutically stages the encounter between philosophy and Talmud in his *Talmudic Readings*. At this point, I wish to indicate how the post-1968 phenomenology of *Otherwise Than Being* may be read as a Pauline intervention in Levinas's pre-1968 phenomenology of *Totality and Infinity*. This critical reading suggests that Levinas's resistance to the West deploys a very Western tradition.

Alienus

The narrative of *Otherwise Than Being* has a similar structure to that of *Totality and Infinity*. Both focus on the phenomenology of the individual subject, setting out from the realm of inner experience and moving outward to exteriority, to an open, general, verbal space where abuse takes place, giving rise to a history of evil and redemption. As noted, the logos of the second book features a subject who constitutes no individual being in contrast with total Being, like in *Totality and Infinity*, but who exists as *other* than being. The phenomenological narrative is shaped by the paradox of presenting the manifestation in being of that which is other than being. As I have argued, this paradox is so fundamentally defining of Levinas's phenomenological enterprise that it establishes a powerful logical structure at the basis of the description. Accordingly, the narrative unfolds as a series of manifestations, or emanations, or hypostases of the same basic logos, manifestations that strongly "echo" one another such that the narrative can be read as the mythical visualization of a conceptual system. It is by the power of this underlying structure that ontology is perfected by its interruption, logos by counterlogos, book by counterbook.

The greatest part of the exposition is dedicated to something analogous—but not identical—to the realm of interiority in *Totality and Infinity*, that is, a preliminary, foundational, existential experience of individual subjectivity. Levinas's descriptions can be read as following the basic paradoxical logic of the being of the other of being, namely as the phenomenology of "the essence of disturbance," which is articulated through three basic moments: sensitivity (chap. 2), closeness (chap. 3), and substitution (chap. 4).

The primal figure in which the subject as other than being manifests itself within being, the first hypostasis of otherness in essence, is strongly negative. The subject emerges in being as an "expulsion outside of being."[24] This means that subjective existence consists not only in retreating from being, which would presuppose substance and power in the realm of being, a power of being, but in pure subjection to negation by being, in pure or super passivity. This "passivity more passive than all passivity" indicates that the subject does not first exist and then become subjected to negation as limitation, to the "no" contradicting his "yes," as it does in *Totality and Infinity*.[25] Rather, negation, or the "expulsion outside of being," *is* the original instance of emergence of the subject.

This constitutive unbeing of subjectivity is verbalized by Levinas through the prefix "ex-." Existence is exile. In contrast to the worldliness of the subject in *Totality and Infinity*, where the self bathes in the elements, dwells in the world, and is essentially economic, "at home," subjectivity in *Otherwise Than Being* is "expelled out of all place, no longer dwelling, no longer 'at home.'"[26] Exiled from the world, the subject does not dwell in another world, in a different place, but exists as the expulsion from all place, in no place—not beyond being, *au-delà*, but prior to or before being, "on this side," *en deça*. This no place may be said to be the subject's exile "in itself," but this "in itself" designates not place, interiority, position, but rather exposition, expulsion, or—a key term in Levinas's exposition—*persecution*.[27]

Terms like *exile*, *expulsion*, and *persecution* clearly evoke tropes of historical Jewish existence, and this evocation becomes central in the political epistemology of Levinas's post-1968 Jewish writings.[28] The same terms also echo figures of biblical myth such as Abraham's emigration or the expulsion of Adam and Eve from paradise. Levinas's exposition points toward an even deeper mytho-phenomenological layer, namely the basic ontological determination of human being in the prophetic said as "creation." The subject's being as other than being manifests itself in the condition of man as created through unworldly agency. The preliminary negative moment in this configuration—the subject's existence as "expelled from being"—presents itself on this ontological level, according to Levinas, in the constitutive feature of the human being as *exposed* to all beings, which is to say in *sensitivity*, the essence of the subject's existence as a living body.[29]

Whereas *Totality and Infinity* portrays sensual, bodily existence as manifesting independence and self-sufficiency and thus as basically happy, *Otherwise Than Being* rereads the body as vulnerability, as exposure to pain. The embodied self is "unwell in his skin."[30] Happiness is given only to be taken away, to enable subjectivity in *suffering*. Suffering is the subject's being as expulsed from his own being, as destitution, concretely visible in senescence, in aging, in the human condition of mortality devoid of transubstantiation. Creation, as the hypostasis of otherwise than being, is essentially finitude, being toward death (Heidegger) or flesh (Paul). This finitude is not utter negativity. As vulnerability, as persecution of the self out of himself, sensitivity originally *grounds* individual subjectivity, producing the self in a way akin to Heidegger's being toward death. Suffering as hyperpassivity, "passivity more passive than all passivity," is at the same time *passion*, the very life of the subject.

Whereas *Totality and Infinity* is oriented around the phenomenological development of the subject as motivated by the need to interrupt the self's self-assertion and absorption in the world (bathing in elements, appropriating things), the need to counter the totalization of being into Being by negation, *Otherwise Than Being* is driven by the opposite motivation: to intensify the inscription of the subject (who is *other* than being) into being. The *second* hypostasis of the subject as otherness in essence intensifies his ontic engagement by transforming his initial negativity into positivity. The first moment of Levinas's exposition features subjective being as an "expulsion out of being" manifested in negative existence, in the suffering body, in the body as suffering, as finitude. The second moment indicates how the suffering body *at the same time* entails the manifestation of subjectivity as something else, as something interconnected with the finite body but different from the body.

The second ontic manifestation of the subject is existence in the body beyond the body, that is, soul. In Levinas's early—Philonic—phenomenology, the body is animated by the soul as the organic principle of the subject's self-identification in the world, by the soul as *physis*, which by virtue of its immanent self-identity is capable of bearing a relation with transcendent otherness, with *metaphysis*. By contrast, *Otherwise Than Being* characterizes the soul not as the principle of self-identity but as "alterity-in-the-same," as "the other in me."[31] The soul does not signify the subject's worldliness; rather, it is a further emanation of "expulsion from being." If the suffering body is other-than-being that exists as finite being, the soul is its affirmative existence as more than being, as otherworldly.

In biblical terms, the finitude of the created human being, of being in flesh, is coupled with a divine element: "And the Lord God formed man of the dust of the ground, and breathed into his nostrils the breath of life; and man became a living soul" (Gen. 2, 7).[32] The soul here is the unworldly as placed in the world, in the suffering human body, which is therefore not an organism but an incarnation. In a stronger rendering of this verse—I am thinking of those of the Greek Septuagint, the Latin Vulgate and the Aramaic Targum—man becomes, through God's breath, not just soul (*psyche, nefesh*) but spirit, Greek *pneuma*, Hebrew *ruach*, literally, wind. Wind, moving air, is the unworldliest element; Genesis features it as God's first manifestation prior to the world.[33] The semantic shift from soul to spirit underlines the conceptual shift from worldly to unworldly human being.[34] *Otherwise Than Being* subscribes to this pneumatic anthropology by asserting, in multiple formulations, beyond the subject as suffering body, the subject as spirit, *esprit*.[35] Subjectivity here is the other-than-being that dwells in being as spirit, as inspiration, respiration, expiration—as a "relation to air."[36]

Spirit is a relation to otherness. Levinas's fundamental insight, as discussed above, is that the relation to otherness may not be founded on the paradigm of vision, on theory, but on the paradigm of practice, on *ethics*. Whereas *Totality and Infinity* characterizes the ethical relation to otherness as desire, going from the separate self to the transcendent, *distant* other, *Otherwise Than Being* portrays it as "proximity" or "closeness," a relatedness to the other as *close* to me, not only spatially near me but *close to me in me*. Being "in me" does not mean dialectically absorbed in my self-consciousness. Levinas describes closeness, that is, spirituality, as an "inversion of consciousness."[37] The other who is close to me is not brought by my consciousness to appear before me as my phenomenon, as being for me; his closeness to me, his presence in me, which is my spirit, manifests as an opposite vector that pulls me out of myself and toward the other. This pull is not some desire or *eros* as that would arise from the independent, happy self. Closeness is not liberty; it is imposition, coercion. In this regard, Levinas speaks of obsession or convocation, of being subjected to authority, to command.

The third principal manifestation of subjectivity is *substitution*, which Levinas describes as the "centerpiece" of his later book.[38] Substitution is the most accomplished hypostasis of the subject, going beyond sensitivity and closeness to fully developed existence, to "the being of the entity that is me."[39] What substitution names is the consequence of closeness. It names the other in the self as "inversed consciousness," as that which does not consist in the other's being for me as phenomenon or object or even as voice or face but in my being for the other. Substitution is subjectivity as *being for the other*.

The basic thrust of *Otherwise Than Being*, as noted, not only counters the primacy of theory in our conception of subjectivity in favor of ethics, as achieved in *Totality and Infinity*. More importantly, it counters worldly subjectivity as an ethics of essence, as self-preservation, being for being, that is, as being for oneself. This contestation is directed not only against Heidegger's Dasein, as that which cares for its own being, but also against Levinas's own earlier phenomenology of subjectivity as separation. As substitution, subjective being does not consist in being for oneself or being the other but rather in being *for* the other. Levinas here posits ascetic ethics as fundamental ontology. The subject's basic performance as other than being thus consists in rejecting self-preservation. It consists in disinterestedness, in existing for the sake of others. The subject, Levinas explains, is *subjectum*; it is being "under the weight of the universe." "Expulsion from being" thus comes to mean "subjection to everything."[40]

In the emanation of subjectivity from sensitivity to substitution, the singling out of the subject from all beings, which translates "otherwise than being" into being, no longer takes the negative form of expulsion, exile, expiration, or mortality but the positive form of *election* or *chosenness*.[41] If sensitivity is manifest as suffering flesh, then substitution, the subject's election, is revealed in its constitutive *responsibility*. Responsibility is a central category of Levinas's later phenomenology, a perfect example of ethics as optics, in which the fundamental human being is conceived vis-à-vis the world not as seeing but as owing or answering. "Subjection to everything" means that the subject "responds for everything and everyone."[42]

It is crucial to insist on the *ontological* significance of substitution and responsibility in Levinas's exposition. The subject, which is fundamentally other than being, comes into being as responsible for being. Responsibility echoes suffering: the subject's responsibility for being is a spiritual pendant to finitude. Responsibility means that suffering, being unto death, is not just extinction, disappearance from being, but, on the contrary, *expiation*—whereby the subject substitutes being and *becomes*. As "expiation for being," which reconciles passivity and activity, identity and alterity, the subject, an other to being, comes into being as the very subject and agent of being, as responsible for being.[43]

The notion of existence as expiation, as atoning for being, calls to mind the biblical discourse of atonement and the Day of Atonements, *yom ha-kippurim*. In rabbinic atonement, the person who atones by suffering, by fasting, atones for his own sins. In contrast, in the biblical text, atonement is not suffered by sinners themselves but by a substitute, an innocent animal, a now well-known scapegoat (Lev. 16) or a *victim* more generally. It is this notion of responsibility without guilt, of expiation for someone else's sins, of victimhood, that Levinas's exposition evokes—and therewith also the entire discourse of *sacrifice*, which is foundational for the prophetic archive on its most "barbaric" level. The subject, as other to being, enters being as substitution, as a sacrificial victim (in Hebrew, *korban* is a cognate of *karov*, meaning close or closeness). The subject is a victim in the sense that his suffering body, his death, renders him not meaningless but meaningful; this suffering body signifies absolute responsibility—existence as sacrifice. Suffering thus takes on the meaning of an offering that is self-offering, *suffrant*, *s'offrant*.[44] Subjectivity is self-sacrifice.

It is through self-sacrifice that the subject, as other than being, *is*. The subject exists for as long and inasmuch as he is responsible, and so "the more I respond, the more I am responsible."[45] In this sense, the subject's responsibility is infinite; it is infinity in him, his divinity, his spirit. Here Levinas makes ample use of the superlative, which intensifies subjectivity as a disturbance of essence, as disinterestedness, self-sacrifice. At the same time, he amplifies subjective existence as the essence of disturbance. The infinity of the subject's responsibility also means "responsibility for the responsibility of the other," "bearing the fault of the other."[46] I have indicated how expiating the other's sins defines the sacrificial victim. But Levinas pushes the hyperbole further. My suffering, my persecution and expulsion from being, expiates not only the sins of others but also their sins *against me*. By taking responsibility for being, by existing as a subject, I take responsibility for my own persecution. Infinite responsibility signifies that "the persecuted is liable to answer for the persecutor."[47]

One central figure that embodies this concept in *Otherwise Than Being* is "maternity, which is bearing par excellence, bear[ing] even responsibility for the persecuting by the persecutor."[48] The mother offers her body to the child who consumes her, standing in contrast to early Levinas's portrayal of the father as perpetuating himself through his son. Levinas explicitly links this phenomenology to biblical and "rabbinic thought."[49] He invokes another biblical trope from Lamentations 3, 30, "Let him give his cheek to the one who strikes him," though without mentioning Jesus's more famous cover version on the Mount: "If anyone slaps you on the right cheek, turn to him the other also" (Matthew 5, 39; cf. Luke 6, 29).[50]

Levinas's exposition pushes this logic of self-sacrificial ethics to a further extreme by pointing out that, in order to be absolutely certain that the sacrifice is not done for one's own sake but for the other's, that it is not an act of egoism, of essence, but of pure disinterestedness, the act of self-sacrifice must potentially make no sense at all: an act of suffering "for nothing." The paradox here consists in wanting to ensure nonegoism even at the price of making no sense to others, in focusing on a negation of the ego insofar as it reinforces subjectivity. As we will see, the very nonsense of self-sacrifice is precisely what constitutes its meaning, what reveals it as a pure act of meaning, signifying—saying. I have already noted how, in Levinas's analysis, saying is revealed by unsaying, for which a central strategy in philosophical discourse is the reduction to nonsense. Self-sacrifice for nothing, subjectivity as substitution, is the nonsense that reveals ultimate sense, subjectivity as signification.

One remarkable footnote in the text speaks about the subject suffering for "the guilt of my persecutors, which amounts to suffering the ultimate persecution, suffering absolutely." "This element of a 'pure burning,'" Levinas continues, "for nothing, in suffering, is the passivity of suffering which prevents its reverting into 'assumed suffering,' in which the 'for-the-other' of sensibility, that is, its very *sense*, would be annulled. This moment of 'for nothing' in suffering is the surplus of non-sense over sense by which the sense of suffering is possible."

He concludes by saying that "there is an anarchic trace of God in passivity, a suffering 'for God' who suffers from my suffering."[51] The nonsense of suffering for nothing constitutes the sense of subjectivity as signifying, as manifesting the otherwise than being, as a trace of God, as the paradigmatic *sign*.

Before exploring this movement from substitution to signification further, let us decode a specific reference Levinas makes to the prophetic archive—more specifically, to its victims. In the passage above, ultimate persecution, absolute suffering, suffering for nothing, is designated as a "pure burning."[52] Purely or entirely burned, in Greek *holokauston*, in Latin *holocaustum*, often translated as "burned offering," is how the Bible describes a type of sacrifice in which the victim, or sacrificed animal, is burned in its entirety, leaving nothing to be eaten, nothing to enjoy. In Hebrew, this senseless sacrifice is called *olah*, the sacrifice that "ascends," "goes up." In the biblical story, *olah* is offered to God on various occasions, for instance, by Noah after the flood. A more famous holocaust is that of Isaac's binding, where God tells Abraham, "Take now your son, your only son Isaac, whom you love, and go to the land of Moriah, and offer him there as a burnt offering [*olah, holocuastum*] on one of the mountains of which I shall tell you" (Genesis 22, 2). Abraham's sacrifice of his only son is also a self-sacrifice, the annihilation of his own lineage. Apart from featuring in Christian theology as prefiguring the self-sacrifice of Jesus, or God's Lamb, the *olah* of Isaac's binding, the Holocaust, has become a designation for the persecutions and murder committed by the Nazis against the Jews, victims of the West. The expression "pure burning" therefore briefly reveals the self-sacrificing subject, who expiates his own persecution, who signifies by suffering for no reason—a Jewish paradigm that becomes central in the epistemo-politics of Levinas's post-1968 Jewish writings.

"Here I Am"

The systematic nature of the logos that commands Levinas's exposition is most visible in the emergence of language. *Totality and Infinity* is structured as a drama around the event in which the subject, enclosed in silent immanence, encounters absolute otherness in the interdiction "You shall not murder," spoken by the encountered face of the other; interiority encounters exteriority in ethical language, in commandment. Levinas's early phenomenology is a drama of encounter. *Otherwise Than Being* posits otherness from the outset as the principle of subjectivity, such that its phenomenological exposition is, paradoxically, less dramatic and more systematic: it is not centered on any encounter but features a continuous process of emanation of that which is other than being. Speech, the central event of *Totality and Infinity*, emerges in Levinas's later book as a further emanation. *Otherwise Than Being*'s introduction of difference into the logos via the logo-hermeneutical difference between Said and Saying, even as it echoes throughout the book, only finds its phenomenological place in the last chapter of the exposition, at a late stage of the conceptual trajectory.

Whereas in *Totality and Infinity*, speech emerges as a dimension of negativity, of resistance to the subject's power of being, speech in *Otherwise Than Being* arises as an advanced stage in the subject's positive incarnation in being. The emergence of speech epitomizes the inscription of otherness into being, of disturbance into essence. I have shown how the main part of the exposition articulates the ontic incarnation of the alien subject through three consecutive hypostases: the suffering body (expulsion from being, sensitivity), spirit (the other in the self, closeness), and self-sacrifice (being for the other, substitution, and responsibility). I have indicated how this trajectory features an advance from negative hypostases to more affirmative ones, whereby passivity constantly translates to agency and suffering emerges as *self*-sacrifice. My analysis has followed Levinas's hyperbole in offering the paradigm of self-sacrifice "for nothing," which radically negates subjectivity and at the same time radicalizes the importance of (negating) the subject: self-sacrifice empowers the self. The culmination of this logic saw the transformation of nonsense (self-sacrifice for nothing) into the very *sense* of subjectivity as nonessence, as signifying beyond being, which is the basic meaning of all *signification*, the function of the *sign*. Accordingly, subjectivity, or other-than-being, gets hypostasized in being as the very dimension of signification, of making sense—of Saying.

Levinas's exposition introduces the realm of signification through the manifestation of subjectivity as *glory*. The term *glory* resonates deep within the prophetic archive. The Latin term *gloria* translates the Greek *doxa*, which translates the Hebrew *kavod*. In English, *kavod* means respect, dignity, importance, and weight and features in biblical discourse as the phenomenon through which God appears directly to humans: "Now it came to pass, as Aaron spoke to the whole congregation of the children of Israel, that they looked toward the wilderness, and behold, the *kavod* of the LORD appeared in the cloud" (Exodus 16, 10). The translation of *kavod* into Greek by *doxa*, "to show," interprets glory as a paradigm of appearance, visibility, phenomenality.

In Levinas's phenomenology, glory arises from senseless self-sacrifice; it is connected with the cross. Self-sacrifice glorifies the suffering body, effecting an apotheosis of the subject from victimhood to divinity. We see this occur in chapter 5, section 2 of *Otherwise Than Being*, titled "The Glory of the Infinite." "Glory," Levinas writes, "is nothing but the other face of the subject's passivity."[53] More passive than all passivity, suffering is passion, self-sacrifice for nothing, infinite responsibility. "The more I respond, the more I am responsible," writes Levinas, to mark the "glorious increase of obligation."[54] Infinite responsibility glorifies the suffering, tortured body, which becomes a sign, the first sign, the sign for signification: "saying saying saying itself."[55] Might the cross be the first sign?

Here Levinas is envisaging the subject—who, by existing, offers himself to senseless suffering, to persecution, to life as dying, thus becoming a sign of transcendence—as a *martyr*. Subjectivity is "persecution and martyrdom."[56] Following the original meaning of μάρτυς as "witness," Levinas describes the manifestation of subjectivity as signification using the concept of "testimony." In self-sacrifice, subjectivity manifests in being as testimony to otherwise than being, to the infinite, the divine. Being a subject, Levinas writes, is "testimony to the Infinite, but a testimony that does not thematize what it bears witness of, and whose truth is not the truth of representation, is not evidence. . . . The Infinite does not appear to him that testifies to it. On the contrary testimony belongs to the glory of the Infinite. It is by the voice of the witness that the glory of the Infinite is glorified."[57] The subject does not, as in *Totality and Infinity*, encounter the infinite but *manifests* the infinite in its very existence, as a living testimony, a sign in flesh.

At this point in the narrative, language explicitly emerges. In *Totality and Infinity*, speech is the original manifestation of otherness in immanence, the subject's encounter with prophecy. The original prophecy is God's word in the Mosaic torah, which teaches through the ethical commandment of the *rav*—"You shall not murder"—and provides the "no" through which the sovereign self originates. Problematizing Levinas's narrative, I have argued that the notion of *speech* has a logocentric function that precludes language as signification, as absence, and instead posits language as *presence*, as something that is in one's face.

Otherwise Than Being radicalizes otherness. The Other, the infinite to whom the subject testifies, is not a presence and does not appear. The absolute Other is never a "you," whether a familiar *tu* or a distant *vous*. Instead, it is an absent *il*, a "he," to whom Levinas attributes the quality of *illeity*, of being-he, of absence. The Other is never encountered. Language does not emerge in the encounter with otherness but instead arises as a further emanation of the subject. Preoriginal saying proceeds from the subject, as the exposition of subjectivity, which is glory, the *manifestation* par excellence. Since subjective being, "expulsion from being," is essentially exposure, vulnerability, suffering, Levinas describes language, "saying," as a second-order exposure, an "exposition of exposition."[58] Primal Saying, "Saying without Said," which is "anterior to all civilization and all beginning of spoken language," or "saying saying saying itself," arises from subjective existence as testifying to otherwise than being in the martyrdom of glorious self-sacrifice.[59]

Accordingly, while Levinas's later phenomenology concurs with his earlier phenomenology in identifying original language with prophecy, the meaning of prophecy changes, as does the location of the seminal moment in historical prophetic discourse. *Totality and Infinity* shows prophecy to be the revealed speech of the Other, which (through the vulnerability of his face) expresses the ethical "no" of the sixth commandment. By contrast, in *Otherwise Than Being* seminal prophecy is not the negation of the subject but the subject's self-affirmation, its self-presentation, coming through a pronouncing of his own being in his own voice, which Levinas writes as a quote: "*me voici*," "here I am."

Just like the interdiction "You shall not murder," "here I am" also quotes a biblical verse, this time from an earlier episode in the prophetic myth, namely Isaac's binding, which we have deciphered as the original scene of total self-sacrifice (*holocaustum*, "pure burning"). "Here I am," *me voici*, translates the Hebrew *hineni*, which is Abraham's response to God's calling him to sacrifice his own son (Genesis 22, 1; 22, 11). Levinas more explicitly refers to another instance of *hineni* in Isaiah.[60] *Hineni*, like *me voici*, does not even contain the verb "being." It is, as Levinas explains, not a doxic statement about the state of things, about existence or nonexistence, but a speech act that *performs* subjectivity as ethical presence, as responsiveness and availability, as self-offering. Note the shifting of prophecy here from the Philonic perspective, from the Mosaic law received on Sinai, to a Paulinian perspective in which the paradigm of Jewish subjectivity is taken back to the individual prior to the people, to Abraham prior to Moses, to faith prior to law. Levinas emphasizes, against tendencies to understand faith as doxic rather than ethical, that prophetic testimony does not speak *of* the transcendent Other; it does not state "God." Prophecy is not theology or any other logos or sort of indicative speech. Glory is the doxa before dogma, the Saying before the Said.[61]

Yet it is crucial to see how Levinas's radicalized conception of otherness as constitutive of subjectivity paradoxically generates a more robust hypostasis of subjectivity as *presence*. My analysis of *Totality and Infinity* has indicated how the ethical limitation of the subject at the same time generates the original presence of the subject. The hyperbolic phenomenology of *Otherwise Than Being* generates an even more radical constellation. In the statement "here I am," other-than-being manifests itself as self-affirming, namely as self-presence, as the presence of the subject to himself, manifested in the paradigmatic phenomenon of the voice.[62] The speaking subject thus transforms (translates? betrays?) radical otherness, absolute absence, *illeity*, into absolute presence. "The infinitely exterior," Levinas writes, "becomes 'interior' voice."[63]

This conversion of otherness to identity already takes place *in ethics*. "Here I am," *hineni*, the response of responsibility, is not, in Levinas's exposition, the original ethical moment in the constitution of subjectivity. Rather, subjectivity emerges in suffering from evil—expulsion, exile, persecution—evil that is then transformed into glorious self-sacrifice. "Here I am" marks the culmination of this process, in which hyperbolic passivity becomes hyperbolic agency. "Here I am" is ethical language by which I take responsibility for my own persecution as if it is my *own* command, my law—to myself. *Totality and Infinity* presents the paradigm of ethical language in the sixth commandment, "You shall not murder," as transcendent law. *Otherwise Than Being*, by shifting prophecy from Moses to Abraham, does not merely shift ethics from law to faith but redefines the essence of law, moving from a position of transcendence revealed to me through a "no" to the statement "here I am," the law I speak to myself, which "commands me by my mouth."[64] Reading "here I am" as the first commandment challenges not only the priority given to the sixth commandment in Levinas's earlier phenomenology but also the biblical first commandment, "I am the Lord your God" (Exodus 20, 2; Deuteronomy 5, 6). Whereas the latter founds the law on the transcendent, heterogeneous lawgiver, "here I am" defines it as given by the subject to himself, as self-law, as the *auto-nomos*.[65]

"Here I am," the Saying without the Said, thus emerges as a hypostasis of subjectivity—a subjectivity beyond the suffering body, beyond any self-sacrificing spirit or glorious martyrdom, as autonomy, as sovereignty. It is here that Levinas explicitly names what I argue is the fundamental principle behind his entire exposition in *Otherwise Than Being*, namely the transformation of otherness to essence in subjectivity, as he writes, the "reverting of heteronomy into autonomy": "Receiving the order out of oneself, this reverting of heteronomy into autonomy, is the very way the Infinite occurs [*se passe*]. The metaphor of the inscription of the law in consciousness expresses this in a remarkable way, reconciling autonomy and heteronomy."[66]

At this point, Levinas invokes a foundational trope in the history of prophecy, in prophecy as history of metaphor, namely the "circumcision of the heart." This trope posits circumcision as the paradigmatic law, the law given not to Moses but to Abraham before Isaac's binding, in a prefiguration of self-sacrifice. The law of circumcision is the foundation of an absolutely heterogeneous law, a command to command, whereby the father is ordered to subject his infant son's body to the law before autonomy. Circumcision literally turns the male body into a sign, a written testimony for transcendence. The trope "circumcision of the heart" shifts the locus of law from exterior to interior. In this shift, the law, written on the body, is radicalized (literally circumcising the baby's heart would kill him and thus complete Abraham's unfinished *holocaustum*) and therewith abolished (since Abraham's sacrifice was stopped), although not by abrogation but by metaphor, allegory. "Circumcision of the heart" thus does not mean physically to cut one's heart but rather to change one's mind, to generate an inner transformation that produces "consciousness." "The metaphor of the inscription of the law in consciousness" signifies the emergence of consciousness out of the abolition of external law, body and text, and the "reverting of heteronomy into autonomy."

This hypermetaphor, first coined in Moses's eschatology, reappears in Jeremiah's and then becomes a centerpiece of Paul's metaphysical anthropology: "he is a Jew who is one inwardly; and circumcision is that of the heart, in the Spirit, not in the letter" (Romans 2, 29).[67] Levinas's exposition accordingly re-creates a critical moment within the history of prophetic discourse, that is, the Greek Jewish emergence of the proto-Western subject from a metaphor, the translation and reversion of heteronomy to autonomy, of exteriority to interiority, of difference to identity, of God to man as a glorified victim—the essence of disturbance.

Justice for Me

The last step in Levinas's exposition, which constitutes the ultimate *telos* of the demonstration it is designed to provide, is the passage—"a latent birth"—from Saying to Said. I have noted ambivalence in this genealogy, insofar as it reveals difference (Saying) as the basis of homogeneous essence (Said) and thus undermines the primacy of homogeneity while grounding it in difference. The same ambivalence is evident in *Totality and Infinity*'s attempt to base totality on the rupture with totality. My claim is that in *Otherwise Than Being*, as this ambivalence becomes the very principle of subjectivity, the paradox intensifies. I have shown how Saying, the preoriginal dimension of difference, nevertheless emerges as explicit self-affirmation— "here I am." The passage from Saying to Said reproduces the same logic, constituting a further, even more immanent emanation, the emanation of immanence itself, the hypostasis of subjectivity *as essence*.

"Here I am" is, as explained, a statement not about the subject's mere existence or location but about the hypostasis of subjectivity as signification, as the realm of saying, the realm of appearance and truth. Levinas's Saying is similar to Heidegger's *Seyn*, "Beyng." Beyng is not yet the Being of beings; it opens the space through which appearance and truth, a world of beings, becomes possible, but it does not imply any specific regime of being. Similarly, Saying is initially "without Said." Yet in Levinas's exposition, since Saying already arises as a—late—moment in the plot of subjectivity, it immediately entails a specific regime of signification, a specific Said, namely logos, with its constitutive ambivalence of verb and noun, Being and beings. This ontology gives presence not just to the subject but to the world.

The Said, in Levinas's exposition, follows the line of emanations, going from suffering to self-sacrifice, from martyrdom and glory, and then emerging in the form of *justice*. Justice is the regime of signification that constitutes a meaningful world for the subject as infinite responsibility. Justice makes sense. It provides the basic grid of intelligibility, experiencability, being: "Everything appears for justice."[68] This phrase reflects the basic insight of Levinas's epistemology of difference, according to which "optics is ethics" or, otherwise put, knowledge is not pure theory but knowledge of good and bad. Something like an ontology of justice also resonates with prophetic discourse. In this vein, Levinas provides an explicit reference to the Psalms, *Tehilim*, the biblical verses of glory, where he finds the "strange affirmation that through injustice 'all the foundations of the earth are shaken'" (Psalms 11, 3).[69]

It is crucial to underline the function of justice in Levinas's analysis as that which generates ontology and therefore constitutes the Said as logos. Justice, he writes, consists in "putting together, assembling, the being of beings."[70] Justice, generated as language, is the explicit transformation of subjectivity into being. This motif is also a feature of *Totality and Infinity*, where justice figures as the mode in which the constitution of reality, thanks to the essentializing operation of the self, is subjected to the ethical limitation of nonviolence in order to produce a rational, Cartesian order. Levinas understands this ethic-based rationality, called justice, as the origin of the Western abuse of ontology, and it leads him to develop his counter-phenomenology in *Otherwise Than Being*. Otherness and ethics here figure no longer as the limit of the subject but as the principle of subjectivity. Yet in its coming into existence, subjectivity, the other of being, takes the form of being—that is, the otherness of subjectivity transforms to essence, such that "justice" comes once again to designate ontological ethics. This time, however, onto-ethics does not arise from an ethical limitation on egoistic being but, on the contrary, consists in the ontological delimitation of the subject's uncompromising *ascetic* morality. Justice, Levinas writes, is the "correction of the asymmetry of closeness,"[71] the limitation of a glorious but senseless self-sacrifice.

This *inversion in the function of justice* lies at the heart of Levinas's later political thought, which shifts from the common conception of the institution of justice (ultimately, the state) as the limitation of natural violence to the opposite conception of this institution as limiting a natural state of extreme morality.[72] The reader might recall Levinas's epigraphic quote of Pascal, in which all attempts to base social order on self-interest are criticized as a "false image of charity." With this inverted conception of justice, Levinas seeks to emancipate morality from politics and subject the state to individual ethics and the bonds of "friendship."[73] Yet in this inverted perspective, justice assumes the function of *limiting* morality for the glory of the subject's existence. Accordingly, justice becomes the paradigmatic hypostasis of subjectivity as the essence of disturbance. Justice—the Said, the being of beings—appears as the principle of a world constituted by a logic of abuse, a world that is basically evil, an eon. This configuration echoes a motif present in various locations within the prophetic archive, where the struggle between good and bad is transfigured into a struggle between good and bad forms of justice. In these transfigurations, bad justice often appears as instituted, rationalized, ordered, worldly justice, justice as nomos, law, or *din*—justice as violence. Bad justice is then contrasted to a good, unworldly form of justice as faith, charity, grace, *hesed*—justice as infinite love.

This ambivalent logic is central to Levinas's succinct discussion of justice in his exposition. In it, justice functions as *the* principle of reason, the principle of principles, the *arche* that establishes a world, which is to say, an order and essence, out of subjectivity as nonsensical self-sacrifice. Similarly to his early phenomenology, Levinas's late phenomenology links justice to what he calls "the entrance of the third [*le tiers*]," a third person or "third party" that comes in addition to the self and the other, such that the asymmetrical field within which the self is oriented toward the absolute Other is reconfigured, by dint of triangulation, as an objective, "panoramic" space of relative positions.[74] In *Otherwise Than Being*, this reconfiguration is more dramatic, since absolute otherness no longer appears originally in the face of the other person, as absolute objectivity, but is the generative principle of the self. The absolutely other is not the other person but the I. Accordingly, the manifestation of objective otherness, as the otherness of the other person, is already relative, already triangulated and generalized: "The other is from the beginning the brother of all other men."[75]

In the state of justice, the subject's infinite responsibility comes to be rationalized, normalized, legalized. This means that subjectivity itself is rationalized, that it becomes reason, and transforms from the pneumatic figure, "spirit," into a worldly figure, more properly epistemic or cognitive, namely "consciousness." Justice is, writes Levinas, "the foundation of consciousness."[76] The ambivalence that pertains to works of justice transpires more clearly as a further consequence of rationalization, where the subject emerges not only as objectifying reason but as an *object* of reason, that is, as himself a "third," existing as another other. "Here I am" thus comes to signify "I am another for the others."[77]

Even as Levinas insists that this shift of perspective does not diminish my infinite responsibility, infinite responsibility, by "correcting the asymmetry," is nonetheless objectified within a system of justice, in which the original vector of responsibility, from me to the other, reverses direction, such that "there is also justice for me."[78] The manifestation of the subject, who is originally other than being, *in* being and *as* being, is now not only explained or excused but *justified*. Let us critically reflect on this. That I am and *should* be—is this not the onto-ethical grounding for self-preservation? Does not justice then become the foundation of *conatus*? We may further wonder whether "I" am just another other among all others or whether there is something unique in me, as the *absolute* Other. Is justice there *also* for me, or perhaps—how to avoid this next step?—*especially* for me, a martyred witness to the glory of justice through self-sacrifice? How could infinite self-sacrifice, holocaust and cross, *not* give rise to infinite right?

That this movement from inversion to perversion is not only possible but necessary through the constitutive logic that commands the entire system of emanations becomes evident as Levinas further determines justice in terms of *politics*. Justice in Levinas's exposition is defined as the institution of justice and thus essentially as a state. The entrance of "the third" turns "the incomparable subject into a member of society," for whom Levinas imagines "the egalitarian and just state in which man is fulfilled."[79] *Otherwise Than Being* only makes a fleeting mention of the *just state*, of the state of justice, which we saw was central to Levinas's pre-1968 conception of the State of Israel. Nonetheless, the very suggestion of this notion of a good *polis* seems to put Levinas's second book at odds with *Totality and Infinity*'s fundamental critique of politics in the name of morality and of the state in the name of the nation.[80]

And yet the emergence of the Said from the Saying, as noted, figures in *Otherwise Than Being* as the site of *abuse*, the site of difference that generates essence. It is indeed only at this late stage of Levinas's exposition, which charts the passage from the Saying to the Said, that the notion of abuse arises explicitly. My analysis of *Totality and Infinity* has shown how, in order to render the evil of abuse possible, the narrative's structural necessity is interrupted by contingency, through *time*, whereby the system opens onto history and the split between polis and people. By contrast, my analysis of *Otherwise Than Being* underlines how the appearance of abuse in the transformation of the Saying into the Said is deeply embedded in the logic of perversion that commands the entire system of emanations through which the Other comes into being. In Levinas's later phenomenology, the phase of abuse of difference emerges not as a real event but rather as an explicit manifestation of the logic that governs the entire exposition.

The act of abuse is not a contingency; it stands as the essence of the "latent birth" of the Said from Saying. Saying, which signifies that which is *otherwise* than being, manifests itself in the Said, in "the *essence* of *essence*,"[81] which can manifest Saying only by *betraying* it, that is, by subordinating otherness "to the linguistic system and to ontology."[82] The abuse of difference through forcing difference into a system of essence is an act of language, of language as abuse, which Levinas, both early and late, sees in the paradigm of *writing*. Writing is intimately related to institutional justice: "Saying is fixed in Said, is precisely written, becomes a book, law and science."[83] Saying is betrayed in the Said, which is essentially letter, just as infinite responsibility is betrayed in a system of justice, which consists essentially of law.

The abuse that language inflicts on difference is an abuse of justice, justice as abuse. The paradigmatic figure of the abuse that is justice in *Otherwise Than Being* is the notion of justified violence. The book presents two forms of justified violence, which constitute two modes of abusive justice in the figure of the state.

The first form is *repressive justice*, which for Levinas refers to how the systematic application of justice through the state ends up repressing individual responsibility, the foundation of justice, similarly to how totalitarianism suppresses individual morality in *Totality and Infinity*.[84] The second form, central to Levinas's self-critique, is *just war*. In contrast to repressive justice, this second mode of abusive justice does not suppress subjectivity but becomes its most powerful emanation, in the form of "pure egoism."[85] The state here stands not for impersonal totality but for essentialized collective, for plural individuality, for a "we": "The State issued from the closeness of the neighbor is always on the verge of integrating him into a we, which congeals both me and the neighbor. The act of consciousness would thus be political simultaneousness, but also in reference to God, to a God always subject to repudiation and in permanent danger of turning into a protector of all the egoisms."[86]

The collective, congealed through justice, does not erase individuality but, through reference to a God, posits itself as a collective individual that embodies absolute justice. God's nation does not counterbalance state violence, as it did in *Totality and Infinity*; rather, it *grounds* this violence.

The second paradigm for justified violence is, accordingly, not the repression of the individual through the universal but the aggression of the collective individual, enacted in the name of justice. Just war is the constellation in which ethics, as envisioned in *Totality and Infinity*—"You shall not commit murder," the ethics of nonviolence, interrupting essence as self-preservation—gets "inverted into 'essence of disturbance,' [in order] to surround itself like every essence, inevitably jealous for its perseverance, with military honors and virtues," leading to "war in good conscience."[87] Levinas's second book understands this necessary form of the abuse of justice, the abuse of the prophetic "here I am," as constitutive of the powerful constellation of—Greco-Jewish—collective egoism, "of which European history itself has been the conquest and jealous defense."[88] This abuse is so constitutive of the Western subject that even the Western tradition of self-disabuse, its tradition of unsaying its said—namely, *philosophy*—has, in Levinas's view, most often betrayed its calling by once again becoming, on a higher, more self-reflective level, the instrument of nationalism, as in the case of Heidegger but also in Levinas's early work.

Accordingly, the ultimate intervention of *Otherwise Than Being*'s counter-phenomeno-logos is to identify something like a counterpolis, a figure of the political before or beyond politics (which calls to mind the notion of the state beyond the state from Levinas's Jewish writings—see chap. 4) that is simultaneously a superpolitics. Levinas draws explicitly on prophecy, notably by referring to "the biblical notion of the Reign of God." In the glory of infinite responsibility, he writes,

> Not a world but a Reign [*un Règne*] is signified. But a Reign of an invisible King. The Reign of the Good whose *idea* is already an *eon*! The Good that reigns in its goodness cannot enter into the present of consciousness, not even as a remembered present. In consciousness it is anarchy. The biblical notion of the Reign of God—Reign of a non-thematizable God—a non-contemporaneous, that is, non-present, God—must not be conceived as an ontic image of a certain "epoque" of the "history of Being," as a modality of essence. Rather, essence is already an *Eon* of the Reign. One has to go back from the Eon to the Reign of God, which signifies in the form of subjectivity.[89]

In this passage, the Reign of God, a kingdom of good, stands in opposition to the state. This Reign *is* precisely the disruption of ontically instituted justice, which for Levinas already constitutes an eon, namely an essentially evil world order—a world that is evil because, as world, it is an order, because it necessarily suppresses *spirit*. Even Plato's idea of the good, the main philosophical trope for ethics in *Totality and Infinity*, represents this eon. The biblical Reign of God undoes every affirmative manifestation of ethics in being. It undoes all justice, which, as the being of beings, is fundamentally abusive. "Not a world but a Reign," writes Levinas—this phrase refers to a nonworldly reign. In the world, "in consciousness," the Reign of God can only be described negatively, as the reign of no reign, as a reign of *anarchy*, a term that, for Levinas, "has a meaning prior to the political (or antipolitical) meaning commonly attributed to it. . . . Anarchy cannot be sovereign, like an *arche*. It can only disturb the State."[90]

The most affirmative vision Levinas gives of this apolitical politics is briefly offered in the last pages of *Otherwise Than Being*, where he develops the notion of the good place that is no place—*utopia*. To the hypothetical reproach that his conception of an apolitical politics is utopian, Levinas answers, first, that he is not proposing any ideal state or place, any *arche*, only disruption, and second, that this disruption is not theoretical but has already taken place, notably with the prophetic origin of the West. He alludes to "an event in which the no-place, becoming a place, would have exceptionally entered into the spaces of history," evoking the biblical myth of revelation, biblical revelation as myth, situating it concretely in a "place"—Israel, Jerusalem, the Temple ("where I have chosen to establish my Name," 1 Kings 11: 36). Levinas, however, does not mention any of these names or places here. Rather, he displaces, demythologizes—unsays—prophecy; he undoes its logos of origin, its *arche*, by *dismissing* the need to refer to this specific event, to any particularity beyond the universal "human," since *"what took place humanly could never remain closed up in its place."*[91]

The Reign of God is not utopian because it has already taken place and left that place, left not in order to leave the world but on the contrary to reign over it. Levinas's concluding indication as to the concrete phenomenon that manifests the Reign of God, which is the ultimate manifestation of subjectivity, of that which is otherwise than being *in* being, is not a place or a state but indeed a world, defined not by space but by order and time; properly speaking, it is an eon, namely "the modern world."

> The modern world is above all an order—or a dis-order—in which the elites can no longer leave peoples to their customs, their wretchedness and their illusions, nor even to their redemptive systems, which, abandoned to their proper logic, are implacably inverted. Elites that are sometimes called "the intellectuals." Peoples of whom we find the agglomerations or dispersions in the deserts without manna of this earth. But each individual of these peoples is virtually a chosen one, called to leave in his turn, or without awaiting his turn, the concept of the Me, its extension in the people, to respond with responsibility: *me*, that is, *here I am for the others*, to lose his place radically, or his shelter in being, to enter into ubiquity which is also a utopia.[92]

The modern world, the eon that is the West, so the claim goes, is an order of disorder, an eon with no eons. The epistemo-political agents of this anti-eon, namely intellectuals and philosophers, have the mission of disillusioning national collectives, or "peoples" more broadly, working to disabuse them of their particular "redemptive systems."[93] Modernity thus appears to Levinas as the ultimate disabuse of God's people, as a second-order disruption of essence that manifests the Reign of God in the disruption of political justice through infinite individual responsibility, through the radical self-sacrifice of love. This modern gospel once again contains an implicit Abrahamic reference, this time to his seminal exile—"The LORD said to Abraham, 'Go forth from your native land and from your father's house to the land that I will show you'" (Genesis 12, 1). However, the new, modern Abraham is sent to an exile in "ubiquity," without, according to Levinas's late philosophy, any promised land.

* * *

This ubiquitous utopia of the modern world, whose modern gospel, the new New Testament of individual self-sacrifice, proclaims the dissolution of all peoples, this eon without eons—is it not the supereon, this superempire of the West, that bears its glorious cross? This counterpolis as superpolis— how can we not hear its kerygma, expressed through the power of its hyperbolic counterlogos, generating the very same monologos Levinas identifies as underlying Western rejection of—epistemic—difference? Levinas writes, "The philosophical discourse of the West knows how to find again, under the ruins or in the hieroglyphs, the interrupted discourses of every civilization and of the prehistory of civilizations that were set up as separated. This discourse will affirm itself to be coherent and one."[94]

Has this Western discourse ever been more one than when it asserted the other? This assertion of difference abuses difference—this is the basic lesson of Levinas's two performances of the inter-epistemic encounter between philosophy and nonphilosophy, philosophy and prophecy, within philosophical discourse. *Totality and Infinity* asserts, against a philosophical, Greek episteme of totality, a prophetic, Jewish, episteme of otherness: against theory, it asserts ethics, against logos—language, against the state— the nation. *Otherwise Than Being* points to the amplified identity that arises from this assertion of otherness, to the West as consisting in the abuse of prophecy, as an identity built on difference, an essence of disturbance, as God's nation-state and just war. Levinas's most powerful observation in this regard is to identify the Western episteme of disabuse, called to perform a second-order disturbance through interrupting the coherence of discourse, unsaying logos, revealing hermeneutics beyond or before all logic. Nonetheless, Levinas's counterlogos remains a "more rigorous logic," one replete with an apophantic superpower that performs unsaying by the hermeneutics of one book, the old, surpassed by another, the new—God's nation superseded by God's empire, Israel in flesh by Israel in spirit.

Against this structural ambivalence of the counterlogos, as that which both interrupts and intensifies the said, that intensifies *by* interrupting, the ultimate resort of Levinas's philosophical discourse to epistemic difference amounts to a recurrent performance of *skeptical* self-unsaying. This move appears numerous times in *Totality and Infinity*, as, for instance, when Levinas writes, "The very utterance by which I state [the absolute exteriority of the other] and whose claim to truth, postulating a total reflection, refutes the unsurpassable character of the face to face relation, nonetheless confirms it by the very fact of stating this truth—of telling it to the Other,"[95] which is to say, "to the reader who appears anew behind my discourse and my wisdom."[96] In *Otherwise Than Being*, he writes, "The very discussion which we are at this moment elaborating is a thematizing, a synchronizing of terms, a recourse to systematic language," yet, he continues, "I still interrupt the ultimate discourse in which all the discourses are stated, in saying it to one that listens to it, and who is situated outside the said that the discourse says, outside all it includes."[97]

In this self-affirming skepticism, which epitomizes Levinas's discourse of difference, the counterlogos turns against itself; it exposes, accuses, and denounces itself as reproducing essence. Through the power of self-accusation, the text posits—outside of itself but at the same time as its own embodiment—the individual subject, the "I," which now stands for discourse, for which the discursive self-denunciation signifies confession, and which performs self-critique as self-sacrifice. Nonetheless, by invoking the absent other—the reader—the self-negating subject reaffirms himself in his discourse of difference, which paradoxically generates a higher, collective identity between me and my silent readers, a hermeneutic community of intellectuals, of brethren-apostles of the modern world. Does this community correspond to a more concrete political constellation in Levinas's post-1968 eschatology?

PROPHECY

CONCERNING THE DRAMA OF LEVINAS'S PHILOSOPHICAL DISCOURSE, the previous two chapters have presented Levinas's self-criticism within the conceptual relations between the book of 1961 and the book of 1974. Our discussion of the historiographical, eschatological narrative featured in Levinas's Jewish texts will now allow us to situate his philosophical self-criticism in the broader intellectual context of 1968 and its aftermath—and thus to better appreciate the more concrete epistemo-political implications, implications only hinted at in his phenomenology.

The "central piece" of *Otherwise Than Being* was published as an article called "The Substitution" in October 1968.[1] As Levinas's work on this philosophical book advanced, post-1968 Jewish essays—included in the second edition of *Difficult Freedom* of 1976—started expressing radical anti-Western critique in the spirit of decolonial discourse.

The next two chapters are dedicated to presenting this turn in Levinas's historiographical narrative after 1968. They lay out and analyze the basic articulation of his late eschatology, which we could qualify as decolonial. At the basis of this new narrative, as we shall see, is Levinas's realization of the consequences of a decolonial critique of the West for his own pre-1968 eschatological vision of Israel as the messianic agent of Western humanism.

8

1967 AFTER 1968

Decolonial Anti-Israelism

A short text by Levinas from 1972 on Jewish intellectual and educator Jacob Gordin criticizes Western history in terms reminiscent of Walter Benjamin's *Concept of History*: "Written by the victors, and meditating on the victories, our Western history and our philosophy of history announce the realization of a humanist ideal while ignoring the vanquished, the victims and the persecuted, as if they were of no significance. They denounce the violence through which this history was nonetheless achieved without being concerned by this contradiction. This is a humanism for the arrogant!"[1]

Like Western culture for Benjamin, Western humanism for Levinas is the violence perpetrated by the conqueror that represents his conquest as the triumph of nonviolence. Just like "irenics" for Derrida, Western humanism for Levinas is not just another form of violence but the manifestation, within history, of the worst kind of violence, the worst war, namely the "bellicosity" of just war: "The denunciation of violence risks turning into the installation of violence and arrogance: the alienation of Stalinism. The war against war perpetuates war by ridding itself of all bad conscience."[2] Matching Fanon and Sartre in fervor, Levinas calls for "the end of Western 'triumphalism,' a new history."

Another essay that is highly important for Levinas's post-1968 turn, "Antihumanism and Education" from 1973, similarly discusses "the crisis of humanism which began with the inhuman events of recent history," namely "the 1914 War, the Russian Revolution refuting itself in Stalinism, fascism, Hitlerism, the 1939–45 War, atomic bombings, genocide and uninterrupted war." All these inhuman Western feats do not arise from an abandonment or forgetfulness of humanism. Rather, Levinas identifies them as featuring "a whole series of reversals, inversions and perversions of man and his humanism!"³ Western inhumanism thus arises from Western humanism itself, from its own perversion, its abuse. Consequently, in this essay Levinas acknowledges the legitimacy of anti-Western Western thought, of antihumanism, in which he recognizes a protest "against the decency that covers hypocrisy, the anti-violence that perpetuates abuse."⁴

This realization of the inhuman perversion of Western humanism leads Levinas, in his post-1968 philosophy formulated in 1974 in *Otherwise Than Being*—to take a self-critical distance from his earlier attempt to found human being on an ethics of nonviolence ("You shall not murder"). He declares the vocation of philosophy, on the contrary, to be *undoing*—unsaying—the foundation of being on the ethical break with being, undoing the "essence of disturbance." In chapter 6, I indicated how this self-critical turn leads Levinas to valorize as representative of philosophy not foundational figures in Western intellectual history, such as Plato, but antifoundational figures such as the skeptics. Similarly, figures such as Hegel and Heidegger, denounced in *Totality and Infinity* for abolishing humanity in the system, dissolving beings in Being, are acknowledged in *Otherwise Than Being* as having, through these same operations, critically *undone* the established Western order of beings, deconstructed the "eon," the empire built by Western powers on the title of Judeo-Greek humanism. With a nod to 1968 and the thought of Foucault and Derrida, Levinas upholds the truth of "modern antihumanism, which denies the primacy that the human person, free and for itself, would have for the signification of being": "Its inspired intuition is to have abandoned the idea of person, goal and origin of itself, in which the ego is still a thing because it is still a being. . . . Humanism has to be denounced only because it is not sufficiently human."⁵

In the context of our present concern with Levinas's historiographical project in his Jewish writings, it is now crucial to underline that his post-1968 embrace of Western anti-Occidentalism calls into question the entire project of a humanistic West not only as Greco-Roman but also as *Jewish*. In other words, Levinas's critique of the abuse of ethics and justice targets the Western eon not as simply oblivious of the Jew at its origin, who accordingly should be reinstated as the true king; as empire, as colonial, the West equally constitutes an abuse of Judaism. Westernized Judaism, too—namely Judaism insofar as it became colonial ideology—must be unsaid.

Accordingly, Levinas displays a paradoxical sympathy for Nietzsche. Notwithstanding the avowed "infidelity to Nietzsche," *Otherwise Than Being* rejects Husserl's transcendental constitutionalism in favor of "the nihilism of Nietzsche's poetic writing," "the laughter which refuses language," and so contests the order of discourse and power, of history.[6] Levinas's sympathy extends to Nietzsche's contestation of the West as the eon of the Jewish God, his liberating declaration of "the death of God." Levinas does not object to this declaration; on the contrary, he *appropriates* it, such as when he indicates that "after the death of a certain god inhabiting the world behind the scenes," an empty space is opened for the trace of "he" who "does not enter into any present."[7] The death of the World God makes room for the present absence of the Jewish God, the essentially nonpresent, nonworldly "He." To undo Western (in-)humanism, to undo colonial imperialism, de-essentialize ethics, and prevent just war, the Jewish God must be saved from the world.

From the perspective of Levinas's intellectual historiography, the turn from worldly God to absent God reorients Levinas's thought toward the same Gnostic separation between transcendence and immanence, otherness and being, which he reproached of Christianity.[8] Does decolonialism preclude the project of giving effect to otherness, to transcendence, within being, the project of establishing a dwelling for God in the world? At this point, where post-1968 Levinas is confronted with pre-1968 Levinas, we gain insight into the specific problem the anti-Western West of French 1968 posed for Levinas.

We discussed the philosophical, phenomenological problem in chapter 6 when analyzing *Otherwise Than Being*'s position vis-à-vis *Totality and Infinity*. As I showed, inasmuch as the later Levinas embraced the radically deconstructive operation of what he now understood as the essence of philosophy, namely the skeptic operation of unsaying, he was *simultaneously* concerned that deconstruction would reduce all differences and thereby reinstitute a repressive totality, that the ontic would be absorbed in the ontological, beings in Being. Inasmuch as Levinas subscribes to the critical thrust of antihumanism, he is concerned by the risk of suppressing all subjectivity: "effacing of the living man behind the mathematical structures that think themselves out in him, rather than he be thinking them."[9] For Levinas, the effacing of subjectivity signifies the elimination of all otherness in being and thus of all responsibility and action—in short, all ethics.[10]

This conceptual problem takes concrete historical features in the narrative discourse of Levinas's Jewish writings. I have indicated how the radical critique of the Western eon displays all the traits of—what Levinas identifies as—Gnosticism, namely the radical separation between otherness (the good, God, transcendence) and being (history, the world, immanence). As discussed, early Levinas diagnosed Gnosticism as inhabiting Christianity and argued that Gnosticism, by asserting the Other as absolutely separated from being, simultaneously asserts being as absolutely separated from the Other; it asserts the world as absolutely separated from the good and so, ultimately, becomes complicit in evil's domination over the world. Such was the complicity, Levinas argued, that existed between Christianity and Hitlerism. Recall that in Levinas's analysis, the sinister collaboration to keep God out of the world translated into a collaboration that fought against any attempt to assert God in the world and within history, namely in the figure of a collective subject, a people, as Israel. For Gnosticism, as for Hitlerism, Levinas writes in "Simone Weil against the Bible" from 1952, "evil is specifically Judaic."[11]

It is this "anti-Semitism of the Gnostic type" that Levinas identifies in the radical anti-Western Occidentalism of 1968, which later becomes known as the *new* anti-Semitism. Just as the ontological deconstruction of the total order of beings dissolves all subjectivity in the totality of being, the epistemo-political deconstruction of the humanist order of the West, declaring dead its Judeo-Christian God, entails declaring death for the collective agent of this God in history, namely declaring war on Israel.

Levinas writes in 1973 that "anti-humanism, which begins by paying better attention to the human, makes the antagonisms between Law and Freedom, which we had thought resolved, erupt again and, by a progressive subtraction of elements, finally announces the end of the essence of the man whose irreducibility and supremacy are the basis of the Old Testament."[12]

Levinas understood that radical self-critique of the West in the process of decolonization must entail radical critique of the specific figure within the West that, according to Levinas's own epistemic historiography, epitomizes the Western *mission civilisatrice* and symbolizes the just conquest that is colonialism, the wars of Joshua, namely, the figure of Israel. Inasmuch as Levinas subscribed to Western self-critique, to disabusing humanism, he also realized that anti-Western Occidentalism translates—in the very language Levinas himself had been promoting—into a *Western anti-Israelism*.

1967 after 1968: The Trauma of French Jews

This realization was not merely conceptual. It constituted an existential shock at a concrete moment in history. The Israeli-Arab War of 1967, the so-called Six-Day War, deeply defined the horizon for the positioning of Jews in relation to 1968 and its aftermath, and it continues to do so to this day. It was in 1967–1968, 1967 after 1968, that Israel, the project of the Jewish state, officially emerged as a project of occupation and thus as the enemy of decolonialization. France, which after the Algerian War officially embraced decolonization and became, as it were, the anti-Western Western state, saw a new anti-Israeli consensus produce a deep rupture between Jews and society, a rupture that, for many French Jews like Levinas, shook the very foundation of modern Jewish existence. This trauma set the terms of a still current discursive constellation that links postcolonialism and anti-Semitism.[13]

To get a sense of this formative moment, consider the testimony of French philosopher Raymond Aron. In stark contrast to Levinas, who embraced Judaism as a tradition of militant epistemo-political agency, Aron described himself as completely "de-Judaized." "I was never a Zionist," he wrote in his 1968 account of the situation of Jews in France after 1967, *De Gaulle, Israël et les juifs*, "first and foremost because I don't feel Jewish."[14] This declaration of nonidentification makes it all the more significant that Aron's analysis not only, as its title indicates, identifies the Jews as party to the relations between the French and the Israeli states but also constructs this triangular constellation around a central moment of antisemitism.

The central text of Aron's book is dedicated to the event that motivated him to publish it, as he states in the preface, namely De Gaulle's press conference on November 27, 1967, in which the French president, offering a broad albeit concise historical reflection on the Jewish state, designated the Jews as "elite people, self-confident and domineering" (peuple d'élite, sûr de lui-même et dominateur).[15] Note that this description echoes Levinas's own pre-1968 vision of Jews as the avant-garde of moral humanity, which is how all colonial power, French included, had justified itself. Yet Aron understood De Gaulle to be not praising Jews but blaming them for the State of Israel's politics, "explaining Israeli imperialism by the eternal nature, the dominating instinct of the Jewish people."[16] In De Gaulle's statement, the anticolonial critique of Israel comes out as anti-Jewish by relating Judaism to colonialism.

Aron analyzes De Gaulle's anti-Jewish statement as expressing a fundamental "reversal" in France's postwar alliance with the State of Israel in line with the new French politics of decolonization. The French-Israeli friendship, Aron argues, was due in large part to the similar situation of both states as waging wars against Arabs—Israel in the Middle East and France in North Africa.[17] When France ended the Algerian War in 1962 and gave its colonies independence, it embarked on a process of reconciliation with the Arab world and consequently cooled its relations to Israel. France was now on the side of the colonized, and Israel of colonialism. This process culminated in the 1967 Six-Day War, when "Israeli soldiers transformed into occupiers." At this moment, on Aron's account, a new consensus crystallized in France—"Zionism, a colonial deed; Israel, outpost of imperialism"—uniting Left and Right in hostility toward Israel, "Communists, by anti-imperialism, Gaullists, by nationalism or by anti-Israelism."[18]

The French president's words demonstrated how the new French anti-Israelism was deeply intertwined with anti-Judaism and so with the emergence of decolonial France as the new anti-Jewish state. This was a shocking realization for Jews in France, a profound shock that made even the de-Judaized Aron feel Jewish once more, by persecution. De Gaulle's press conference, Aron wrote ominously, "opened a new period in Jewish history and maybe of anti-Semitism. Everything becomes possible again. Everything recommences."[19] Recall Arendt's claim that Nazi death camps became imaginable with totalitarianism's guiding motto that "everything is possible."[20] Gaullist France was not Hitler's Germany, Aron acknowledged; French Jews were not facing actual persecution, but persecution was no longer unimaginable. France's Jews were entering "The Era of Suspicion," as Aron titled his main essay. The loss of trust in France was worse than the memory of German atrocities as, for Aron as well as for Levinas, in the aftermath of the Holocaust, the alliance with France signified the *unbroken* alliance of Jews with Western modernity—the lasting nature, in spite of Auschwitz, of "the ideas of 1789."[21] Perceiving that a *new* anti-Judaism had been officially espoused by the *post*-Holocaust, *post*-Vichy French state, Jews were now, Aron wrote, "mourning their love": "How many Jews, in France and outside, were crying after the press conference, not because they feared persecutions, but because they lost their heroes!"[22] De Gaulle, the general of liberation from Nazism, was now embracing anti-Semitism.

Aron's account renders visible how the constellation of 1967 after 1968—Israel's military victory, conquest, and occupation as perceived in the era of French decolonization—produced a decolonized and repentant anti-Western West, a new Europe whose own self-criticism translated into anti-Zionism and anti-Israelism. For many Jews, this decolonialism seemed like a new, post-Holocaust anti-Semitism—a worse one than before, since it was historically informed of potential consequences. A profound break transpired between French Jews and the French state, generating trans-generational trauma and a basic sense of "suspicion" toward the post-1968 West. Precisely to this moment of rupture could we perhaps trace a powerful political activation of the memory of the Holocaust that is, to a certain extent, the reconfiguration of collective Jewish subjectivity as constituted by the Holocaust, a memory more prevalent in subsequent decades, distinctly so in Levinas's writings.

The traumatic impact of the events of 1967–1968 on Levinas's own perception of the relationship between France and its Jews is clearly discernible in his essay "Space Is Not One-Dimensional," included in the second edition from 1976 of *Difficult Freedom* and originally published in *Esprit* in 1968. In this essay, Levinas describes the crisis "of French Jews in 1967": "Unable to accept with an untroubled soul the possible disappearance of Israel and extermination of the Israelis, they were no longer to accord with the definition of a French person."[23] We will discuss later the application of Holocaust tropes ("extermination") to the Israeli-Arab War. The point here is the rupture that identification with the State of Israel signified for Levinas vis-à-vis the Republic of France. Recall that in Levinas's pre-1968 narrative, for modern Jews, "France was the country in which prophecies came to pass."[24] This paragon of the modern nation-state figures in this narrative as the exemplary modern manifestation of the Davidic state, the first modern State of Israel. France was the country in which Jews entered the realm of the state, became citizens, entered modernity, entered history, and joined the West. If we recall this, we can understand the profundity of the question posed by Levinas in the essay of 1968: "Is there a new way of being Jewish in France since June 1967?"[25]

The most distinct manifestation of the shock of 1967–1968 in Levinas's work, and his most significant response, is the talmudic readings. The direct thematization of this trauma in the talmudic readings is initially concise and semi-explicit. In the introduction to the first volume, *Four Talmudic Readings*, published in 1968, Levinas, like Aron in the same year, registers the anti-Israeli sentiment in the aftermath of the 1967 war and land conquest: "at the moment in which Jewish history wishes also to be a land upon the earth that its concrete universalism contributed to unite and upon which the rigidity of the alternative national-universal is weakening, immortal anti-Semitism continues in the form of anti-Zionism."[26] Like Aron, Levinas experiences hostility toward Israel as anti-Jewish.

However, whereas Aron condemns (de Gaulle's) anti-Semitism for relating Israeli occupation politics to a distinctly Jewish elitism, the existence
of which Aron categorically denies in the name of "the ideas of 1789," Levinas, on the contrary, laments as anti-Semitic the *denial* of Jewish excellence
that the State of Israel manifests. We saw that the Jewish people, Israel, features in Levinas's early epistemo-political historiography as the particular
historical agent of the universal humanist cause, as "concrete universality" that stands for "the unity of the consciousness of one humanity."[27] The
contestation of this exceptionality is what Levinas identifies at the basis of
1968's anti-Israeli critique, when "humanity, now conscious of its oneness,
allows itself to challenge Israel's vocation."[28]

Note that Levinas's understanding of post-1967 anti-Semitism not
only diverges from Aron's conception but actually *applies* to it as object of
critique: Aron counters anti-Semitism by rejecting the idea of Israel having a vocation as an anti-Semitic myth. In addition, Levinas's insistence
on the epistemo-political reality of historical collectives such as "Israel"
enables us to perceive deeper ideological and discursive transformations
beyond Aron's analysis of post-1967 anti-Israelism as a mere slur arising
from shifts in geopolitical alliances (and his famous analysis of 1968 as a
"psychodrama"). Levinas's broad perspective allows us to appreciate the
already noted irony in De Gaulle's denouncing of Jews—or anyone—for
domineering arrogance, which was indeed the anticolonialist accusation
leveled against a West of which France was a prominent representative. In
De Gaulle's speech, the new, postcolonial France redeemed itself by condemning colonialist virtues and so its old self—"elite people, self-confident
and domineering"—as *Jewish*. If for Aron this operation was scandalous,
Levinas's narrative, which posits Israel as the elite spearhead of Western
humanism, made it *necessary*. As I have shown, for Levinas, the West's
own critique of Western humanism as imperialism, by dint of the "bloody
operation" that Sartre prescribed for the West as a way of "removing the
colonizer inside each one of us," had to signify "the end of the essence of
the man whose irreducibility and supremacy are the basis of the Old Testament."[29] Following Levinas's own pre-1968 logic, decolonization, which,
like Nietzsche, revaluates Western good as evil, can only be anti-Jewish.

The Weakest

The first talmudic reading delivered by Levinas after 1968, "Judaism and
Revolution" from 1969, makes more precise references to current events

and begins to articulate Levinas's response. In this text, Levinas sees the "death of Judaism in the revolutionary man," not, namely, De Gaulle but the Left, which remained closer to France's tradition of enacting humanism by executing the aristocracy, or elite. But Levinas is referring more specifically to the anti-Israelism of 1968. His essay quotes a letter sent to him by someone, probably Maurice Blanchot, who "occupies a prominent place in today's French literary world, if it could be said of a man like him that he occupies a place without shocking him by all that the very idea of occupying a place—even if it were sheer metaphor—evokes of the bourgeois and of comfort." Having "participated in the May events," remaining "deeply associated with them beyond the month of May," this person explains in the letter that he "separated himself from his revolutionary friends when they opted against Israel." Levinas then quotes the letter, with barely any commentary, authorizing us to read it as expressing, or inspiring, Levinas's own thoughts. The key phrase of the letter is a concise early formulation of Levinas's complex position toward the decolonial critique of Israel, which he developed in years to come, a position of simultaneous rejection and incorporation: the author's critique of his anti-Israeli "revolutionary friends" for "the usage of empty concepts (imperialism, colonization) and also the feeling that it is the Palestinians who are the weakest, and one must be on the side of the weak (as if Israel were not extremely, dreadfully vulnerable)."[30]

What the letter dismisses as "empty concepts," imperialism and colonization, is the anti-Western Western discourse of decolonization. This discourse, as I have already argued, forswears any justification of Western power through Western humanism and rejects any legitimacy of conquest by the moral superiority of the Old Testament, all the more so when literally executed in the name of Israel. In other words, in contrast to historical anti-Semitism, which insisted on Jewish exception notwithstanding Jewish assimilation, decolonialism criticizes any exception claimed on behalf of Israel as the Jewish state. "It is not true that anti-Zionism is the anti-Semitism of today," the letter observes. Post-1968 anti-Israeli critique *also* arises from proper anti-Semitism, from "those who want to exterminate the Jew because he is a Jew" and "those who are completely ignorant of what it is to be Jewish," namely from the young revolutionaries of 1968, whom "the meaning of Israel itself, in its most obvious aspect, absolutely escapes."[31]

What is this complete ignorance of "what it is to be Jewish" that, the author alleges to Levinas, causes decolonial anti-Israeli critique and turns its criticism into "empty concepts"? What is this "most obvious aspect" of "the meaning of Israel" that escapes Israel's decolonial critics? Obviously, what escaped them was *not* the meaning of Israel as Levinas had been elaborating it for two decades in his Jewish writings, namely as the moral elite of the West. The decolonial critique of the State of Israel's conquest and occupation in 1967 stemmed not from ignorance about how "the essential task" of the Hebrew University of Jerusalem was "the translation 'in Greek' of the wisdom of the Talmud," which would turn Jerusalem into the city of justice.[32] Rather, anticolonial voices criticized the very vetero-testamentary logic of just conquest, condemning the proposition that just Jerusalem may be built on occupied territory. In short, Levinas's pre-1968 narrative, according to which Israel is the spearhead of Western humanism, cannot provide a response to the post-1967 decolonial critique of Israel, as his narrative is precisely the target of this critique.

In fact, the letter does not suggest that Israel's moral excellence and eschatological mission are a justification for Israeli occupation, and thus it marks a profound shift in Levinas's narrative. My claim is that Levinas basically accepts the decolonial perspective, accepts antihumanism insofar as humanism has been abused to justify wars. If being can be moral, if historical collective subjectivity can be based on ethics, if such an ethics based subjectivity can have a concrete historical agent, if "Israel" is possible, then, in Levinas's understanding, "the meaning of Israel," its "most obvious aspect," cannot be the ontic success of its cause, its worldly power. Within decolonial discourse, Israel can be embodied neither by the conqueror Joshua nor by King David. Rather, as the letter notes, the revolutionaries of 1968 espouse a different, contrary figure of collective moral agency. They do not reject all forms of "concrete universality," of "universalist particularism"; rather, they acknowledge that universalism may be historically represented by a specific collective, by the existence of a specific people of moral excellence. In other words, structurally, conceptually, decolonialism does not completely reject "Israel" and the justice of its cause. However, the decolonial cause lies not with the colonizer but with the colonized, not with the conqueror king but with the oppressed, not with power but with weakness. In post-1967 Jerusalem, decolonial "Israel" is therefore not the State of Israel, the occupier, but, as the letter notes, the occupied Palestinians: "it is the Palestinians who are the weakest, and one must be on the side of the weak."

Accordingly, the Palestinians emerge in decolonial discourse as the incarnation of collective moral subjectivity, as the historical agent of justice whose excellence arises not from its success in instilling justice in the world, in enforcing or observing the law, but rather from its lack of power, its existential weakness. Justice is weakness; weakness is justice, and to fight for justice, "one must be on the side of the weak." This categorical imperative constitutes what may be called the negative political epistemology of postcolonialism, which imagines the collective agency of justice in history in the figure of the victim.

The most significant point in the letter quoted by Levinas in 1969 is not that it cites decolonial discourse, with its negative figure of moral agency, but that it *subscribes* to it. Inasmuch as the letter dismisses as "empty concepts" the critique of the State of Israel's occupation as "imperialist" and "colonialist," it does *not* dismiss the underlying decolonial claim that occupation cannot be justified by moral eschatology or placed under the banner of holy war or *mission civilisatrice*. In response to the decolonial figuration of moral agency (Israel) as the oppressed, weak collective subjectivity ("it is the Palestinians who are the weakest, and one must be on the side of the weak"), the author of the letter does not posit the counterfigure of David, the righteous king, the power of justice. The author's response fully subscribes to weakness as "the most obvious aspect" of Israel—but for him, the real weakness in the Israeli-Palestinian war lies not with the Palestinians but with the State of Israel, as he parenthetically counters pro-Palestinian decolonialism: "(as if Israel were not extremely, dreadfully vulnerable)." It is at this point that Levinas makes his only comment on the letter, adding his own parenthesis: "[The two Israels, I think: Mr. Israel and the State of Israel, for Israel is vulnerability itself.]"[33] Levinas considers not that the paradigmatic victim of history, the Israel of 1968, can become a metaphor for the Palestinians but that it should remain the literal designation of historical Israel, both the Jews ("Mr. Israel") and the Jewish state. *This is the shift in Levinas's post-1968 narrative: Israel is no longer the spearhead of Western civilization but its ultimate victim, and to the anti-Western West, he offers Israel as the ultimate anti-West.*[34]

The Decolonial Subject

Let us consider this shift in the broader context of Levinas's response to 1968, of his decolonial turn. As analyzed so far, Levinas's basic dilemma concerns the status of the subject. Within the discourse of philosophy, Levinas *first* recognizes the fundamental problem of his earlier notion of ethics-based subjectivity, namely the essentialization of this subject ("essence of disturbance," "perseverance") and the consequent humanistic just war. He *second* acknowledges the importance of antihumanism in disabusing (unsaying) humanistic imperialism, and he nonetheless *third* also identifies a threat of returning to totalitarianism in the complete dissolution of the individual ethical agent.

Chapters 6 and 7 analyzed in detail Levinas's response to this threat, which consists in the proposition in *Otherwise Than Being* of a new phenomenology of ethics-based subjectivity. Levinas's post-1968 phenomenology features the subject not as joyful ontic positivity, as being-for-itself that self-restrains only in view of the other, but as always already existing by way of being-for-the-other (substitution), namely a subject who *is* only through suffering, who only persists through self-sacrifice. Levinas's post-1968 ethics is not about a subjectivity curtailed through nonviolence ("You shall not murder") but about a self-offering through which subjective being is originally *posited*: Abraham's "here I am."

My analysis has indicated several difficulties in Levinas's later phenomenology, not least with respect to its political implications, which are not fully articulated in Levinas's second book. Nonetheless, a certain ambivalence is discernible.

On the one hand, the notion of the self-sacrificing subject seems to entail a radically individualistic conception that resists any instituted collective agency, any "essentialization," any people, law, or state. Indeed, in the last sections of the book, Levinas discusses how any institution of individual responsibility as a system of justice ineluctably leads to ontic abuse by establishing an "eon" and grounding just war. To counter this abuse, Levinas suggests a constellation he terms the "Reign of God," described in the book's last pages as an anarchic disorder, a utopia of infinitely responsible individuals who break with all collective ties, with every logic of the "people," just like Abraham did. Situating his utopia in the "modern world," we may read Levinas's words—I quote them again—as a post-1968 vision of radical Abrahamic individualism for the postcolonial age, for the Wretched of the Earth.

> The modern world is above all an order—or a dis-order—in which the elites can no longer leave peoples to their customs, their wretchedness and their illusions, nor even to their redemptive systems, which, abandoned to their proper logic, are implacably inverted. Elites that are sometimes called "the intellectuals." Peoples of whom we find the agglomerations or dispersions in the deserts without manna of this earth. But each individual of these peoples is virtually a chosen one, called to leave in his turn, or without awaiting his turn, the concept of the Me, its extension in the people, to respond with responsibility: *me,*

that is, *here I am for the others*, to lose his place radically, or his shelter in being, to enter into ubiquity which is also a utopia.[35]

On the other hand, this vision, in its very message of radical individuality, simultaneously activates a certain collective archive, reclaims a specific memory, and thereby summons a concrete congregation. Did not Abraham leave one place *for another*, did not he quit his people in order to become *the* "father of many nations" (Gen 17, 4), the patriarch of an Abrahamic civilization? Who are, in fact, the "intellectuals" who dissolve the peoples, the—again this word—elites? Are they simply individual philosophers, isolated skeptics, solitary prophets? This intellectual, ethical elite rather stands for a certain order, be it anarchic and for the "Reign of God," an order that is not merely nonworldly and ahistorical but that takes place as the "modern world." Is this order not, once again, the ultimate eschaton of Levinas's pre-1968 historiography, the West?

As indicated at the end of chapter 7, *Otherwise Than Being* may be read in this way. The broader perspective of Levinas's post-1968 turn, I am suggesting, provides another reading. *Otherwise Than Being* subscribes to the decolonial critique of European history as an abuse of humanism, as a history of "conquest and jealous defense." In this perspective, modern redemption does not lie with the colonial West but with the decolonial anti-West, or *other* West, the Other within the West. Accordingly, if the "elite" agents of God's reign constitute not only a multitude of individuals but also a collective historical subject, this anti-imperial collective is situated by Levinas neither as the West nor as any triumphant, Davidic power but as the historical agency of weakness—as that which, within the "history of the West," we could call "the victims of the triumphs which entitle the eras of History."[36] Considering how *Otherwise Than Being* features victimhood as the very essence of the infinitely responsible, self-sacrificing subject, and, in so doing—as shown in chapter 7—invokes Abraham's binding of Isaac and Auschwitz through the term *holocaustum*, then it is only a small step to seeing the paradigmatic victim of the West as residing in the collective figure of Israel *qua* the Jewish people. *Levinas's post-1968 Israel emerges as the absolute anti-West, as the collective messiah of decolonization.*

My claim is that this decolonial Israel, toward which Levinas's later philosophy only hints, lies at the heart of Levinas's post-1968 eschatological historiography as it unfolds in his later Jewish writings. This story is told in the next chapter.

9

DECOLONIAL ESCHATOLOGY

L ET US LOOK AT THE MAIN FEATURES OF Levinas's post-1968, decolonial historiography and its shifts from the pre-1968 narrative. These two narratives are not separated by any clear, chronological break and continue to coexist in Levinas's texts after 1968. I indicate here a process whereby new motifs emerge or specific arguments become more central or accentuated, thus generating a palpable tendency that makes sense and provides intelligibility within a broader context of discursive transformation, as described in the previous chapters.

Israel as Anti-West

The *first* crucial development in Levinas's post-1968 narrative is the collapse of the clear distinction between Western and non-Western epistemes, a distinction foundational for Levinas's narrative since 1934. The basic notion underlying this distinction is that, in contrast to non-Western, pre-Socratic, Germanic, or Arab attachment to absolute immanence and ontic power pursued through racial imperialism, the Western project (Christian, Greco-Roman, Jewish) has consisted in asserting transcendence, otherness, as that which overcomes egoism through ethics and particularism through universal justice. The challenge of the West, according to this narrative, is to avoid the suppression of the particular by the universal, to prevent the erasure of being by Being, the repression of the individual by the state—that is, to avert totality. This should be carried out, early Levinas suggests, through an ethics-based individual existence able *to replace* the self-interested egoism of the non-Western episteme.

Chapters 6 and 7 showed how Levinas's post-1968 philosophy reformulates his critique of Western thought. Western ontology is no longer perceived only as that which threatens to erase individual beings in Being; it no longer poses just the risk of totality. It is now also held responsible for the ontic principle of individual being, that which, by the force of "perseverance," of self-interestedness, is liable to abuse ethics in the name of self-expansion, of imperialism. Western philosophy, then, no longer stands for a formal universalism that subordinates racial particularism; it emerges—this is the decolonial critique of Western humanism—as the imperial ideology of European racism. Within the historiographical narrative Levinas develops in his Jewish writings, this shift in his appreciation of Western philosophy signifies, as noted, the collapse of the distinction between Western and non-Western episteme.

This collapse is noticeable, for instance, in the talmudic reading of 1978, "Who Plays Last?" In it, Levinas provides a civilizational typology of the ancient world. The Oriental power of Persia comes to be characterized by the same features early Levinas attributed to non-Western humanity, those pertaining to the immanent, corporeal, biological, and racial principle, to "animal energies of attachment to being." Yet, Levinas goes on to argue, this racial principle is not countered by reason, as the West's universal principle, but completely consistent with Western rationality, such that the animal attachment to being is "the rigour of logic itself, . . . the strength of reasoning."[1] Ontic particularism is no longer non-Western, but Western anthropology itself stands for, as the 1975 talmudic reading states, "the perseverance in being, [i.e.,] the famous *conatus* describing the *essence* of man."[2]

If the non-West comes to be equated with the West, then Western civilization loses its supremacy. The same reading of 1978 describes Greece not as the cradle of philosophy, liberty, and humanism but as "the empire of Alexander"—described in a later Levinas reading as a "colonial enterprise."[3] Accordingly, Greek discourse consists in "rhetoric and pure courtesy, a 'courtly language' that veils cruelties and malevolence, the extreme fragility of all this refinement capable of ending up in Auschwitz."[4] That Greco-Roman culture in Levinas's post-1968 narrative stands no longer for formal universalism (totality) but for the most powerful particularistic, racist imperialism can be seen in "State of Cesar and State of David," an important essay published in 1971 that describes Rome as "the pagan State, jealous of its sovereignty, the State in search of hegemony, the conquering, imperialist, totalitarian, oppressive State, attached to realist egoism."[5] In a late talmudic reading from 1986, "The Nations and the Presence of Israel," Levinas refers, as regards the rabbinic discussion over the expression "wild beast" in Psalm 68:31, to the savage, bestial violence of Rome, evoking "an entire unsettling aspect of our Western world, its so often bloody history, with its cult of heroism and military nobility, its nationalistic exclusionism, its racial, social and economic injustice."[6] Western humanism is thus identified with the racism of Western man, the ideology of European imperialist colonialism.

This brings us to the *second* crucial development in Levinas's post-1968 historiography, which concerns the status of Israel. As noted, the decolonial abnegation of the notion of the West as a superior, preferential, or exceptional historical agent of wisdom and justice is related to a general repudiation of the notion of epistemic and moral agency vested in any historical collective. Insofar as "Israel" is the paradigm of such a collective, as in the case of Levinas's pre-1968 narrative, anti-Western decolonialism is essentially anti-Israel. It would seem that post-1968 political epistemology can only acknowledge individual, personal moral agency, namely the Abrahamic individual featured by Levinas at the end of *Otherwise Than Being* who is "called to leave . . . the concept of the Me, its extension in the people, to respond with responsibility."[7]

However, I have indicated how the *Abrahamic* paradigm of the moral individual already evokes a specific collective memory, summoning up Israel again. This dialectics of the collective of anticollective individuals, which remains implicit in the philosophical work Levinas published in 1974, is articulated explicitly a year earlier in the aforementioned 1973 essay on "Antihumanism and Education." "Yes, a particularism. Like that of Abraham," Levinas affirms as a decolonial response to the abuse of humanism by Western imperialism: "The salvation of human universality perhaps once more requires paths that do not lead to the great metropolis. . . . The age of Abraham has returned: one must accept obedience personally." However, he immediately refutes the purely individual essence of this decolonial particularism and points toward its collective manifestation in a very specific historical-political community: "This personal acceptance is not egoist, nor is the other mode of existence for itself: the withdrawal into itself which the Jewish people achieves through the State of Israel."[8] The post-1967 State of Israel, Levinas claims, embodies *the decolonial, anti-Western moral subject.*

How so? To understand this claim, we must examine the post-1968 historiography that Levinas develops in his Jewish writings. Before we do, however, we are already given the hermeneutic key to this new narrative in "Antihumanism and Education," which provides the fundamental characteristic of the drama's main figure of decolonial Israel. In this text, Levinas no longer presents the Jewish episteme only as the historical agent of nonviolence ("we must ask if Jewish education has ever raised violent people. Has it asked anyone to believe in violence devoid of justice?"), an agent justifying and even requiring state power, legitimizing just conquest. Rather, Levinas goes a step further to claim that Judaism rejects not only unjust but also *just* war: "Is it Judaism which has perpetuated the war within the war waged on war? Has its humanism been able to remain content with the peace of the conqueror? Has it ever ceased to be the humanism of patience? Has it ever eliminated the vanquished from history?"[9]

The key word here is *patience*. Israel, the collective Jewish subject, is reaffirmed as the historical agent of morality, ethics, and humanism. However, the agency of this agent is based on patience and passivity, that is, on nonaction or, rather, on the radical action of refraining from action, on the action of suffering—in short, on *passion*. This notion of Israel, further articulated in Levinas's post-1968 historiography, clearly corresponds to the notion of the subject developed in his later philosophy, in which the subject is based on being for the other, a *substitution* that manifests in suffering, self-offering, responsibility, and self-sacrifice—in martyrdom. Textual support for this way of understanding and imagining the Jewish project, which constitutes a significant shift from the Davidic, royal, and conquering image of Israel prevalent in Levinas's pre-1968 texts, can be found in Levinas's post-1968 reference in "Antihumanism and Education" to the famous figure of the "suffering servant" from Deutero-Isaiah (Isa 40–55, especially 53): "In the symbol of the suffering servant we find all the suffering that demands justice until the end of time, a justice beyond the triumph of the triumphant."[10]

This martyr image has historically played a crucial role in the formation of the Christian figure of the crucified Messiah. It is therefore all the more noteworthy that Levinas reclaims this figure for his post-1968, decolonial Jewish Israel as standing for weakness ("Israel is vulnerability itself")—the ultimate victim, the paradigmatic figure of persecuted of Western civilization, itself the very civilization built on the Cross. The anti-West here is posited in and through the foundational figure of the West. Insofar as victimhood actually becomes an epistemo-political paradigm of decolonial discourse, this operation raises the question of the extent to which Western logos survives, and perhaps even thrives, in anti-Occidentalism, of whether colonialism's greatest triumph has not been to preconfigure the power that would bring its demise—or even whether this preconfiguration has not been the essence of Western colonialism, the Glory of the Cross.

Holy History and the Passion of Israel

Let us take a closer look at how Levinas revisits his historiographical narrative in his talmudic readings after 1968, recasting the decolonial figure of Israel not as a messiah-king but as a messiah-victim, not as lawgiver but as persecuted, not as conqueror but as martyr. The first point to note is the intimate relation between the nature of Israel's historical agency and the essence of historiography itself: the reconceptualization of Israel as a martyr entails a reconfiguration of the historiographical operation (Levinas's, to be sure) that seeks to render this victimhood visible and attest to the martyr's testimony.

Levinas indicates this relation between agency and historiography in his 1968 essay "From the Rise of Nihilism to the Carnal Jew."[11] "No matter what Sartre may say," Levinas writes some months after the Six-Day War, Judaism is not created by anti-Semitism: "perhaps the ultimate essence of Israel, its carnal essence prior to the freedom that will mark its history, this manifestly universal history, this history for all, visible to all, perhaps the ultimate essence of Israel, derives from its innate predisposition to involuntary sacrifice, its exposure to persecution."[12]

Here history is visibility, the realm of objective, universal existence, of positive, affirmative, successful being. The victim, as oppressed and persecuted, exists prior to or outside of history, in a history of nonhistory. If Jewish election means that "one accepts martyrdom," to "die for an idea," then "we can recall that besides the Israel that is interpreted spiritually, where there is an obvious equation between Israel and the Universal, there exists an Israel of Fact, a particular reality that has traversed history as a victim, bearing a tradition and certainties that did not wait to win acclaim from the end of History."[13]

Even more explicit in this regard is Levinas's 1972 essay "Jacob Gordin," which decries the Western abuse of humanism ("the denunciation of violence risks turning into the installation of a violence and an arrogance," "the war against war perpetuates war") by pointing to the contradiction of humanist history: "Written by the victors, and meditating on the victories, our Western history and our philosophy of history announce the realization of a humanist ideal while ignoring the vanquished, the victims and the persecuted, as if they were of no significance. They denounce the violence through which this history was nonetheless achieved without being concerned by this contradiction."[14]

Western historiography, even as it claims to counter power through humanist ideals (Benjamin called it "culture"), remains the narrative of power, of the victors, of affirmative being. Levinas's response to this challenge of "our age" is, beyond nonviolence, the notion of moral agency as "passivity, and a certain weakness that is not cowardice," which he finds exemplified— once again referring to Isaiah's suffering Messiah—in the Jewish people: "The martyrology of this people becomes a palpable example, a concrete projection of calvary and all suffering humanity. This painracked 'Slave of God' who condenses the world's tortures in his destiny becomes a concrete symbol of the humanity that learns to know itself, and a providential prefiguration of the future messianic humanity."[15]

This passive, suffering, self-sacrificing agency is by definition effaced from the triumphal historiography of the West, and so, as he says, "the humanism of the suffering servant—the history of Israel—invites us to create a new anthropology, a new historiography, and perhaps, by bringing about the end of Western 'triumphalism,' a new history."[16]

This "new historiography" is the central project of the post-1968 talmudic readings, under the explicit title *Talmudic Readings*. The fundamental thrust of the project lies in redefining the notion of history, which amounts to redefining the notion of temporal being, of being as time. Against the old notion of history, the notion that underlies "our Western history and our philosophy of history" and that guides Levinas's own pre-1968 historiography, Levinas now posits and elaborates a new conception of history, which he designates as "holy history," often with capitals, Holy History.[17]

This concept appears in the introduction to the first collection of talmudic readings from 1968.[18] Its exact meaning in this text is obscure, but its discursive function is already clear, as is its political import. The concept appears in the context of Levinas's discussion about the legitimacy of Zionism as the ideology used to justify Israeli land conquest, such as that which occurred in 1967. Against a vulgar notion of Zionism as based on the "will to power" of egoistic nationalism, Levinas asserts the idea, inspired by the Talmud, of "noble Zionism." According to the "sages of the Talmud," he writes, the right to the land of Israel is not based on occupation, on physical possession, on presence, but on heritage. It lies with "the patriarchs, fathers of holy history, the only ones with a right to possession": "The history of this land cannot be separated from holy history."[19] The legitimacy of occupying the land of Israel derives only from the historical significance of this land within the holy history, meaning with the heirs of the patriarchs, the de facto *agents* of holy history—otherwise put, with the holy people, Israel, acting in its messianic capacity. The eschaton of holy history, Jerusalem as the city of justice, therefore *conditions* the legitimacy of Israel's land occupation, which is justified only if just. This is Levinas's morally critical point. It also means, however, that holy history provides the condition that justifies Israeli occupation.

What exactly is "holy" history? In what does its "holiness" consist? What distinguishes it from unholy, profane, or mere history? Here, we might think of Karl Löwith's analyses of the Judeo-Christian idea of *Heilsgeschichte*, the "history of salvation," which, in different periods and forms, has been used to discern within historical time—but beyond the secular, prosaic, and meaningless chain of events—the unfolding of an eschatological drama, replete with a comprehensive meaning and an overarching teleology.[20] The same holds for Levinas's conception. However, finding "meaning in history" (Löwith) can mean providing eschatological signification to historical developments in order to justify history *as it is*: sanctifying the victors, damning the losers. This type of *Heilsgeschichte* corresponds to Levinas's pre-1968 historiography, where Israel, the main protagonist of history, manifests itself as David, as king, as state. Levinas's post-1968, "new" historiography, however, seeks to *counter* Western messianic triumphalism, to provide a counternarrative, a history—to evoke Benjamin again—that runs "against the grain." What makes this new history holy is that it *inverts* the meaning of hegemonic historiography; positive becomes negative, negative turns positive. Where hegemony celebrates triumph, holy history marks downfall, and the protagonist, the hero, of holy history is not the victor but the victim, the "suffering servant." Holy history is the *history of the loser*.

Accordingly, the fundamental shift in Levinas's post-1968 historiography of Israel vis-à-vis his earlier narrative consists in a revaluation of the meaning of diaspora. As we saw, the long period of statelessness in Jewish history, the many centuries of *galuth*, exile, feature in Levinas's initial historiography as sheer negativity. Diasporic statelessness is described as existence outside of history, insofar as Israel, deprived of a state due to nations' "misunderstanding" of its concrete universalism as particularism, was also deprived of any historical role and limited in its activity, as Levinas wrote in 1951, to "the fervent mysticism that overexcites the orthodox or liberal tendencies of the diaspora living alongside Christianity."[21] But in the new, decolonial Haggadah, the perspective of holy history means that Israel's exilic condition is no longer interpreted as negativity, as nonhistory, but on the contrary as counterhistory, as *actual* history.

This revaluation of Jewish diaspora in Levinas's post-1968 historiography is clearly articulated in 1988 in his introduction to *A l'heure des nations*, "In the Time of the Nations," a collection of talmudic readings and essays from the mid-to-late 1980s. As the collection's title indicates, its guiding theme is collective time, or history. The introduction speaks of a "time lag," a "diachrony" between, on the one hand, "Universal History," which is "the time of the nations" based on presence and actuality, and, on the other, Israel's proper time of "Holy History."[22] The two histories, universal and holy, are not separated. Rather, holy history unfolds "*in* the Time of the Nations." Holiness shines in universal history thanks to the "illumination of the seventy nations through Christianity and Islam," that is, the successful monotheistic religions.[23]

The primary holy light is, however, Israel's torah, manifested in the time of nations through Jewish diaspora among nations: "The diaspora of Israel itself is assigned the mission of monotheism, the bearer of justice."[24] Diaspora, dispersion, does not only mean the propagation of religious wisdom among other peoples, which Christianity and Islam had done far more effectively. Levinas emphasizes the specific political and existential *negativity* of the exilic condition, which is powerlessness and constitutes the properly Jewish manifestation of holy history in universal history.[25] Judaism manifests holiness not in triumphs, as with Islam and Christianity, but on the contrary, "in the suffering, disdain and blood brought down upon the carrier of the Torah by so many triumphant bursts of its borrowed light."[26]

Holy history is the historical unfolding of holiness, or justice, within universal history, within the time of nations and nation-states, within the history of presence, action, and triumph; it is the manifestation of justice in Jewish suffering. The suffering of exilic Israel is the historical manifestation of justice. Suffering Israel is testimony, martyrdom. To designate the basic event or happening, the basic *act* of holy history, Levinas often uses the expression "the Passion of Israel." The 1978 talmudic reading, for instance, describes holy history as consisting in "the biblical message and the history of a people of survivors, and the Passion of Israel throughout history that they evoke."[27] Passion is a key concept in *Otherwise Than Being*, where it designates the existence of a subject whose being consists in subjecting himself to others, in self-exposing, self-offering, suffering, in a passivity that is "more passive than any passivity."[28] The term *passion* has been used traditionally in Christian representations of the suffering Christ through the figure of the Passion of Jesus.[29] Levinas's post-1968 historiography performs a remarkable (re)appropriation of Christian tropes in order to revisit the history of Jewish statelessness, for example, in the 1985 talmudic reading, where he speaks of "eschatology through the Passion of Israel among the nations. Passion of Humanity bleeding in the wounds of Israel."[30]

One striking example of Levinas's deployment of his new, diasporic historiography in the post-1968 talmudic readings is the 1981 reading, "For a Place in the Bible." This text discusses—through readings in tractate *Megillah*—the canonization of the Book of Esther and its story of Purim. Esther is the exilic biblical book *par excellence*, the only book in the Bible that takes place entirely in—Persian—exile, making reference neither to the land of Israel nor to the God of Israel. To explain why Esther nonetheless got "a place in the Bible," Levinas, commenting on a talmudic midrash (bMegilah 7a), explains that Purim belongs to the holy book that is the Bible because it belongs to holy history: "The History of Israel and the Passion of Israel through its History would constitute, as it were, the very unfolding of the will of God."[31] The Book of Esther is part of holy history because it evokes the danger, catastrophe, and potential holocaust that constantly threaten Jews in exile: "the History of Israel in its daily patience, in its Passion and even in its despair and death in the concentration camps." Levinas adds, simultaneously responding to De Gaulle and his own pre-1968 narrative, that "there is nothing here that resembles the pride of election for which Israel's enemies reproach her."[32]

Cursed Race

The notions of holy history and the Passion of Israel delineate a specific phenomenal horizon for imagining the concrete figure of the Jewish people. Within this horizon, the collective of Israel, in its historical agency, appears not primarily in the active, assertive forms of law, justice, or the city but instead in the form of extreme passivity. I note that this shift entails an important process of de-epistemization of the collective agency of Israel, a shift from a conception of Israel based on a shared body of knowledge, customs, norms, and performances to an Israel based on a shared lived experience, situation, destiny, or—to speak in existentialist terms—"thrownness."[33] One concrete shape of collective passivity, one concrete figure of the collective as passion, that defines Levinas's post-1968, postcolonial Israel is the figure of race.

Race as a collective figure stands for radical difference, difference that does not arise from any specific action, practice, choice, or volition but is imposed and given on the level of being, of passive bodily existence, by a heterogeneous, external, transcendent election. A racialized collective may emerge from racial self-perception, from race theory. This is not so for Levinas, who explicitly rejects any racialized understanding of Israel, defining it instead in epistemo-political terms. But a collective may be racialized through an external imposition, that is, through racial discrimination and persecution, generating a sociopolitical condition of radical, ontical difference at the level of being. Within decolonial discourse, this condition of radical discrimination, brought about by colonization, is precisely what characterizes the political situation of colonized peoples. As Fanon observes, in the Manichean dualism of the colonial situation, the colonized are not just "wretched" but *damnés*, "damned," fated, predestined to damnation due to their non-European being. In these conditions, decolonization, through which the colonized assert themselves and transform themselves from victims into political actors, begins by appropriating the imposed difference, that is, by the militant assertion and transvaluation of racial identity. "This antiracist racism is the only way that can lead to the abolition of race difference," wrote Sartre in his support of *négritude*.[34]

A similar logic can be observed in Levinas's post-1968 conception of Israel as the ultimate victim of Western history. One of the first texts to articulate this conception is the 1969 talmudic reading, "Judaism and Revolution," where Levinas directly confronts the anti-Israelism of 1968. At a certain point in the text, he recalls that a watchword of May 1968's demonstrators, launched in response to Daniel Cohn-Bendit's deprecation by his opponents as a "German Jew," was the call of solidarity "We are all German Jews." Levinas comments on this remarkable deployment of Jews as identificatory figures for the revolutionary cause: "German Jews in 1933, foreigners to the course of history and the world, Jews *tout court*, this signifies the most fragile, most persecuted thing in the world. More persecuted than the proletariat itself—who is exploited, but not persecuted."[35] Levinas interprets the revolution's identification with Jews as identification with the world's victim, the figure that marks the absolute site of opposition to the world's injustice. This logic is the same that led Marx to see the proletariat as the revolutionary class and that Sartre applied to Jews, Black people, and the colonized.

Levinas insists on the supreme status of Jewish victimhood; Jews are the elite of all suffering, the "most persecuted thing in the world." This superlative directly arises from his post-1968 conception of Israel as the collective agent of ethics and justice in history, whose agency nonetheless consists in the extreme passivity of passion. Judaism as "responsibility towards the entire universe" manifests historically as "universally persecuted Judaism." Whereas workers are defined by work, which is only exploitation under the conditions of capitalism, Jews, according to Levinas, are essentially constituted by the ethics of self-sacrifice, of martyrdom. Judaism thus emerges in the 1969 talmudic reading as the model for the subject described in Levinas's later phenomenology in *Otherwise Than Being*, namely the subject based on infinite responsibility, which means an ontological condition of persecution. "To be responsible despite oneself is to be persecuted. Only the persecuted must answer for everyone, even for his persecutor."[36]

Jews are the "most persecuted thing in the world" because they are persecuted in their very Jewish being, which is the messianic existence of the suffering servant. A central endeavor of "Judaism and Revolution" consists in showing that Judaism is persecuted by the revolution itself, as attested by the young 1968 revolutionaries, that is, by those who "opted against Israel."[37] It is this conception of ontological suffering that leads Levinas to describe Jews not as a class, like the proletariat, but as a *race*: "a race cursed, not through its genes, but through its destiny of misfortune, and probably through its books, which call misfortune upon those who are faithful to them and who transmit them outside of any chromosomes. People of our God, in this very precise sense."[38]

It is the Jews who are *the damned on Earth*.

Passion of the Holocaust

If the collective of Israel, as Levinas reconceptualizes and reimagines it after the decolonial turn of 1968, as a suffering collective, appears within history in the paradigmatic figure of a persecuted race, it is easy to understand the enhanced significance that Levinas's new historiography lends to the Holocaust. In Levinas's post-1968 narrative, the great racial persecution and destruction of Jews in the twentieth century takes the same place the foundation of the French Republic occupied in his pre-1968 discourse, namely as the defining event of modernity. The event of the Holocaust has an apocalyptic quality in the sense that it reveals the truth of holy history by exposing Israel for what it really is: an accursed race. The Passion of Israel is revealed in the Passion of the Holocaust.

It is instructive to reflect, through Levinas's work, on the role played by Holocaust memory in post-1967 Jewish historiography, which developed in response to and in terms of decolonial discourse. One noteworthy feature that can be identified in Levinas's case is the affinity between Jewish inscriptions of the Holocaust in holy history as the apocalypse of the victim-messiah and similar Christian interpretations. We have already noted elements in Levinas's discourse that strongly resonate with elements of Christian theology, such as the image of the "suffering servant" and the notion of the Passion. In a more general manner, Levinas's post-1968 reconfiguration of the Jewish project as based less on positive agency, on the moral conquest of being, and more on passion and suffering drives Judaism closer to the figure of Christianity as featured in Levinas's pre-1968 historiography. Recall that Levinas sees the essence of Christian operation in affirming otherness as absolutely distinct from being, in asserting goodness as absolutely separate from the world. The existential significance of this dualism is that *within the world*, any identification with goodness, any moral agency, is essentially estranged, which is to say, persecuted. This same logic also applies to post-1968 Levinas's radical opposition between universal history and Israel's history, the holy history featuring the Passion of Israel in "the Time of the Nations."

It is unsurprising, therefore, that one of the earliest occurrences of an apocalyptic understanding of the Holocaust in Levinas's writings appears in a quote of Paul Claudel, who, as we saw, served for Levinas as a locus for confrontation with Christianity. In his 1969 essay on Claudel, "Poetry and the Impossible," Levinas writes that "it is incredible that Claudel could write on 1 August 1939: 'all the sacred writers call Israel a witness, but the Greek word *witness* means *martyr*.'"[39] Claudel is presented as a seer, a prophet who acts as a precursor to Levinas's "new historiography," having, at a relatively early moment, perceived the revelation, meaning, and sacred testimony that transpired in the Nazi persecution of the Jews. This Catholic author was able to see the Holocaust as a key event of holy history, a moment of truth that rendered the Passion of Israel universally visible. Against all the "explanations of the events that took place in these dark years by the historical and social sciences, Claudel," Levinas writes, "places the martyr-dom of Auschwitz out on its own."[40]

Levinas develops his notion of the Passion of the Holocaust in later texts. Two texts from 1982 articulate this question especially clearly. The first is "The Thought of Moses Mendelssohn," which comprises Levinas's preface to Dominique Bourel's French translation of Mendelssohn's *Jerusalem*. The essay attributes to Mendelssohn the same messianic vision of modernity as consisting in the redemption of Israel ("the new fraternity . . ., within the modern nation-states, between Jews and Gentiles") that Levinas himself proclaims in his early historiography. Now, however, Levinas deems that "the ordeals undergone during the Hitler years of Europe and their current fallout have made it impossible to assume the quasi-Messianic style of the emancipation announced by Mendelssohn."[41] In contrast to his pre-1968 narrative, Levinas now presents emancipation as bringing about the *loss* of Judaism through assimilation, dejudaization, and conversion. The end of statelessness, the end of diasporic existence, no longer means, as in the pre-1968 narrative, the *beginning* of Jewish agency in history but, on the contrary, its *end*—the end of the Passion. Remarkably, but in adherence with this logic of holy history, the Holocaust represents not the ultimate destruction but rather the *restoration* of Israel. Levinas writes,

> Must we not insist on all the unforeseeable and unforeseen dimensions that the very desperation brought about by National Socialist persecution opened up within Israel's ancient faith: the Passion of the Shoah, its meaning for the survivors who to this day feel they have been incomprehensibly, as it were unjustly, spared? Ordeals, abysmal depths conferring an unexpected meaning on very ancient texts—texts already bearing the trace of an extraordinary spiritual history, but that in the course of the nineteenth century, in the enlightened atmosphere of emancipation, were beginning to be seen as old scribblings of interest to no one except historians and doxographers.[42]

In the Passion of the Shoah, Israel is said to have returned to its suffering self after self-alienation occasioned by modern assimilation into the West. In the same year of 1982, Levinas's collection of talmudic readings *Beyond the Verse*, a key text for this period, expounds more clearly the political implications of this narrative. Fifteen years after the 1967 war and subsequent occupation, and in the same year as the first Lebanon War and the Sabra and Shatila massacre, Levinas explicates in his introduction how his decolonial reconfiguration of Israel as victim of the West, universally revealed in the martyrdom of Auschwitz, provides the "raison d'être of Zionism."

In the post-1968 logic Levinas embraces, justice manifests in weakness. The moral legitimacy of political claims is measured by the level of suffering. "Can we understand the suffering of others? Nobody could weigh up and compare sufferings which do not have, like the elements of matter, different 'atomic weights,'" Levinas notes. The Shoah, however, is exceptional, exemplary: "Can one deny, in the Passion of the Holocaust, the despair of all human sufferings! Can one compare Hegel's 'unhappy consciousness' with a millennial history of outrages and tears, of permanent insecurity and of the shedding of real, warm blood? That is where the concrete cause and real raison d'être of Zionism lies, not in any biblical exaltation of hope and domination, nor in an inversion of paranoia into persecution—too new a movement for a very ancient people."[43]

Contrary to all decolonial assertions that—as Levinas quoted in "Judaism and Revolution" of 1969—"it is the Palestinians who are the weakest," the Passion of the Holocaust attests to the fact that "Israel is vulnerability itself."[44]

Self-Defense

Accordingly, the Passion of the Holocaust is the argument Levinas develops in his talmudic readings to provide decolonial justification for the post-1967 State of Israel. Here we come to the nerve center of Levinas's post-1968 narrative and its ultimate challenge. The challenge consists in applying the notion of passion, of victimhood and weakness, to support the ultimate institution of violence, namely the use of military power by a sovereign state on stateless civilians. More precisely, the challenge consists in asserting the ultimate moral agency of the Jewish collective by virtue of its factual historical persecution to justify the *de facto* military occupation carried out by the State of Israel. In keeping with Levinas's own post-1968 logic, both in his philosophy and in his talmudic readings, is not *weakness* the only guarantee that the ethics of nonviolence is not abused for justifying imperial wars? Is not Israel justified because it is the "suffering servant," as attested by the martyrdom of Auschwitz? Does not the military violence of the State of Israel signify the end of this testimony, and so the end of historic Israel? What is Levinas's post-1968 justification for the State of Israel?

Before answering this question, let us recall that Levinas's pre- and post-1968 discourses in the talmudic readings are not neatly separated but remain intertwined. Post-1968 arguments are prefigured in earlier texts, while later texts continue to feature elements of the pre-1968 narrative side by side with "new historiography" due to the nonsystematic, fragmentary nature of the talmudic readings. Accordingly, even after Levinas's decolonial turn, which deemphasizes advocating the Israeli state as a resurrected Davidic Zion, his texts still occasionally play to the tune of messianic triumphalism. The basic eschatology remains. As discussed, the doctrinal 1971 essay "State of Cesar and State of David" articulates the vision of the State of Israel as the Davidic state that will deliver to humanity "the formulation of monotheistic politics that no one has yet formulated."[45] Another important text for our discussion, "Politics After!" from 1979, written in view of the peace process between Israel and Egypt, confirms that the "ultimate purpose of Zionism" is "to create on [Israel's] land the concrete conditions for the political invention." "For two thousand years," Levinas writes, pointing beyond the politics of victimhood, "the Jewish people was only the object [of history] in an innocent politics that it owed to its role as victim. It is not enough for its vocation. Since 1948, here it is, surrounded by enemies and always in question, but also engaged in the facts, for thinking—and for doing and redoing—a State where the prophetic moral and the idea of its peace should be realized."[46]

And yet, after 1968, the assertive, proactive, messianic mission of the Jewish people becomes a secondary justification for the Israeli state. The main legitimacy for Jewish state violence provided in Levinas's post-1968 talmudic readings is no longer grounded in the paradigm of a Davidic, triumphant Israel but in that of a suffering, persecuted, *weak* Israel. Levinas's new justification for violence is no longer based on the colonial logic of just conquest, on military power deployed for the sake of building a just society, but on the anticolonial logic of *defense*—that is, the self-defense of the wretched against persecution. Levinas does not go as far as Frantz Fanon and argue for the *necessity* of violence in the process of decolonization, for liberating the decolonized subject by completely *breaking* the colonial order. Levinas's colonized subject, the collective of Israel, is constituted by nonviolence and by weakness. Accordingly, Israel may only be justified in exercising violence for the sake of preserving itself as nonviolent and weak. The violence of the victim as victim (rather than as new aggressor) is the violence of *self-defense*.

Levinas developed his doctrine of self-defense as the basis for the State of Israel in texts from the mid-1970s and early 1980s. In the 1979 essay "Politics After!" he describes the historical process of the founding of the Jewish state in these terms: "The human perfectly human which unfolds in historical events in the form of Judaism, patience and a Passion that are forever beginning afresh right until they revert to action in order to rescue the human."[47] Reverting from passion to action is necessary to rescue the "perfectly human," that is, not to overcome passion but to preserve its existence.

Levinas's clearest articulation of this idea can be found in his 1981 introduction to the collection of talmudic readings *Beyond the Verse*. Even if the Jewish state reactivates prophetic politics, the "real raison d'être of Zionism," Levinas emphasizes, "lies not in any biblical exaltation of hope and domination" but in the "Passion of the Holocaust." The Holocaust showed "the necessity for the Jewish people . . . to not continue being a minority in its political structure . . . in order for the attack and murder of Jews in the world to lose their character of an uncontrollable and unpunished phenomenon."[48] The Holocaust thus revealed the necessity for Jews to be strong in order to remain weak, the need to not be a political minority in order to survive as an ethical elite—otherwise put, the necessity of a Jewish state to protect the stateless essence of Judaism.

The paradox here is evident. Would not self-defense, inasmuch as it defends a weak, persecuted, suffering people, at the same time end suffering and weakness and so bring an end to this people, Israel, as "vulnerability itself"? Would not the State of Israel bring an end to the Passion of Israel? Recall that, in Levinas's post-1968 decolonial narrative, "passion" designates the constitutive weakness of Israel as the agent of morality in Western history, the agent who not only embraces nonviolence but also resists the abusing of nonviolence through just war by embracing weakness. Weakness *is* the Jewish people's existence. Would not the Jewish state, as Jewish self-defense, put an end to Jewish weakness not only, or not necessarily, as a factual condition but also, more importantly, as an onto-ethical principle of Jewish being? Furthermore, would justifying the State of Israel as necessary to Jewish self-defense in view of the *Passion* of the Holocaust signify the abolishment of weakness through violence and posit weakness (radical nonviolence) as a *justification of* violence? Would this not simply repeat the very structure of abuse (of nonviolence by just war) that post-1968 Levinas diagnoses in Western civilization?

These difficulties are visible in Levinas's attempts to formulate his position. We have already revisited two sites in Levinas's post-1968 corpus where the basic parameters of this problem (passion as justifying state, victimhood as justifying violence) are negotiated.

One site is Levinas's polemics with Christianity, which Levinas understands as the radical, dualistic separation between the Other and being, between the good and the world. I noted how this dualism is intimately related to the notion that moral agency *in* the world, as that which represents good in the realm of evil, can only be an agency of suffering, a crucified messiah. Levinas's post-1968 doctrine of Israel as passion accordingly situates his thought in proximity to (his understanding of) Christianity, which requires him to mark his distance.

In his 1987 exchange with Bishop Klaus Hemmerle, "Judaism 'and' Christianity," Levinas marks this distance in relation to the question of passion and power. As discussed above, Levinas strongly criticizes Hemmerle's notion of the "defenseless" Christ, protesting that in view of crimes like Auschwitz, the "*kenosis* of powerlessness costs man too much! Defenseless Christ on the cross eventually found himself leading the armies of the Crusades!"[49] Levinas problematizes the notion of the defenseless, suffering Messiah by pointing at its historical abuse to justify political power. Paradoxically, Levinas's countervision—namely, that the suffering servant, Israel on the Cross of Auschwitz, may not be left defenseless but must be defended by state power—does not counter the logic of the Crusaders but reproduces the same abuse: Christ needs military defense, and suffering Israel needs a state.

A *second site* at which Levinas struggles with the fundamental difficulty of his post-1968 discourse is *Otherwise Than Being*. My analysis has indicated how this book is dedicated to showing and countering the process through which the ethical disturbance of ontology is reinscribed in the logic of being ("essence of disturbance") such that the ethics of nonviolence is abused for the sake of justifying violence ("just war"). Levinas argues that this abuse is necessary for the positive consolidation of language, narrative, world, and being. He suggests that it may be countered only by the sort of human being that is based on undoing its own being, namely on a subjectivity based on sacrificing itself for others, on passion. Nonetheless, my analysis has shown how Levinas's phenomenology of the self-sacrificing subject restages the same abuse it seeks to counter. In the transformation of ethics to *justice*, the subject's self-positioning through the Abrahamic "here I am" shifts from signifying my self-offering for others to signifying "I am other for the others," the self-offering of others unto me. When infinite responsibility becomes objectified as a system of justice, the original vector of responsibility from me to the other reverses its direction, such that "there is also justice for me."[50] I have critically indicated how this inversion generates in Levinas's later phenomenology an argument that leads from the weak, self-sacrificing subject to the just state, which is hardly distinguishable from the abusive deployment of the ethics of nonviolence to justify war.

The same inversion of passion to power—and the same abuse, to take up Levinas's own insight—is also at work in Levinas's post-1968 justification of Israeli state violence. In the introduction to the talmudic readings published in 1981, *Beyond the Verse*, Levinas makes clear that the Holocaust revealed the necessity of defending powerless, stateless Jews not just to *maintain* them in their statelessness, in diaspora, in weakness. He now formulates the lesson of Israel's passion in stronger terms. To begin with, he draws a clear distinction between the individual and the collective: "The great—the greatest—ethical idea of existence for one's neighbour applies unreservedly to me, to the individual and the person that I am. An idea that cannot be thought to include demanding the existence of a people of martyrs, whose model many beautiful souls reproach Zionism for distorting."[51]

Levinas's ethics of subjectivity as self-sacrifice, as an infinite responsibility for others, applies only to the individual, not the collective. Notwithstanding his new historiography of the Jewish people as the suffering servant of Western history ("Passion of Humanity bleeding in the wounds of Israel"), which Zionism and the State of Israel seem to contradict, here Levinas categorically dismisses the notion of "a people of martyrs." This notion is now presented as the idea of "beautiful souls," by which he means Christians and leftist intellectuals. Instituting Israel as the name of state, of military violence, Levinas insists now, is no contradiction.

But Levinas is not content with arguing that political power and state violence, on the collective level, merely do not contradict, pervert, or *abuse* the individual ethics of infinite responsibility for others. The same text from 1981 deploys this logic of defense to articulate a stronger argument that posits the Jewish ethics of self-sacrifice as capable of *justifying* nation-state violence. Levinas writes, "In the responsibility for others prescribed by a non-archaic monotheism, it reminds us that it should not be forgotten that my family and my people, despite the possessive pronouns, are my 'others,' like strangers, and demand justice and protection. The love of the other—the love of one's neighbour. Those near to me are also my neighbours."[52]

That people are allowed and expected to protect their family is trivial. The force of Levinas's argument here lies in the operation it performs on his own theory of subjectivity as substitution and self-sacrifice, notably concerning its political implication. Not only is martyrdom for others incumbent solely on the individual, not on the collective, but the collective here also assumes the role of the others, such that the infinite responsibility of the individual comes to be directed toward *his own* collective: "my family and my people." The Passion of Israel, Jewish suffering for others, translates into Jews taking care of themselves against others.[53] The risk of abuse is obvious. It exceeds the abuse of individual responsibility in formal universalistic justice, as we saw in *Otherwise Than Being*. Here, the ethics of self-sacrifice permutates into patriotic martyrdom for national self-defense. *Israel would be an army of martyrs who sacrifice themselves for the defenseless victims they themselves are.*

Levinas's deployment of Israel's passion to justify the Jewish state as collective self-defense is carried out in the *Talmudic Readings* through the sanctification of Israeli defense as a holy war. The 1975 talmudic reading, "Damages due to Fire," ends with Levinas commenting on a talmudic aggadah according to which "the Holy One, Blessed be He, said: I kindled a fire on Zion and I will rebuild it one day with fire, as it is said (Zechariah 2:9): 'And I myself will be a wall of fire all around it and I will be a glory inside it.'"[54] Having linked the discussion a little earlier to the Holocaust, Levinas now reads this passage as promising "the reconstruction of Jerusalem in its glory, the reconstruction by the same means that were used to destroy it, precisely by the fire that becomes protective. But where is the glory of His Presence among us, if not in the transfiguration of the devouring and avenging fire in protective wall, in wall of defense?"[55] The Israel Defense Force replaces the Passion of Israel as the avatar of God's glory.

Or consider the 1981 talmudic reading, "For a Place in the Bible," where Levinas contemplates verses in the Book of Esther that, according to the rabbis, demonstrate that this book is the work of the Holy Spirit. One verse states that the victorious Jews killed their enemies, but "on the spoil they laid not their hand" (Esther 9:15). Here Levinas reads the holiness of Jewish violence as residing in "the story of a defensive combat, free of all attachment to possessions, of all greed, all conquest, the account of Israel's defensive struggle, the disinterestedness of which we still have so much trouble convincing the world."[56] Israel's self-defense is a holy war: the struggle of a minority community in Persian exile combating persecutions *just as much as* the wars waged by the State of Israel's military forces.

Palestinians as the West

This comparison is clearly problematic in the context of Levinas's own post-1968 narrative. The problem lies not only with the questionable analogy between the defense of stateless Jews and the self-defense of a sovereign Jewish state. There is one constitutive feature of his decolonial holy historiography that nonetheless allows Levinas to make this analogy, namely the notion of the Passion of Israel, according to which the Jewish collective is the suffering Messiah who exists in history as the ultimate victim of the West. Whether diaspora or state, Israel is persecuted by, and needs defending from, Western civilization. But—and here we reach the heart of the matter and ongoing dispute—is the State of Israel really threatened by the West, by the victors and hegemons of history? In its wars, the Jewish state has rather confronted Arabs. Can they be identified with the West? From a decolonial perspective, do Arabs not belong to the peoples and regions that Europe colonized rather than to the colonizing powers? Did the French colonial war in Algeria, for example, not feature a decolonial struggle between Europe and the Arab world? Recall that according to Raymond Aron, the relation to the Arab world was the basis for the French-Israeli alliance *prior to* France's turn to decolonization and the reason for the break of this alliance *afterward*. Have not Arab peoples, Palestinians included, been, like Jews, victims of the West? That they in fact *have* is a central pillar of decolonial and postcolonial discourse. Even if it is not the case that "it is the Palestinians who are the weakest," are they not among the weak?

Arguing that this is *not* the case constitutes a crucial element in Levinas's decolonial defense of the post-1967 State of Israel. Not only are the Palestinians not weakest, or even weak—the main thrust of Levinas's argument consists in identifying them with the *imperial West*. He does so by deploying the ethics of infinite responsibility for others and the narrative of the Passion of the Holocaust.

The operation is articulated in the most integral way in the aforementioned 1969 essay on Paul Claudel, "Poetry and the Impossible," where Levinas draws on the Catholic poet to trace the basic lines of holy history and the "martyrdom of Auschwitz." At a certain point in this short essay, Levinas confirms that "the rights to their 'native land' invoked by the Arab refugees can certainly not be treated unjustly."[57] Thus, there is some—reserved—acknowledgment of Palestinian claims vis-à-vis the State of Israel and even of the Palestinian suffering and statelessness caused by the

Jewish state, both in 1948 and in 1967. Is not the State of Israel a source and name of injustice here? Can Levinas's post-1968 justification of the Jewish state, namely the defense of Jews against Western persecution in view of Auschwitz, apply to the dispossession of Palestinians? Levinas, aware of the difficulty, evokes a strong argument that may be leveled *against* the attempt to justify the dispossession of Palestinians in the name of the Holocaust: "The Arab peoples would not have to answer for German atrocities, or cede their lands to the victims of Hitlerism!"[58] Or, as he writes in his introduction to *Beyond the Verse* from 1981, "of course, it is the West, not the Arab world, which bears the responsibility for Auschwitz."[59] Can the defense of persecuted Jews in Europe justify violence against Arabs in the Middle East? Ought Palestinians be forced to bear the responsibility for and consequences of the Holocaust?

This proposition unsettles common notions of justice. Yet here is precisely the point at which Levinas deploys his uncommon ethics of infinite responsibility for others. The claim that Arabs bear no responsibility for Auschwitz is correct, he states in the 1981 introduction, "unless one accepts that the responsibility of men cannot be divided, and that all men are responsible for all others."[60] Each person is responsible for all others. This rule is symmetrical. It means not only that Arabs are responsible for Jews but also that Jews—and everyone else—are responsible for Arabs. But Levinas's ethics is asymmetrical. It states that "I am infinitely responsible for others." Through the Passion of the Holocaust, this asymmetry is transposed from individual phenomenology into collective historiography. The Holocaust revealed the absolute victims of humanity, the people of Israel, who in their passion testify to the superhuman ethics of infinite responsibility for others. According to this logic, however, by virtue of radical martyrdom performed for the sake of others, the Jewish people become the paradigmatic Other of the West—and, accordingly, the ultimate object of all human responsibility. *The Other is Israel.*

To make this point, the 1981 introduction explicitly refers back to the 1969 essay: "Can anyone amongst mankind wash his hands of all this flesh gone up in smoke?" Indeed, here Levinas proclaims (emphasis in the original), "*every survivor of the Hitlerian massacres—whether or not a Jew—is other in relation to martyrs.* He is consequently responsible and unable to remain silent. He is obligated to Israel for the reasons that oblige every man. These reasons are therefore common to Jew and Arab and ought to help them to talk to each other."[61]

While every person is infinitely responsible for all others, nevertheless the Passion of Israel as manifested in the Holocaust presents an extreme, exceptional kind of victimhood, an elite of suffering, of absolute otherness toward which everyone else is the self-same and therefore bears infinite responsibility. This absolute responsibility to Israel has an eschatological, messianic character, inasmuch as it—very much like Saint Paul's faith in Christ—transcends all religious and ethnics divides and so unites humanity "beyond all national differences."[62] Not only Jews and Germans, not only Europeans and Westerners, but every man, Arabs included, is "obligated to Israel." Palestinian refugees and those under occupation may have rights, but they also have to carry obligations vis-à-vis the Jewish people.

A visible inversion—and I think perversion—of a basic principle of Levinas's ethics of otherness occurs here, one based on the asymmetry of infinite responsibility of myself for others: the infinite responsibility of the Jewish people for humanity generates an infinite obligation of humanity to Israel. This obligation justifies the dispossession carried out by the military power of the Jewish state against Palestinians, whose "rights to their 'native land' . . . can certainly not be treated unjustly." Does Levinas have to be read this way? Could his statement that the responsibility of all post-Holocaust humanity to martyrs is "common to Jew and Arab and ought to help them to talk to each other" be interpreted as saying that Jews should also acknowledge the suffering of Arabs from violence exercised by the Jewish nation-state? Could Levinas be understood as calling to take transnational responsibility for all victims, both Jews and Arabs?

Levinas's texts make such an interpretation difficult. His argument proceeds to make exactly the opposite claim, namely that *no* comparison, symmetry, or reciprocity exists between Jewish and Arab suffering. According to his analysis, the basic problem of the Israeli-Arab and Israeli-Palestinian conflict is precisely the commonly stated *false* perception that their suffering is symmetrical. This false symmetry is established by applying the categories of the Western episteme: those of reason, light, formal universalism, and humanism, the same that subjugate ethics to politics. The 1981 introduction bemoans, as the very *cause* of the conflict around the State of Israel, the "abstract nakedness" of ideas such as democracy and human rights when detached from prophetic ethics and alienated in "the purely political game."[63] "Politics, arising everywhere," we read in his essay from 1969, "falsifies" the actual moral reality,[64] which, according to Levinas, is defined by the absolute victimhood of—and accordingly the absolute obligation of responsibility toward—the persecuted Jewish people.

In Levinas's essay, not only is the comparison of Jewish and Palestinian suffering a false Western perception, but the very assertion of Palestinian rights also becomes a performance of Western immorality, which to his eyes establishes an *identification between the West and the Palestinians*. The responsibility for the Shoah accordingly lies with the Palestinians as humans and as representatives of European moral turpitude. "What deafness to the call of consciousness!" decries Levinas against the claim that Arabs are not responsible for the Holocaust. And in response to the suggestion that Palestinians have also suffered, and at the hands of Jews, he asks: "Can every human relationship be reduced to assessing damage and interest and every problem to balancing the accounts? The right to a 'birthplace' invoked by Arab refugees can certainly not be treated unjustly. . . . But can the call of the land silence the cries of Auschwitz which will echo until the end of time?"[65]

The claims of Palestinian refugees, dispossessed and rendered homeless and stateless by Jewish military violence, are presented here as voicing the "call of the land," not the transcendent holiness of victimhood but instead the immanence of autochthonous, powerful, and triumphant being: "Will the vast spaces inhabited by the Arabs not lose some of their majestic dimensions and the Arab Fatherland lose its heart through the amputation of a tract of land whose immensity is measured only in centuries of Holy History, a history never interrupted in the soul of Israel?"[66]

Once again, we encounter the identification of Arabs with immanence, territory, and racial imperialism observed in Levinas's pre-1968 historiography. The difference is that the earlier narrative featured this territorial imperialism as characterizing non-Western, pagan, and Germanic barbarism in contrast to Western humanism, whereas the post-1968, decolonial narrative, as we saw, collapses the distinction and posits European humanism itself as imperialist. Accordingly, by asserting land rights against the State of Israel and thereby against the protection of Jews sent to Auschwitz, Palestinians turn out not to be "the weakest," as anti-imperialist leftists would have it, but rather to represent, at least in the Israeli-Arab conflict, immoral and anti-Jewish Western imperialism.

The Persecuted State

Consequently, this inversion of perspective allows Levinas to develop a further, more radical interpretation of the meaning of the Jewish state in holy history. This interpretation does not posit the State of Israel as the *end* of Jewish defenselessness, that is, as marking the overcoming of Jewish martyrdom through Jewish military self-defense: the State of Israel is the *continuation* of the Passion of Israel, not its *end*. Since the Arabs may be considered an extension of the imperial violence of Europe, of the Germans, the State of Israel can be considered as presenting not defense or redemption from suffering but on the contrary an extended condition of Jewish victimhood, of anti-Jewish persecution. Note that in Levinas's discourse, the Jewish state does not end or attenuate anything, nor does it merely relocate the site of anti-Judaism from Europe to the Middle East; rather, it brings about the *expansion* of European Jew-hatred. "Immortal anti-Semitism continues in the form of anti-Zionism," writes Levinas in the introduction to the first talmudic readings from 1968, thereby melding Europe and the Arab world into one great anti-Israeli civilization.[67]

The notion of the State of Israel as continuing the history of Israel's passion—the messianic essence of the Jewish people as the "suffering servant"—is articulated in strong terms in another essay of the same fateful year of 1968, "From the Rise of Nihilism and the Carnal Jew." We have noted Levinas's call for a reconfiguration of the French Jewish worldview after the crisis of French Jews in 1967. In describing this deep crisis, Levinas writes that Jews in France were "unable to accept with an untroubled soul the possible disappearance of Israel and extermination of the Israelis."[68] Levinas's words suggest that French Jews like himself relived in the 1967 war the trauma of the Holocaust—and the additional trauma caused by the "untroubled soul" of non-Jews in the face of a new extermination.

It is now noteworthy for us how in "From the Rise of Nihilism and the Carnal Jew," the return of Auschwitz signifies not the failure of the Jewish State (to protect Jews from persecution) but rather its very essence. Recall how Levinas's pre-1968 narrative already presents the conflicted State of Israel as restoring "danger" to Jewish existence, thereby fostering Jewish disassimilation and renewal. This logic is radicalized in the post-1968 narrative, in which hardship is no longer just a tool of redetaching Jews from Europe. Rather, suffering becomes the essence of Jewish being: "In the Jewish life in the West which tried to be completely inner, the State of Israel achieves the return of the possibility of abnegation: as in the period when people went to the stake rather than be baptized, we once again have a Jewish value that, to those most assimilated into it, appears worthy of an ultimate sacrifice. The State of Israel, in this sense, constitutes the greatest event in modern Judaism."[69]

The creation of a Jewish state is presented as the greatest event in modern Judaism not because it ended the historical weakness of Jews but, *on the contrary*, because it countered Jewish assimilation in the West, the conversion of Jews to European citizens, and to hegemony and *reaffirmed* the vulnerability, exposure, and self-sacrifice of the Jewish people—it *renewed* the Passion of Israel.

Levinas's perception of the State of Israel as reenacting the martyrdom of the Holocaust and thus restoring the Jewish people's moral agency in victimhood is vividly presented in his 1979 essay "Politics After!" which deals with the peace process with Egypt. In this text, Levinas dismisses the portrayal of the Jewish state in post-1967 decolonial France as "an armed and dominating State, one of the great military powers of the Mediterranean basin, against the unarmed Palestinian people whose existence Israel does not recognize," an "imperialist endeavour" that has arisen from "Western ideologies."[70] The real situation is the opposite. The sovereign State of Israel in fact "still carries pain and dereliction in its depths": "In its very real strength, is not Israel also the most fragile, the most vulnerable thing in the world, in the midst of its neighbours, undisputed nations, rich in natural allies, and surrounded by their lands? Lands, lands and lands, as far as the eye can see."[71] The actual agents of imperialism are the Arabs, whereas Israel remains the victim, now doubly persecuted, by Arab violence and by misguided European critique.

In contrast to the territorial imperialism of the Arab world, possessing "lands, lands and lands," and in contrast to Palestinian refugees' attachment to their "native land," the relation of the State of Israel to the land it occupies is argued to arise from the basic Jewish condition of landlessness. The Jewish state holds its land as "a final place in which to entrench itself," as the "dead end" (*impasse*): "It is to this position of dead end that the words heard in Israel refer: *en bererah*, 'no choice'!"[72] The Israeli military is accordingly not an army of conquerors and occupiers; it is the Israel Defense Force, "the defenders of the last ramparts." Levinas goes on to inscribe the violence exercised by the State of Israel in a long line of acts of Jewish martyrdom in anti-imperial struggles, stretching from the Roman Empire to the Third Reich: "the struggle of the Warsaw ghetto up in arms but with no ground to which to withdraw, where each step taken in retreat counts and costs as if it were everything, a struggle from which the memory of Massada is never absent, and which one dares to denounce as dependent on Western ideologies."[73]

The State of Israel figures as the last manifestation of the Passion of Israel, forever persecuted and tortured, forever the weak Messiah crucified by the powers of this world, the powers that be—the Romans, the Germans, and now the Arabs.[74]

The sharpest formulation of Levinas's post-1968 narrative of the State of Israel as the suffering Messiah, the very paradigm of the human, is provided in the 1975 talmudic reading, "Damages due to Fire." We have seen how Levinas uses a midrashic passage in this text to present the defense of the State of Israel as a holy war. Let us turn now to another midrash he comments on in the same text. In the passage in question, the Talmud stages a confrontation between two biblical verses. The *first verse* instructs people in times of danger to go inside, to stay home: "Go my people, enter your chambers, and lock your doors behind you" (Isaiah 26:20). The *second verse*, however, can be read as saying that the inside, too, is dangerous, terrifying: "The sword shall deal death without; within, there shall be terror" (Deuteronomy 32:25). The world can be so threatening that one feels persecuted even at home. Levinas deploys this midrashic notion as key to historiography: this "is the twentieth century." At the center of this history stands the State of Israel. In the figure of radical persecution, which threatens even at home, "you will see the entire problem of present-day Israel appear."[75] The State of Israel is thus the difficult situation of the Jewish people in the violent twentieth century. Living outside any state, in diasporic statelessness, they faced Auschwitz, and living in their own state, at home, they face Arab terror.

And yet, in this impossible situation, in this *impasse*, Levinas affirms, "one must go back inside, even if there is terror inside." Even if Jews are threatened both outside and inside Israel, they nonetheless ought to be in the Jewish state: "That inside in which there is fear is still the only refuge. It is the no-exit. It is the no-place, the non-place." The State of Israel is the paradoxical nonplace of the Jews, the home of their homeless existence, the state of their essential statelessness, the glory of their cross. We recognize here Levinas's post-1968 phenomenology, that of *Otherwise Than Being*, where the subject's proper being consists in relinquishing his proper being, in suffering, self-offering, and martyrdom. In the 1975 talmudic reading, Levinas proceeds to posit the—midrashically portrayed—State of Israel explicitly as the paradigm of humanity: "the no-exit of Israel is probably the human no-exit," and "all men are on the verge of being in the situation of the State of Israel. The State of Israel is a category."[76]

But the Jewish state is more than just a category, a model for potential humanity—it is *the* agent of true, moral humanity in history. Eschatologically speaking, it *is* humanity. Terror, or Israel's internal troubles, "is the suffering of Israel as universal suffering." To seal the semantic merger between the persecuted Jews in the Holocaust and the State of Israel in decolonial discourse, Levinas concludes by paraphrasing the famous identification of the May '68 revolutionaries with diasporic Jews—"We are all German Jews"—by inverting its meaning: "All men are of Israel. In my way, I would say: 'We are all Israeli Jews.' We, that is, all human beings."[77] It is not as diaspora but as members of their own state that the Jewish people come to constitute the messianic collective of the decolonial age. The State of Israel is the State of the Passion, the instituted violence necessary to sustain the existence of the victimized community as a victim. And the Talmud, where Levinas reads this vision, is nothing less than the Torah of the decolonial state.

CONCLUSION
From Logos to Talmud

IT IS A DEEP EPISTEMIC CRISIS OF OUR time that Western universalism has been intertwined with Western imperialism and modern European philosophy and science with colonialism. In an attempt to break out of this epistemo-political predicament and decolonize itself, the Western episteme has turned from universality toward difference. It has sought to interrupt sameness and make room for otherness—for diversity, multiplicity, plurality.

But making room for the other is simultaneously a form of integration. Acknowledging and accommodating difference is a form of containment. In other words, the turn to difference risks becoming yet another instrument of universalism, and decolonization risks becoming a new element of imperialism.

To examine this contemporary syndrome more closely, this book has presented a study of the work of Emmanuel Levinas. It has shown how Levinas offered more than an individual ethics of alterity that disrupts structures of knowledge, politics, and history. My analyses have pointed in Levinas's texts to an intervention that does not bid farewell to philosophy, thought, and knowledge but, on the contrary, seeks to transform them from within. Levinas offers otherness not only as the basis of ethics but also as the basis of knowledge, as "optics," as first philosophy. He offers an epistemology of otherness.

The studies collected in this book further show how Levinas posits an actual episteme of otherness, that is, a concrete historical culture of knowledge founded on the relation to the other—Judaism. For hegemonic knowledge, which is founded on sameness, Judaism, the episteme of otherness, appears as epistemic otherness, as the other. The epistemo-political argument of this book is that, for Levinas, the epistemology of otherness embodied in Judaism is intertwined with the politics of otherness incarnated in the collective of Israel.

The readings I have presented in this book render visible two periods in the development of Levinas's work: one before 1968 and one after. These two periods represent phases in the elaboration of his epistemology of otherness and his reflection on the political epistemology of Jewish otherness. I have characterized the first period as colonial and the second as decolonial and have argued that the latter represents a critical reflection on the former. My analyses have revealed how the two periods of Levinas's Jewish discourse of otherness also feature phases of abuse of Jewish discourse by the imperial sameness of Western logos, each time a double abuse—one in phenomenology and one in eschatology, one in the name of philosophy and one in the name of prophecy.

Before 1968, Levinas established the conceptual foundations for every approach to otherness. A relation to otherness, he argued, can only take place from the position of a self and as a movement of transcendence from this position to an elsewhere, to an exteriority. Insofar as this relation is an epistemological principle ("optics"), I call it knowledge. But the knowledge of otherness, Levinas stresses, is no theory, no consciousness of objects that brings the other to the self. Rather, this knowledge, which drives the self beyond itself, takes the form of command, law, responsibility. Otherness is known, seen, through ethics.

The medium in which this ethical relation to the other takes place, where the self is commanded by exteriority, is language. For early Levinas, the seminal speech that introduced otherness into human history is prophecy, founded on the commandment laid down in the Hebrew Bible, "You shall not murder."

This early insight into knowledge of otherness as ethics is presented—and betrayed—by Levinas in the language of sameness and, more precisely, in two forms of Western logos. In his pre-1968 phenomenology, Levinas narrates the experience of otherness, the encounter with a command, as constituting the self as separate, the revealed infinite as instituting totality. Ethics justifies ontology, and prophecy grounds philosophy. In short, the positing of otherness as the condition of sameness does not unsettle the self but reaffirms it.

This reaffirmation takes concrete historical and political form in Levinas's pre-1968 eschatology. This logos presents otherness as the founding principle of Western civilization and places Israel at the heart of the West as *the* people of the other. The people of the other is, in relation to other peoples, the people of others, whose political form is the state of others.

Knowledge of otherness defines the State of Israel as an ethical state, whose violent conquest is just. In Levinas's early eschatology, the epistemology of otherness serves to justify Israel's war against the Palestinians in colonial terms, that is, as spearheading Western humanism.

My analysis has suggested a decolonial turn in Levinas's work after 1968. The abuse of otherness for the sake of the self becomes a central concern of his thinking, in an act of profound self-critique. Levinas's later epistemology clearly locates this abuse of otherness as taking place in language—more specifically, in perfected, completed speech, in language as that which has been "said." The said functions as a logos that inscribes every revelation of otherness within a unifying system, within the same fabric. In contrast to the said, Levinas posits language in the mode of saying as the dimension of sense making, of signifying. If the said generates a continuum of logical homogeneity, the saying opens up a heterogeneous space of hermeneutic events in which otherness is encountered as a new site of meaning. To counter the abuse of otherness in logos, Levinas points to the necessity of reducing the said back to the saying, of returning from logic to hermeneutics, through a logoclastic operation of unsaying, which is the true vocation of philosophy.

But beyond philosophy, the said of which is always logos and which can therefore only encounter otherness through unsaying, Levinas also points to the possibility of other modes of said, poetic or prophetic, which would give rise to other, nonabusive, nonreductive modes of knowing otherness. The specific mode the thinker of otherness chooses for his later book is what he calls the prophetic, consisting in an ethical language characterized by hyperbole, by the superlative—by the "beyond." Within the concrete historical archive of biblical prophecy, I have suggested that this mode of speech, which has the function of disabusing and surpassing a preliminary, primary prophetic said, corresponds to postbiblical forms of hyperbolic discourse such as those found in Kabbalah, negative theology, and the New Testament.

My reading has problematized Levinas's later decolonial and more radical turn to otherness beyond logos by showing how his superlative speech, rather than countering logos, produces a superlative mode of logos, a superlogos that reproduces and amplifies the abuse of the other for the interests of the self. His post-1968 phenomenology posits, beyond the early self constituted by the ethical encounter with the other, a self who *is* the other, whose own being consists in otherness than being. The existence of this subject consists not in enjoyment but in exile, suffering, and self-sacrifice. The ethical relation, described as being-for-the-other, or responsibility, does not only limit the ontic powers of the subject through a negation ("You shall not murder"). Rather, being-for-the-other constitutes the positive being of the self: "Here I am." My analysis shows how radicalized inscription of otherness into the being of the self also radicalizes the abuse. The hyperbolic responsibility for the other distinguishes the self as a martyr, a holy other, a victim with a special claim to justice.

Levinas's post-1968 eschatology translates this abuse into a concrete political situation. Colonial Israel, a righteous messianic conqueror, the avant-garde of Western civilization, is replaced by a decolonial figure of Israel: a weak, persecuted, paradigmatic victim of the West. What epitomizes Jewish alterity and distinguishes Israel as *the* state of others, demanding infinite responsibility from the world, including the Palestinians, is not the prophetic vision of justice so much as the martyrdom of the Holocaust. The ontological weakness of the alterity-based Jewish collective provides a justification for the warring Jewish state in terms of self-defense. Moreover, the ongoing state of war, together with the international condemnation of Israeli politics, ensures Israel's continued existence in a state of victimhood.

I have noted that the conceptual dynamics and epistemo-political constellations and paradoxes this study traces in Levinas's work may serve as a general key for understanding the development of post-Holocaust Jewish and Israeli thought and politics, especially after 1967/8. In recent months, in response to the Hamas attacks on October 7, 2023, a new, more radicalized and explicit discourse has emerged, putting forth notions of transhistorical, ontological Jewish victimhood. These notions serve to detach violence from its geopolitical context, that is, the decades-long oppression of Palestinians by the State of Israel, to posit this state as the current victim of a timeless, metaphysical, theological anti-Jewish hatred and portray the Palestinian armed struggle as a new Holocaust. This assertion of otherness, weakness, and victimhood generates, motivates, and serves to justify the genocidal brutality of Israel's mass destruction of Gaza. Levinas would have been appalled at how easily, for the Jewish state today, "Here I am" trumps "You shall not murder."

Is this perversion of otherness in logos necessary? Is an epistemology of otherness at all possible in the language of philosophy? If so, at what point exactly is it betrayed in Levinas's narratives? Does the distortion of ethics take place in the justification of war, of state violence, or of the state itself? Or does the betrayal of otherness occur when it is mobilized to constitute the self, the collective one and perhaps even the individual subject? Can we conceive, imagine, or narrate a different, nonabusive discourse of alterity? Or is the only way to establish a real relation to epistemic otherness, the only way to decolonize philosophy, to undo the systematic structure of logos—as later Levinas called it, to unsay?

In fact, one of Levinas's two main countermeasures against the abuse of otherness in logos—first and foremost in phenomenology—is the skeptical self-unsaying of his own narrative through occasional invocation of the author's individual "I," whereby he distances himself from his own words and deplores "the very utterance by which I state [the absolute exteriority of the other] and whose claim to truth refutes the unsurpassable character of the face-to-face relation."[1]

But Levinas's oeuvre puts forward another alternative—the Talmud. I propose to understand his turn to the discursive form of talmudic readings, especially after 1968, as his most radical attempt to turn away from the philosophical logos, not only by reducing its said to saying but by turning to a different mode of saying altogether, a different kind of said. The talmudic text can indeed be described as a mode of discourse not shaped by the systematic, linear, coherent form of philosophical logos. This text is woven around utterances that can be characterized, in philosophical terminology, as ethical. Talmudic ethics, however, does not speak in superlatives; it does not produce a hyperlogos. Instead, the Talmud is said in the language of law, commandment, or mitzvah.

Most importantly, the universe generated by the talmudic said, the cosmos that holds its individual sayings together as one archive, is not governed by logical relations that produce a single narrative, a book. The talmudic archive, this collection of commandments, is held together not by a logical force but by a hermeneutic one, that is, by mutual interactions between instances of meaning, by acts of quoting, reciting, reading, and interpreting, in a word, by acts of learning, of *talmud*. Could not the talmudic or rabbinic discourse be seen, in terms of historical epistemology, as a radical deconstructive intervention in the prophetic archive, a powerful resistance to logos—philosophical or theological—and a sustained dispersion, a diasporization of the unified book, the Bible?

Was Levinas able through his readings to provide access to the Talmud as an episteme of otherness, a world of knowledge that accommodates difference, an archive for epistemic decolonization? The answer to this question requires a study of Levinas's talmudic hermeneutics.

NOTES

Introduction

1. On the question of Levinas and the feminine, see Chanter, "Ontological Difference, Sexual Difference, and Time," 106; Irigaray, "The Fecundity of the Caress"; Vasey, "Faceless Women and Serious Others"; Katz, "From Eros to Maternity"; Katz, "Reinhabiting the House of Ruth."

2. Derrida, "Violence."

3. Emmanuel, *Is It Righteous to Be?*, 137.

4. Emmanuel, *Éthique et infini*, 89, 85 (EI). References to Levinas's works in this book mention the page in the French edition followed by the page in the English translation. All the translations below follow the published translations, with my adjustments.

5. Judith Butler, in *Parting Ways*, argues that the idea of diasporic ethics finds expression in Judaism as in a specific "idiom" (9); the political application of this idea requires translating it into other idioms, thereby ceding its specific textual or historical grounding in Jewish tradition. As we will see, translating Jewish ethics "into Greek" was a key notion for Levinas. For a similar recent critique of Levinas that also references Butler's book, see Marsh, *Saying Peace*. In her *The Figural Jew: Politics and Identity in Postwar French Thought*, Sarah Hammerschlag argues that Levinas asserts the Jewish ethics of uprootedness as a "universal idea . . . disassociated from a people, a race, an ethnicity" (149) and criticizes the exception he makes of Zionism as incoherence. In her later book *Broken Tablets: Levinas, Derrida, and the Literary Afterlife of Religion*, she acknowledges that Levinas's Zionism correctly follows from his identification of ethics as Jewish: "The tradition that produced this ethical teaching had to be protected" (160). To counter this identification, Hammerschlag suggests that "we engage with being Jewish as a literary figure," "as a trope" (*Figural Jew*, 266). In his recent *Levinas's Talmudic Turn: Philosophy and Jewish Thought*, Ethan Kleinberg has made a more complex argument, suggesting that it is in the Jewish tradition, in the Talmud, in contrast to philosophy, that Levinas finds "a site of understanding uncoupled from historical development" (163), such that his *Talmudic Readings* offer a "logic of Jewish identity . . . predicated on a displacement of the self" (173). Kleinberg proposes to "follow Levinas away from Levinas" by deriving from his Talmud "an understanding of ethics and responsibilities that does not allow itself to rest on its historical past or its status in the present" (179). Reading in the Talmud the notion that "to achieve human universality . . . we must be prepared to jettison our prior and proper identity" (181) sounds to me like a form of Paulinism.

6. Fagenblat, *Covenant*, xii and passim.

7. Moten, "There Is No Racism Intended," in *The Universal Machine*, 31. Moten initially reiterates the critique formulated by Andrew McGettigan in "The Philosopher's Fear of Alterity: Levinas, Europe and Humanities 'without Sacred History,'" which points out that Levinas's notion of alterity does not imply horizontal difference but vertical transcendence, "height." As such, it fosters not cultural pluralism but monotheism, which, for McGettigan, features a Judeo-Christian specificity to the exclusion of other cultures and is "not a universal

possibility" (15). Moten, however, goes on to diagnose in the "specific and exclusionary Judeo-Christian monotheism" (6) the working of the "Universal Machine" of philosophy itself, which always strives to surpass the particular being of "things"—"the way we are right here right now" (22). The specific *"omnicidal* drive" of Greco-Judeo-Christian civilization lies in its universalist desire. Resistance to universalism, Moten suggests, lies in the dissident performance of the "thingly" that refuses generalized comprehension, namely in a "gesture of incomprehension," in "phonochoreographic performance," (9) which he identifies in "black radical tradition" and in Derrida, in contrast to Levinas and "German-Jewish tradition" (42). See also Bernasconi, "Who Is My Neighbor?"; Critchley, "Five Problems in Levinas's View of Politics"; Eisenstadt, "Eurocentrism and Colorblindness."

8. John Drabinski, *Levinas and the Postcolonial: Race, Nation, Other,* criticizes Levinas's ethics for its detachment from "historical experience" (193), his Other being abstracted from all national, racial, and cultural identity and his philosophical work lacking reference to the concrete contexts of colonialism and the Holocaust. Drabinski proposes "decolonizing Levinas's thought" (2) through "incarnate historiography" (10). I later show how Levinas's thought is engaged in very concrete historiography, including colonialism and Holocaust, in his Jewish writings and through the figure of the Jewish. Drabinski dismisses the philosophical relevance of Levinas's investment in the Jewish episteme as confining it to the "particularity of a geography of ideas" (xi), which is hard to reconcile with Drabinski's decolonizing insistence on situating thought in concrete historical embodiments.

9. Samuel Moyn, *Origins of the Other: Emmanuel Levinas between Revelation and Ethics,* describes Levinas as "an insider to European philosophy" (23) who invented an "imagined Judaism" (16). In the same year, Leora Batnitzky argued in *Leo Strauss and Emmanuel Levinas: Philosophy and the Politics of Revelation* that "in the context of a philosophy and ethics of the 'other,' Levinas does not recognize the 'otherness' of the Jewish tradition" (202). Benny Lévy, in *Etre juif,* thinking "with Levinas, in spite of Levinas" (16), criticizes Levinas's "philosophical conversion" of Judaism, claiming that his work "converts a proposition of Jewish facticity into a supposedly universal proposition, into Greek, into 'university language'" (40, my translations).

10. Bernasconi, "Who Is My Neighbor?": "if one wants to find resources in Levinas to counteract what is most totalizing in Levinas and dismissive of ethnic difference, cannot one find it in his own understanding of what it means to be a Jew?" (18).

11. For critiques of this operation of secularism, see Asad, *Formations of the Secular;* Anidjar, *The Jew, the Arab;* Masuzawa, *The Invention of World Religions.*

12. Levinas and Kearny, "Dialogue with Emmanuel Levinas," 18.

13. Simon Critchley, for instance, in his introduction to *The Cambridge Companion to Levinas,* explains why Levinas, in his philosophical work, cites Plato rather than Jewish texts through his "basic belief in reason," commending him for not "reducing philosophical universality to the particularism of a specific religious tradition" (23; I note that Critchley sees no universality compromised in citing Shakespeare). John Drabinski, *Levinas and the Postcolonial,* does see the universality of Levinas's philosophy compromised by the "insular" (xvi) specificity of his commitment to Judaism as "religious" (xvi), which Drabinski considers "chauvinistic, even just plainly violent, in a transnational context" (18). Andrew McGettigan, "The Philosopher's Fear," decrys traces of "religious inheritance" (15) in Levinas's philosophy, denouncing notions such as the Other, infinite, and exteriority as drawing validity not from "phenomenological analysis" (18) but from the "representation of a specific

religious tradition," an illegitimate inspiration he harshly castigates as "fidelity and ignorance trump[ing] science" (23). Fred Moten, *The Universal Machine*, joins the denunciation of "a specific religious tradition" (8) that undermines the universality of Levinas's philosophy (an idea of universality that Moten himself then critically proceeds to undermine), noting that "his face-to-face encounters are mediated by a highly circumscribed textual canon" (19). Sarah Hammerschlag, in "Reading May '68 through a Levinasian Lens," also contrasts Levinas's "movement back to textual study, back to the rabbis" with the "universalization of the modality of 'being-Jewish'" as "a philosophical position" (551).

14. Michael Fagenblat, in *Covenant of Creatures*, characterizes Levinas's project as a secularizing attempt to offer a "philosophical interpretation of Judaism" (xxii) that would establish the "unity of Judaism and philosophy" (xvii), which Fagenblat demonstrates in the work of Maimonides, a paragon of Jewish philosophy. Levinas's project would thus counter the problematic "partitioning" of Judaism and philosophy and reunite them as two origins of Western thought—as Marlène Zarader claims Heidegger did earlier without admitting it; see *The Unthought Debt: Heidegger and the Hebraic Heritage*. Consequently, Fagenblat describes Levinas's division between his philosophy and Jewish thought as "denying the Jewish element of his thought [that] was quite simply the price of its admission into the arena of French philosophy" (xiv). Similarly, in *Correlations in Rosenzweig and Levinas*, Robert Gibbs, although he acknowledges that for Levinas the "Hebrew" and the "Greek" feature as two different "modes of thought" (157), describes the division between Levinas's philosophical and Jewish writings as a "segregation" due to "the regnant postreligious consciousness, combined with a never completely absent anti-Semitic scent, [that] makes the reception of boldly Jewish thought by the philosophical community difficult" (22).

15. In his *Levinas's Talmudic Turn* of 2021, Ethan Kleinberg formulates this position by suggesting that Levinas's talmudic readings evoke an epistemic difference between a secular academic discourse and a talmudic one and offering a reflection on Levinas's talmudic readings that proceeds in two parallel perspectives, secular and talmudic. I subscribe to Kleinberg's daring intervention, which attempts to mobilize talmudic epistemology to internally challenge academic forms of knowledge. Nonetheless, as I explain in this introduction, my epistemological analysis is different from Kleinberg's, even opposite to it. I also consider as a position of epistemic difference, which is closer to mine, Annabel Herzog's *Levinas's Politics: Justice, Mercy, Universality*. Indeed, Herzog—referencing Fagenblat—insists that for Levinas there is "no irreducible difference between the philosophical and Jewish traditions" (4), such that his two corpora, the philosophical and the talmudic, are in fact two "kinds of philosophical writings" (14), different only in "style and language" (4). Yet Herzog's basic claim is that Levinas's two corpora express different "philosophical concerns" (5), ethics and politics/ontology. She describes this division as a difference between "mode[s] of thought" (5) and traces it back to Levinas's distinction between "said" and "saying," which is "arguably the most important . . . conceptual distinction of his work" (15). The diverging "language and style" would signify that the philosophical and talmudic corpora are divided by Levinas's most important epistemic difference.

16. Levinas and Kearny, "Dialogue with Emmanuel Levinas," 18–19.

17. Cf. Butler, "Can the 'Other' of Philosophy Speak?"

18. Derrida, "Violence."

19. Levinas, *Totalité et infini*, 33, 43 (TI).

20. TI 33, 43.

21. See, for instance, Heidegger, "Aus einem Gespräch."

22. Jonas, *Gnosis und spätantiker Geist: Die mythologische Gnosis*; Jonas, *Gnosis und spätantiker Geist: Von der Mythologie zur mystischen Philosophie*; Jonas, *Gnostic Religion*; on Jonas's project see Lapidot, "Gnosis und Spätantiker Geist II."

23. Other scholars have noted this coding. Sarah Hammerschlag indicates Biblical "tropes" in Levinas's philosophy and suggests that in his philosophical writings, "the proper name of Judaism is called *ethics*" (*Figural Jew*, 142). I would rather say that in Levinas's Jewish writings, the proper name of ethics is called *Judaism*.

24. Levinas, *Autrement qu'être ou au-delà de l'essence*, 169, 262 (AE).

25. The question of politics has become central in current readings, discussions, and critiques of Levinas. The most systematic analysis so far is Howard Caygill, *Levinas and the Political*. See also Horowitz and Horowitz, *Difficult Justice*; and more recently Herzog, "Levinas's Ethics, Politics, and Zionism." In her even more recent book, *Levinas's Politics*, Herzog argues that Levinas's philosophical work is too purely ethical and nonpolitical or even antipolitical; she finds his politics rather in the talmudic readings. I think Herzog has a point, but I see more continuity between Levinas's two corpora.

26. Michael Fagenblat, *Covenant*, speaks of "Levinas 1 and Levinas 2" (xxv, 98), pointing at the "seismic shift" between Levinas's two great philosophy works, which he characterizes as a turn "from a metaphysical to a post-metaphysical account of ethics" (98). I accept this characterization without further political and historical contextualization.

27. The main volumes are Emmanuel Levinas, *Difficile liberté: Essai sur le judaïsme* (1963) (DL), translated by Sean Hand as *Difficult Freedom* (1990); Levinas, *Quatre lectures tal-mudiques* (1968) (QLT); Levinas, *Du sacré au saint: Cinq nouvelles lectures talmudiques* (1977) (DSS). The two last books are translated by Annette Aronowicz as *Nine Talmudic Readings* (1990). Levinas, *L'au-delà du verset: Lectures et discours talmudiques* (1982) (ADV), translated by G. D. Mole as *Beyond the Verse: Talmudic Readings and Lectures* (1994); Levinas, *A l'heure des nations* (1988) (HN), translated by M. B. Smith as *In the Time of the Nations* (1994).

28. See Annabel Herzog, *Levinas's Politics*, focused on the talmudic readings. Oona Eisenstadt, "Anti-utopianism Revisited," argues that Levinas's Jewish writings are not "confessional" but "social-political" or "communal" (121); see also Eisenstadt, "Levinas's Jewish Writings."

29. Here lies my disagreement with John Drabinski, *Levinas and the Postcolonial*, who claims that "the question [of historicity] does not seem to have occurred to him and, in the end, Levinas seems to have had very little interest in world affairs" (xi) and that "historical experience is alien to Levinasian thinking" (193). It is here that I also part ways with Ethan Kleinberg's *Levinas's Talmudic Turn*, although I share his gesture of asserting a fundamental difference between modern academic and talmudic epistemes—between "Philosophy and Jewish Thought," as his subtitle reads. Kleinberg argues that "secular" episteme ("Philosophy") is deeply *historical*, focused on finitude and politics, whereas the Talmud ("Jewish Thought") offers a "counter-historical claim that divine and ethical meaning transcends time or particular historical context" (10). My analysis emphasizes rather the opposite, i.e., the more abstract, timeless, Platonic nature of—also Levinas's—philosophy versus the concrete, historically and politically situatedness of his Jewish talmudic writings. Chapters 3 and 4 show how this division corresponds to Levinas's own analysis of the epistemic difference between Greco-Roman and Jewish universalism. My analysis is in this sense more similar to Annabel Herzog's in *Levinas's Politics*, where phenomenology stands for abstract ethics and Talmud for concrete politics. Nonetheless, Herzog—in the name of anti-Hegelianism—categorically removes thought, also political thought, from history, such that to her, in reading the Talmud philosophically, as "universal," Levinas completely detaches it from its historical,

Jewish context: "The Jewish context has little value as Jewish context" (26). I think that this analysis oversees Levinas's fundamental critique of Greco-Roman-Christian universalism— see chapter 3.

30. Cf. Lapidot, "Carl Schmitt's Warring Wars." On Levinas and Schmitt, see Rae, *The Problem of Political Foundations*; Botwinick, "Same/Other versus Friend/Enemy."

31. Löwith, *Meaning in History*; Taubes, *Abendländische Eschatologie*.

32. Oona Eisenstadt, "Levinas versus Levinas: Hebrew, Greek, and Linguistic Justice," argues that Levinas's Jewish writings are even more "Greek" in generating an epistemic totality than his philosophy, which she suggests is more dialogical—and therefore, in Levinas's terms, more "Hebrew."

33. Foucault, *L'Archéologie du savoir*.

34. DL 9, x.

35. Althusser, "Idéologie et appareils idéologiques d'État."

36. QLT 32, 14.

37. DSS 18, 98.

38. Robert Bernasconi, "Who Is My Neighbor?": for Levinas, "the designation 'Jew' is, at the very least primarily, not to be understood as an ethnic term. The term Israel applies to 'all humanity'" (19). Simon Critchley, "Five Problems": "Israel is the name of any people . . . any people that has submitted to the Law, non-Jewish as well as Jewish" (175). Michael Fagenblat, *Covenant*: "Jewishness, for Levinas, is a matter of ethical indifference—pure adiaphora, as Paul rightly calls it" (25); "Levinas's secularized political theology makes no assumptions about the identity of members of the body politic. If Levinas thinks of ethics as implying a model of political fraternity realized, for example, in the State of Israel, that is not because of Jews but because of Judaism" (187). Sarah Hammerschlag, *Figural Jew*: Judaism for Levinas is a "universal idea" "disassociated from a people, a race, an ethnicity" (149). Michael Morgan, *Cambridge Introduction to Emmanuel Levinas*: "terms such as 'Hebrew,' 'Greek,' 'Jew,' 'Israel,' and 'Zionism' ultimately are metaphors for Levinas, signifying fundamental features of the human condition, and the Jewish people, is, as it were, a living metaphor" (235). Annabel Herzog, *Levinas's Politics*: Israel is "not a specific people but humanity in its entirety" (27). Ethan Kleinberg, *Levinas's Talmudic Turn*: Levinas's talmudic readings "let go of essentialist notions of identity predicated on a particular history or people" (165).

39. QLT 76, 35.

40. That Levinas's talmudic readings are timeless is a basic claim of Ethan Kleinberg in *Levinas's Talmudic Turn*.

41. Scholars have already noticed this shift. Leora Batnitzky, *Leo Strauss and Emmanuel Levinas* (160), and Sarah Hammerschlag, *Figural Jew* (161), both diagnose enhanced affinity to "religious Zionism" in Levinas's work after 1967, which I think is not accurate enough to mark the turn. Annabel Herzog points at a shift in Levinas's thought around the publication of "Substitution" in 1968 without, however, referring to the historical context. See "Benny Levy versus Emmanuel Levinas on 'Being Jewish.'"

42. See Hammerschlag, "Reading May '68."

1. Ethics as Optics

1. I wonder whether it would not be more in line with Levinas's thought to translate the French *l'infini* not as the impersonal noun "infinity" but as "the infinite," an attribute that refers to something or someone with whom we can be in relation—see below.

2. Cf. Bernasconi, "Rereading Totality and Infinity," 33. See also Caygill, *Levinas and the Political*, 95; Batnitzky, *Leo Strauss and Emmanuel Levinas*, 32.

3. TI 9, 24.

4. David Klemm, "Levinas's Phenomenology of the Other and Language as the Other of Phenomenology," identifies not two but three different "voices" in *Totality and Infinity*: "the philosophical, the religious, and the prophetic" (407).

5. TI 75, 77.

6. TI 107, 104.

7. For the use of the term *religion*, see, for instance, TI 58, 64.

8. TI 105, 102.

9. On the discourse of "Semitism" and its deepistemizing effect, see Lapidot, *Jews out of the Question*.

10. Chapter 3 reveals in Levinas's Jewish writings the broader context of his pre-1968 geo-epistemology.

11. TI 241, 218.

12. TI 105, 102; 327, 294.

13. Leora Batnitzky describes this operation as Levinas's attempt to use Jewish thought to "challenge philosophy's hegemony from within" (*Leo Strauss and Emmanuel Levinas*, 28).

14. TI 5, 21.

15. TI 105, 102.

16. This is one of Derrida's central observations in "Violence and Metaphysics," for instance, 125–137.

17. TI 32, 34.

18. TI 327–328, 294.

19. TI 32, 34. Levinas has here in mind Heidegger's notion of Being (*Sein*), which is what we must necessarily already understand in order to enter into relation with anything, namely something that exists, that *is*. Being is the light we must already see in order to see everything else. In the light of Being, all things, as different and diverse as they may be, nonetheless *are* and so are accessible, knowable, visible as *beings*, which in Heidegger's *Being and Time* are mostly totalized into "the being" (*das Seiende*; not to be confused with Being, *Sein*). Heidegger is analyzed in *Totality and Infinity* as an accomplished and especially articulated version of Western philosophy, which "has for the most part been ontology" (TI 33, 43) and, as such, epistemology of totality.

20. TI 87, 87–88.

21. TI 5, 21.

22. TI 5, 21.

23. A similar understanding of nontotality in the sense of *plurality* as a condition for ethics can be found in Hermann Cohen, as noted by Gibbs, *Correlations*, 18; on Cohen's ethics see more recently Hollander, *Ethics out of Law*.

24. TI 5, 21.

25. Arendt, *Origins of Totalitarianism*, 427.

26. Arendt, *Origins of Totalitarianism*, 427; TI 37, 46.

27. TI 37–38, 46; 35, 44.

28. For a thoughtful reflection on the affinity and complementarity between Arendt's political thought and Levinas's ethics, see Topolki, *Arendt, Levinas and a Politics of Relationality*.

29. TI 104, 102; 269, 301. See Derrida's critique, "Violence," 186.

30. TI 197, 180; 326, 293.

31. TI 24–25, 36; 237; 340. Cf. to Husserl's definition of conscience (*Bewußtsein*) as "conscience of . . . ," namely as intention. Husserl, *Cartesianische Meditationen und Pariser Vorträge*, 8 and passim.

32. There is here an analogy to the epistemological implication of Carl Schmitt's Friend/ Foe distinction, which is always perceivable "only through existential interest and participation." See Schmitt, *Der Begriff des Politischen*, 26.

33. TI 11, 26. I concur with Leora Batnitzky that Levinas's "central argument in *Totality and Infinity* is for a separable, independent subject." See Batnitzky, *Leo Strauss and Emmanuel Levinas*, 30. For the same reason, I can only partly agree with Sarah Hammerschlag that in *Totality and Infinity*, "the other uproots me from myself" (*Figural Jew*, 130), since the encounter with the other also constitutes and grounds the self—see chapter 2. Similarly, I question Simon Critchley's reading of Levinas's entire philosophy as based on the problem of "how to escape" (*Problem with Levinas*, 26).

34. TI 29, 40. This notion clearly echoes Heidegger's fundamental characterization of Dasein's existence as "in each case mine, *je meines*." See Heidegger, *Sein und Zeit*, 41, 67 (SZ). References to this work are made with the page number of the German edition followed by the page number of the English translation.

35. TI 7, 22; 14, 28.

36. Scholem, *Major Trends in Jewish Mysticism*, 208.

37. TI 43, 51.

38. TI 126, 121; 8, 23. I therefore disagree with readings of Levinas's ethics as simply excluding knowledge, such as Simon Critchly's introduction to *Cambridge Companion to Levinas*, which states that for Levinas, "ethics is otherwise than knowledge" (11). My claim is that "ethics is optics" signifies a different kind of knowledge. I am more inclined to agree with Michael Fagenblat, *A Covenant of Creatures*, who reads Levinas as rejecting epistemology but clarifies that "Levinas never intended, much less proposed, to throw out the baby of truth with the bathwater of epistemology but rather provided an account that illuminated the ethical face of truth and belief" (163). Adrian Peperzak, *To the Other*, also warns against overlooking that ethics in Levinas is a common source for both activity and theory (124).

39. TI 15, 29. As already noted, within philosophy, Levinas indicates Plato's idea of the Good beyond Being as a subversive emergence of ethical knowledge within a basically ontological episteme. Beyond philosophy, he evokes the notions of revelation and "teaching," which can be translated into *torah*. I suggest that within Greek knowledge discourse, Levinas's notion of ethics-based knowledge, founded on the acknowledgment of radical otherness, is akin to what Hans Jonas identifies with the category *gnosis*. For Jonas, gnosis means knowledge that is essentially—in Levinas's sense—ethics. Gnosis is how the forbidden knowledge in the constitutive ethico-epistemic myth of the prophetic discourse, "knowledge of good and evil" (Genesis 2, 17), was called in its Greek translation, γνωστὸν καλοῦ καὶ πονηροῦ. See Jonas, *Gnostic Religion*, xviii. On Levinas and Jonas, see Vogel, "Jewish Philosophies after Heidegger"; and Lapidot, "Divine Invisibility and Ethical Epistemology in Late Modernity."

40. TI 212, 195.

2. The Philonic Encounter

1. TI 14, 28.

2. TI 14, 28; 9–10, 24.

3. This logic is the heart of Husserl's exercise, which seeks to show how perception of objects is founded in intention toward objects. Levinas calls this the "literal" meaning of Husserl's method, which Levinas spiritualizes so as to lead perception back behind objectal, theoretical intention, to a more fundamental, nonobjectal experience of difference. However, by doing so, Levinas not just extends or deepens Husserl's deduction; he twists its logic. To base totalizing knowledge on totalizing intention is straightforward—to base totality on nontotality less so. See Derrida's critique in "Violence," 128. Bernasconi, "Rereading," draws from the same observation of the foundation of totality on nontotality the opposite conclusion: "The conditions for the possibility of the experience of totality are at the same time the conditions for the impossibility of the experience of totality, in the sense that the rupture with totality shows that there never was a totality" (33).

4. TI 104, 102. Cf. Derrida, "Violence," passim.

5. Michael Fagenblat's book *Covenant* presents a compelling demonstration of how to read Levinas as a twentieth-century pendant of another paradigmatic Jewish philosopher, namely Maimonides. The paradigm of Philo, which I do not discuss in detail here, has in this context the advantage of constituting a preliminary intellectual connection between Athens and Jerusalem before the more complex intellectual history of Maimonides, who was facing at least three traditions of Greek Jewishness, namely the Christian, the Islamic, and the rabbinic. Leora Batnitzky also identifies—and contrasts with Leo Strauss's conception—the "fundamental harmony" of Athens and Jerusalem in Levinas. I later show how the situation changes in Levinas's post-1968 work.

6. The question of narrativity in Levinas's writing has been debated by scholars. Robert Bernasconi criticizes "attempts to shape [Levinas's] account into a narrative" ("Levinas's Ethical Critique," 255), My reading is more in line with Simon Critchley's reading of Levinas as a "linear narrative": "as if *Totality and Infinity* were an anti-Hegelian rewriting of the *Phenomenology of Spirit*" ("Il y a," 79). See also Critchley, *Problem with Levinas*, 10. Michael Fagenblat suggests that Levinas offers a "mythology of post-metaphysical reason" (*A Covenant of Creatures*, 44), while Michael Morgan speaks of "a philosophical story or fable" (*Cambridge Introduction*, 30). With respect to the eschatological nature of Levinas's fable, Leora Batnitzky recognizes in Levinas (similarly to Hermann Cohen) the same "messianic aspirations" that characterize the "Christianization of philosophy that defines German metaphysics" (*Leo Strauss and Emmanuel Levinas*, 68). Elliot Wolfson offers a precise analysis of the dynamics by the force of which attempts, such as Levinas's, of thinking transcendence beyond all imagination end up in new, powerful forms of figuration: "The disclosure of transcendence in any form of revelatory giving suggests that the mind submits in the end to imaging the unimaginable rather than remaining speechless in apophantic unknowing and aporetic suspension." See Wolfson, *Giving beyond the Gift*, 142. In the context of Levinas, Wolfson describes this dynamic as the "effacement of the nonphenomenolizable," which presents "too much of a hazard of making the anti-idolatry of formlessness into a form of idolatry" (138).

7. This difficulty is related to a critical observation concerning the interdependency of transcendental and factual or empirical analysis in Levinas's phenomenology offered by Derrida and later Bernasconi, as recently discussed in detail by Jack Marsh, *Saying Peace*. Marsh notes that "separation is both the ground and the result of the other's appearance" (60, 86), diagnoses in Levinas a "vicious circularity" (10), and concludes that "Levinas's entire method is premised in a systematic failure to distinguish between real and transcendental conditionality, real and transcendental genesis" (85). It seems to me that this formulation rather

expresses the basic challenge of phenomenology, which Heidegger summarizes under the onto-ontological difference, namely the challenge to distinguish between Being and beings.

8. TI 115, 112; 157, 107.

9. TI 176, 163. For earlier and more detailed discussion of the "il y a," see Levinas, *Le temps et l'autre*, 24–30, 44–50 (TA); Levinas, *De l'existence à l'existant*, 93–105, 57–64 (DEE).

10. On the difficult question of gender roles in Levinas, see Chanter, *Feminist Interpretations of Emmanuel Levinas*, and the further references listed in the first note in the introduction to this book.

11. TI 163, 153.

12. This dialectics of immanent worldliness—self-identification through others that at the same time signifies self-alienation in others—echoes the initial stages of modern philosophical narratives that influenced Levinas. One is reminded of Dasein's being-in-the-world, in Heidegger's *Being and Time*, where the human subject "initially and most often" loses himself in the world in which he dwells, but also of the initial stage in Descartes's thought experiment in *Meditations*, where the distinctive existence of the ego and its world melt in mere seeming and self-doubt. More explicitly Jewish Greek, the initial "experience of totality" in Levinas's phenomenology calls to mind the first stage in Rosenzweig's narrative in *The Star of Redemption*, Creation before Revelation. Both Rosenzweig and Levinas portray initial worldliness as a primal disposition in the evolution of individual conscience and at the same time as a primary form of culture, which not only is intersubjective but also enacts a primitive form of relation to absolute otherness, to the otherness of god, a form described by Levinas as pagan religion of "mythical divinity," of "faceless gods, impersonal gods" (TI 151, 142).

13. TI 185, 170; 183, 169; 161, 151.

14. For a broader reflection on the relations between Levinas and Rosenzweig, see Robert Gibbs, *Correlations in Rosenzweig and Levinas*, who specifically indicates the similar structure between the narrative of *Totality and Infinity* and Rosenzweig's *Star* (26). See also in Moyn, *Origins of the Other*, 145–167.

15. Derrida, "En ce moment même dans cet ouvrage me voici," 168.

16. TI 186, 171.

17. TI 85, 86.

18. TI 216, 198. See Wyschogrod, *Emmanuel Levinas*, 86: "We can only wish to kill one whom we cannot incorporate into the totality." It is interesting to compare this to Carl Schmitt's characterization of politics as the intensified level of any conflict in which the conflicted parties stand in ontic opposition to each other, are opposed to each other's very existence, and pose for each other the threat of "ontic negation," whose paradigmatic phenomenon is "physical killing" (*The Concept of the Political*, 31). It is noteworthy that for both Levinas and Schmitt, the relation to otherness is characterized in terms of radical adversity, of existential negation, of killing.

19. TI 237, 215.

20. TI 217, 199.

21. See *Mekhilta of Rabbi Ishmael*, Bahodesh, 8 (on Exodus 20, 14) for a midrashic reflection on the relation between the first and sixth commandments: "I am the Lord your G-d" and opposite it "You shall not kill."

22. TI 185, 171.

23. I therefore agree with Robert Bernasconi's claim that the commandment of nonviolence is "not addressed to the will and so could be said to displace the notion of the 'ought,'"

see Bernasconi, "The Ethics of Suspicion," 33. But I argue that this original commandment *constitutes* the very experience of "ought" and "shall."

24. Hence the notion, which becomes more central in *Otherwise Than Being*, that my responsibility is infinite in the sense that it is "increasing in the measure that it is assumed; duties become greater in the measure that they are accomplished. The better I accomplish my duty the fewer rights I have; the more I am just the more guilty I am" (TI 274, 244). This results from the fact that responsibility—my self-limitation vis-à-vis the Other—constitutes my individual being.

25. TI 224, 204; 189, 174. My analyses show why I cannot share Leora Batnitzky's appraisal that "Levinas maintains that the will of the other person dictates the laws of reason" and so gives "primacy of the other human being's will over reason" (*Leo Strauss and Emmanuel Levinas*, 90). I think that the Other in Levinas stands not for "will" but for "being."

26. HN 155, 133.

27. TI 188, 172–173; 197, 181.

28. TI 188, 173.

29. Here lies the foundation for what Robert Bernasconi diagnoses as Levinas's ethical "suspicion of ethics." See Bernasconi, "The Ethics of Suspicion," 40: "Ethics in [Levinas's] sense interrupts the complacency of any specific ethics. Everything which passes for justice is under the suspicion of producing injustice."

30. TI 68, 71; 98, 162; 198, 181; 200, 183.

31. TI 199, 182; 191, 176. Levinas takes here a clear position on what Derrida will a few years later call "logocentrism," which consists, among others, in "phonocentrism," namely in giving preference to the "absolute proximity of voice and being, of voice and the meaning of being, of voice and the ideality of meaning." See Derrida, *De la grammatologie*, 23, translated by Spivak, *On Grammatology*, 11.

32. TI 192, 176; 199, 182.

33. TI 191, 176.

34. TI 270, 241.

35. TI 272, 242; 239, 217.

36. TI 239, 216; 271, 242.

37. TI 271, 242.

38. This is another obvious parallel to Hermann Cohen's *Religion der Vernunft*.

39. TI 271, 242; 273, 244; 336, 301.

40. My interpretation here is very much in line with one offered by Robert Bernasconi in "Levinas's Ethical Critique of Levinasian Ethics." Bernasconi points out that scholarship "tended to ignore that whole of the fourth section of *Totality and Infinity* on eros and fecundity" (256) and notes that even Levinas himself suppresses this section "in the *précis* of the book that he wrote to accompany its presentation to the University of Paris as his principle thesis" (260). In contrast, Bernasconi underlines, as I do, the crucial role of this section in the book's architecture, namely as "the fulfillment of the ethical relation" (260) with "a political meaning" (265). Bernasconi shows how the last section's "infinite time of triumph" provides the answer to the book's opening question of "whether or not we are duped by morality" (267). See also Caygill, *Levinas and the Political*, 97, who indicates how the book's final section returns to the basic theme posited in its opening, "war and peace" (97). Cf. also Critchley, *The Ethics of Deconstruction*, 223 ("politics provides the continual horizon of Levinas's ethics"), and also *Problem with Levinas*, 91. Michael Fagenblat identifies in this section the

"key to the teleological structure" of the book (*A Covenant of Creatures*, 93); more recently, Marsh, *Saying Peace*, 63.

41. TI 294–295, 263.

42. Even though Levinas states that the erotic relation is "no knowledge" (309), it should be noted that this may be true for visual knowledge, for the knowledge of philosophers, for *theoria*, but surely not for prophetic epistemology. In one of the first prophetic records of knowledge, in the first chapters of Genesis, right after Adam and Eve gained knowledge of good and bad (Genesis 2,17), "knew they are naked" (Genesis 3,7), and were expelled from Eden, we are told that "Adam knew Eva" (Genesis 4,1), which is the first erotic act, the rise of carnal knowledge. All these instances use the standard Hebrew root for knowledge, ידע, and in the Greek translation, cognates of *gnosis*. Eros is a central theme, among the other themes of *Totality and Infinity*'s last section, in Levinas's earlier phenomenology, especially in *Time and the Other* (77–84, 84–89).

43. TI 298, 269; 301, 269.

44. This is where I question Sarah Hammerschlag's understanding of "religion" for Levinas as signifying "not a lineage, but an encounter" (*Figural Jew*, 152).

45. TI 342, 306.

46. Leora Batnitzky, for instance, argues that Levinas's philosophy of "subjective interiority" "cannot be extended into the public realm" (*Leo Strauss and Emmanuel Levinas*, 51).

47. Robert Bernasconi, in "Levinas's Ethical Critique," reads the "political meaning" of Levinas's "family" in asserting, against the state, "private life" (265). The "privatization" (or decollectivization) of family is consistent with Bernasconi's claim, in the article "The Third Party," that "fraternity" is for Levinas the model for "human society that did not depend on the idea of the human race as a biological genus" and "challenges the conception of politics that reduces it to a network of relations organized with reference to the species, the people, the race" (53). I agree that Levinas objects to reducing politics to race, but I claim that he also objects to the abstraction of society from sexuality, family, and peoplehood. For similar reasons, I disagree with Simon Critchley's reading of Levinas's "fecundity" as pointing to "plurality that is neither individuality nor collectivity," beyond any model of peoplehood or even "monastic community," which can be best approximated to "the writing of female, medieval Christian mystics" (*Problem with Levinas*, 138). Michael Fagenblat, *Covenant*, similarly only sees in *Totality and Infinity*, as Levinas's political model, a "pluralist society of speakers" (92), which features a "we" that shares a history but constitutes no people. Rather, as Caygill argues, it is bound by the fraternity of the "republican state" (182–183). The deeper sources of difficulty transpire in the reading of Adrian Peperzak, *To the Other*, who is unsure "to what extent the categories of the erotic and the family are taken in a restricted sense [biological] or rather are meant as metaphors for moral or religious communities, spiritual families, traditions and practices" (199). This question arises from a categorical division between religion (i.e., spirit) and family (i.e., flesh), which, as we see in the next chapter, Levinas contests as Christian by asserting Judaism. My interpretation is more in line with the reading of Robert Gibbs, who identifies in Levinas's notion of fecundity a clear reference to "Rosenzweig's own contentious discussion of the Jewish people . . . [whereby] Judaism rested in the blood of the people, from generation to generation" (*Correlations*, 29), and accordingly points out that Levinas here "is not canonizing the nuclear family as much as finding it a model for all sociality" (239). Cf. Rosenzweig, *Star*, 331–332. Next to Rosenzweig, I offer, as a clear precursor to Levinas's family, Martin Buber's early notion of the Jewish people as connected through

"blood." See "Das Judentum und die Juden" (1909), in *Reden über das Judentum*, 8. See also Marsh, *Saying Peace*, 64.

48. Levinas, "Messianic Texts," in Hand, *Difficult Freedom*, 149. On the "vexed question of Israel," see Simon Critchley, "Five Problems in Levinas's View of Politics and the Sketch of a Solution to Them." My reading challenges Caygill's appraisal that "in *Totality and Infinity* the translation of the work of justice into a political project is accomplished in a way that makes any identification of it with a state such as the 'State of Israel' extremely difficult"; see *Levinas and the Political*, 124. Caygill notes that "Levinas does not fully explore the implications of the 'elected' ethical subject" (126). My claim is that these implications are developed in the Jewish writings and explicitly lead to Israel—see chapter 5. Bernasconi, "Who Is My Neighbor?" 18–19, recognizes the role of Israel in Levinas's political thought but limits his reading to the Jewish writings, not connecting it to the figure of the family in *Totality and Infinity*.

49. Commentators have noticed this affinity; see Michael Fagenblat, *Covenant*: "cohistoricizing of *Dasein*" (181–182); William Large, *Levinas's Totality and Infinity*, who however argues that Levinas's idea here is "entirely opposite" to Heidegger's, since in "the ethical community . . . the future is not ours, but the others'" (111). This assessment, I argue, fails to take into account that Levinas's ethical community is based on fecundity, where the child is "at the same time other and myself."

50. SZ 384, 436.

51. See, for example, Brumlik, "Everyday Life, Hatred of Jews, and the Identitarian Movement."

52. Arendt, *Origins of Totalitarianism*, 239.

53. Bernasconi, "Levinas's Ethical Critique of Levinasian Ethics," evokes the formal affinity of Levinas's "fecundity" to Heidegger's *Volk* but characterizes Levinas's notion of "infinite of time" in opposition to Heidegger's "finitude of being" (263). My argument undermines this opposition by showing how fecundity constitutes infinite time that is nonetheless individualized, i.e., genealogical, historical, and, in this sense, finite. Bernasconi further interprets Levinas's notion of the family as a paradigm not of the nation but of the private sphere, and for this reason as agreeing with Arendt's "observation that totalitarianism destroys private life" (265).

54. TI 318, 284–285.

55. As Franz Rosenzweig shows, both performances of God's people generate the collective identity, the "we," as the agent of God's kingdom.

3. Our Old Europe

1. Simon Critchley notes that "Levinas's philosophy [is] defined and threatened by 'Hitlerism' until the very end," *The Problem*, 32. It is therefore hard to understand John Drabinski's critique of "how little Levinas engages with the central issues of post-Shoah theorizing" (*Levinas and the Postcolonial*, 135) unless one excludes the Jewish writings from Levinas's "philosophical work," as Drabinski does. See in contrast Caygill, *Levinas and the Political*: "The event of National Socialism, feared and mourned, marks all of Levinas's writings, from the early phenomenological texts of the 1930s to the late essays on prophetic politics and human rights" (5).

2. Levinas, "Quelques réflexions sur la philosophie de l'hitlérisme" (PH).

3. PH 23; 24; 26; 24.

4. Chaouat, "Being and Jewishness," 100–103. Samuel Moyn, *Origins of the Other*, situates Levinas in the landscape of "interwar theology," such as the work of Karl Barth, which in response to the moral collapse of liberal theology's idea of "culture" asserts the "absolute transcendence of God"—"*totaliter alter!*" (137).

5. PH 28; 26; 32. Fred Moten has already indicated the colonial and imperial vectors of Levinas's notion of Europe globally propagating its Judeo-Christian truth; see *Universal Machine*, 7. We will see that this vector in fact gains momentum in Levinas's Jewish writings and orients his entire pre-1968 historiography.

6. PH 30; 24–25; 31; 30.

7. PH 31; 32.

8. Quoted and discussed in Lapidot, *Jews out of the Question*, 116–119.

9. QLT 185–186, 87.

10. Fred Moten, *The Universal Machine*, offers a powerful articulation of this paradox, whereby the philosophical resistance to racism as too attached to "thingly" existence generates resistance to what philosophy perceives as "thingly" existence, which for European philosophy would be the essence of non-European cultures. Accordingly, philosophical resistance to racism generates racism. Commenting on Levinas's statement in an interview that Europe is "Bible and the Greeks" and "everything else is dancing . . . no racism intended," Moten writes, "Levinas becomes the thing he denigrates in his disavowal of the thingly by way of a liquidation of the thingly in his own work that cannot be fully accomplished" (10). Opposition to the thing generates a thingly ("unintended," thoughtless) racism.

11. DL 9–10, xiii.

12. HN 190–191, 162.

13. HN 191, 163.

14. HN 190, 162.

15. Levinas, *Etre juif* (EJ).

16. PH 26; EJ 57, 207.

17. EJ 62, 209.

18. Sarah Hammerschlag, in *Broken Tablets*, argues that *Difficult Freedom*, Levinas's early Jewish essays, set Judaism "in opposition to the two prominent ideologies of the 1950s," liberalism and Marxism (105), which I refer, in Levinas's eschatological historiography, to the figures of Christianity and Greco-Roman universalism, respectively.

19. See Jonas, "Gnosticism, Existentialism, Nihilism," in *Gnostic Religion*, 320–341.

20. EJ 55, 207.

21. This also explains the ambivalence, even contradiction, both in Levinas and in Jonas, between a critique of transcendence and a critique of immanence that, in different moments, address one and the same target—namely Heidegger. See the tension between Levinas's "Being Jewish" of 1947 versus "Heidegger, Gagarin and Us" of 1961 (DL 347–351, 231–234), and Jonas's "Gnosticism and Modern Nihilism," first published in 1952, versus "Heidegger and Theology" (1964).

22. Cf. Hammerschlag, *Figural Jew*, 119; Critchley, *The Problem*, 32, 40; Eisenstadt, "Anti-utopianism Revisited," 134; Caygill, *Levinas and the Political*, 35–40.

23. DL 154, 99–100.

24. DL 156–157, 101; QLT 75, 34.

25. DL 206–207, 134; 214, 139.

26. DL 228–229, 149.

27. DL 207, 134.

28. DL 207, 134. For the Christian myth of passion, of suffering, Levinas writes in his 1950 critique of Claudel's *Emmaüs*, "does not Cain prefigure the Jewish people and Abel the Sacrificed Lamb? This is a courtly explanation of all our woes subsequent to exile, Auschwitz included," only to add, underlying the ambivalence of sacrifice (is Cain—the Jewish people—the murder or the ultimate victim?): "A prefiguration that we accept" (DL 189, 122).

29. DL 162–163, 105; DL 167, 108; HN 165, 142.

30. DL 27–46; 11–23.

31. ADV 165, 135.

32. This is Levinas's response to Leora Batnitzky's critique of his "understanding of philosophy as providing a messianic and universal cure for the ills of concrete political life," which for her renders his "political thought meaningless" (*Leo Strauss and Emmanuel Levinas*, 160). For Levinas, the significance of both philosophy and Judaism, vis-à-vis Christianity, lies in their political intentionality.

33. My analysis therefore offers to nuance readings of Levinas's intellectual historiography as based on a fundamental tension between Judaism and "paganism" (Hammerschlag, *Figural Jew*, 135). I distinguish in Levinas between non-Western paganism (Greek tragedy, Germanic and Persian racism) and the equally pagan but nonetheless Western Greco-Roman civilization.

34. HN 47, 37; 63, 52; 65, 53.

35. ADV 229–231, 196–198.

36. DL 109, 68; QLT 11–12, 4; HN 59, 48; QLT 24, 10.

37. QLT 75, 34.

38. QLT 77, 35; DL 144–145, 94.

39. QLT 76, 35; DSS 96–97, 145; QLT 71, 32.

40. QLT 74, 33; 77, 35; 74, 33; 76, 34.

41. QLT 76, 35; TI 5, 21; QLT 75, 34.

42. DL 144–145, 94.

43. HN 101, 89.

44. Bereshit Rabba, 9:13, to Genesis 1:31 (ed. Theodor-Albeck, 2:480); translated by Levinas in ADV 215, 183; see also ADV 85, 66.

45. ADV 215, 183.

46. ADV 72, 54.

47. mAvot 3, 2; translated by Levinas in ADV 84, 65; see also ADV 215, 183.

48. ADV 85, 66.

49. ADV 84–85, 65–66; ADV 216, 183. Cf. Herzog, *Levinas's Politics*, chap. 4.

50. ADV 85, 66; ADV 84, 65.

51. ADV 84–86, 65–67.

52. See Schmitt, *Der Nomos der Erde*, 31.

53. ADV 85, 66.

54. DL 146, 95.

55. ADV 216, 184.

56. ADV 57, 40; ADV 56–57, 40; Cf. Eisenstadt, "The Problem of the Promise"; see also Herzog, *Levinas's Politics*, 49.

57. ADV 84, 65.

58. Once again, note the affinity to Hannah Arendt, whose notion of "totalitarianism" in *The Origins of Totalitarianism* refers both to Nazism and to Communism.

59. DL 242, 160; DL 250, 165.

60. DL 311, 208; DL 314, 210; DL 311, 208; DL 405, 272.

61. DL 309–310, 206–207.

62. Levinas, "Le débat russo-chinois et la dialectique," in *Les imprévus de l'histoire*, 149–151. Note that in the figure of Maoist China, the non-Western collaborates with the Christian-Gnostic to generate not Hitlerism but the perfect Roman state.

63. HN 102, 88.

64. DSS 43, 112; DSS 39, 110; DSS 38, 110. Fifteen years later, in an interview with Richard Kearney, Levinas says: "Marxism was, of course, utterly compromised by Stalinism. The 1968 Revolt in Paris was a revolt of sadness, because it came after the Khrushchev Report and the exposure of the corruption of the Communist Church. The year 1968 epitomized the joy of despair, a last grasping at human justice, happiness, and perfection—after the truth had dawned that the communist ideal had degenerated into totalitarian bureaucracy. By 1968 only dispersed groups and rebellious pockets of individuals remained to seek their surreal-ist forms of salvation, no longer confident of a collective movement of humanity, no longer assured that Marxism could survive the Stalinist catastrophe as the prophetic messenger of history." See Cohen, *Face to Face with Levinas*, 33. On Levinas's ambivalent relation to Marx-ism, see Gibbs, *Correlations*, 229–255.

4. The State of David

1. See "For a Jewish Humanism," 1956 (DL 409, 275); "A Religion of Adults," 1957 (DL 37, 11); "Jewish Thought Today," 1961 (DL 241, 159).

2. Levinas, *Humanisme de l'autre homme*.

3. In a forthcoming study, I show how a similar dynamic also operates in Levinas's hermeneutical approach to *the* Jewish text, the Talmud, in generating a shift from Mishnah to midrash, from law to verse, letter to book.

4. QLT 75, 34.

5. QLT 85, 39.

6. QLT 107, 49. It should be noted that the talmudic discussion of this midrash goes on to argue, in hermeneutical means, that Israel ultimately *did* willingly accept the Torah in the days of Esther. Commenting on the words "the Jews fulfilled and accepted" (*kiymu ve-kiblu*, Esther 9, 27), the talmudic sage Rava says, "They fulfilled what they already accepted." Rashi explains that the Jews accepted the Torah in Esther's time "for the love of the miracle" that was done to them. In contrast to Rava and Rashi, Levinas reads the words "they fulfilled and accepted" to say that "practice precedes adhesion," which makes sense literally but contradicts the Talmud's point.

7. QLT 104, 48; QLT 106, 49.

8. QLT 109, 50.

9. QLT 85, 39.

10. QLT 82, 37.

11. Simon Critchley, in *The Problem with Levinas*, calls it, in reference to Levinas's 1934 text on Hitlerism, an attempt to produce "alternative elemental philosophy" (44), a "rethink-ing of the body" (37).

12. For a discussion on the idea of exemplarity in Levinas and of Derrida's critique, see Hammerschlag, "Another, Other Abraham." For a discussion on the question of exemplarity in modern Jewish thought in general, see Hollander, *Exemplarity and Chosenness*.

13. EJ 60. This idea appears already in 1939, Emmanuel Levinas, "A propos de la mort du Pape Pie XI," *Paix et Droit* 3 (March 1939): "Jews have the obscure feeling that Hitlerism is like a renewal of their vocation and their destiny" (3).

14. EJ 67.

15. DL 130, 82. The *locus classicus* for this discussion, as noted in the introduction, is in the talmudic reading "Judaism and Revolution" of 1969: "each time Israel is mentioned in the Talmud one is certainly free to understand by it a particular ethnic group which is probably fulfilling an incomparable destiny. But to interpret in this manner would be to reduce the general principle in the idea enunciated in the Talmudic passage, to forget that Israel means a people who has received the Law and, as a result, a human nature which has reached the fullness of its responsibilities and its self-consciousness" (DSS 18, 98).

16. DL 148, 96.

17. DL 146, 94.

18. DL 146, 94.

19. QLT 178, 83; ADV 232–233, 199–200. The exception to this principle is a small number of basic principles, like prohibiting murder or idolatry, the so-called Seven Laws of Noah. In this sense, I do not completely share Leora Batnitzky's critical observation that "Jewish law, far from reflecting the outer structure of communal and political life, is for Levinas the inner meaning not only of Judaism but of civilization and humanity as well" (*Leo Strauss and Emmanuel Levinas*, 199). I think that for Levinas, it is precisely because Jewish law expresses the *nonsymmetrical* inner meaning of humanity that it reflects the outer structure of Jewish communal existence. I do agree with Batnitzky that in his talmudic hermeneutics, Levinas tends to reduce Jewish law to a universal "message."

20. DL 130, 82; QLT 174, 82.

21. DSS 18, 98.

22. DL 130, 82.

23. Moten, *Universal Machine*, 8.

24. QLT 175, 82.

25. DSS 18, 98.

26. ADV 70, 50.

27. Levinas's conception also diverges from Rosenzweig's understanding of Jews as the "eternal people" of "eternal life" who already stand and wait at the end of history, leaving Christians with the political-historical work of the mission, the "eternal way." See Rosenzweig, *Star*, part III. For Levinas, it is rather the Christians who are outside of history.

28. ADV 209, 217.

29. DSS 45, 113. Cf. Hammerschlag, *Figural Jew*, 149–150.

30. ADV 73, 55.

31. Maimonides, *Mishneh Torah*; Maimonides, "Kings and Wars," in *Mishneh Torah*, 11–12.

32. ADV 213, 180.

33. ADV 218, 186.

34. ADV 219, 186.

35. ADV 219, 186.

36. DL 44, 23. See, for instance, TB Avodah Zarah 2b, where the Romans state before God: "Master of the Universe, we have established many marketplaces, we have built many bathhouses, and we have increased much silver and gold," or TB Shabbat 33b, where a rabbi praises the Romans: "They have made streets, they have built bridges, they have erected baths."

37. DL 44, 22; DL 146, 94. See also in "L'inspiration religieuse de l'Alliance," *Paix et Droit* 8 (October 1935): 4: "To forget the religious essence of the fact of diaspora is to betray the very meaning of Jewish history."

38. TI 247, 158.

39. QLT 108, 50.

40. ADV 14, xvii.

41. DSS 18, 98; ADV 55, 38.

42. QLT 137, 64; QLT 138, 64; QLT 144, 146; ADV 14, 184; QLT 125, 58.

43. QLT 56, 25; QLT 185, 87; AE 121, 75; QLT 186, 87.

44. HN 148, 129; HN 148n3; 187n6.

45. HN 149, 129. For a critique of Levinas's Volozhin-inspired theodicy, whereby "all suffering is deserved" (46), as "obscene," see Martin Kavka, "For It Is God's Way to Sweeten Bitter with Bitter: Prayer in Levinas and R. Hayyim of Volozhin." Kavka interprets the identification of Israel's suffering with God's, in Volozhin and in Levinas, as reinforcing the justification of suffering and not limiting it, like I do for the sake of my argument here.

46. HN 194–195, 166.

47. ADV 209, 177.

48. Samuel Moyn calls it a "polity beyond politics" (*Origins of the Other*, 233).

49. ADV 211, 179.

50. See Schmitt, *Der Nomos der Erde*, 31.

51. ADV 212, 180; ADV 68, 50; ADV 55, 83; ADV 70, 50. Accordingly, even though I agree with Oona Eisenstadt's argument in "Levinas's Jewish Writings" that Levinas's State of Israel is different from other states in that "it knows itself *merely* to be a state" (5), I do not think that this implies for Levinas that the Jewish state "knows itself to be an imperfect state" (id.)—on the contrary.

5. States of Israel

1. For a recent reading of the Jewish Bible as theo-political myth, see Naiweld, *The Age of the Parakletos*.

2. See Boyarin, *A Traveling Homeland*.

3. Amnon Raz-Krakotzkin, "galut be-tokh ribonut—le-bikoret 'shlilat ha-galut' ba-tarbut ha-yisraelit" [Exile in Sovereignty—Critique of 'Negation of Exile' in the Israeli Culture].

4. See Rosenzweig, *Star*, part III, book I. I therefore disagree with Robert Gibbs that both Levinas and Rosenzweig formulate similar visions of "Jewish people living outside of history, as an eternal people" (*Correlations*, 25; see also Kleinberg, *Levinas's Talmudic Turn*, 153), and even more with Samuel Moyn's assessment that Levinas broke with "Rosenzweig's communitarianism and historicism" (*Origins of the Other*, 167), although there are moments in Levinas that, as I show, point in this direction. My interpretation concurs with Annabel Herzog's in *Levinas's Politics*, which recognizes that for Levinas, in contrast to Rosenzweig, "political history is the instrument that allows redemption to enter the phenomenal world" (120). She points out that Jean Wahl, in reaction to Levinas's lecture on Rosenzweig in 1960, had already criticized him for reproducing Hegelian historicism despite his own criticisms of it (117). I do not think that any acknowledgment of the necessity of historical process must be Hegelian, but I agree that some moments in Levinas do support this interpretation.

5. In his 1982 preface to Dominque Bourel's French translation of Mendelssohn's *Jerusalem*, see HN 159–168, 138–145.

6. "Exclusive Rights," DL 358–364, 239–244; DL 360, 240.

7. ADV 232, 199. In the 1980 essay "Assimilation and New Culture." See also the 1988 preface to HN, where Israel is misunderstood as based on the "pride of withdrawal into itself" (HN 10, 3).

8. DL 326, 218.

9. DL 345, 230.

10. ADV 219, 187.

11. DL 147, 95.

12. EJ 50.

13. DL 18, 5—the English translation erroneously renders "philosophical morality."

14. DL 45, 23.

15. Renan, *Qu'est-ce qu'une nation?* 4–5; QLT 16, 6.

16. DL 324, 215–216.

17. Renan, *Qu'est-ce qu'une nation?* 10; DL 389, 261–262. See Hammerschlag, *Figural Jew*, 148; Critchley, "Five Problems," 176. Samuel Moyn argues that the work of the *Alliance israélite universelle*, whose school, *École Normale Israelite Orientale*, designed to provide Parisian education to "oriental" Jews, Levinas was the director of for thirty-four years, was "a French-Jewish version of the French *mission civilisatrice*" (*Origins of the Other*, 90–91). See also Kleinberg, *Levinas's Talmudic Turn*, 14, 147; Fagenblat, *A Covenant of Creatures*, 183–184. I therefore disagree with Howard Caygill that "the two historic vehicles of prophetic politics [identified by Levinas]—universal human rights and the State of Israel—collide" (*Levinas and the Political*, 174). Annabel Herzog has recently concluded her analysis of Levinas's political thought by suggesting that "politics in the Talmudic readings is an original interweaving of the French tradition of secular rights and the Talmudic emphasis on hesed" (*Levinas's Politics*, 136).

18. DL 278–279, 185–186.

19. QLT 167, 78; DL 320, 214; "The Meaning of History," DL 339, 227; Arendt, *Origins of Totalitarianism*, 243.

20. DL 320, 214; DL 280, 186.

21. This line of thought can already be traced in Levinas's letter to Maurice Blanchot of May 21, 1948, shortly after the founding of the State of Israel, published in Levinas, *Etre juif*, 71–77. In this letter, Levinas expresses his admiration for France as representing an "almost eternal order of things that nothing . . . can spoil" (73). In this respect, the State of Israel is an "anachronism," and Levinas, echoing Hermann Cohen, confesses his misgivings about this new development in Jewish history. Nevertheless, he ends his letter on a hopeful note, pointing out that the reference to God and the prophets in the Israeli Declaration of Independence is different from such references in the founding documents of other states, since here "it is the original text that was pronounced" (76): "The great alienation of Scripture that was the Septuagint—where we ourselves study the Bible—is over" (77).

22. DL 147, 95.

23. HN 165, 142; "The Spinoza Case," DL 164–170, 106–110, and "Have you Re-read Baruch?" DL 171–183, 111–118; DL 167, 108; QLT 40, 17–18. See "How Judaism Is Possible?" from 1959, DL 365–379, 245–254.

24. HN 165–166, 142.

25. QLT 24, 9.
26. DSS 165, 187.
27. DSS 166, 188.
28. ADV 219, 187; QLT 24, 9.
29. EJ 60; DL 381, 255; DL 28, 12; DL 244, 161.
30. DL 148, 96.
31. DL 148, 96; DL 370, 248; DL 249, 164; QLT 24, 9.
32. DL 326, 218; DL 327, 218; DL 248–249, 164.
33. DL 149, 96; DL 327, 219; DL 248–249, 164.
34. DL 329, 220; DL 328, 219.
35. DL 373, 250.
36. ADV 219, 186.
37. QLT 24, 10.
38. QLT 24, 9.
39. This idea is mentioned in the speeches of Hayyim Nahman Bialik and R. Kook at the inauguration of the Hebrew University of Jerusalem on April 1, 1925; see Davide Mano and Ron Naiweld, "Hayyim Nahman Bialik's Inaugural Speech at the Hebrew University of Jerusalem"; Shnayer Z. Leiman, "Rabbi Isaac Ha-Kohen Kook: Invocation at the Inauguration of the Hebrew University."
40. ADV 234, 201; QLT 24, 9–10.
41. ADV 224, 191.
42. DL 327–328, 218–219.
43. QLT 33, 14.
44. QLT 129, 60; QLT 130, 60. See the discussion in Herzog, *Levinas's Politics*, 100–103.
45. QLT 131, 61.
46. Giladi, "L'invention d'un macro-nationalisme 'hébreu.'"
47. DL 327, 218.
48. ADV 224, 191. This ambivalence has been noted by Sarah Hammerschlag: "The definition of Judaism and the people of Israel as carriers of a moral message ultimately serves as a justification for unconditional support of a state that has failed to embody the ideals ascribed to it" (*Figural Jew*, 161; see also Hammerschlag, "Literary Unrest," 666). Hammerschlag identifies this operation as occurring mostly in Levinas's work after the Six-Day War and characterizes it as "religious Zionist" (162). The claim that Levinas's "religious Zionism" emerged after 1967 is one that Leora Batnitzky made previously in *Leo Strauss and Emmanuel Levinas*, 160. I argue that Levinas's religious Zionism is already present in the 1950s and that after 1967/1968, it takes a decolonial turn. Cf. Michael Fagenblat, *A Covenant of Creatures*: Levinas enables ethical critique of the State of Israel, but "indulged the Occupation" (186–187).
49. Levinas, Finkielkraut, and Malka, "Ethics and Politics," 294.
50. Butler, *Parting Ways*, 23.
51. Chaouat, "Débat." Chaouat notes that "had Levinas uttered such a thing, there could be no doubting the inherent complicity between Zionism and colonialist racism and much worse." Eisenstadt and Katz, "The Faceless Palestinian," 19. Butler, "Levinas trahi?." A similar critique was already offered by Jason Caro in "Levinas and the Palestinians," recently referenced by Jack Marsh in *Saying Peace*, 136. Caygill, *Levinas and the Political*, 132–143.
52. ADV 13, xv; ADV 12, xv.
53. DL 370, 248; DL 202–204, 131–132; ADV 226, 192.

54. DL 45, 23; QLT 185, 87. Levinas performs a similar operation in "Le débat russo-chinois et la dialectique" (*Les Imprévus de l'histoire*, 172), which Howard Caygill describes as "Levinas's ugliest and most disturbing published work" (*Levinas and the Political*, 183). This little text, which is quite vague, first relates the Soviet break with China to Russia's fidelity to European, Greco-Judeo-Christian civilization and its fear of "Asian civilization" ("The yellow peril! It is not racial, it's spiritual. It's not about inferior values; it's about radical foreignness, foreign in all the density of its past, where no voice with a familiar inflection filters through, a lunar or martian past," 150). It then expresses an understanding of Chinese Communism's fear of post-Stalinist Russia's embrace of third-world (according to Caygill, Arab) nationalism, which reveals "the shadow of national-socialism" (151).

55. QLT 146, 68.

56. QLT 131, 61.

57. QLT 137, 64; QLT 138, 64; QLT 144, 67; QLT 146, 68; QLT 125, 58; QLT 144, 67; QLT 125, 58; QLT 143, 67; QLT 124, 57.

58. QLT 137, 64; QLT 141, 66.

59. QLT 141–142, 66.

60. QLT 147, 68.

61. DL 328, 219; QLT 147, 69.

62. QLT 145, 67–68.

63. QLT 146, 68.

64. QLT 146, 68.

65. The motif of Israel facing "one hundred million Arabs" is common. There is a speech of Mao given to a PLO delegation on May 15, 1965, a few months before Levinas gave his reading (October 1965), in which Mao says: "You are not only two million Palestinians facing Israel, but one hundred million Arabs." Quoted in Cooley, "China and the Palestinians," 25.

Part II. State of Persecution: Levinas after 1968

1. On the representation and meaning of 1968 in later politics, culture, and thought, see Ross, *May '68 and Its Afterlives*; see also Starr, *Logics of Failed Revolt*; Jackson, Milne, and Williams, *May 68*; Freenberg and Freedman, *When Poetry Ruled the Streets*; Hanley and Kerr, *May '68*; Pawling, *Critical Theory and Political Engagement*; Reader and Wadia, *The May 1968 Events in France*.

2. On the political, cultural, and intellectual history of French decolonization, see Kalter, *The Discovery of the Third World*; Shepard, *The Invention of Decolonization*; Naylor, *France and Algeria*; Just, *Literature, Ethics, and Decolonization in Postwar France*; Chafer, *The End of Empire in French West Africa*; Boittin, *Colonial Metropolis*.

3. Fanon, *Les damnés de la terre*, translated as *The Wretched of the Earth*.

4. Fanon, *Les damnés de la terre*, 42.

5. Fanon, *Les damnés de la terre*, 41.

6. For general discussions, see Hudis, *Frantz Fanon*; Nayar, *Frantz Fanon*; Cherki, *Frantz Fanon*, translated by Nadia Benabid; Haddour, *Frantz Fanon*; Byrd and Miri, *Frantz Fanon and Emancipatory Social Theory*; Rabaka, *Forms of Fanonism*.

7. Fanon, *Les damnés de la terre*, 28, 31, 31–32, 33. For discussions of Sartre, decolonialism, and antiracism, see Judaken, *Race after Sartre*; Consonni and Liska, *Sartre, Jews, and the Other*.

8. On the complex relations between Levinas and Derrida, see Hammerschlag, "Another, Other Abraham." Hammerschlag, *Broken Tablets* argues that Derrida, in the footsteps of Blanchot, engages in "subversion of Levinas's thought" (x). Hammerschlag notes that both Levinas and Derrida, in contrast to Blanchot, refrained from actively participating in the 1968 protests (115).

9. Derrida, "Violence," 172, 145–146; 190–191, 162; 226, 191; 172, 145–146; 172, 145–146.

10. Derrida, "Violence," 190–191, 162; 191, 162; 219, 185.

11. Derrida, "Violence," 173, 146.

12. The complex relations between Levinas and Derrida have been treated by a number of scholars. For instance, Critchley, *The Ethics of Deconstruction*, highlights continuity; Hammerschlag, *Broken Tablets*, underscores the tensions. See also Cohen-Levinas and Crépon, *Levinas-Derrida*; Foran and Uljée, *Heidegger, Levinas, Derrida*; and Llewelyn, *Appositions of Jacques Derrida and Emmanuel Levinas*.

13. *Pace* John Drabinski's claim that "Levinas's work shows no signs of engagement with these events [of decolonization]" (*Levinas and the Postcolonial*, 145).

Philosophy

1. See, for instance, Adrian Peperzak, *To the Other*, who argues that there is no "turn" in Levinas between *Totality and Infinity* and *Otherwise Than Being* but rather a process of "radicalizing" the quest of "transcendence" (7, 32). More recently, Michael Morgan, *Cambridge Introduction*, 126, describes the move from the first to the second book as a process of elaborating, clarifying, and deepening. Jacques Derrida, too, writes that *Otherwise Than Being* "brings forward, certainly, in a very continuous way . . . the impetus and the 'logic' of *Totality and Infinity*, but to dislodge even more seriously the primacy of intentionality"; Derrida, *Adieu à Emmanuel Levinas*, 103.

6. Unsaying

1. Underscoring Derrida's influence on Levinas, Simon Critchley characterizes Levinas's post-1968 philosophy book as his "deconstructive turn" (*Ethics of Deconstruction*, 8; *Cambridge Companion*, 18).

2. Perhaps in contrast to Heidegger's *da*?

3. AE 19, 11.

4. AE 5, vii.

5. Or as Levinas preliminarily notes, "ess*a*nce": a noun which designates no substantive, no being, but is an "abstract name of action." AE 9, xlvii.

6. AE 14, 5.

7. AE 15, 4.

8. AE 283, 185.

9. AE 51, 29.

10. Compare to Hegel's description of conscience: "consciousness distinguishes from itself something to which it at the same time relates itself." Hegel, *Phenomenology of Spirit*, translated by Michael Inwood, 39.

11. AE 257, 165.

12. Cf. Jonas, *Gnostic Religion*, 51f.

13. AE 75, 43–44.

14. This is the emphasis of the famous preface. Later in the book, Levinas also indicates that war presupposes the absence of totality, namely, the fact of plurality: "In war beings refuse to belong to a totality, refuse community, refuse law; no frontier stops one being by another, nor defines them. They affirm themselves as transcending the totality, each identifying itself not by its place in the whole, but by its *self*" (TI 245–246, 222).

15. AE 15, 4.

16. AE 271, 176–177.

17. See Lapidot, "People of Knowers."

18. Cf. Caputo, "People of God, People of Being," 88.

19. AE 251, 161.

20. Schmitt, *Der Nomos der Erde*, 219.

21. AE 283, 185.

22. AE 249, 160.

23. TI 5, 21.

24. "La guerre à la guerre." The English translation only says "the war," which of course obfuscates the self-critical complexity of Levinas's argument.

25. AE 271–272, 177.

26. AE 67n1, 189n28.

27. AE 61, 35.

28. AE 65, 37.

29. AE 69, 40.

30. AE 70, 40.

31. Cf. Edmund Husserl, *Ideen zu einer reinen Phänomenologie und phänomenologischen Philosophie*, vol. 1, *Allgemeine Einführung in die reine Phänomenologie*: "Jeder 'Satz,' z.B. jeder Wunschsatz, kann daher in einen doxischen Satz umgewandelt" (243), namely, that every sentence can be formulated as a being-sentence (doxic).

32. "Die Sprache spricht als das Geläut der Stille." Heidegger, "Die Sprache," 27; translated by Albert Hofstadter, "Language," 205. AE 70, 40; AE 69, 40.

33. AE 242, 155.

34. AE 258, 166.

35. AE 46–47, 25.

36. AE 224n1, 198n6.

37. AE 64, 38.

38. AE 243, 162.

39. Heidegger, SZ, § 34. *Da-sein und Rede. Die Sprache*. See Lapidot, "Die Versammlung."

40. See, for instance, Heidegger, "Vom Wesen der Wahrheit,"201: "Weil zu ihm lichtendes Bergen gehört, erscheint Seyn anfänglich im Licht des verbergenden Entzugs."

41. AE 17–18, 6.

42. AE 158n1, 194n2.

43. "Nous autres Occidentaux," literally "we other Westerners." The English translation "us Westerners," with no "other," is idiomatic and no doubt closer to Levinas's intention, which—following standard linguistic usage—is to speak of Westerners themselves as "others," as others against those who are non-Western. Nevertheless, I have taken the

hermeneutic—midrashic—liberty of reading these words in the direction of the actual meaning of this passage, which indicates or calls for an inner self-distancing of Westerners with respect to the West itself.

44. AE 271–272, 177.

45. AE 283, 185. Howard Caygill interprets this passage as a concession made by Levinas to the possibility of "war waged against war, a just war at whose justice we shudder and for whose violence we repent, but a war nevertheless" (*Levinas and the Political*, 143), which Caygill finds "disappointing." As my analysis shows, I read in this passage the fear of just war as motivating the fundamental turn in Levinas's post-1968 thought.

46. AE 30, 14.

47. AE 19, 7.

48. This idea is even traceable in *Totality and Infinity*, where language is described explicitly as "unsaying," namely, as "continually undoing its phrase by the foreword or the exegesis, in unsaying the said" (TI 16, 30).

49. AE 75, 26.

50. AE 237, 243, 252.

51. AE 21, 8.

52. AE 21, 8.

53. AE 96–97, 57–58.

54. AE 21–22, 8.

55. Lit. "examination, observation"—that is, a discipline of vision, phenomenology. I doubt whether Leora Batnitzky's claim that, in contrast to Strauss, "Levinas wants to reject skepticism" (*Leo Strauss and Emmanuel Levinas*, 130) applies to Levinas's later philosophy.

56. AE 274, 178.

57. AE 76, 44.

58. AE 256, 165.

59. AE 262, 169; "l'histoire de la philosophie occidentale n'a été que la réfutation du scepticisme autant que la réfutation de la transcendance." The English translation renders: "the history of Western philosophy has not been the refutation of skepticism as much as the refutation of transcendence." This—I think inaccurate—rendering covers over the dramatic anti-Platonism and anti-Cartesianism of the statement, as well as Levinas's profound self-critique, which, on my reading, are evident in this passage.

60. Socrates can also be read as having founded the tradition of skepticism. See Hazlett, *A Critical Introduction to Skepticism*, 4–5.

61. AE 263, 169–170.

62. AE 39, 20.

63. AE 264–265, 170–171.

64. AE 262, 169.

65. AE 263, 169–170.

7. The Self as Other

1. AE 37, 19.

2. AE 37, 19; AE 244, 157.

3. AE 280, 183; AE 273, 178; AE 97, 58.

4. AE 150n1, 193n35; AE 191, 120.

5. AE 191n1, 187n5.

6. AE 281–282, 183–184.

7. Michael Fagenblat indeed describes OB as negative theology (*A Covenant of Creatures*, 101). On negative theology in modern Jewish thought, see Fagenblat, *Negative Theology as Jewish Modernity*.

8. AE 281–282, 183–184.

9. AE 30, 14.

10. Michael Fagenblat identifies and emphasizes the Paulinian turn of Levinas's post-1968 philosophy; see *A Covenant of Creatures*, 176. For a careful analysis of the Christian nature of the turn taken by Levinas in his later philosophy, see David Brezis, "Messianisme et pensée sacrificielle: Sur la 'dérive christianisante' de Levinas." Brezis's analyses converge in many points with my own. He suggests that Levinas, by placing his later phenomenology "under the sign of Christian sensibility or spirituality," can be read as trying to "rejudaize" Christianity, as it were, by showing that "the true Passion is Israel's" (243).

11. In his *Covenant*, Michael Fagenblat makes a contrast between the centrality of the "face" in *Totality and Infinity* and the "defacement of the Other" in *Otherwise Than Being* (99), namely, the nonphenomenality, nonpresence, nonencounter, such that "ethical obligation is no longer derived from moral experience" (99). Levinas's later phenomenology is based not on "revelation" (100) but on "incarnation" (102). Adrian Peperzak also indicates a movement in later Levinas from the "other's visage" to "the Self" (217). See his *To the Other*.

12. AE 37, 19.

13. He is referring here to *Totality and Infinity*, but I think the description is even more pertinent to *Otherwise Than Being*. See Derrida, "Violence," 124, 164; Peperzak, *To the Other*, 220–221. Paul Ricoeur notes that in Levinas's text, "we notice no visible progression in the argument." See *Autrement Levinas*, 3.

14. AE 51, 28–29.

15. AE 85–86, 50. The English translation systematically rewrites—betrays—these structures by adding "there is" or other verbal forms.

16. AE 274, 178.

17. Benjamin, "Über den Begriff der Geschichte," 695. For a comparison between Levinas and Benjamin, see Herzog, "Levinas, Benjamin, and the Oppressed."

18. AE 10, xlviii.

19. AE 272, 177.

20. Heidegger, *Holzwege*, 295.

21. Barth, *Der Römerbrief*; see Moyn, *Origins of the Other*.

22. On Gnosticism in twentieth-century philosophy, see Styfhals, *No Spiritual Investment in the World*.

23. On Levinas and Kabbalah, see Elliot Wolfson, "Secrecy, Modesty, and the Feminine: Kabbalistic Traces in the Thought of Levinas," and the references cited there; Jacob Meskin, "The Role of Lurianic Kabbalah in the Early Philosophy of Emmanuel Levinas." Concerning neo-Platonism, Simon Critchley argues that Levinas's "apophatic" language owes "a deep debt to Plotinus, neo-Platonism, and Plato" (*Problem with Levinas*, 71) and compares it to the negative theology of Pseudo-Dionysius and Eckhart (75). Michael Fagenblat, in his *Covenant*, suggests that there are "echoes of mystical and martyrological exegetical traditions," of "apophatic traditions" (106) and "Neoplatonic traditions" (107), such as Plotinus (108) and

Ibn Gabirol's Fons Vitae (109), and speaks of Levinas's "Jewish via eminentia" (106). In *To the Other*, Adrian Peperzak also identifies in Levinas motifs of *via eminentia* and refers to Pseudo-Dionysius (233).

24. AE 163, 103.

25. AE 85, 50.

26. AE 83, 48–49. For this reason, Levinas's later ethics can no longer be said to be based on generosity or "hospitality." See Bernasconi, "Strangers and Slaves": "Derrida's claim in *Adieu* that hospitality is 'ethicity itself: the whole and principle of ethics' . . . is, at best, misleading when extended to *Otherwise than Being*" (254). Cf. Derrida, *Adieu*, 119–129.

27. AE 163, 103.

28. In *Broken Tablets*, Sarah Hammerschlag points to the use of the trope of persecution already in Levinas's early notebooks (63).

29. The English translation of *sensibilité* by "sensibility" thus seems to me to miss the point.

30. AE 87, 51.

31. AE 109, 126; AE 111, 141.

32. Levinas explicitly refers to this verse in "Judaïsme et Kénose," HN 133–151, and 114–132, where he connects the notion of "living soul" to the notion of "God's image" (TI 144, 125).

33. "And the earth was without form, and void; and darkness was upon the face of the deep; and the *ruach* of God moved upon the face of the waters."

34. The Pauline and Gnostic traditions, among others, go on to assert a Greek Jewish pneuma against a Jewish Greek psyche: "the man of soul [*psychikos*] does not accept the things of the spirit [*pneumatos*] of God" (1 Cor. 2, 14). See Jonas, *Gnostic Religion*, 124.

35. The rendering of *esprit* in English as "mind" erases the entire prophetic tradition—its spirit, the pneuma—and relocates Levinas in the Greek anthropology of soul and *nous*.

36. AE 277, 181.

37. AE 160, 111. Is there here a proximity to Heidegger's *Da*?

38. AE 10, xlvii.

39. AE 185n1.

40. AE 183, 116; AE 185, 117.

41. We have already seen how Levinas employs this category at the heart of his phenomenology, whereby he deploys "barbaric" discourse within philosophy—that is, not just prophetic discourse, but more specifically a category of discourse that has been a bone of contention, a *skandalon*, a barbarism within the prophetic tradition itself, not in the least between Christianity as the Universal Church, and Judaism as the Chosen People. Levinas's operation, inasmuch as it generates a certain shock, stumble, or interruption in the philosophical logos, immediately overcomes the scandal by universalizing chosenness into a basic feature of all human subjectivity, of every individual as a spirit in flesh.

42. AE 181, 114.

43. AE 188, 118.

44. AE 87, 51.

45. AE 149, 93.

46. AE 186, 117; AE 177, 112.

47. AE 175, 111.

48. AE 121, 75.

49. He does so by referring to Rashi's commentary on Numbers 11, 12. In this verse, Moses, who can no longer stand the people's complaints, says to God: "Did I conceive all this people, did I bear them, that You should say to me, 'Carry them in your bosom as a nurse carries an infant'?" In his comment, Rashi quotes an earlier rabbinic midrash, *Sifrei*, which invokes other verses to show that God entrusted the people of Israel to Moses, that is, "on the understanding that they will curse you and stone you." Rabbinic thought thus, Levinas writes, "says the extent of responsibility: '. . . to the point of being delivered over to stoning and insults' on the part of the very one for whom the responsible one answers" (139n2, 192n24). The reference stated in Levinas's book is actually to Rashi's commentary on the following chapter of Numbers, namely on Numbers 12, 12. However, the words quoted by Levinas appear not in Rashi's commentary on Numbers 12, 12 but in Rashi on Numbers 11, 12, a verse Levinas himself quotes a few pages later (145, 91), so it seems that the printed reference is erroneous. For a nice attempt to explain Levinas's note nevertheless in reference to Numbers 12, 12, which interestingly also invokes motherhood, see Botwinick, *Emmanuel Levinas and the Limits of Ethics*, 208–209. For a discussion of Levinas's reference to this verse, see Guenther, "'Like a Maternal Body."

50. AE 176, 111.

51. AE 186n1; 196n21.

52. "Pure brûlure." The English translation reads "pure born," which should perhaps have been "pure burn," and in any case mutes the deep prophetic echo I attempt here to reconstruct. See "Judaïsme et Kénose": "The sacrifices that were made every day in the Temple—were they not daily holocausts? And the flesh offered up in the Temple—was it not to be burned completely away, leaving nothing behind for the giver of the sacrifice? Can the individual, then, speak in prayer of his or her selfish needs, when that would compromise the pure dis-inter-estment of the burnt-offering?" (HN 148, 128).

53. AE 220, 140; AE 226, 144.

54. AE 149–150, 94.

55. AE 223, 143.

56. AE 228, 146.

57. AE 229, 146.

58. AE 72–73, 42.

59. AE 231, 143; AE 225n1, 198n6.

60. Isaiah 6, 8: "Then I heard the voice of my Lord saying, 'Whom shall I send? Who will go for us?' And I said, 'Here am I; send me.'" In a footnote, Levinas comments: "'here I am' means 'send me'" (228n1, 199n11).

61. "'Here I am, in the name of God,' without referring myself directly to his presence. 'Here I am,' just that! The word God is still absent from the phrase in which God is for the first time involved in words. It does not at all state 'I believe in God.' To bear witness to God is precisely not to state this extra-ordinary word, as though glory would be lodged in a theme and be posited as a thesis, or become being's essence. As a sign given to the other of this very signification, the 'here I am' signifies me in the name of God, at the service of men that concern me, without having anything to identify myself with, but the sound of my voice or the figure of my gesture—the saying itself" (AE 233, 149).

62. Cf. Derrida, *De la grammatologie*, 23, 12: "s'entendre-parler," "hearing-oneself-speak."

63. AE 230, 147.

64. AE 230, 147.

65. Leora Batnitzky notes how in Levinas's philosophy "the externality of law is ultimately unredeemable. Law must be made internal. It must be inscribed 'in me'" (*Leo Strauss and Emmanuel Levinas*, 91).

66. AE 232, 148.

67. Cf. Deuteronomy 30, 6: "The LORD your God will circumcise your hearts and the hearts of your descendants, and you will love Him with all your heart and all your soul, so that you may live." Jeremiah 4, 4: "Circumcise yourselves to the LORD, remove the foreskins of your hearts, O men of Judah and people of Jerusalem."

68. AE 253, 163.

69. AE 77, 45.

70. AE 251, 161. This brings to mind two motifs in Heidegger's late philosophy. First, in his writings on language, Heidegger works with a conceptual distinction similar to Levinas's differentiation between Saying and Said, namely, between language as a generative happening, *Sprechen* (speaking), or *Sagen* (saying), on the one hand, and language as already perfected semantic product, *das Gesprochene* (the spoken), *das Gesagte* (the said), or *die Sage* (the saying, saga, epos, tale), on the other. One of the ways in which Heidegger describes the latter notion, akin to Levinas's Said, is that it features *Versammlung*, assembling, gathering. The Said gathers the dispersed moments of Saying. "In what has been spoken [das Gesprochene] speaking [das Sprechen] assembles/gathers the ways in which it persists as well as that which persists by it—its persistence, its subsistence [Wesen]." See Heidegger, "Die Sprache," 14, 192. See also "Die Sage ist die alles Scheinen fügende Versammlung des in sich vielfältigen Zeigens, das überall das Gezeigte bei ihm selbst bleiben lässt" ("Das Wort," in von Herrmann, *Unterwegs*, 246). The notion that the Said gathers the Saying, thereby generating essence from speech, is supported by the morphology of German grammar, in which the perfect form of the verb is constructed with the prefix "ge-" (*gesprochen, gesagt, gewesen*), also used in the construction of nouns that designate the collection, group, or assembly of numerous individual objects, such as *Gebrige* (a group of mountains, *Berge*), or *Gebüsch* (a group of bushes), *Gefieder* (the set of a bird's feathers), and so on. See Lapidot, "Die Versammlung." The second motif relevant here is Heidegger's reinterpretation of the Greek *dike*, "justice," in terms of *Fug*, order or jointure, and *Gefüge*, assembled order, that is, structure or system. "Being is fittingness that enjoins (fügender Fug): dike" (*Einführung in die Metaphysik*, 123, translated by Fried and Polt, *Introduction to Metaphysics*, 171). "The human being's emerging into order and his standing within order [Fug] or dike, which is orderliness [Fügsamkeit]" (*Parmenides*, 137, translated by Schuwer and Rojcewicz, *Parmenides*, 93). See Bambach, *Thinking the Poetic Measure of Justice*. It is easy to see the cooperation between the Said, an operation of gathering, and justice, an operation of structuring, combined into the production of being in Heidegger as well as in Levinas.

71. AE 246, 158.

72. See also EI 75, 80.

73. AE 249, 160.

74. AE 245, 157.

75. AE 246, 158. It is for this reason that I find it hard to accept Howard Caygill's interpretation whereby in *Otherwise Than Being*, the "responsibility for the other is given precedence over responsibility for the third" (*Levinas and the Political*, 143). I agree with Caygill that Levinas's analysis opens up the threat of a just war, but I attribute this problem not to the

distinction between the other and the third but to the nondistinction between the other and the I—see below.

76. AE 249, 160.

77. AE 247, 158.

78. AE 247, 158.

79. AE 247, 158; AE 249, 159.

80. Cf. Gibbs, *Correlations*, 241.

81. AE 69, 40.

82. AE 17–18, 6.

83. AE 247, 159.

84. AE 263, 170.

85. AE 204, 128.

86. AE 251, 161.

87. AE 283, 185.

88. AE 274, 178.

89. AE 88–89, 52.

90. AE 160n1, 194n3.

91. AE 282, 184.

92. AE 282–283, 184–185. On Levinas and utopia, see Abensour, "To Think Utopia Otherwise."

93. Simon Critchley, in *Ethics of Deconstruction*, accordingly describes Levinas's political vision as "an open community, an interrupted community" that enacts "plurality, multiplicity" (225) through "a political discourse of reflection and interrogation, a language of decision, judgment, and critique that is informed and interrupted by the responsibility of the ethical Saying" (233). In another text, Critchley relates Levinas's political vision to Blanchot's (and later Jean-Luc Nancy's) *communauté désoeuvrée*. See Critchley, "Il y a," 77. In "Five Problems," against Levinas's insistence on "Israel," Critchley refers to Rancière's "anarchist metapolitics": "the radical manifestation of the people, the people not as *das Volk* or *le peuple* shaped by the state, but as *die Leute*, or *les gens*, the people in their irreducible plurality" (182).

94. AE 262, 169.

95. TI 244, 221.

96. TI 329, 295.

97. AE 242, 155; AE 264, 170.

Prophecy

1. See AE 9, xlvii, reporting that the essay was published in the *Revue philosophique de Louvain* of October 1968.

8. 1967 after 1968

1. DL 257, 170. A French translation of Benjamin's essay ("Sur le concept d'histoire") by Pierre Missac appeared in Sartre's journal *Les temps modernes* no. 25. It would be interesting to compare Benjamin's disappointment in Marxism (following the 1939 Molotov–Ribbentrop

Pact)—which, according to Gershom Scholem, was the background for this essay—and Levinas's disappointment in French humanism, both disappointments having led to a radical questioning of Western historiography.

2. DL 258, 170–171.

3. DL 417–418, 281.

4. DL 420; 282–283. Levinas also identifies in antihumanism "a protest against belles-lettres and the declamation that takes the place of necessary activities" and "equally against the violence of the verbal indignation of revolutionaries themselves, who immediately become inverted into a cultural pastime as they turn themselves into a revolutionary literature, in which literature coats revolution and so refreshes a dulled artistic palate. It is an antihumanism that protests against all-powerful literature and finds its way even into the graffiti that call for such literature's destruction. It is an antihumanism as old as the prophecy of Ezekiel, in which the real prophetic spirit is offered as the only thing capable of putting an end to all such writing" (DL 420, 282–283).

5. AE 203, 127–128.

6. AE 272, 177; AE 22, 8.

7. AE 284, 185.

8. We already saw how decolonial critique of the West (which unveils the humanist project of the West, namely Western "good," as evil) activated Gnostic motifs, such as Fanon's description of the colonial situation as "Manichaeism."

9. AE 96–97, 57–58. Sarah Hammerschlag, in *Broken Tablets*, notes Levinas's ambivalent relation to antihumanism, writing that Levinas "reclaimed the banner of antihumanism not to side with Foucault or Derrida but to suggest that in the wake of an antihumanist critique of autonomy . . . one might find another form of heteronomy" (73)—not the heteronomy offered by literature but the heteronomy offered by religion. Simon Critchley makes a similar argument in contrasting Levinas with Blanchot ("Il y a," 83). By contrast, my analyses highlight a profound hermeneutic engagement in Levinas's post-1968 work, such as the difference of said/saying, the motif of unsaying, and the turn to the Talmud.

10. Michael Morgan argues that Levinas was responding to the crisis of ethics generated by the antihumanist critique of colonialism. See Morgan, *Cambridge Introduction*, 6–11.

11. DL 207, 134.

12. DL 423, 284.

13. Sarah Hammerschlag, in *Figural Jew*, already suggests "a shift in Levinas's . . . political sensibilities" representing "a shift in the general zeitgeist of French Jews, who became more vocally pro-Zionist and communitarian after the Six-Day-War" (161).

14. Aron, *De Gaulle, Israël et les juifs*, 55.

15. Aron, *De Gaulle*, 25.

16. Aron, *De Gaulle*, 35. Some commentators, including De Gaulle himself, understood his words as praise to Jews. See, for instance, Romain Gary in his interview in *L'Arche*, April 26–May 25, 1970, 40–45.

17. Aron, *De Gaulle*, 40–41.

18. Aron, *De Gaulle*, 49, 55, 62.

19. Aron, *De Gaulle*, 37.

20. Arendt, *Origins of Totalitarianism*, 427.

21. Aron, *De Gaulle*, 53.

22. Aron, *De Gaulle*, 44, 63.

23. DL 385, 259.
24. DL 389, 261–262.
25. DL 386, 262.
26. QLT 16, 6.
27. QLT 16, 6.
28. QLT 16, 6.
29. Fanon, *Les damnés de la terre*, 31; DL 423, 284.
30. DSS 48, 115. On Levinas and Blanchot, see Critchley, "Il y a."
31. DSS 48–49, 115–116.
32. QLT 24, 9.
33. DSS 48, 115.
34. I wonder to what extent Levinas draws inspiration here from the figure of subjectivity Sarah Hammerschlag describes as developed by Blanchot in response to the Algerian War based on "power of refusal": as "unwillingness *even* to resist as an active force, to find an alternative to forms of political expression that reify agency as something transparent, that accept a version of the subject who can be invoked and convoked by the political law" (*Broken Tablets*, 175–176). Hammerschlag argues for Blanchot's inspiration on Derrida, both featuring in her book as counterfigures to Levinasian affirmative Jewish identitarianism. I share Hammerschlag's critical appraisal of Levinas's Zionist commitment; however, I claim that after 1967/68, Levinas moves to ground this commitment on a model of subjectivity that closely corresponds to what Hammerschlag finds in Blanchot and Derrida. Annabel Herzog, *Levinas's Politics*, identifies the two different Zionist narratives in Levinas's talmudic readings—the one where the State of Israel has the vocation of realizing prophetic politics and the one where its purpose is Jewish self-defense. However, she analyzes these two narratives not as alternative and corresponding to different periods in Levinas's thought but rather as simultaneous and complementary: "the modern State of Israel allows a survival that is necessary for the implementation of its specific justice" (99). Nonetheless, Herzog does identify a shift from messianic to survivalist Zionism in Levinas after "the First Lebanon War and the Sabra and Shatila massacres of September 1982" (105), a shift that I date earlier, to 1967/8.
35. AE 282–283, 184–185.
36. AE 274, 178.

9. Decolonial Eschatology

1. ADV 76–77, 58. On animality in Levinas as a type of evil, see Herzog, *Levinas's Politics*, 76–79.
2. DSS 167, 188.
3. ADV 79, 60; Levinas, *Nouvelles lectures talmudiques*, 71.
4. ADV 80, 61. See discussion in Herzog, *Levinas's Politics*, 72–73.
5. ADV 216, 184.
6. HN 119, 103.
7. AE 282–283, 184–185.
8. DL 429, 288.
9. DL 427, 287.
10. DL 427, 287.

11. Originally published in Isaac Schneersohn, ed., *D'Auschwitz à Israël, vingt ans après la Libération* (1968).

12. DL 336, 225.

13. DL 335, 224; DL 334, 223.

14. DL 257–8, 170.

15. DL 257–258, 170.

16. DL 258, 171.

17. The alternative English translation "sacred history," used by Aronowitz (*Nine Talmudic Readings*, 9), strikes me as problematic in view of Levinas's distinction between—as Aronowitz herself translates in the same volume—the "sacred" (*sacré*) and the "holy" (*saint*) (89 and passim).

18. For earlier, pre-1968 uses, see already in 1935 "L'inspiration religieuse de l'Alliance," and in 1939, "A propos de la mort du Pape Pie XI."

19. QLT 23, 9.

20. Löwith, *Meaning in History*.

21. DL 326, 218.

22. HN 10, 2.

23. HN 11, 3.

24. HN 12, 4.

25. Cf. TB Pesachim 87b: "And Rabbi Elazar said: The Holy One, Blessed be He, exiled Israel among the nations only so that converts would join them."

26. HN 11, 3.

27. ADV 82, 63.

28. AE 30, 14.

29. Cf. Caygill, *Levinas and the Political*, 162.

30. HN 101, 88.

31. HN 38, 29.

32. HN 39, 30.

33. I am grateful to Annabel Herzog for drawing my attention to this point. In "Benny Levy versus Emmanuel Levinas," contra Benny Levy's stressing in Levinas the idea of "being Jewish" as opposed to philosophy, Herzog indicates that Levinas since the publication of "Substitution" in 1968 "stopped emphasizing the Jewish 'difference'" (20). My analysis introduces a nuance by saying that in his post-1968 thought, Levinas downplays Jewish *epistemic* difference and emphasizes the historical-existential—indeed (*pace* Herzog's point against Levy) *ontic*—difference of Israel versus Europe.

34. Sartre, "Orphée noir," xiv.

35. DSS 44, 113.

36. DSS 46, 114–115.

37. DSS 48, 115.

38. DSS 44, 113.

39. DL 198, 128. It is not entirely clear whether Levinas reproaches or approves of Claudel's note. As I show below, Levinas proceeds to appropriate Claudel's position on the Israeli-Arab conflict.

40. DL 200, 129.

41. HN 164, 141; HN 165, 142.

42. HN 166, 143.

43. ADV 13, xvi.
44. DSS 48, 115.
45. ADV 219, 186.
46. ADV 227–228, 194.
47. ADV 227, 193.
48. ADV 14, xvii.
49. HN 194–195, 166.
50. AE 247, 158.
51. ADV 14, xvii.
52. ADV 14, xvii.
53. Howard Caygill analyzes the problem here as arising from what he reads as the privilege of "the other" over "the third" in later Levinas; see *Levinas and the Political*, 190. I analyze the problem as arising from the conflation of the Other and the I.
54. DSS 180, 196; TB Baba Kama 60b.
55. DSS 180, 196.
56. HN 35, 26–27.
57. DL 203, 131. Howard Caygill, *Levinas and the Political*, justly notes Levinas's complex operation—"a complexity that verges on the irresponsible" (186)—whereby he "reports Claudel's position, but without marking any distance from it, thus giving the impression that Levinas is speaking through a mask" (187), "as if Levinas has not spoken, but allowed his voice to be confused with that of a Christian with a questionable record with respect to anti-Semitic and anti-Islamic sentiment" (189).
58. DL 202, 131.
59. ADV 13, xvi.
60. ADV 13, xvi.
61. DL 203, 132.
62. DL 202, 131.
63. ADV 13, xv.
64. DL 204, 132.
65. DF 203, 131.
66. DL 203, 131–132.
67. QLT 16, 6.
68. DL 385, 259.
69. DL 335–336, 224–225.
70. ADV 226, 193.
71. ADV 226, 193.
72. ADV 226, 193.
73. ADV 227, 193–194.
74. Cf. Judith Butler's critique of Levinas's analogy between the "suffering of Jews and Nazism and the suffering of Israel" (*Parting Ways*, 45).
75. DSS 170, 191; DSS 169, 190.
76. DSS 170–171, 191.
77. DSS 171, 191.

Conclusion

1. TI 244.

BIBLIOGRAPHY

Abensour, Miguel. 1998. "To Think Utopia Otherwise." *Graduate Faculty Philosophy Journal* 20.2–21.1: 251–279.

Althusser, Louis. 1970. "Idéologie et appareils idéologiques d'État: Notes pour une recherche." *La Pensée* 151: 3–38. Translated by Ben Brewster, "Ideology, and Ideological State Apparatuses (Notes towards an Investigation)." In *Lenin and Philosophy and Other Essays*, 127–186. New York: Monthly Review Press, 1971.

Anidjar, Gil. 2003. *The Jew, The Arab: A History of the Enemy*. Stanford, CA: Stanford University Press.

Arendt, Hannah. 1979 [1951]. *The Origins of Totalitarianism*. New York: Harcourt Brace.

Aron, Raymond. 1968. *De Gaulle, Israël et les juifs*. Paris: Plon. Reprinted with a preface by Frédéric Brahami. Paris: Les Belles Lettres, 2020.

Aronowitz, Annette. 1990. "Translator's Introduction." In Levinas, *Nine Talmudic Readings*, edited by Emmanuel Levinas, ix–xxxix. Bloomington: Indiana University Press.

Asad, Talal. 2003. *Formations of the Secular: Christianity, Islam, Modernity*. Stanford, CA: Stanford University Press.

Bambach, Charles. 2013. *Thinking the Poetic Measure of Justice: Hölerlin-Heidegger-Celan*. Albany: SUNY Press.

Barth, Karl. 1985 [1919]. *Der Römerbrief*. 1st ed. Edited by H. Schmidt. Zurich: Karl-Barth-Gesamtausgabe, Band II.

Batnitzky, Leora. 2005. *Leo Strauss and Emmanuel Levinas: Philosophy and the Politics of Revelation*. Cambridge: Cambridge University Press.

Benjamin, Walter. 1974 [1940]. "Über den Begriff der Geschichte." In *Gesammelte Schriften* I.2, edited by Rolf Tiedemann and Hermann Schweppenhäuser, 691–707. Frankfurt a. Main: Suhrkamp.

Bernasconi, Robert. 2012. "Levinas's Ethical Critique of Levinasian Ethics." In *Totality and Infinity at 50*, edited by Scott Davidson and Diane Perpich, 253–270. Pittsburgh: Duquesne University Press.

Bernasconi, Robert. 2006. "Strangers and Slaves in the Land of Egypt: Levinas and the Politics of Otherness." In *Difficult Justice. Commentaries on Levinas and Politics*, edited by Asher Horowitz and Gad Horowitz, 246–261. Toronto: University of Toronto Press.

Bernasconi, Robert, 1999. "The Third Party. Levinas on the Intersection of the Ethical and the Political." *Journal of the British Society for Phenomenology* 30, no. 1: 76–87. Reprinted in Katz, *Levinas*, 1:45–57.

Bernasconi, Robert. 1992. "Who Is My Neighbor? Who Is the Other? Questioning 'the Generosity of Western Thought.'" In *Ethics and Responsibility in the Phenomenological Tradition*, edited by Robert Bernasconi, 1–31. Pittsburgh: Simon Silverman Phenomenology Center, Duquesne University. Reprinted in Katz, *Levinas*, 4:5–30.

Bernasconi, Robert. 1990. "The Ethics of Suspicion." *Research in Phenomenology* 20: 3–18. Reprinted in Katz, *Levinas*, 3:29–43.

Bernasconi, Robert. 1989. "Rereading Totality and Infinity." In *The Question of the Other: Essays in Contemporary Continental Philosophy*, edited by A. Dallery and C. Scott, 23–34. Albany: SUNY Press. Reprinted in Katz, *Levinas*, 1:32–44.

Boittin, Jennifer Anne. 2010. *Colonial Metropolis: The Urban Grounds of Anti-imperialism and Feminism in Interwar France*. Lincoln: University of Nebraska Press.

Botwinick, Aryeh. 2014. *Emmanuel Levinas and the Limits of Ethics: A Critique and Reappropriation*. London: Routledge.

Botwinick, Aryeh. 2005. "Same/Other versus Friend/Enemy: Levinas contra Schmitt." *Telos: Critical Theory of the Contemporary* 132: 46–63.

Bourg, Julian. 2005. "The Red Guards of Paris: French Student Maoism of the 1960s." *History of European Ideas* 31, no. 4: 472–490.

Boyarin, Daniel. 2015. *A Traveling Homeland: The Babylonian Talmud as Diaspora*. Philadelphia: University of Pennsylvania Press.

Brezis, David. 2011. "Messianisme et pensée sacrificielle: Sur la 'dérive christianisante' de Levinas." *Europe—revue littéraire mensuelle* 991–992: 242–268.

Brumlik, Micha. 2018. "Everyday Life, Hatred of Jews, and the Identitarian Movement: The Present-Day Heritage of Martin Heidegger." In *Heidegger and Jewish Thought: Difficult Others*, edited by Elad Lapidot and Micha Brumlik, 41–54. London: Rowman & Littlefield.

Buber, Martin. 1923. *Reden über das Judentum*. Frankfurt a. Main: Literarische Anstalt Rütten & Loening.

Butler, Judith. 2013. "Levinas trahi? La réponse de Judith Butler." *Le Monde*, March 21, 2013. https://www.lemonde.fr/idees/article/2013/03/21/levinas-trahi-la-reponse-de-judith -butler_5994702_3232.html.

Butler, Judith. 2012. *Parting Ways: Jewishness and the Critique of Zionism*. New York: Columbia University Press.

Butler, Judith. 2004. "Can the 'Other' of Philosophy Speak?" In *Undoing Gender*, 232–250. New York: Routledge.

Byrd, Dustin J., and Seyed Javad Miri, eds. 2020. *Frantz Fanon and Emancipatory Social Theory: A View from the Wretched*. Leiden: Brill.

Caputo, John. 2000. "People of God, People of Being: The Theological Presuppositions of Heidegger's Path of Thought." In *Appropriating Heidegger*, edited by James E. Falconer and Mark A. Wrathall, 85–100. Cambridge: Cambridge University Press.

Caro, Jason. 2009. "Levinas and the Palestinians." *Philosophy & Social Criticism* 35, no. 6: 671–668.

Caygill, Howard. 2002. *Levinas and the Political*. London: Routledge.

Chafer, Tony. 2002. *The End of Empire in French West Africa: France's Successful Decolonization?* Oxford: Berg.

Chanter, Tina. 2005. "Ontological Difference, Sexual Difference, and Time." In Katz, *Levinas*, 4:101–131.

Chanter, Tina, ed. 2001. *Feminist Interpretations of Emmanuel Levinas*. University Park: Pennsylvania State University Press.

Chaouat, Bruno. 2020. "Being and Jewishness: Levinas Reader of Sartre." In *Sartre, Jews, and the Other: Rethinking Antisemitism, Race, and Gender*, edited by Manuela Consonni and Vivian Liska, 90–106. Oldenbourg: De Gruyter.

Chaouat, Bruno. 2013. "Débat: Judith Butler ou Levinas trahi ?" *Le Monde*, March 13, 2013. Translated by Alan Astro, "Judith Butler and the Critique of Zionist Reason."

https://www.lemonde.fr/idees/article/2013/03/13/debat-judith-butler-ou-levinas
-trahi_5994697_3232.html.

Cherki, Alice. 2006. *Frantz Fanon: A Portrait*. Translated by Nadia Benabid. Ithaca, NY: Cornell University Press.

Claudel, Paul. 1964. *Emmaüs*. In *Oeuvres completes de Paul Claudel*, edited by Pierre Claudel and Jacques Petit, and Gallimard, 23:73–439. Paris: Gallimard.

Claudel, Paul. 1950. *Une voix sur Israël*. Paris: Editions Librairie Gallimard.

Cohen, Hermann. 2008. *Religion der Vernunft aus den Quellen des Judentums*. Hrsg. Bruno Strauss, neu eingeleitet von Ulrich Oelschläger. Wiesbaden: Marix.

Cohen-Levinas, Danielle, and Marc Crépon, eds. 2015. *Levinas-Derrida: Lire ensemble*. Paris: Hermann Editeurs.

Colson, F. H., and G. H. Whitaker, trans. 1949. *Philo in Eleven Volumes*. Vol. I–VI. Cambridge, MA: Harvard University Press.

Consonni, Manuela, and Vivian Liska, eds. 2020. *Sartre, Jews, and the Other: Rethinking Antisemitism, Race, and Gender*. Oldenbourg: De Gruyter.

Cooley, John K. 1972. "China and the Palestinians." *Journal of Palestine Studies* 1, no. 2: 19–34.

Critchley, Simon. 2015. *The Problem with Levinas*. Edited by Alexis Dianda. Oxford: Oxford University Press.

Critchley, Simon. 2014 [1992]. *The Ethics of Deconstruction: Derrida and Levinas*. Edinburgh: Edinburgh University Press.

Critchley, Simon. 2004a. "Five Problems in Levinas's View of Politics and the Sketch of a Solution to Them." *Political Theory* 32, no. 2: 172–185.

Critchley, Simon. 2004b. "Introduction." In *The Cambridge Companion to Levinas*, edited by Simon Critchley and Robert Bernasconi, 1–32. Cambridge: Cambridge University Press.

Critchley, Simon. 1996. "Il y a—Holding Levinas's Hand to Blanchot's Fire." In *Maurice Blanchot: The Demand of Writing*, edited by C. B. Gill, 75–87. London: Routledge.

Derrida, Jacques. 1998 [1987]. "En ce moment même dans cet ouvrage me voici." In *Psyché: Inventions de l'autre*, 159–202. Paris: Galilée.

Derrida, Jacques. 1997. *Adieu à Emmanuel Levinas*. Paris: Galilée.

Derrida, Jacques. 1967a. *De la grammatologie*. Paris: Les éditions de minuit. Translated by Gayatri Chakrovarty Spivak, *On Grammatology*. Baltimore: Johns Hopkins University Press, 1976 [1974].

Derrida, Jacques. 1967b. "Violence et métaphysique." In *L'écriture et la difference*, 117–228. Paris: Seuil. Translated by A. Bass, "Violence and Metaphysics." In Derrida, *Writing and Difference*, 79–153. London: Routledge & Kegan Paul, 1978.

Drabinski, John. 2011. *Levinas and the Postcolonial: Race, Nation, Other*. Edinburgh: Edinburgh University Press.

Eisenstadt, Oona. 2018. "Levinas's Jewish Writings." In *The Oxford Handbook of Levinas*, edited by Michael Morgan, 459–472. Oxford: Oxford University Press.

Eisenstadt, Oona. 2012. "Eurocentrism and Colorblindness." *Levinas Studies* 7: 43–62.

Eisenstadt, Oona. 2008. "Anti-utopianism Revisited." *Shofar* 26, no. 4: 120–138.

Eisenstadt, Oona. 2005. "Levinas versus Levinas: Hebrew, Greek, and Linguistic Justice." *Philosophy and Rhetoric* 38, no. 2: 145–158.

Eisenstadt, Oona. 2003. "The Problem of the Promise: Derrida on Levinas on the Cities of Refuge." *CrossCurrents* 52, no. 4: 474–482.

Eisenstadt, Oona, and Claire Elise Katz. 2016. "The Faceless Palestinian: A History of an Error." *Telos* 174: 9–32.

Fagenblat, Michael, ed. 2017. *Negative Theology as Jewish Modernity*. Bloomington: Indiana University Press.

Fagenblat, Michael. 2010. *A Covenant of Creatures: Levinas's Philosophy of Judaism*. Stanford, CA: Stanford University Press.

Fanon, Frantz. 2002 [1961]. *Les damnés de la terre*. Paris: La découverte. Translated by Constance Farrington, *The Wretched of the Earth*. New York: Grove Press, 1963.

Fields, Belden. 1988. *Trotskyism and Maoism: Theory and Practice in France and the United States*. New York: Praeger.

Fields, Belden. 1984. "French Maoism." *Social Text* 9/10: 148–177.

Foran, Lisa, and Rozemund Uljée, eds. 2016. *Heidegger, Levinas, Derrida: The Question of Difference*. Dordrecht: Springer.

Foucault, Michel. 1969. *L'Archéologie du savoir*. Paris: Gallimard. Translated by A. M. Sheridan Smith, *The Archaeology of Knowledge*. London: Routledge, 2002.

Freenberg, Andrew, and Jim Freedman. 2011. *When Poetry Ruled the Streets: The French May Events of 1968*. Albany: SUNY Press.

Gibbs, Robert. 1992. *Correlations in Rosenzweig and Levinas*. Princeton, NJ: Princeton University Press.

Giladi, Amotz. 2018. "L'invention d'un macro-nationalisme 'hébreu.'" *Les Dossiers du Grihl* 12-1. https://doi.org/10.4000/dossiersgrihl.7052.

Guenther, Lisa. 2006. "'Like a Maternal Body': Emmanuel Levinas and the Motherhood of Moses." *Hypatia* 21, no. 1: 119–136.

Haddour, Azzedine. 2019. *Frantz Fanon, Postcolonialism and the Ethics of Difference*. Manchester: Manchester University Press.

Hammerschlag, Sarah. 2016. *Broken Tablets: Levinas, Derrida, and the Literary Afterlife of Religion*. New York: Columbia University Press.

Hammerschlag, Sarah. 2010a. *The Figural Jew: Politics and Identity in Postwar French Thought*. Chicago: University of Chicago Press.

Hammerschlag, Sarah. 2010b. "Literary Unrest: Blanchot, Levinas and the Proximity of Judaism." *Critical Inquiry* 36, no. 4: 652–672.

Hammerschlag, Sarah. 2008a. "Another, Other Abraham: Derrida's Figuring of Levinas's Judaism." *Shofar* 26, no. 4: 74–96.

Hammerschlag, Sarah. 2008b. "Reading May '68 through a Levinasian Lens: Alain Finkelkraut, Maurice Blanchot, and the Politics of Identity." *Jewish Quarterly Review* 98, no. 4: 522–551.

Hanley, D. L., and A. P. Kerr. 1989. *May '68: Coming of Age*. Basingstoke: Palgrave Macmillan.

Hazlett, Allan. 2014. *A Critical Introduction to Skepticism*. London: Bloomsbury.

Hegel, G. W. F. 2018. *The Phenomenology of Spirit*. Translated by Michael Inwood. Oxford: Oxford University Press.

Heidegger, Martin. 2003 [1959]. "Aus einem Gespräch von der Sprache, zwischen einem Japaner und einem Fragenden." In *Unterwegs zur Sprache*, 84–155. Stuttgart: Klett-Cotta. Translated by Peter Hertz, "A Dialogue on Language, between a Japanese and an Inquirer." In *On the Way to Language*, 1–54. New York: Harper & Row, 1971.

Heidegger, Martin. 2003. *Holzwege*. Edited by Friedrich-Wilhelm von Herrmann. Frankfurt am Main: Vittorio Klostermann. Translated by Julian Young and Kenneth Haynes, *Off the Beaten Track*. New York: Cambridge University Press, 2002.

Heidegger, Martin. 2001 [1927]. *Sein und Zeit*. Tübingen: Max Niemeyer Verlag. Translated by John Macquarrie and Edward Robinson, *Being and Time*. New York: Harper Row, 1962.

Heidegger, Martin. 1992. *Parmenides*. Edited by Manfred S. Frings. Frankfurt am Main: Vittorio Klostermann. Translated Andre Schuwer and Richard Rojcewicz, *Parmenides*. Bloomington: Indiana University Press, 1992.

Heidegger, Martin. 1985. "Die Sprache." In *Unterwegs zu Sprache*, edited by F.-W. von Herrmann, 30–60. Frankfurt am Main: Vittorio Klostermann. Translated by Albert Hofstadter, "Language." In *Poetry, Language, Thought*. New York: Harper & Row, 1971.

Heidegger, Martin. 1983. *Einführung in die Metaphysik*. Edited by Petra Jaeger. Frankfurt am Main: Vittorio Klostermann. Translated by Gregory Fried and Richard Polt, *Introduction to Metaphysics*. New Haven, CT: Yale University Press, 2000.

Heidegger, Martin. 1980. *Hölderlins Hymnen "Germanien" und "Der Rhein."* Edited by Susanne Ziegler. Frankfurt am Main: Vittorio Klostermann. Translated by William McNeill and Julia Ireland, *Hölderlin's Hymn "Germanien" and "Der Rhein."* Bloomington: Indiana University Press, 2014.

Heidegger, Martin. 1976 [1930]. "Vom Wesen der Wahrheit." In *Wegmarken*, edited by Friedrich-Wilhelm von Herrrmann, 15–45. Frankfurt am Main: Vittoria Klostermann. Translated by John Sallis, "On the Essence of Truth." In *Pathmarks*, edited by William McNeill, 136–154. New York: Cambridge University Press, 1998.

Herzog, Annabel. 2020. *Levinas's Politics: Justice, Mercy, Universality*. Philadelphia: University of Pennsylvania Press.

Herzog, Annabel. 2019. "Levinas's Ethics, Politics, and Zionism." In *The Oxford Handbook of Levinas*, edited by Michael Morgan, 473–491. Oxford: Oxford University Press.

Herzog, Annabel. 2006. "Benny Levy versus Emmanuel Levinas on 'Being Jewish.'" *Modern Judaism* 26, no. 1: 15–30.

Herzog, Annabel. 2003. "Levinas, Benjamin, and the Oppressed." *Journal of Jewish Thought and Philosophy* 12, no. 2: 123–138.

Hollander, Dana. 2022. *Ethics out of Law: Hermann Cohen and the "Neighbor."* Toronto: University of Toronto Press.

Hollander, Dana. 2008. *Exemplarity and Chosenness: Rosenzweig and Derrida on the Nation of Philosophy*. Stanford, CA: Stanford University Press.

Horowitz, A., and G. Horowitz, eds. 2006. *Difficult Justice: Commentaries on Levinas and Politics*. Toronto: Toronto University Press.

Hudis, Peter. 2015. *Frantz Fanon: Philosopher of the Barricades*. London: Pluto Press.

Husserl, Edmund. 1976. *Ideen zu einer reinen Phänomenologie und phänomenologischen Philosophie*. Vol. I, *Allgemeine Einführung in die reine Phänomenologie*. Edited by Karl Schuhmann. The Hague: Martinus Nijhoff.

Husserl, Edmund. 1973. *Cartesianische Meditationen*. Edited by S. Strasser. The Hague: Martinus Nijhoff.

Husserl, Edmund. 1963. *Cartesianische Meditationen und Pariser Vorträge*. Edited by S. Strasser. The Hague: Nijhoff.

Irigaray, Luce. 2005. "The Fecundity of the Caress: A Reading of Levinas, *Totality and Infinity*, Section IV, B, 'The Phenomenology of Eros.'" In Katz, *Levinas*, 227–248.

Jackson, Julian, Anne-Louise Milne, and James S. Williams, eds. 2011. *May 68: Rethinking France's Last Revolution*. Basingstoke: Palgrave Macmillan.

Jonas, Hans. 1964. "Heidegger and Theology." *Review of Metaphysics* 18, no. 2: 207–233.

Jonas, Hans. 1958. *The Gnostic Religion: The Message of the Alien God and the Beginnings of Christianity*. Boston: Beacon Press.

Jonas, Hans. 1954. *Gnosis und spätantiker Geist: Von der Mythologie zur mystischen Philosophie*. Göttingen: Vandenhoeck und Rupprecht.

Jonas, Hans. 1952. "Gnosticism and modern Nihilism." In: *Social Research* 19.4: 430-452.

Jonas, Hans. 1934. *Gnosis und spätantiker Geis: Die mythologische Gnosis*. Göttingen: Vandenhoeck und Rupprecht.

Judaken, Jonathan, ed. 2008. *Race after Sartre: Antiracism, Africana Existentialism, Postcolonialism*. Albany: SUNY Press.

Just, Daniel. 2015. *Literature, Ethics, and Decolonization in Postwar France: The Politics of Disengagement*. Cambridge: Cambridge University Press.

Kalter, Christoph. 2016. *The Discovery of the Third World: Decolonization and the Rise of the New Left in France, c. 1950–1976*. Cambridge: Cambridge University Press.

Katz, Claire Elise, ed. 2005. *Emmanuel Levinas: Critical Assessments of Leadings Philosophers*. Vol. IV. London: Routledge.

Katz, Claire Elise. 2005. "Reinhabiting the House of Ruth. Exceeding the Limits of the Feminine in Levinas." In Katz, *Levinas*, 4:259–282.

Katz, Claire Elise. 2005. "From Eros to Maternity: Love, Death, and 'the Feminine' in the Philosophy of Emmanuel Levinas." In Katz, *Levinas*, 3:190–211.

Kavka, Martin. 2019. "For It Is God's Way to Sweeten Bitter with Bitter: Prayer in Levinas and R. Hayyim of Volozhin." *Levinas Studies* 13: 43–67.

Kleinberg, Ethan. 2021. *Levinas's Talmudic Turn: Philosophy and Jewish Thought*. Stanford, CA: Stanford University Press.

Klemm, David. 1989. "Levinas's Phenomenology of the Other and Language as the Other of Phenomenology." *Man and World* 22: 403–426.

Lacoue-Labarthe, Philippe. 2002. *Heidegger: La politique du poème*. Paris: Galilée. Translated by Jeff Fort, *Heidegger and the Politics of Poetry*. Urbana: University of Illinois Press, 2007.

Lacoue-Labarthe, Philippe. 1998 [1987]. *La Fiction du politique: Heidegger, l'art et la politique*. Paris: Christian Bourgois. Translated by Chris Turner, *Heidegger, Art and Politics: The Fiction of the Political*. Oxford: Blackwell, 1990.

Lapidot, Elad. 2023. "Divine Invisibility and Ethical Epistemology in Late Modernity: Heidegger, Jonas and Levinas." In *Der Mensch als Bild des unergründlichen Gottes*, edited by Rainer Hirsch-Luipold and Georgiana Huian, 71–83. Berlin: De Gruyter.

Lapidot, Elad. 2021. "Gnosis und Spätantiker Geist II. Hans Jonas' The Lost Book." In *Hans Jonas—Handbook*, edited by Michael Bongardt, Holger Burckhart, John-Stewart Gordon, and Jürgen Nielsen-Sikora, 88–95. Stuttgart: J. B. Metzler Verlag.

Lapidot, Elad. 2020a. "Carl Schmitt's Warring Wars." *Philosophical Journal for Conflict and Violence* 2020, no. 1: 36–53.

Lapidot, Elad. 2020b. *Jews out of the Question: A Critique of Anti-Anti-Semitism*. Albany: SUNY Press.

Lapidot, Elad. 2018. "People of Knowers. On Heideggerian and Jewish Political Epistemologies." In Lapidot and Brumlik, *Heidegger and Jewish Thought*, 269–290.

Lapidot, Elad. 2017. "Die Versammlung: Heideggers Logopolitik." In *Martin Heidegger: Die Falte der Sprache*, edited by Michael Friedmann and Angelika Seppi, 227–252. Vienna: Turia + Kant.

Lapidot, Elad, and Micha Brumlik, eds. 2018. *Heidegger and Jewish Thought: Difficult Others*. New York: Rowman & Littlefield.

Large, William. 2015. *Levinas's Totality and Infinity*. London: Bloomsbury Academic.

Last Stone, Suzanne. 1993. "In Pursuit of the Counter-text: The Turn to the Jewish Legal Model in Contemporary American Legal Theory." *Harvard Law Review* 106, no. 4: 813–894.

Leiman, Shnayer Z. 1994. "Rabbi Isaac Ha-Kohen Kook: Invocation at the Inauguration of the Hebrew University." *Tradition* 29, no. 1: 87–92.

Levinas, Emmanuel. 2015 [1947]. *Etre juif: Suivi d'une lettre à Maurice Blanchot*. Paris: Payot & Rivages. Translated by Mary Beth Mader, "Being Jewish." *Continental Philosophy Review* 40 (2007): 205–210.

Levinas, Emmanuel. 2001. *Is It Righteous to Be? Interviews with Emmanuel Levinas*. Edited by Jill Robbins. Stanford, CA: Stanford University Press.

Levinas, Emmanuel. 1996. *Nouvelles lectures talmudiques*. Paris: Les éditions de minuit. Translated by Richard A. Cohen, *New Talmudic Readings*. Pittsburgh: Duquesne University Press, 1999.

Levinas, Emmanuel. 1994a. *Les Imprévus de l'histoire*. Montpellier: Fata Morgana.

Levinas, Emmanuel. 1994b [1934]. "Quelques réflexions sur la philosophie de l'hitlérisme." In *Les Imprévus de* l'histoire, 23–33. Montpellier: Fata Morgana. Originally published in *Esprit* 26 (1934): 199–208.

Levinas, Emmanuel. 1990 [1947]. *De l'existence à l'existant*. Paris: Vrin. Translated by Alphonso Lingis, *Existence and Existents*. The Hague: Martinus Nijhoff, 1978.

Levinas, Emmanuel. 1988. *A l'heure des nations*. Paris: Les éditions de minuit. Translated by M. B. Smith, *In the Time of the Nations*. Bloomington: Indiana University Press, 1994.

Levinas, Emmanuel. 1983 [1947]. *Le temps et l'autre*. Paris: Presses Universitaires de France. Translated by Richard Cohen, *Time and the Other*. Pittsburgh: Duquesne University Press, 1987.

Levinas, Emmanuel. 1982a. *Éthique et infini: Dialogues avec Philippe Nemo*. Paris: Fayard. Translated by Richard A. Cohen, *Ethics and Infinity*. Pittsburgh: Duquesne University Press, 1985.

Levinas, Emmanuel. 1982b. *L'au-delà du verset: Lectures et discours talmudiques*. Paris: Les éditions de minuit. Translated by G. D. Mole, *Beyond the Verse: Talmudic Readings and Lectures*. Bloomington: Indiana University Press, 1994.

Levinas, Emmanuel. 1977. *Du sacré au saint: Cinq nouvelles lectures talmudiques*. Paris: Les éditions de minuit. Translated by Annette Aronowicz, *Nine Talmudic Readings*. Bloomington: Indiana University Press, 1990.

Levinas, Emmanuel. 1974. *Autrement qu'être ou au-delà de l'essence*. The Hague: Martinus Nijhoff. Translated by Alphonso Lingis, *Otherwise Than Being or Beyond Essence*. Dordrecht: Kluwer Academic, 1978.

Levinas, Emmanuel. 1972. *Humanisme de l'autre homme*. Montpellier: Fata Morgana. Translated by Nidra Poller, *Humanism of the Other*. Champaign: University of Illinois Press, 2006.

Levinas, Emmanuel. 1968. *Quatre lectures talmudiques*. Paris: Les éditions de minuit. Translated by Annette Aronowicz, *Nine Talmudic Readings*. Bloomington: Indiana University Press, 1990.

Levinas, Emmanuel. 1963. *Difficile liberté: Essai sur le judaïsme*. Paris: Albin Michel. Translated by Sean Hand, *Difficult Freedom*. Baltimore: John Hopkins University Press, 1990.

Levinas, Emmanuel. 1961. *Totalité et infini: Essai sur l'extériorité*. The Hague: Martinus Nijhoff. Translated by Alphonso Lingis, *Totality and Infinity: An Essay on Exteriority*. Pittsburgh: Duquesne University Press, 1969.

Levinas, Emmanuel. 1939. "A propos de la mort du Pape Pie XI." *Paix et Droit* 3: 3.

Levinas, Emmanuel. 1935. "L'inspiration religieuse de l'Alliance." *Paix et Droit* 8 (October): 4.

Levinas, Emmanuel, Alain Finkielkraut, and Shlomo Malka. 1989. "Ethics and Politics." In *The Levinas Reader*, edited by Sean Hand, 289–297. New York: Routledge.

Levinas, Emmanuel, and Richard Kearny. 1986. "Dialogue with Emmanuel Levinas." In *Face to Face with Levinas*, edited by Richard A. Cohen, 13–34. Albany: SUNY Press.

Lévy, Benny. 2003. *Etre juif*. Lagrasse: Verdier.

Llewelyn, John. 2002. *Appositions of Jacques Derrida and Emmanuel Levinas*. Bloomington: Indiana University Press.

Löwith, Karl. 1949. *Meaning in History: The Theological Implications of the Philosophy of History*. Chicago: University of Chicago Press.

Maimonides, Moses. 1980. *Mishneh Torah: Hu Ha-Yad Ha-Ḥazaḳah*. Vol. 14. Jerusalem: Mosad ha-Rav Ḳuḳ.

Mano, Davide, and Ron Naiweld. 2022. "Hayyim Nahman Bialik's Inaugural Speech at the Hebrew University of Jerusalem." *La Revue K*, June 23, 2022.

Marsh, Jack. 2021. *Saying Peace: Levinas, Eurocentrism, Solidarity*. Albany: SUNY Press.

Masuzawa, Tomoko. 2005. *The Invention of World Religions, Or, How European Universalism Was Preserved in the Language of Pluralism*. Chicago: University of Chicago Press.

McGettigan, Andrew. 2006. "The Philosopher's Fear of Alterity: Levinas, Europe and Humanities 'without Sacred History.'" *Radical Philosophy* 140: 15–25.

Meskin, Jacob. 2007. "The Role of Lurianic Kabbalah in the Early Philosophy of Emmanuel Levinas." *Levinas Studies* 2: 49–78.

Morgan, Michael. 2011. *The Cambridge Introduction to Emmanuel Levinas*. Cambridge: Cambridge University Press.

Moten, Fred. 2018. *The Universal Machine*. Durham, NC: Duke University Press.

Moyn, Samuel. 2005. *Origins of the Other: Emmanuel Levinas between Revelation and Ethics*. Ithaca, NY: Cornell University Press.

Moyn, Samuel. 2003. "Emmanuel Levinas's Talmudic Readings: Between Tradition and Invention." *Prooftexts* 23, no. 3: 338–336.

Naiweld, Ron. 2022. *The Age of the Parakletos: A Historical Defense of Rabbinic Knowledge*. Lanham: Rowman & Littlefield.

Nancy, Jean-Luc. 1990 [1986]. *La communauté désoeuvrée*. Paris: Christian Bourgois Editeur.

Nayar, Pramond K. 2013. *Frantz Fanon*. London: Routledge.

Naylor, Phillip C. 2000. *France and Algeria: A History of Decolonization and Transformation*. Gainesville: University Press of Florida.

Pawling, Christopher. 2013. *Critical Theory and Political Engagement: From May '68 to the Arab Spring*. Basingstoke: Palgrave Macmillan.

Peperzak, Adrian. 1993. *To the Other: An Introduction to the Philosophy of Emmanuel Levinas*. West Lafayette, IN: Perdue University Press.

Rabaka, Reiland. 2015. *The Negritude Movement: W. E. B. Du Bois, Leon Damas, Aime Cesaire, Leopold Senghor, Frantz Fanon, and the Evolution of an Insurgent Idea*. Lanham: Lexington Books.

Rabaka, Reiland. 2010. *Forms of Fanonism: Frantz Fanon's Critical Theory and the Dialectics of Decolonization*. Lanham: Rowman & Littlefield.

Rae, Gavin. 2016. *The Problem of Political Foundations in Carl Schmitt and Emmanuel Levinas*. London: Palgrave McMillan.

Raz-Krakotzkin, Amnon. 1993–1994. "galut be-tokh ribonut—le-bikoret 'shlilat ha-galut' ba-tarbut ha-yisraelit" [Exile in Sovereignty—Critique of 'Negation of Exile' in the Israeli Culture]. *teoria u-bikoret* 4: 23–55; and 5: 113–132.

Reader, Keith A., and Khursheed Wadia. 1993. *The May 1968 Events in France: Reproductions and Interpretations*. Basingstoke: Macmillan Press.

Renan, Ernest. 1882. *Qu'est-ce qu'une nation? Conférence faite en Sorbonne, Le 11 mars 1882*. Paris: Calmann Lévy.

Ricoeur, Paul. 1997. *Autrement: Lecture d'autrement qu'être ou au-delà de l'essence d'Emmanuel Levinas*. Paris: Presses universitaires de France.

Rosenzweig, Franz. 1976 [1921]. *Der Stern der Erlösung*. The Hague: Martin Nijhoff. Translated by Barbara E. Galli, *The Star of Redemption*. Madison: University of Wisconsin Press, 2005.

Ross, Kristin. 2002. *May '68 and Its Afterlives*. Chicago: University of Chicago Press.

Sartre, Jean-Paul. 1948. "Orphée noir." In *Anthologie de la nouvelle poésie nègre et malgache de langue française*, edited by Léopold Sédar Senghor, ix–xliv. Paris: PUF. Translated by John MacCombie, "Black Orpheus." *Massachusetts Review* 6, no. 1 (autumn 1964–winter 1965): 13–52.

Schmitt, Carl. 2011 [1950]. *Der Nomos der Erde im Völkerrecht des Jus Publicum Europaeum*. Berlin: Duncker & Humbolt.

Schmitt, Carl. 2009 [1932]. *Der Begriff des Politischen: Text von 1932 mit einem Vorwort und drei Corollarien*. Berlin: Duncker & Humblot. Translated by Georg Schwab, *The Concept of the Political*. Chicago: University of Chicago Press, 2007 [1996].

Schneersohn, Isaac, ed. 1968. *D'Auschwitz à Israël, vingt ans après la Libération*. Paris: Centre de documentation juive contemporaine.

Scholem, Gershom. 1995 [1946]. *Major Trends in Jewish Mysticism*. New York: Schocken Books.

Shepard, Todd. 2006. *The Invention of Decolonization: The Algerian War and the Remaking of France*. Ithaca, NY: Cornell University Press.

Sorek, Yoav, and Paz Uri. 2014. "The Sting of the Giant of Knowledge—on Mr. Chouchani." [Hebrew] https://shorturl.at/wBqEF.

Starr, Peter. 1995. *Logics of Failed Revolt: French Theory after May '68*. Stanford, CA: Stanford University Press.

Styfhals, Willem. 2019. *No Spiritual Investment in the World: Gnosticism and Postwar German Philosophy*. Ithaca, NY: Cornell University Press.

Szwarc, Sandrine. 2022. *Fascinant Chouchani*. Paris: Hermann.

Tambling, Jeremy. 2009. *Allegory*. London: Routledge.

Taubes, Jacob. 1947. *Abendländische Eschatologie*. Bern: Francke. Translated by David Ratmoko, *Occidental Eschatology*. Stanford, CA: Stanford University Press, 2009.

Topolki, Anya. 2015. *Arendt, Levinas and a Politics of Relationality*. London: Rowman & Littlefield.

Vasey, Craig R. 2005. "Faceless Women and Serious Others." In Katz, *Levinas*, 4:388–399.

Vogel, Lawrence. 2001. "Jewish Philosophies after Heidegger: Levinas and Jonas on Responsibility." In *Taking Responsibilities: Comparative Perspectives*, edited by Winston Davis, 121–148. Charlottesville: University of Virginia Press.

Whitman, Jon. 2003. *Interpretation and Allegory: Antiquity to the Modern Period*. Boston: Brill.

Wolfson, Elliot. 2014. *Giving beyond the Gift: Apophasis and Overcoming Theomania*. New York: Fordham University Press.

Wolfson, Elliot. 2006. "Secrecy, Modesty, and the Feminine: Kabbalistic Traces in the Thought of Levinas." *Journal of Jewish Thought and Philosophy* 14, no. 1–2: 193–224.

Wolin, Richard. 2010. *The Wind from the East: French Intellectuals, the Cultural Revolution, and the Legacy of the 1960s*. Princeton, NJ: Princeton University Press.

Wright, Benjamin G. 2015. *The Letter of Aristeas*. Berlin: Walter de Gruyter.

Wyschogrod, Edith. 1974. *Emmanuel Levinas. The Problem of Ethical Metaphysics*. The Hague: Martinus Nijhoff.

Zarader, Marlène. 1990. *La Dette impensée. Heidegger et l'héritage hébraïque*. Paris: Seuil. Translated by Bettina Bergo, *The Unthought Debt: Heidegger and the Hebraic Heritage*. Stanford, CA: Stanford University Press, 2006.

INDEX

ELAD LAPIDOT is Professor of Hebraic Studies at the University of Lille. He is author of *Jews Out of the Question: A Critique of Anti-Anti-Semitism.*

FOR INDIANA UNIVERSITY PRESS

Lesley Bolton, *Project Manager/Editor*
Gary Dunham, *Acquisitions Editor and Director*
Anna Francis, *Assistant Acquisitions Editor*
Anna Garnai, *Production Coordinator*
Katie Huggins, *Production Manager*
Dan Pyle, *Online Publishing Manager*
Alyssa Nicole Lucas, *Marketing and Publicity Manager*
Jennifer Witzke, *Senior Artist and Book Designer*

www.ingramcontent.com/pod-product-compliance
Ingram Content Group UK Ltd.
Pitfield, Milton Keynes, MK11 3LW, UK
UKHW041955140725
460777UK00001B/1